THE COLLECTED WORKS OF JEREMY BENTHAM

General Editor

J. H. Burns

Principles of Legislation

OF LAWS
IN GENERAL

—————

edited by
H. L. A. HART

—————

UNIVERSITY OF LONDON
THE ATHLONE PRESS
1970

Published by
THE ATHLONE PRESS
UNIVERSITY OF LONDON
at 2 Gower Street, London wc1
Distributed by Tiptree Book Services Ltd
Tiptree, Essex

Australia and New Zealand
Melbourne University Press

U.S.A.
Oxford University Press Inc
New York

0 485 13210 9

Printed in Great Britain by
WILLIAM CLOWES AND SONS, LIMITED
LONDON AND BECCLES

PREFACE

The thanks of the Bentham Committee are due to the following bodies for financial assistance towards the cost of editorial work on this volume: The Rockefeller Foundation; The British Academy; The Pilgrim Trust; University College London. The Committee also wishes to thank the Librarian of University College and his staff for access to Mss. and for other assistance.

The editor wishes to express his gratitude to the Nuffield Foundation for the award of a research fellowship enabling him to devote part of his time to this edition of Bentham's works.

The editor is greatly indebted to the General Editor, Professor J. H. Burns, both for valuable assistance and advice on many detailed points and for his expert general organization and supervision of work by many hands on this volume. His thanks are also due to Mr G. L. Williams, whose initial appreciation of the textual problems much lightened his task, and to the following whose work as research assistants was of the greatest value: Mrs Sandra Hole; Mrs Deborah Paton; Miss Helen Nowell; Mr Jan Phillips. He wishes also to thank Mr Hardy Wieting, Jr. and Mr M. H. James for additional help in preparing the indices; and Mrs Valerie Bottomley for secretarial assistance.

H. L. A. H.

CONTENTS

I A LAW DEFINED AND DISTINGUISHED   1

1. A law defined   1

2. It may be considered with relation to   1
its source; its subjects; its objects; its extent; its aspects;
its force; its expression; its occasional appendages
Parts contained in a law. Blackstone, 2 n.

3. The idea exhibited by this definition more extensive
than what is commonly annexed to the word *law*   3

4. —more extensive than it ought to be to correspond to
the phrases *legislation* and *legislative power*, viz. by
including   3
domestic orders, 4; temporary orders of administration, 4;
judicial orders, 4; monarchical orders if particular and *sua
natura* temporary, 5; laws made by a magistrate the most
conspicuous part of whose power is of the judicial kind, 6;
—or of the executive kind, 7; —or by one whose legislative
power is derived, 8

5. Necessity of these verbal discussions   8

6. Reason of extending the import of the word *law* so as to
make it include the articles above mentioned   9

7. No other word would answer the purpose as well, viz. 10
command, 10; commandment, 10; order, 10; injunction, 11;
decree, 11; precept, 11; statute, 11; ordinance and edict,
12; constitution, 12; regulation, 12; establishment, 13;
institution, 13; mandate, 13

8. Concessions of sovereign are not laws   16

9. No more are treaties between sovereigns   16

10. Local names of statutes dismissed   17

II SOURCE OF A LAW   18

1. A law must come from a sovereign   18

2. —to whose power the party in question is subject   20

3. This it may do (1) in the way of conception or (2) of
adoption   21

4. Adoption is either (1) susception or (2) pre-adoption   21

5. Persons whose mandates he adopts—(1) Former sovereigns   21

6. (2) Subordinate power-holders   22

7. Concern which the sovereign has in giving legality to conveyances and covenants   23

8. Degrees of adoption   27

9. Forms of adoption   27

10. By-laws, what   28

11. Analytical sketch of the different sorts of mandates distinguished according to their source   29

III   ENDS WHICH A LAW MAY HAVE IN VIEW   31

1. The end of a law is the external motive which he whose law it is had in prospect   31

2. This end may in certain cases be the private interest of him from whom the law immediately emanes   31

3. But the most conspicuous cases are those in which it ought to be the public at large   32

4. Analysis of this common or general end into the specific ends that are subordinate to it   32

IV   SUBJECTS OF A LAW   34

1. Subjects of a law, persons, things—as agents or patients   34

2. Persons may be subjects of a law in a physical or in a pathological way   34

3. Pathological termination of an act—its various modifications   35

4. An act may have a physical termination and not a pathological   36

5. —or a pathological and no physical   36

6. or a physical and a pathological in distinct subjects   36

7. In as far as the consequences are of a public or semi-public nature the pathological termination of the act is contingent   37

8. Different senses of the word *upon* as applied to a person who is a passible subject of the law   38

9. Direct and indirect subjects of the law   38

10. Example of such as are indirect   39

V   OBJECTS OF A LAW   41

1. Acts may be directly or indirectly the objects of a law   41

2. Necessity of introducing the words *circumstance* and *case*   41

3. Specificant circumstances in a law, what   41

4. Specificant circumstances are to an act what specificant properties are to a substance   42

5. Example   43

6. [*No marginal heading*]   43

7. [*No marginal heading*]   44

8. A case, what   44

9. Use of the above disquisition   45
'Circumstance' not applied to real entities, 45 n.

10. Collateral circumstances   46

11. Example—a law against killing expressed without the help of any specificant circumstances   48

12. —with specificant circumstances   49

13. —with circumstances that are not specificant   50

14. The law narrowed with or without adding circumstances—e.g. where the person killed is a judge   50

15. So, where the act is performed by poison   50

16. —or with premeditation   51

17. Why in some cases it may appear to have a necessary respect to circumstances   51

VI   OF THE PARTIES WHICH MAY BE AFFECTED BY A LAW   53

1. Different ways in which persons may be affected by the law viz. by being (1) bound or coerced: (2) made to suffer: or (3) favoured by it   53

2. This source of distinction different from that concerning the *Subjects* of a law   53

3. That there must be (1) a party bound or coerced   54

4. (2) a party made to suffer   54

5. (3) a party favoured — 55

6. There are no other ways in which a party can be affected than the above — 56

7. In what sense a party may be said to be favoured in point of agency — 56

   Autocheiristic power not originally the work of law, 57 n.

8. By favouring one party in point of interest the law gives another a right to *services* — 57

9. A party so favoured may be an individual, a subordinate class, or the community — 58

   This distinction inapplicable to the party bound — 58

10. A party may in point of agency be favoured for his own sake or another's — 59

11. But to complete the favour designed for such beneficiary requires another law — 59

12. Parties affected in laws concerning — 59

   offences against person, 59; and reputation, 59;—property, 60; —condition, 61; semi-public and public offences, 61

   Punitory laws — 61

13. In a remote way many sets of parties may be exposed to suffer or favoured by the same law — 62

14. Use and importance of the above distinctions — 63

15. Constitutional laws *in principem* — 64

16. They may be addressed to the law-giver, his successors or both together — 64

17. How *leges in principem* come to be adopted by successors — 65

18. In what sense the sovereign may be said to bind himself — 67

19. —by what means — 68

20. Necessity of promulgation — 71

VII OF THE LOCAL EXTENT WHICH A LAW MAY HAVE — 72

1. Local extent of a law may be direct or indirect — 72

2. This head reducible to the preceding — 73

CONTENTS

VIII OF THE DURATION OF A LAW   74

1. Extent in point of time is also reducible to the preceding heads   74
2. Why mentioned separately   74
3. A law temporary by nature, by institution   74

IX THE GENERALITY OF A LAW   76

1. A law may be particular, general, or both in one   76
   Imperfection of the language with relation to this topic, 76 n.
2. *Privilegia*, what   77
3. Domestic mandates the only ones that are particular throughout   77
4. Examples of laws which are particular *ex parte*. Domestic mandates   77
5. Military, judicial and other public orders   78
6. Covenants   78
7. Conveyances—in what respect general, and in what particular   79
8. Use of the distinction between general laws and particular   80
9. Power of legislation is but a part of the whole power of imperation in any given case   81
10. The *power of aggregation* or *accensitive power* is the other   82
11. Accensitive power—its five branches   83
12. Accensitive power *in personam* has the effect of *investitive*   83
    Difference between accensitive power *in personam* and investitive power, 84 n.
13. Modification of the accensitive power *in personam*   84
14. The other branches of accensitive power are productive ultimately of the same effects   85
15. Disaccensitive power, what   85
16. Correspondency between investitive power, power of conveyance, power of *jurisdation* and endynamistic power   85
17. Instances of the exercise of accensitive and disaccensitive power—as applied to the matrimonial condition   86

18. —to various constitutional powers, such as that of appointing and displacing officers of various sorts 87
19. —declaring war and making peace 87
20. Convicting delinquents 88
21. Regulating the coin—an instance of the accensitive power *in rem* 88
22. Accensitive power *in actum* needs no separate exemplification 89
23. Instances of accensitive power *in locum* 90
24. Accensitive power *in tempus* 90
25. Imperfection of the power of imperation *de singulis* 91

X ASPECTS OF A LAW 93

§ i. *Plan of this Chapter*

1. A law may take for its objects either acts alone, or other laws as well as acts 93
2. Four heads under which what concerns the aspect of a law may be arranged 94

§ ii. *Primordial*

1. Aspect primordial, superventitious 95
2. Aspect decisive or neutral: mandate decisive or indecisive 95
3. A command—prohibition—non-command—non-prohibition or permission 95
4. Aspect and mandate affirmative—negative 95
5. A negative aspect towards an affirmative act equipollent to an affirmative towards a negative 95
6. Mandate imperative, obligative, coercive, or unimperative etc. 96
7. Opposition and concomitancy among mandates 97
8. Aspects for which there are no corresponding mandates 97
9. The state of the mind may be expressed partly by words and partly by silence 98
10. Use of the undecisive mandates 99

§ iii. *Reiterative*

1. Mandates reiterative, what 100

2. Subalternation of acts   100

3. Reiteration *in genere* and *in specie*   100

4. —*in toto* or *pro tanto*   101

5. Purposes to which reiterative mandates may be applied —confirmation—continuation—admonition—exposition   101

    An expository mandate, what   102

    An expository mandate the only one that must vary in tenor from the primordial one   102

6. The reiteration may be with or without notice taken of the primordial   102

7. How in an expository mandate the style of imperation is dropped   104

8. A declaratory mandate, what   107

    —its uses   108

§ iv. *Alterative*

1. Superventitious aspect unconformable, superventitious provision contradictive—contrariant   110

2. Primordial aspect active, superventitious provision if contrariant, deobligative—a countermandate   110

3. A countermand—a repermission   110

4. Primordial aspect inactive, superventitious provision if contradictive a command or a prohibition   111

5. Primordial aspect active, superventitious provision if contrariant, a prohibition or a command   111

6. Primordial aspect inactive, superventitious provision can not be contrariant   111

    Countermand—does not match in every case with permission, 111 n.; Cause of this want of symmetry in language, 112 n.; Dispensation, what, 112 n.

7. Command etc. conditional—unconditional   112

8. Limitative circumstances—words—clause—proposition   113

9. Exceptive circumstances   114

10. In what cases the words are limitative; in what, exceptive   114

11. Example of a conditional law reduced to the unconditional form   114

12. Circumstances etc. whether limitative or exceptive may be termed qualificative   115

13. Provisions conditional and unconditional interconvertible   115

14. Qualificative matter may be placed all of it on either side   116

15. An unqualified law to be explicit must be translated into a qualified one   116
Words of limitation and exception various, 116 n.

16. Use of non-commanding and originally-permissive provisions   119

17. Limitations and exceptions to preceding limitations and exceptions   120

18. An offence, what. Circumstances and clauses justificative, exculpative or de-obligative   120
The word 'exemptive', why not used, 121 n.

19. Circumstances and clauses etc. inculpative or criminative   121
The word *criminative* not applicable to all cases, 122 n.; Objection to the term *inculpative*, 122 n.; The word *delinquefying or delinquefactive* proposed, 122 n.

20. In what cases exculpative circumstances come first; in what, inculpative   122

21. Inculpative circumstances to be found in most laws   123

22. Exculpative and inculpative circumstances of the 1st, 2nd, etc. orders   123
Pleadings in a cause explained, 123 n.

23. In unconditional mandates inculpative circumstances may be termed reinculpative   124

24. Principal or leading provision, what   124

§ v. *Extensive*

1. Provision extensive   125

2. Provisions indirectly or virtually extensive   126

3. Provisions may be issued *uno* or *diverso flatu*—difference between a provision, a law and a statute   126

4. Provisions expositive and qualificative, how reducible to independent provisions   127

5. Recapitulation   128

§ vi. *Repugnancy*

Repugnancy, what   129

XI FORCE OF A LAW   133

1. Motives a law relies on, alluring or coercive—reward or punishment   133
2. Sources from whence they may issue—the moral, religious, or political sanctions   133
3. When from the political, they may be announced by written or by customary law   134
4. When by written law, it consists of two parts: (1) the directive (2) the incitative or sanctional   134
5. The incitative may be (1) comminatory or (2) invitative   134
6. It is more frequently the former than the latter   134
7. Why—punishment the only force that can be depended on   134
     Why government cannot be carried on by reward alone, 135 n.
8. Hence the idea of punishment is with difficulty separable from that of law   136
9. An invitative or praemiary law   136
10. A law with an alternative sanction   136
11. Law principal—subsidiary   137
     Of perfect dominion power of imperation is but one half; power of contrectation being the other, 137 n.
12. The subsidiary law addressed commonly to the judge   139
13. Who must have assistants—hence more subsidiary laws   139
14. On what circumstances the number of these depends   140
15. Subsidiary laws proximate—remote: the proximate punitory or remunerative   140
16. Laws substantive—adjective   140
17. Connection between the principal law and its proximate subsidiary   142
18. One expression may serve for both the principal law and the subsidiary   143
19. The principal most commonly serves for both   144
20. To a praemiary law when principal, the next subsidiary must be penal   144
21. Exemptive circumstances   145
22. Difference between exculpative and exemptive   146

23. How laws of procedure apply exemptions to substantive laws   146

24. Disexemptive circumstances   147

25. Limitations which are annexed of course to a punitory law   147

26. —and which are made obligative on the other side   148

27. Law anaetiosostic, the antagonist to the punitory   148

XII   APPENDAGES OF A LAW   149

1. Appendages or remedial laws—another species of subsidiary   149

2. Procedure *in compensandum—compescendum—avertendum*   151

3. Satisfactive clauses added to the substantive law   151

XIII   SIGNS OF A LAW   152

1. Signs by which a law may stand *expressed.* Law written—traditionary—customary   152

2. Customary laws are expressed by acts only, not by words   152

3. No assignable laws to be found in books of customary law   153

4. Various modes of expression that may be given to the same written law   154

XIV   IDEA OF A COMPLETE LAW   156

1. The definition of a complete law varies according to the fullness of the pattern   156

2. A law of the first or narrowest pattern in what respects it may be complete or incomplete   156

3. In point of expression   157

4. In a complete code there can be no law that is not complete   158

5. In point of connection   159

6. In point of design: which may happen through want (1) of discrimination, (2) of amplitude, original or residuary   160

7. Example of a law incomplete in point of design 161

8. Interpretation strict—liberal; liberal—extensive—restrictive 162

9. A law takes more words to complete it than an ordinary command—why 164

10. Unity of a law of the foregoing pattern 165

11. Language on this head unsteady 166

12. A law with a comminative part when complete in point of connection 167

13. In point of design 168

14. Unity of an obligative law of the second pattern 168

15. Integrality and unity of obligative laws of the two remaining patterns 168

16. —of a de-obligative law 168

17. If the superventitious law is not de-obligative *in toto*, it is only qualificative; if it is, then by destroying the mandate the qualifications fall to the ground with it 168

18. Obligative laws the only standards to measure by 169

19. Unity of a law to be determined by the occasions for distinguishing offences 170

20. A complete code being given, the number of laws in it is given 172

21. *Genera infima* of offences 172

22. *Species infimae* constituted by circumstances of aggravation and extenuation applied to the above *genera* 172

23. Necessity of mixing with the *genera infima* those which have others under them 174

24. The establishment of *genera* liable to vary in different languages 174

25. Necessity of such establishment for the purposes of discourse 174

26. Reference of inculpative and exculpative circumstances to such generic names 175

27. Integrality of the laws of the three remaining patterns 175

28. First conception of the laws of property to be taken from the offence of wrongful occupation 176

29. Example where the proprietary subject is a particular field 176

30. This law may be resolved into (1) a general prohibition and (2) a particular permission taken out of it   177

31. Infinitude of the laws of property upon this plan   177

32. That infinitude may be reduced by translating the laws out of the imperative into the assertive form   178

     Expansion and consolidation both throw a law out of the imperative into the assertive form, 179 n.

33. Among the laws which create property conveyances are included in which the imperation is performed by the law and the right-giver conjointly   179

34. Cases in which the property is established by the law alone in the first instance   181

35. Of the expositive matter belonging to the law against wrongful occupation a great part belongs in common to the law correlative to the other offences against property   181

36. The laws relative to the offence of wrongful occupation are all reducible to one—(1) in the conditional form   181

37. (2) In the unconditional form with exceptions   182

38. The last formulary the plainest   182

39. What is necessary to make it appear complete   182

40. In what respects laws are apt to fail of being complete in this point   183

XV   NO CUSTOMARY LAW COMPLETE   184

1. A customary law can never be complete   184

2. The original elements of it are acts of autocratico-judicial power   184

3. Sources of customary law—Records   185

4. Reports—their deficiencies   186
   —redundancy and confusion   188

5. Treatises   188

6. Manuscript Reports   188

7. Formularies of Precedents   189

8. Preference not settled   190

9. Utility—original and derivative   190

10. Competition between documents of different orders   191

11. Uncertainty of this branch of law ... 192

12. Conclusion ... 194

Unaccommodatingness of the customary law, 194 n.

XVI SEPARATION OF THE CIVIL BRANCH FROM THE PENAL ... 196

1. The generality of laws have each a penal as well as a civil branch ... 196

2. Law-books in which no mention is made of punishment accounted for ... 196

3. According to the order of the ideas the penal and civil branches would stand together ... 197

4. But must be separated for the convenience of discourse ... 197

5. Foundation of the penal and civil codes ... 198

6. Expository matter ... 198

7. Of the expository matter the circumstantiative will be the most copious ... 198

8. Circumstantiative matter, how it may come to stand apart from the penalising matter ... 199

9. The circumstantiative matter forms the civil branch of the law: the penalising the penal ... 199

10. Circumstantiative matter belonging to the several penal titles ... 200

In offences against person it excepts power viz. over persons ... 200

11. In offences against property it excepts title, viz. power over things ... 201

12. In offences against reputation, there is little place for it ... 202

13. In offences against condition ... 203

14. In semi-public offences it is of the same tenor as in the corresponding private ones ... 204

15. In self-regarding offences ... 204

16. In offences against the external security of the state ... 205

17. In offences against the preventive branch of the police ... 205

18. In offences against justice ... 205

19. In offences against the public force ... 206

20. In offences against the positive increase of the national felicity — 206

21. In offences against the public wealth — 206

22. In offences against population — 207

23. In offences against the national wealth — 207

24. In offences against the sovereignty — 207

25. In offences against religion — 208

26. In offences against the national interest in general — 208

XVII DIVISION OF THE LAWS INTO CIVIL AND CRIMINAL — 209

§ i. *Distinction between Civil Law and Criminal*

1. Is *criminal* law more distinct from *civil* than *penal* is? — 209

2. Three senses of the word crime—it imports (1) mischievousness, (2) odiousness, (3) penalty — 209

3. Magnitude of the punishment alone no source of distinction between offences considered with a view to punishment — 210

4. —nor the degree of odiousness — 210

5. —nor the degree of mischievousness — 210

6. Whether an act be a crime depends on all three circumstances together — 210

7. Easier to point out some acts that are crimes, than to say what are not — 210

8. Particularly in as much as it depends upon *degree* — 211

9. Offences if punished with an ordinary measure of punishment may be deemed civil offences; if with an extra-ordinary, criminal — 211

10. Punishment ordinary, and extra-ordinary — 211

11. Grounds for extra-ordinary punishment — 212

12. Punishment must be extra-ordinary, where the profit is not pecuniary — 212

13. The directory (circumstantiative) part of every law belongs to the civil branch—the comminatory to the criminal — 213

14. Intentionality makes the difference between civil and criminal offences — 214

15. Influence which this has on the mischief of the act   214

§ ii. *Limits between the Criminal Branch and the Civil*

1. Some cases appear more manifestly to belong to the criminal branch than others   214
2. Consciousness of criminality or criminal consciousness presumed from the nature of the offence: where it affects a person   215
—not where it affects a thing   215
—unless the circumstance of his having no right to meddle with it be too clear to admit of doubt   216
3. The line is drawn by the magnitude of the punishment   216
—which is made to depend in most cases upon criminal consciousness   216
which is sometimes taken for granted as following of course   216
4. To mark out rights belongs not to penal law   216
5. Sometimes punishment where no criminal consciousness: sometimes no punishment where there is   217
6. Variableness of the distinction   217

§ iii. *Limits between the Criminal Branch and the Civil. Offences against Property*

1. Difference between criminal and civil offences against property   217
2. A line if drawn could not be permanent   218
3. Limits with the penal branch marked out by the manner in which punishment is concerned   218
4. Dictates of ethics include what ought to be dictates of jurisprudence and something more   219

XVIII DISTINCTION BETWEEN PENAL AND CIVIL PROCEDURE   220

1. Division of judicial procedure into penal and civil   220
2. —with respect to the defendant   221
Judgment of conviction   221
3. Judgment of acquittal   221
4. Judgment of adjudication   222

5. Judgment of non-adjudication — 223

6. Recapitulation — 223

7. All suits reducible to the above standards — 224

8. Suits defective by the want of a plaintiff — 224

9. Many accusations in one, may claims in one — 225
   Incidental suits arising out of the principal — 225

10. Cross claims — 225

11. The judgment may be the same in a civil suit as in a penal one — 225

12. What it is that civil suits have to do with offences — 226

13. A judgment must pass into an act of the will — 226

14. Rights unliquidated and liquid — 227

15. Sometimes the suit may be indifferently a civil or a penal one — 227
    A suit may be tried either way when there is no punishment — 228
    Example in claims to land, 228 n.

16. Cases where there is no ground for a penal suit—(1) where the right claimed has not been violated — 229

17. (2) where it is as yet unliquidated as in the case of a *debt* — 229

18. —unless it be for the offence of not conferring the right — 230

19. Recapitulation — 230

20. A civil and a penal suit are distinguishable even where either may be brought indifferently, and where the steps taken in them may be the same — 231

21. Conclusion — 231

XIX USES OF THE EIGHTEEN PRECEDING CHAPTERS — 232

1. Uses — 232

2. It gives the plan of a complete body of statute law — 233

3. —which includes a complete digest of the customary law — 235

4. It gives room for making amendments without inconvenience — 236

5. It will serve to ensure their propriety in point of matter — 236

6. It tends to check the licence of interpretation — 239

7. —and to facilitate a comparison between the laws of different nations 242

8. —and to facilitate the communication of the science to beginners 243
School 244
Model 244
Harmony 244
New code 244

9. Connection of this and preceding chapters with the next ensuing[1] 245

10. Plan 246

11. Nothing need be omitted, nothing unprepared for 246

APPENDIX A DISTINCTION BETWEEN PENAL LAW AND CIVIL 247

1. Limits between penal law and civil indiscernible 247

2. It is not every sentence of the penal law that mentions punishment 247

3. Nor is there any command that belongs exclusively to the civil branch supposing there were two distinct branches of jurisprudence 247

4. A law may be penal without mentioning punishment 248

5. The distinction between penal and civil applies not to the laws themselves, but to the books that treat of them 248

6. Example in the law relative to wills 248
Ambiguous import of the epithet *civil* as applied to law, 248 n.

7. So in the law concerning the appointment of persons to public trusts 249

8. The whole business of law reducible to that of creating duties. This takes two operations 249
Rights created by prescribing duties, 249 n.

9. Which however may be expressed in one sentence 250

10. Instance in a law against theft 250

11. Or a part of it may take up volumes in many of which nothing should be said about punishment 250

12. Conclusion—that book relates to penal law, which dwells most upon punishment 250

[1] For elucidation of this heading see below, 245 n. 1.

APPENDIX B PART I   251

   1. Rights, powers, and other fictitious legal entities to be
      explained by their relation to real entities   251

   2. Legal fictitious entities are created by creating offences 252

   3. Before the law acts liberty is universal   253

   4. Restraint produced on the one part: personal security
      and protection afforded on the other   254

   5. Restraint produced on the one part—liberty on the
      other   254

   6. Restraint on the one part—protection for reputation
      on the other   254

   7. To all an inexclusive power over or property in a thing 255

   8. A power over a thing inexclusive as against some,
      exclusive as against others   255

   9. A property exclusive with respect to all   256

  10. This case is never strictly verified   256

  11. Power over things, corroborated by prohibition of
      disturbance   256

  12. One though not the only way of corroborating a power
      over things is by rendering it exclusive   257

  13. Powers subservient to powers over things   257

  14. Subservient powers over things impeding   258

  15. It is the essence of such power to be but occasional   258

  16. Power over persons is either over their passive or their
      active faculties   258

  17. Distinctions observable in regard to power over the
      active faculty   259

  18. Power over the active faculty precarious   260

  19. Power over the passive faculties of persons, un-
      corroborated   260

  20. Corroborated by prohibition of disturbance   261

  21. —by prohibition of disobedience   261

  22. Power over the passive faculty includes power over the
      active. Power over the active faculty constituted by
      power of punishment   261

CONTENTS

23. Power over the active faculty constituted by power of coercive influence   262
24. —by power of alluring influence   262
25. No property constituted by either kind of influence   262
26. Yet both come under the notion of power   262
      Power of coercive influence—what sorts of acts (instrumental) it may extend to, 262 n.
27. By what powers over persons power over things may be corroborated   263
28. —by power over the passive faculty   263
29. —by power of punishment   263
      Power of alluring influence—what acts of power it does and does not extend to, 263 n.
30. Subservient powers corroborated—(1) by permission of assistance, (2) by command of assistance   264
31. Restraint or constraint on one part—a right to services on the other   264
31a. Rights to the use of things   265
32. To constraint correspond active services, to restraint services of forbearance   266
33. Services corporal and mental   266
34. Services *in personam* and *in rem*   267
35. Power (and right) direct and indirect   268
36. Power indirect—investitive and divestitive   268
37. Power investitive how created   268
38. Power divestitive   268
39. Exercise of an indirect power, what   268
40. Rights direct and indirect   269
41. Investitive and divestitive powers of the 1st, 2nd, 3rd, etc. orders   269
42. Conditional investitive power—power to control by non-assent   269
43. Defeasible investitive power—power of control by dissent   269
44. Principal modifications of which the indirect powers are susceptible   269
45. Other modifications of indirect powers dismissed   269
46. Buying and selling a mutual exercise of the investitive power   270

47. Buying and selling, where money is concerned   270

48. Giving, what   270

49. Conveying, what   270

50. Different modes of buying and selling   270

51. A compact or contract is to be distinguished from a conveyance   270

52. Persons for whose benefit a power is designed. Power beneficial or fiduciary   271

53. Fiduciary private, semi-public or public   271

54. Power fiduciary how created   271

55. Power fiduciary imports right to services   271

56. The operations of the executive magistrate are liable not to quadrate with those of the legislative   272

57. Occupation, what   272

58. Various senses of the word *possession* analysed   273

59. Physical possession as against physical obstacles   273

60. Physical possession as against human obstacles   273

61. Legal possession *de jure*   273

62. Legal possession *de facto*   274

63. Title may be good, lawful, valid: or actual, effectual   274

64. Investitive and divestitive event   274

65. The two species of legal possession and title commonly go together   274

66. Investitive event purely natural or voluntary   275

67. Investitive event may be simple or complex   275

68. Possession is permanent—occupation instantaneous   275

69. Right of possession is the same as right to a thing   276

70. Protection for property   276

71. Impossibility of ascertaining the whole number of possible modifications by an exhaustive process   277

72. Conclusion. Intricacy of the subject   278

APPENDIX B PART II   279

Actual title depends upon the disposition of the judge paramount   279

How by an offence a man may lose the legal possession   279

The duty of the executive magistrate is to make the legal possession *de facto* coincide with that *de jure*   280

Ways in which it may happen he fails of doing so   280

Means by which such failure may be brought about   280

The exercise of the right consists in an act: viz in the occupation of the thing   281

Occupation of an incorporeal different from a corporeal article   281

Occupation of a person   282

Trust a species of property   283

Articles to be considered in relation to property   284

The object of property—Property corporeal and incorporeal   284

1. Object of a corporeal property—a person *or* a thing   285
Line between movable and immovable objects not clear, 285, n.

2. Relation—A legal relation what   285

Number of the relations is equal to that of the persons concerned multiplied by that of the aspects   285

3. Acts of occupation—property direct or occupied *per se,* indirect or occupied *per alium*   286

Legal relation constitutes a condition   286

Condition—its commencement and termination—an investitive event—a divestitive event   286

Act of investment communicates a legal relation, and a condition however transient   286

Investitive event purely natural or voluntary   286

Weakness of power investitive without the divestitive—in this case the interest remaining to the investor is next to nothing   287

Strength of, when accompanied by the divestitive—in this case the interest of the derivative occupant is what is nothing   287

Example—servant and guardian   287

It is in the latter case only that the acts of the derivative occupant are spoken of as being the acts of the original investor   287

In the former case the occupation is considered as totally severed from the exercise of the investitive power   287

Not that the investitive power has no influence on the acts of occupation   288

Recapitulation—Power either direct or indirect   288

APPENDIX C   289

1. Connection   289

2. Objects of legislation—producing good, avoiding to produce evil   289

3. Two instruments—coercion and reward; coercion is either physical or by punishment   289

4. Method of operation—imposing obligations   289
   Obligations positive and negative   289

5. Objects of the conduct regulated things or persons   290
   Power over things   290
   Power over persons, three degrees of it   290

6. The law where it creates negative offences corresponding to the above positive ones gives right to so many sorts of services   291

7. To give protection to different kinds of property may require different operations   291

8. Power particular or partial in point of use, and given specially or *per exceptionem*—property *in* a thing   291

9. Power general or partial in point of use, but given generally or *sub exceptione*—property *of* a thing   291

10. Power given *generally* usually more ample than power given specially   292

11. Power is not necessarily ample in point of *value*, in proportion to what it is in point of *use*   292

12. Power partial in point of substance   292

13. The beneficiary may be an individual, a class, the public   293

14. [*No marginal heading*]   293

15. Right—how resulting out of duty   293

16. Notion of duty a common measure   294

17. Necessity of the above definition   294

18. Power over persons howsoever corroborated imports not of itself any command addressed to the persons to whom it is given   295

19. Difference between power beneficial and power fiduciary   295

APPENDIX D¹   298

    Imperfection of the nomenclature relative to expressions of the
    will, 298 n.

  4. Aspect inactive—a non-command—an inactive per-
    mission   300

  5. Superventitious provision—consentaneous—alterative   301

  6. Primordial aspect—active, superventitious provision
    if consentaneous a command or a prohibition   301

  7. How by abbreviation a cluster of provisions reiterative
    in specie may drop the imperative form for the
    assertive   302

APPENDIX E *Jeremy Bentham to Lord Ashburton*

    (3 June 1782)   304

APPENDIX F *Of Laws in General: Table of the Chapters*   312

INDEX OF SUBJECTS   315

INDEX OF NAMES   341

¹ See below 298 n. 1 for an explanation of the incomplete series of paragraphs in this appendix.

ABBREVIATIONS

Apart from standard abbreviations, the following should be noted :

Bowring : *The Works of Jeremy Bentham*, published under the superintendence of ... John Bowring (11 vols.), Edinburgh, 1838–43.

CW : *The Collected Works of Jeremy Bentham*, London, 1968 –

U.C. : Bentham papers in the Library of University College London (Roman numerals refer to boxes, Arabic to leaves).

INTRODUCTION

The present work is a continuation of *An Introduction to the Principles of Morals and Legislation*.[1] It was substantially completed in 1782[2] but was never published by Bentham, and remained unknown until it was discovered by Professor Charles Warren Everett among the Bentham Mss. at University College London in 1939. The circumstances of its discovery and identification as the second part of *An Introduction to the Principles* are narrated by Professor Everett in his edition of the work published in 1945 by Columbia University Press, under the title of *The Limits of Jurisprudence Defined*. Through Professor Everett's industry and acumen a substantially correct text of one of Bentham's most original and important works was first made available. The text presented here, however, differs from that of the Everett edition in important respects. Chapters I and II and the first eighteen pages of Chapter XXI of that edition are excluded from the text of the present edition and assigned to Appendices, and two passages of considerable length have been added to the text. The reasons for these and other changes are discussed in this Introduction.

EVOLUTION OF BENTHAM'S CONCEPTION OF THE PRESENT WORK

Bentham's conception of the relation of the present work to *An Introduction to the Principles* changed during its composition, and an understanding of the development of his ideas concerning the work is necessary for an appreciation of the various problems presented by the Mss. The work was originally designed by Bentham to form the third, fourth and fifth sections of the last chapter (XVII) of *An Introduction to the Principles*, which Bentham entitled 'Of the Limits of the Penal Branch of Jurisprudence'. It was later conceived by him as a set of further chapters forming a single work together with *An Introduction to the Principles*, and later still as a separate work and the subject of

[1] Hereafter referred to as *An Introduction to the Principles*.
[2] This date is established by Bentham's letter of 3 June 1782 to Lord Ashburton (Appendix E below) and by several references in the text of the work itself to 1782 as the year of writing.

a separate volume. Bentham's final plan seems[1] to have been that the present work together with an analysis of fundamental legal concepts should constitute the tenth and last of the series of projected works shortly described in paragraphs 17 to 19 of the Preface to *An Introduction to the Principles*.[2] The original design of the work is outlined by Bentham in paragraph 29 of Ch. xvii of *An Introduction to the Principles*, which, according to the long note added to it in 1789, was written not later than November 1780.[3] A number of traces of this original conception survive in the present text in those places where Bentham uses the expression 'this chapter' to refer to the work as a whole.[4] The intermediate stage in which the present work was conceived as a set of further chapters to be added to *An Introduction to the Principles* is evident in the letter, mentioned above, written by Bentham to Lord Ashburton on 3 June 1782,[5] with which he enclosed the printed sheets of *An Introduction to the Principles* as they stood at the end of 1780. In this letter the chapter numbers for the present work run from 18 and Bentham speaks of his abandonment of his original idea that the work was to form sections of Ch. xvii of *An Introduction to the Principles*. The later conception of the work as a separate one is described in great detail by Bentham in the note of January 1789 above mentioned which he added to Ch. xvii of *An Introduction to the Principles* just prior to its publication in that year. It is also attested by a document headed 'Of Laws in General. Table of Chapters'[6] which dates from March 1782 and consists of a list of contents in which the chapters are listed both as a continuation of *An Introduction to the Principles* in Arabic numerals running from 17 to 41 and also as a separate work in Roman numerals running from i to xxi.

Both the list of contents given in the letter to Ashburton and the list headed 'Of Laws in General' include at the end three chapters headed 'Indirect Legislation', 'Place and Time', and 'Corpus Juris'.[7] Though there are references in the present work to both

---

[1] The evidence is in the first paragraph of the long note inserted by Bentham in 1789 at the end of Ch. xvii of *An Introduction to the Principles* (in *CW*, 301).

[2] In *CW*, 5–6.

[3] Ibid., 298–300.

[4] See, esp., Ch. xix *passim*, 232 ff.

[5] See Appendix E, 304–11, for the text. The text given by Everett (pp. 7–10) is not complete.

[6] See Appendix F, 312–3, for the text of this document.

[7] The order differs in the two lists, the Ashburton letter placing 'Corpus Juris' before, while the other list places it after 'Indirect Legislation' and 'Place and Time' (which appears as 'Time and Place' in the Ashburton letter).

'Indirect Legislation' and 'Corpus Juris' as if these were comprised in later chapters, it seems unlikely that Bentham in fact wrote anything substantial on any of these three topics in the form of chapters of the present work.[1] He wrote at length on the subject of 'Indirect Legislation' and these Mss. were subsequently used by Dumont in compiling Part III of *Traités de Législation Civile et Pénale* (1802: cf. Bowring, i, 533–80). The work on the influence of time and place in matters of legislation became a separate essay, also used by Dumont in his *Traités* (cf. Bowring, i, 163–94). Both these works were written in 1782, and Bentham was already envisaging them as separate entities when he wrote his letter to Ashburton in June of that year. The work referred to as 'Corpus Juris' is less easily identified, but it must be in some way related to what Dumont published as 'Vue générale d'un corps complet de législation' (cf. Bowring, iii, 155–210).[2]

The text of the work presented in this edition follows the table of contents given both in the Ashburton letter and in the list 'Of Laws in General' with the following exceptions. For the reasons just given there is nothing corresponding to the final three chapters (on 'Indirect Legislation', 'Place and Time' and 'Corpus Juris') included in these lists. For reasons explained below, the first two chapters in these lists, which are in fact repetitions of the first two sections of Ch. xvii of *An Introduction to the Principles*, are omitted. The present text therefore consists of nineteen chapters corresponding to nos. iii–xxi of the list of contents for 'Of Laws in General' and to nos. 19–37 in the list in the letter to Ashburton.

Title and Scope of the Work

The great bulk of the Mss. of the present work is headed 'Limits'. This is a survival of the original conception of the work as forming the concluding sections of Ch. xvii of *An Introduction to the Principles*, and the title of that chapter ('Of the Limits of the Penal Branch of Jurisprudence') frequently appears in the abbreviated form 'Chapter xvii (Limits)' in footnote references to it in earlier chapters of *An Introduction*.[3] Accordingly, had Bentham not altered his original design, the whole of the present work might

---

[1] On the other hand, a number of Ms. sheets originally written for the 'Corpus Juris' chapter were subsequently incorporated in the present work and re-headed 'Limits'.

[2] These three works will form part of a further volume in this section of the present edition.

[3] See, e.g., op. cit., Ch. xvi, para. 44 n. d4 (in *CW*, 244).

have been entitled *The Limits of the Penal Branch of Jurisprudence*, but there seems no ground whatsoever for following Professor Everett in entitling this work *The Limits of Jurisprudence Defined*. Not only is there no trace of such a title in the Mss. but it fails to convey the character and scope of the present work and has an unfortunate similarity to Austin's *The Province of Jurisprudence Determined*. On the other hand, the title *Of Laws in General* which appears at the head of the list of contents compiled when Bentham determined that these chapters should form a separate work seems entirely appropriate to a volume which, as Bentham stated, was to answer the questions 'what sort of thing *a* law is',[1] 'what the properties are that are to be found in every object which can with propriety receive the appellation of *a* law',[2] and was 'to afford some little insight into the structure and contents of a complete body of laws'[3] and to serve 'for an introduction to the principles of legislation in general'.[4]

This development of a considerable work appropriately entitled *Of Laws in General* from mere sections of a chapter on 'the Limits of the Penal Branch of Jurisprudence', was due to a deepened appreciation on Bentham's part of the great difficulties and profound importance for the understanding of the nature of a legal system of the issues raised by the apparently simple question: What is the nature of the distinction between civil and penal law? He came to see that this question could only be satisfactorily answered as part of a general solution of what a modern logician would term the problem of individuation[5] (What is one law? What is part of a law? What is a complete law?) and that it was necessary to develop as he does in Ch. x of the present work what he termed 'a logic of the will'[6] which corresponds in many ways to what a modern logician calls deontic logic. These are the difficulties which in the letter to Ashburton he rightly describes as 'problems of a most

---

[1] Op. cit., Ch. xvii, para. 1 (in *CW*, 282).

[2] Op. cit., Ch. xvii, para. 29 (in *CW*, 299–300).

[3] Op. cit., Ch. xvii, concluding note, para. 15 (in *CW*, 305).

[4] Letter to Ashburton, Appendix E below, 305.

[5] Bentham himself used the phrase 'the individuation of a law' in what seems to have been an early draft for the beginning of the present work: see below, Appendix A, p. 247. The same phrase occurs in a letter written by Bentham to Lord Shelburne on 18 June 1781: see below, Appendix E, p. 305 n. 2.

[6] For Bentham's explanation of this phrase see *An Introduction to the Principles*, Preface, paras. 35, 36, and Ch. xvii, para. 29 n. b2 (in *CW*, 8–9 and 299–300). The second passage referred to was included by Everett in the present work (ed. cit., pp. 293–5) under the heading *Note [on Logic]*; but there are clear indications that it is a note to para. 29 of Ch. xvii of *An Introduction* (cf. op. cit., in *CW*, Introduction, xlii). See also Bowring, v, 270 n.

intricate kind which no-one hitherto had thought of solving' and to which in the Preface to *An Introduction to the Principles* he attributes the long delay in the publication of that work. Bentham's solution of these problems led him to the radical conclusion that the distinction between civil and penal law was a distinction only in the description and arrangement of law and not in the law itself. He found the only satisfactory criterion by which a single law could be individuated to be the duty imposed by it[1], and that every law when adequately described could be shown to comprise both a penal and a civil element. The penal element is the mandatory or imperative part of the law creating the duty and its sanctions; the civil element is the 'expositive' or 'circumstantiative matter', i.e. the specification, usually in descriptive language, of the often complex conditions, circumstances, exceptions and qualifications to which legal duties are subject. Though different laws are individuated by the different duties which they impose they frequently share vast ranges of common circumstantiative matter or conditions. These common conditions may be collected together and studied separately under such headings as the Law of Property or Constitutional Law, but they are parts of law, not entire laws. A full understanding and description of a single law involves an understanding and description of all the ramified conditions common to it and to other laws, and hence an understanding and description of the entire system. 'A body of laws is a vast and complicated piece of mechanism, of which no part can be fully explained without the rest. To understand the functions of a balance-wheel you must take to pieces the whole watch: to understand the nature of a law you must take to pieces the whole code.'[2]

INITIAL CHAPTER OF THE PRESENT WORK

Bentham's list of contents for 'Of Laws in General' starts with two chapters of which the first is shortly described as 'Limits' and the second as 'Jurisprudence'. It seems clear from Bentham's statement in the letter to Ashburton, where the chapter entitled 'Jurisprudence' is spoken of as 'dismembered from Chapter XVII', that he proposed to use as the first chapter of the separate work section 1 of Ch. XVII of *An Introduction to the Principles*, which was

[1] See below Ch. XIV, para. 18. Bentham usually expounds this doctrine in terms of the notion of an offence which he regards as the counterpart of duty. 'By what circumstance determine the unity of the law? By the unity of the class of acts which it takes for its object; by the unity of the offence' (ibid., para. 19).

[2] *An Introduction to the Principles*, Ch. XVII. para. 29 n. b2 (in *CW*, 299).

entitled 'Limits between Private Ethics and Legislation' and to use section 2 of that chapter, which was entitled 'Jurisprudence, its branches', as the second chapter of the separate work. Nothing is however gained by the repetition in the present work of the last chapter of *An Introduction to the Principles*, and it is accordingly omitted. The full text of it, corrected by the addition of an important and lengthy note (on the 'logic of the will') wrongly included in the Everett edition in the text of the present work, has already been printed in this edition.[1]

Accordingly in the present edition *Of Laws in General* starts with the chapter on the definition of a law which appears as Ch. III in Bentham's list of contents for the work. The Everett edition started with two chapters entitled respectively 'Distinction between Penal Law and Civil' and 'Analysis and Exposition', which are excluded from the text of this edition and relegated to Appendices A and B. The reasons for this course together with the reasons for assigning to Appendices B and C certain passages incorporated in Ch. XXI of the Everett edition are set out below.

APPENDICES TO THE TEXT

1. *Appendix A*[2]

There seems little doubt that this short discussion of the distinction between penal and civil law was originally intended by Bentham to bridge the transition from Ch. XVII of *An Introduction to the Principles* to the present work. However neither the letter to Ashburton nor the list of contents for 'Of Laws in General' include any reference to such a bridge chapter, and the Mss. for these pages are in fact struck out in pencil. Accordingly it seems clear that Bentham came to regard these few pages as a false start, possibly because the work includes a much fuller discussion of the main point made in these pages, viz. that properly understood every law has both a civil and a penal part and the distinction between penal and civil is a distinction not in the law itself but in the exposition and arrangement of law. It is not possible to assign a date to the composition of these pages nor to their deletion in pencil. The Mss. were found together with those for Ch. XVI, which is a virtual restatement of the main point made in these pages.

---

[1] Op. cit., in *CW*, 281–300: the note is on 299–300.
[2] Everett, Ch. I: Distinction between Penal Law and Civil.

2. *Appendix B, Part I*[1]

The subject of these pages (except for one passage inserted in the Everett edition[2] which does not belong to the present work and is omitted from this edition) is the analysis of legal rights and powers and the application of that analysis to the elucidation of the various forms of property which Bentham terms 'the several modifications of which property is susceptible'. Though this subject was certainly held by Bentham to be one of great importance, neither the letter to Ashburton nor the list of contents for 'Of Laws in General' make any reference to the inclusion of this treatment of it. There are many passages in the work which are concerned with 'powers', but none of them has any continuity with the pages under discussion. The origin of these pages is however clear. In the lengthy classification and analysis of Offences to which Ch. xvi of *An Introduction to the Principles* is devoted, Bentham reached in paragraph 25 the topic which he described as 'Offences against Trust'. He there shortly defined the notion of a trust in terms of the notions of 'power' and 'right', but in an elaborate footnote conceded that these latter notions were in equal need of 'exposition', and stated that he had in fact prepared such an 'exposition', but it was too long for inclusion there.[3] In the same footnote however he gives a summary of this exposition of rights and powers and of its application 'to the modifications of which property is susceptible', from which it is clear that the pages now under discussion form a substantial part but probably not the whole of the exposition itself. This conclusion is corroborated by the fact that the Mss. of these pages are headed 'Exposition'. The date of composition (1780) is attested by a letter to Samuel Bentham in which Bentham refers to himself as engaged in revising part of *An Introduction to the Principles* and in 'drawing up without inserting an analysis of the possible modifications of property'.[4]

In the long note to paragraph 25 of Ch. xvi of *An Introduction to the Principles* Bentham states that an analysis of rights and powers, of which those of which property is comprised form only 'one branch', would find 'its proper place in a work which would treat of the civil branch of legislation as distinct from the penal branch'. This passage, written not later than November 1780, is perhaps some evidence that Bentham thought at one time of the 'exposition' as falling within the scope of a work of the same

[1] Everett, Ch. ii: Analysis and Exposition.
[2] Pp. 82–5.
[3] Op. cit., in *CW*, 205.
[4] *Correspondence*, in *CW*, ii, 488: 27 October 1780.

general character as the present one. But by 1782, when the list of contents of the present work was settled, he must have decided not to include it. There is no evidence of any subsequent decision to include it, and he may have come to think that the treatment of the general topic of powers in various parts of the present work rendered its inclusion unnecessary.[1]

3. *Appendix B, Part II*[2]

These pages are also concerned with property and the phrase 'the several modifications of which property is susceptible', which Bentham used in describing the contents of the 'exposition', occurs here (p. 285). It is accordingly conceivable that they form a further part of the 'exposition' and the lack of continuity with the pages assigned to Part I of Appendix B can be ascribed either to Bentham's failure to complete the 'exposition' or to the loss of some of the Mss. There are however good reasons for thinking that these pages are an early draft of part of Ch. xvi of *An Introduction to the Principles*, written before Bentham had decided that the exposition of rights and powers was too long or elaborate for inclusion in Ch. xvi. This is strongly suggested by the fact that the Mss. of these pages are headed 'Division', since this abbreviation of the title of Ch. xvi ('Division of Offences') was frequently used by Bentham both in the present work and in *An Introduction* itself. Moreover the subject matter and some of the phraseology of these pages are very similar to those of paragraph 25 of Ch. xvi, dealing with offences against trust. Thus of the pages under discussion pp. 279 to 283 deal with what Bentham described as 'the means by which the possession of a trust may be offended against', and when that topic is exhausted he begins the next topic with the words 'We come now to offences against Trust', which is the same phrase as that used to introduce paragraph 25 of Ch. xvi of *An Introduction*. There then follows a general discussion of property and investitive and divestitive powers. It thus seems likely that these pages are part of an early draft of a chapter on offences written at a time when Bentham still thought he might include in it the exposition of property and powers. Nothing in the Mss. supports the view taken by Everett that these pages should be included in the final chapter of the present work. Neither of the lists of contents is consistent with this view.

---

[1] British Museum Additional Ms. 33,549 includes (ff. 293–4) a list of marginal headings for the 'exposition'. It seems possible to infer from a note in Bentham's handwriting ('1826 July 2. Seen') that he may still have been considering the material included in Appendix B of this edition as late as 1826.

[2] Everett, Ch. xxi, pp. 320–9.

4. *Appendix C*[1]

Though these pages, the continuity of which is broken at p. 293, are also mainly concerned with the topics of powers and property, the opening paragraph makes it clear that Bentham intended them to form part of a summary of the preceding chapters of the work. There is no place for such a summarizing chapter in either of the lists of contents and for this reason, and also because these pages add very little to previous discussions of the topics with which they deal, they have been assigned to an appendix in this edition.

The Text of Chapter X ('Aspects of a Law')[2]

The Mss. of this chapter, which is of crucial importance to the work as a whole, present certain problems:

(a) The Mss. for the later part of the chapter (pp. 110–32) and also for the pages assigned to Appendix D[3] are of earlier date than those for the earlier part of the chapter (pp. 93–110), which includes a revised and much improved version of the contents of the pages assigned to Appendix D. The difference in date between the two parts of the chapter is evident both from differences in the paper of the Mss. and from the fact that the first part is firmly written, without deletions, where the succeeding pages have all the appearance of a tentative first draft. From these indications it seems clear that Bentham intended to rewrite the whole of this chapter but did not get beyond the point corresponding to p. 110 below. That revision had, however, covered the topics dealt with in that part of the earlier draft which is represented by pp. 199–203 of the Everett edition. These pages are therefore omitted from the text of the present edition, but they are preserved as Appendix D because they contain a valuable footnote not completely covered in Bentham's revised version.

(b) Bentham's revised version of the early part of the chapter envisaged the division of the chapter into numbered sections, and in the outline of his plan on p. 94 below he indicates four topics to be treated under what he describes as 'four heads which may be taken as subjects of so many succeeding sections'.[4] The numbers and headings for three sections (§ i *Introduction*, § ii *Primordial*, § iii *Reiterative*) appear in the Mss., but no further numbers or

[1] Everett, Ch. xxi, pp. 311–20.
[2] Everett, Ch. xii.
[3] Everett, pp. 199–203.
[4] This is one of the rare instances where the Mss. reflect the later conception of the present work as being divided into chapters with their own subdivisions, rather than sections of Ch. xvii of *An Introduction to the Principles*. It supports the hypothesis that the Mss. of the earlier part of Ch. x were written at a relatively late stage.

headings are to be found there. It is however possible from Bentham's descriptions of the topics on p. 94 to identify these sections in accordance with these indications (§ iv *Alterative* and § v *Extensive*). Though these seem plainly warranted, the division of the last parts of the chapter into further numbered sections is more problematic. It is not clear whether Bentham intended § v *Extensive* to include the discussion of limitations and exceptions and related topics which occupies pp. 127–8 or whether these topics should be the subjects of separate sections. Since the brief description of the contents of this chapter in the letter to Ashburton does not refer to distinct headings they have been included in § v *Extensive*.

(c) In the present edition this chapter ends with a section (§ vi) on the topic of Repugnancy, the contents of which appeared in the Everett edition in the middle of the chapter (pp. 195–9). The reason for removing these pages to the end of the chapter is that the list of contents in the letter to Ashburton gives Repugnancy as the last of the topics treated in the chapter and the tentative description given on p. 130 by Bentham of its relevance to the chapter ('it seems to have some claim to be considered here') suggest that it was intended for the conclusion of the chapter.

ADDITIONS TO THE TEXT

Besides numerous minor additions and corrections, two substantial additions have been made of Ms. material not included in the Everett edition. These are represented by pp. 9–17 and 198–208. The first is a valuable discussion of reasons for preferring the word 'law' to other terms for the expression of the legislator's will; the second is a review of the different classes of legal offences undertaken to illustrate Bentham's central distinction (to be made in the case of every law) between the expositive or circumstantiative matter referred to the civil branch of the law and the mandatory or imperative matter referred to the penal branch of the law. The first of these passages clearly belongs to Ch. i of the present edition, where it is continuous with the rest of the text. The second almost certainly belongs (together with the last three paragraphs of Ch. 4 on pp. 98–100 of the Everett edition, which are a continuation of it) to Ch. xvi of the present edition, where it has accordingly been placed (see p. 198 and n. 1).

DESCRIPTION OF THE MANUSCRIPTS

Virtually all the Mss. for the present work are now to be found in

Boxes lxxxviii(a) and lxxxviii(b) of the Bentham papers at University College London. They are almost entirely in Bentham's hand and, apart from an occasional note or insertion, they are in ink. For the most part they are written on double sheets of foolscap, both sides of each leaf being commonly used. It was evidently Bentham's practice, however, to use a fresh sheet for the beginning of each new section of what he wrote, and where the section did not fill all four sides of the sheet he usually left blanks. These sections or paragraphs are frequently, in accordance with the practice established in *An Introduction to the Principles*, numbered for reference. This was not consistently done, and in addition Bentham engaged in extensive renumbering at various stages of composition —a fact which at times causes difficulty both in identifying Bentham's cross-references and in establishing the intended order of his text. In the same way the numbering and renumbering of the Ms. pages is at once a help and a hindrance to the elucidation of the text. The overwhelming majority of the Mss. are headed 'Limits' together, usually, with a subheading. The latter indicates the section of the expanded Ch. xvii of *An Introduction to the Principles* for which the Ms. was intended; and there is virtually no reflection in the Mss. themselves of the subsequent stages, noted above, through which the conception of the work passed. There is, on the other hand, quite extensive evidence of revision and rewriting, and it is sometimes possible, as in the case of Ch. x of the work, already discussed, to distinguish clearly between earlier and later versions of the same material. But while there is no way of dating precisely the various stages through which the Mss. passed, there is nothing to suggest that Bentham worked on them in any significant degree after 1782. He did at some stage 'marginalise' the material in what was already his usual fashion: that is, he entered in the margins (usually in pencil on these Mss.) summaries of each paragraph or section. These, following the pattern of *An Introduction to the Principles*, have been used as shoulder-notes to the text and to provide an analytical table of contents.

It remains to say something of Bentham's frequent deletions and alternative readings. In the case of the latter, his interlinear or marginal 'second thoughts' have usually been preferred, except where the original version gave greater clarity or consistency with the rest of the passage. Deletions have presented a more difficult problem. Firm deletions in ink have in general been regarded as decisive and the passages in question omitted (they are usually replaced by Bentham himself with alternative versions). The more tentative deletions in pencil (sometimes no more than a marginal query) leave more room for editorial discretion, and these cases have been decided on their merits. Where the deleted passage appeared to incorporate material of value not covered elsewhere, or where its exclusion left some incoherence in the text, it has been retained.

PRESENTATION OF THE TEXT

In accordance with the general policy of the present edition spelling has been systematically modernised. In matters of punctuation a similar policy has been adopted, but at the same time an attempt has been made to retain some characteristics of Bentham's own practice. That practice is far from uniform, however, and an attempt to reproduce it exactly could only have impaired the clarity and readability of the text. Brackets occurring in Bentham's text and notes have throughout been printed as round brackets, Bentham himself having been quite unsystematic in his use of different forms. Square brackets are here reserved for editorially inserted words. Perpendicular strokes indicate a gap in the manuscript. Bentham's footnotes are indicated by suprascript letters running in sequence throughout each chapter[1]; footnotes to these notes (usually references) are indicated by asterisks, etc. Bentham's frequent, but often incomplete and therefore unhelpful cross-references within the text have been reproduced only where they could be identified with some certainty; many references in such forms as 'V. *supra*' have been silently suppressed. Editorial footnotes are indicated by suprascript numerals, with a separate numerical sequence for each page of the text.

[1] Where Bentham has more than twenty-six footnotes in a chapter, a second series, a2, b2 . . . etc., has been used, followed, when required, by a third series, a3, b3 . . . etc., and so on.

CHAPTER I

A LAW DEFINED AND DISTINGUISHED

1. A law may be defined as an assemblage of signs declarative of *A law* a volition conceived or adopted by the *sovereign* in a state, concern- *defined* ing the conduct to be observed in a certain *case* by a certain person or class of persons, who in the case in question are or are supposed to be subject to his power: such volition trusting for its accomplish- ment to the expectation of certain events which it is intended such declaration should upon occasion be a means of bringing to pass, and the prospect of which it is intended should act as a motive upon those whose conduct is in question.

2. According to this definition, a law may be considered in eight *It may be* different respects. *considered*

with relation
(1) In respect to its *source*: that is in respect to the person or *to 1. its* persons of whose will it is the expression. *source 2. its*

subjects 3. its
(2) In respect to the quality of its *subjects*: by which I mean the *objects 4. its* persons and things to which it may apply. *extent 5. its*

aspects 6. its
(3) In respect to its *objects*: by which I mean the *acts*, as character- *force 7. its* ized by the *circumstances*, to which it may apply. *expression 8.*

its occasional
(4) In respect to its *extent*, the generality or the amplitude of its *appendages* application: that is in respect to the determinateness of the persons whose conduct it may seek to regulate.

(5) In respect to its *aspects*: that is in respect to the various manners in which the will whereof it is the expression may apply itself to the acts and circumstances which are its objects.

(6) In respect to its *force*: that is, in respect to the *motives* it relies on for enabling it to produce the effect it aims at, and the laws or other means which it relies on for bringing those motives into play: such laws may be styled its *corroborative appendages*.

(7) In respect to its *expression*: that is in respect to the nature of the *signs* by which the will whereof it is the expression may be made known.

(8) In respect to its *remedial appendages*, where it has any: by which I mean certain other laws which may occasionally come to be subjoined to the principal law in question; and of which the design is to obviate the mischief that stands connected with any indi- vidual act of the number of those which are made offences by it, in a more perfect manner than can be done by the sole efficacy

of the subsidiary appendages to which it stands indebted for its force.[a]

Parts contained in a law. Blackstone

[a] According to the great oracle of English jurisprudence, every law consists of four parts: (Blackst. Comm. Introd. § 2, p. 53–56.)[1] a declaratory, a directory, a remedial, and a vindicatory which he calls also the sanction: by the declaratory (to judge from such feeble lights as can be extracted out of the thickest obscurity) he seems to mean that which contains the description of the act: by the vindicatory that which contains the description of the punishment. The directory as he describes it is a vague repetition of the substance of the declaratory and the vindicatory taken together. By the remedial he means one or other or both together of two very different things 1. that part of the law in question which appoints compensation: 2ly, so much of the system of procedure as is subservient to the execution of that law. Now the former of these articles may be considered as a branch of what he calls the vindicatory: being a direction concerning the disposal of the whole or a part of the produce of the punishment: that is in the case where the punishment is any part of it, of that sort the peculiar nature of which it is to be capable of yielding a beneficial transferrable produce. As to this part of the law it is plain there are but two cases in which it can have existence: 1. where the offence is of a private nature: 2. Where being of a semi-public or of a public nature and being levelled against property, the fund to the prejudice of which it operates is assignable. As to what belongs to the head of procedure, this, so far from being a part of the law in question, or indeed a part of any law, is a complex mass consisting of a multitude of laws put together. It contains a multitude of separate regulations or commands: commands which are not so much as addressed to the same person as that is which constitutes the law in question; but to a prodigious variety of other persons.

If the author had made a point with himself to find one example for all these parts as he has done for some of them, he would have given no account of this matter at all or he would have given a different one. 'Stealing is a crime'—that says he is the declaratory part of a law: Thou shalt not steal; this he says is the directory part of the same law. What is the remedial part of it? what the vindicatory? This he has not told us: for he could go no further. To illustrate the remedial he takes up another specimen: and here again he gives us the declaratory part and the directory, as before *in terminis. The field or inheritance which belonged to Titius's father is vested by his death in Titius.* This says he is the declaratory part. *It is forbidden that anyone enter on another's property without leave of the owner.* This he gives for the directory. What then is the remedial? Here for the second time he is at a stand—*bis patriae cecidere manus.** There being no such thing, there was no producing it: instead then of giving the thing itself he gives this general account of it, which let anyone make a meaning of that can. If Gaius after this will presume to take possession of the land, the remedial part of the law will then interpose its office; will make Gaius restore

* Esprit des Loix. Pref.[2]

[1] William Blackstone, *Commentaries on the Laws of England*, 1765–9 and many later editions: the Introduction deals with 'the Nature of Laws in General' and section II with 'municipal law'.

[2] Montesquieu, *De l'Esprit des lois*, Preface, *ad fin.*: in *Oeuvres*, Amsterdam and Leipzig, 1758, I, p. lxii and n.

3. The latitude here given to the import of the word *law* is it must be confessed rather greater than what seems to be given to it in common: the definition being such as is applicable to various objects which are not commonly characterized by that name. Taking this definition for the standard it matters not whether the expression of will in question, so as it have but the authority of the sovereign to back it, were his by immediate conception or only by adoption: whether it be of the most public or of the most private or even domestic nature: whether the sovereign from whom it derives its force be an individual or a body: whether it be issued *propter quid* as the phrase may be, that is on account of some particular act or event which is understood to warrant it (as is the case with an order of the judicial kind made in the course of a cause); or without the assignment of any such special ground: or whether it be susceptible of an indefinite duration or whether it be *suâ naturâ* temporary and undurable: as is most commonly the case with such expressions of will the uttering of which is looked upon as a *measure of administration*: whether it be a command or a countermand: whether it be expressed in the way of statute, or of customary law.[b] Under the term 'law' then if this definition be admitted of, we must include a judicial order, a military or any other kind of executive order, or even the most trivial and momentary order of the domestic kind, so it be not illegal: that is, so as the issuing of it be not forbidden by some other law.

4. Judging however from analogy, it would naturally be expected that the signification given to the word *law* should be correspondent to that of its conjugates *legislation* and *legislative power*: for what, it will be said, is legislation but the act of making laws? or legislative power but the power of making them? that consequently the term

The idea exhibited by this definition more extensive than what is commonly annexed to the word law

—more extensive than it ought to be to correspond to the phrases legislation *and* legislative power

the possession to Titius and also pay him damages for the invasion. *Voces inopes rerum, nugaeque canorae.* There remains still his vindicatory part, which no attempt is made to exemplify, not even as the remedial is exemplified—not even by description. All this for want of the light of genuine metaphysics: wandering in a labyrinth of rights and wrongs, and duties, and obligations and laws of nature, and other fictitious entities, instead of gathering up that clue that might have been afforded by an attentive consideration of such particulars as the acts which are made offences, the circumstances with which they are accompanied, the persons whose acts they are, the persons who are sufferers by them, the pain experienced by those persons, the pain to be inflicted on the offenders and so on throughout the region of real entities.

Of this nature is the analysis, given by that admired writer, of the parts to be found in every law: and his analysis of the content of a whole body of laws is of a piece with it.

[b] These distinctions will all of them be explained at large, as we proceed.

law should be applied to every expression of will, the uttering of which was an act of legislation, an exertion of legislative power; and that on the other hand it should not be applied to any expression of will of which those two propositions could not be predicated. Accordingly in the former of these points it does indeed quadrate with these two expressions: but it can not be said to do so in the latter. It has all the amplitude which they have, but the import of it is not every where confined within the bounds which limit theirs. This will be seen in a variety of examples.

1. viz. by including domestic orders

(1) In the first place, according to the definition, the word *law* should be applicable to any the most trivial order supposing it to be not illegal, which a man may have occasion to give for any of the most inconsiderable purposes of life: to any order which a master may have occasion to give to his servant, a parent to his child, or (where the request of a husband assumes the harsh form of a command) of a husband to his wife. Yet it would seem a strange catachresis to speak of the issuing of any such order as an act of legislation, or as an exercise of legislative power. Not but that in cases like these the word *law* is frequently enough employed: but then it is in the way of figure. Even where there is no strict legal superiority, a man may say to another out of compliment, 'your commands are laws to me': but on occasions like these the impropriety of the expression is the very reason of its being chosen.

2. Temporary orders of administration

(2) With equal propriety (according to the definition) would the word *law* be applicable to a temporary order issued by any magistrate who is spoken of as exercising thereby a branch of *executive* power, or as exercising the functions belonging to any department of *administration*. But the executive power is continually mentioned as distinct from the legislative: and the business of administration is as constantly opposed to that of legislation. Let the Board of Treasury order a sum of money to be paid or issued to such or such a person, let the Commander in chief order such or such a body of troops to march to such a place, let the Navy Board order such or such a ship to be fitted out, let the Board of Ordnance order such or such a train of artillery to be dispatched to such a destination—Who would ever speak of any of these orders as acts of legislative power, as acts of legislation?

3. Judicial orders

(3) With equal propriety again would the word law according to the definition be applicable to any *judicial* order, to any order which in the course of a cause of any kind a man might have occasion to issue in the capacity of a judge. Yet the business of judicature is constantly looked upon as essentially distinct from the

business of legislation and as constantly opposed to it: and the case is the same between the judicial and the legislative power. Even suppose the order to have been ever so general, suppose the persons to whom it is addressed to be ever so numerous and indeterminate, and the duration of it ever so indefinite, still if issued in the course of a forensic contestation, the act of issuing it would not be looked upon in general as coming under the notion of an act of legislation, or as an exercise of legislative power. The fate of a province may be determined by a judicial decree: but the pronouncing of the decree will not on that account be looked upon as being capable with any sort of propriety of being termed an act of legislation.

(4) Of course the term *law* would according to the definition be applicable to any order whatsoever coming directly from the sovereign. But it is not in all cases that the issuing of any such order is looked upon as an act of legislation.

4. *Monarchical orders if particular and* suâ *naturâ temporary*

Where the sovereign is a body corporate, there indeed, if the matter be considered with reference to the English language, there seem to be no exceptions. In Great Britain, for example, the sovereignty is in the King, Lords, and Commons in Parliament assembled: it would be hardly possible for that complex body to issue any order the issuing of which would not be looked upon as an act of legislation. What power was it that it exercised when it made the act by which the Earl of Strafford suffered death,[1] or that by which the Earl of Clarendon was driven into banishment?[2] The answer would I suppose be in both cases, the legislative:[c] and in this case the command which was the result of such act of legislation would accordingly be termed a law. How would it be with a command of the like nature issued by the Diet of Poland or that of Sweden, by the sovereign councils of Berne, Venice, Genoa or Amsterdam? This would depend partly upon the political notions

[c] I choose here for examples such orders as have their physical termination in a man's body, and are capable in their own nature of being fulfilled by a single person. Those which regard property will generally be very complex according to the different articles which a man's property may consist of. In these examples the acts in question would in fact be found resolvable into a variety of orders, issued to different persons: but the effect of the most material articles might by possibility have been obtained by one.

[1] Thomas Wentworth (1593–1641), 1st Earl of Strafford, was executed on 12 May 1641 in accordance with a bill of attainder which had received the royal assent two days previously.

[2] Edward Hyde (1609–74), 1st Earl of Clarendon, went into exile in 1667 after acting as Charles II's chief minister since the Restoration. Articles of impeachment were prepared against him but not proceeded with.

prevalent in the respective states, partly upon the terminology of the respective languages. As to Rome in the time of the Common-wealth we know from Cicero that the language was thus: a command was termed a *privilegium*; which being a conjugate of the word *lex*, shewed that the power of which such command was deemed the exercise, was the legislative.[1]

But where the sovereignty is in a single person and the party who is looked upon as principally affected by it is an individual, neither the word *law* nor any conjugate of it seems, in common speech at least, to be employed. When the King of France orders a man to quit the metropolis, or sends him to the Bastile, the power he exercises is not spoken of as a legislative power, nor the act he performs as an act of legislation. *Lettres de cachet* are not ordinarily termed laws. They are termed *ordres souverains*, sovereign orders, or by some such name. Will it be said that the orders in question are seldom issued but on account of some offence committed or apprehended, and that therefore the power exercised by them is either of the judicial or the *phthano-paranomic*[2] kind? Be it so. But even let the exercise of it be as far as possible from all dependence upon any particular event, as much so as any of the widest extend-ing law can be, in short let the *sic volo* even have no other reason than the *non amo te*, still the power exercised upon the occasion would hardly be looked upon as at all the better entitled to the name of legislative.

Thus much for the *privilegia odiosa*: and the case is the same where the *privilegium* is of the favourable kind; the most striking part of its effects consisting in the *benefit* of which it is productive to an individual. If the Parliament of England order money to be paid to any body it is by an act of legislation, and the command is called a law: but nobody I suppose, thinks of giving that name to a command of the like nature issued by the King of France.

5. *Laws made by a magistrate the most con-spicuous part of whose power is of the judicial kind*

(5) There are even cases in which although the command were in every point a general one, although it were issued *mero motu* and although the party from whom it issued were a complex body, it might be a matter of dispute whether the command itself were according to common notion entitled to the appellation of a law, or the act of issuing it to that of an act of legislation: and perhaps with

[1] Cicero, *De Legibus*, iii.19: 'in privatos homines leges ferri noluerunt: id est enim privilegium'.

[2] For this term cf. *An Introduction to the Principles*, Ch. XVI, para. 17 n. *u* (in *CW*, 198): 'Who would have endured in this place to have seen two such words as the *phthano-paranomic* or *crime-preventing*, and the *phthano-symphoric* or *calamity-preventing*, branches of the police?'

not only equal but still stronger appearance of reason, whether the power in virtue of which such command was issued would admit of the appellation of the legislative power. These are the cases where either the power from whence the magistrates by whom the commands in question are issued take their official name, or that of the magistrate from whose appointment they derive their office, comes under the denomination of either of those powers which are wont to be put in contradistinction to the legislative. In England the same sets of magistrates who exercise the judicial power are allowed, many of them, to establish *ex mero motu* regulations of a durable nature, regulations that are general in all points concerning the conduct of such parties as shall chance thereafter to be anyhow concerned in litigation. These regulations, though in every other circumstance except that of their not emaning[1] directly from the sovereign power they agree with those which are universally and without scruple termed by the name of laws, are not usually characterized by that name: they are called sometimes *orders*, sometimes by a compound sort of name *rules and orders* of the court from which they ensue: and sometimes for distinction's sake *standing orders*; nor would the magistrates who are allowed to issue them be spoken of as exercising acts of legislation or as possessing any share of legislative power.

(6) In the same country the magistrate whose powers taken collectively are commonly termed by the appellation of the executive power, I mean the King, is also allowed to establish of himself and *ex mero motu* a multitude of regulations; regulations which are to such a degree general that the conduct and the fate of large and numerous classes of individuals are regulated and determined by them, and which accordingly in point of duration, though limited by positive institution, are in their own nature susceptible of perpetuity. The articles of war for the government of the army and the instructions given to privateers may serve for examples. I say nothing here of the power of making treaties nor of the power of making war and peace: powers of which the nature is too complicated, and the relation which they bear to legislative too faintly characterized, to be adduced for the purpose of illustration in the present stage of our enquiry. These then are so many other sets of articles which the definition would comprise under the name of laws. At the same time the issuing of the commands referrable to

6.–or of the executive kind

---

[1] The verb *to emane* meaning to issue or emanate is used frequently in the present work and sometimes also in Bentham's other works. It appears to have been of his own coining.

these heads would hardly without some reluctance be acknowledged as acts of legislation; and the power in virtue of which they were issued would probably not without a still greater degree of reluctance be admitted to the title of legislative power.

7.–or by one whose legislative power is derived

(7) Some difficulty there may also be, though perhaps not so much, with regard to various orders (general in point of extension or perpetual in point of duration or both) which are wont to be issued by various sets of magistrates, all of whom derive their authority originally, and many of them immediately, from the King. I am speaking of those for instance, which are issued by the governing part in corporate towns and other corporations for the government of the members of the corporation: as also of those which are issued by Justices of the Peace for the levying of rates in the counties for which they are commissioned. The unwillingness to employ in these cases the terms *law*, *act of legislation*, and *legislative power* will probably increase as the field of dominion becomes less extensive. No man ever made a difficulty about employing them in the case of Ireland, of the American provinces or other distant members of the empire: yet to many it might seem odd to apply the same high sounding appellation to the powers acts and operations of a fraternity of weavers or tallow chandlers in a little town or parish. At the same time it would be impossible perhaps for the most scrupulous to draw any line of separation: the parish of Halifax in Yorkshire is in point of territory not many times less, and in point of population, probably even more considerable, than the Kingdom of Man.

Necessity of these verbal discussions

5. These discussions, local as they are, could scarcely be avoided on account of the influence which local establishments and local actions have on the idiom of the language. Such words as the language a man writes in furnishes, such must he make use of, and whatever word he makes use of on any occasion, he will of course be understood to annex the same idea to as every body else annexes to it, unless he gives warning to the contrary: such warning therefore he must give if he means to be understood, wherever the language is inconsistent with itself. In the present instance, from the confused ideas which men are wont to annex to the terms legislative power and executive power little can be collected but that the former it is thought is something superior to the latter; and where legislature and legislative power are mentioned without any epithet of addition, supreme legislature and supreme legislative power are commonly intended. In constitutional topics like these, and under popular governments more especially, the judgments of men are in continual danger of being disturbed by the influence of their passions: nor is it to be wondered at if a consciousness of the inferences that may be drawn from the significations assigned to particular words should on such occasions dispose them to regard the most phlegmatic and impartial discussions with an eye of jealousy.

In some cases the very proximity which there is in point of importance between two branches of power is the very cause of the repugnance which is felt at the thoughts of extending to the one the appellation which is currently given to the other. The two Houses of Parliament are each allowed to issue their standing orders, as well as the King his proclamations: which orders have every quality (that of sovereignty excepted) which is to be found in those of which the title to the name of *laws* stands clearest from dispute: at the same time it has been a practice of such frequency and a point of such importance to refuse to those orders and proclamations the name of laws in the sense in which the word *law* is put for an object of equal authority with an act of parliament, that it would not be to be wondered at if more aversion should be manifested to the applying of the name in question to these objects than to any other: insomuch that in the eyes of those who are upon the watch for political heresies it might seem a more dangerous solecism to attribute the legislative power in severalty to these high authorities, than to attribute it to an inconsiderable fraternity of petty tradesmen.

6. Such then are the various sorts of expressions of will to which men would be apt for one reason or other to deny the appellation of *a* law: such therefore are the points in which the definition here given of that important word outstretches the idea which common usage has annexed to it. And these excluded objects have in every point except that of the manner of their appertaining to the sovereign, in every point in short except their immediate *source*, the same nature with those whose title to the appellation stands clearest of dispute. They are all referrable *ultimately* to one common source: they have all of them alike their subjects and their objects, their local extent and their duration: in point of logical extent as it may be called they must all of them be either general or particular, and they may in most instances be indifferently either the one or the other: they are all of them susceptible of the same diversities with respect to the *parties* whom they may affect, and the *aspects* which they may present to the acts which are their objects: they require all of them the same *force* to give them effect, and the same *signs* to give them utterance.

Reason of extending the import of the word law so as to make it include the articles above mentioned

9

No other word would answer the purpose as well, viz:

7. To characterize at once a set of objects so intimately allied and to which there would be such continual occasion to apply the same propositions it was necessary to find a common appellation: that which seemed least exceptionable upon the whole was the term *law*. The only words that would come into competition with it in this view seem to be those which follow: command, commandment, order, injunction, precept, decree, statute, ordinance, edict, constitution, regulation, establishment, institution, mandate. Of the reasons for adopting it in preference to all these several appellations it may be proper to give a general idea.

1. Command

(1) The word *command* seemed inadequate in three respects. 1. It gives no intimation that the will in question is in any manner referable to the sovereign. 2. It does not include a countermand, and 3. It is not applicable without some degree of harshness to any material instrument, such as a written or printed paper whereby the will in question is expressed. When applied to anything written, it seems to denote the will which is expressed, in exclusion of the writing by which it is expressed.[d]

2. Commandment

(2) The same objections seem to apply to the word *commandment*: add to which that usage hath in a manner confined the application of it to a few particular commands which are considered as emaning immediately from the Deity: nor is there any word that corresponds to it in the manner that *countermand* does to *command*; unless we were to coin a word and say *countermandment*.

3. Order

(3) The word *order* may perhaps without impropriety be looked upon as free from the second of the above objections: for example in the instance of military orders: and it is indisputably clear from the third. But 1. It is open to the first of the objections which apply to the word *command*. 2. Another objection to it is that it seems confined to such commands as are looked upon either as not being very *general* in respect of the multitude of the persons they extend to, or as not emaning directly from the sovereign authority, or as not of a nature to be perpetual. To speak of the orders of Justinian meaning those contained in the *Corpus Juris* or of the Emperor Charles the 5th meaning those contained in the Carolinian Code[1] would seem little less improper on the one hand than on the other hand it would seem to be were we to apply the name of *laws* to the directions

---

[d] We do not call a written paper a command: but where it is called an *order*, or in a complimental way of speaking put upon the footing of an order, we speak of the commands contained in it, that is expressed by it.

[1] I.e. presumably, the *Constitutio Criminalis Carolina*, an ordinance dealing with penal procedure promulgated by Charles V on 27 June 1532.

a mistress of a family gives to her cook about the dressing of a dinner.

(4) The word *injunction* is open to the objections which apply to **4. *Injunction*** the word *command* as well as to those which apply to the word *order*: add to which that in English it has, besides its ordinary and general sense, a technical and confined sense, in which it is put for a particular kind of order issuable by a particular set of judges in a particular kind of cause.

(5) The word *decree* in its larger sense means rather a resolution to **5. *Decree*** issue a command than a command itself: and it is open to the second of the objections that lie against the word *command*: besides that in this enlarged sense it is seldom applied but to such resolutions as are attributed to the deity or in a figurative way to some fictitious personage such as Fate or Providence. Moreover in English it is embarrassed with a narrow and technical sense somewhat analogous to that which adheres to the word *injunction*.

(6) The word *precept* in its larger sense is applied rather to **6. *Precept*** advices than commands: to such expressions of will as seek their accomplishment rather by motives represented as accruing of themselves from other sources, than by motives which the party represents himself as about to be instrumental in bringing into play. The only sense in which it is unequivocally significative of a command is a narrow technical sense which it has of its own, after the manner of the words preceding.

(7) The word *statute* stands clear of the first of the objections **7. *Statute*** which apply to the words *command, order*, and the like. But it lies open to several objections: 1. It is not applicable to domestic commands. 2. Nor to commands issued *litis causâ*. 3. By reason of certain circumstances peculiar to the British constitution it would seem to exclude (after a few exceptions which could not be reduced to any rule) all other laws but what emaned immediately from the sovereign. 4. It denotes a particular expression of will no otherwise than through the medium of a particular instrument or assemblage of signs denoting the ideas signified, not howsoever signified but only as signified by those signs: being in this respect the reverse of the word *command*. 5. It accordingly means not any determinate portion of the matter of which laws are made; but such a quantity of that matter, be it ever so great or ever so little as happens to be issued at one enactment or as we may say, *uno flatu*.

This objection to the word *statute* regards rather a meaning which I wish to see annexed to the term *law* than one which it has any settled and exclusive possession of already: and as the distinction

11

between this new idea and the idea already annexed to the word *statute* is nice, as well as the use that I propose to make of it an important one, it will demand some attention. The idea for which I want to find an expression is that of so much of the matter of which laws and statutes are made as constitutes one entire command or countermand and nothing more. To this purpose the word *law*, after proper notice given, is capable of being applied. In this very sense indeed it hath no doubt been frequently employed already: all that remains to be done is to appropriate it: for the idea having never yet been distinctly pointed out, the word *law* has hitherto been indiscriminately applied to this and the more variable idea which belongs to the word *statute*. This being premised I will for shortness sake suppose the word *law* to be already fixed in the possession of the particular sense to which I purpose to confine it: which done, the distinction between this and the word *statute* may be further illustrated as follows. The idea of a law (in its primary sense) is the idea of an object which may be purely intellectual existing nowhere but in the mind of him who speaks of it: the idea of a statute is constantly the idea of a material object, copies of which may be had anywhere at the bookseller's. If a coarse allusion may be allowed, a law in comparison with a statute, is what a single but entire muscle as dissected off by an anatomist is to a steak or a joint as cut off by a butcher. The idea of a law as thus determined is what must previously be formed in order to serve as a pattern to which the contents of a statute or any number of statutes may be reduced, and the several parts they consist of referred to the several stations they belong to in the system. Laws in short are the elements of which statutes are composed, and into which in order to be understood they must be resolved.

8. *Ordinance and edict*

(8) The words *ordinance* and *edict* lie open to all the objections except the third, of those which lie against the word *statute*.

9. *Constitution*

(9) The word *constitution* lies open to all the objections which lie against the words *ordinance* and *edict*: besides which, the more confined sense in which it is put for the aggregate of those laws in a state which are styled collectively the public law (*jus publicum*), or rather for a kind of fictitious entity, the supposed product of those laws, renders it in many cases inconvenient for use.

10. *Regulation*

(10) The word *regulation* lies open to the second of the objections which lie against the word *statute*: it being scarcely applicable to commands issued *litis causâ*. With regard to the 4th of these objections, this word is not confined to denote neither more nor less than one entire command or countermand: it may indeed mean

exactly one such expression of will: but it may also include more as well as less; but more naturally less than to any considerable degree, more.

(11) The word *establishment* lies open to the objections following: 1. Although it may in certain cases be employed instead of the word *law* it can no more be made to take the place of it in all cases than a genus can in all cases be put in the place of a species that is contained under it: for *establishment* is no otherwise significative of a law than in as far as it denotes a work of any kind considerable in point of relative importance, and promising a certain degree of stability: or rather perhaps a kind of fictitious entity, looked upon as being the result of the labour employed in such a work; just as the constitution (as above mentioned) is considered as the result of what is done by the laws of which *jus publicum* is composed. 2. It lies open to the second of the objections which lie against the word *law*, not extending to commands issued *litis causâ*. 3. With regard to the fourth of these objections it stands much upon a footing with the word *regulation*. It seems likewise to lie open in a slight degree at least to another objection or two not worth insisting on. In short it is only in a very vague and uncharacteristic as well as imperfect manner that it can serve for representing the word *law*: since it can signify no laws that are not permanent and it signifies any thing else almost that is so.[e]

11. *Establishment*

(12) The word *institution* lies open to the objections following: 1. It lies open to an objection similar to the first of those which lie against the word *establishment*. It is put for the cause of a practice or habit of any kind prevailing among a considerable assemblage of persons, whether that cause were the act of making a positive law or only the act of using persuasion or setting an example, and thence by metonymy for the practise or habit itself so caused.[f] In short it signifies what we mean by law no otherwise than in as far as it signifies any work that has had a beginning, considered in respect to its having had such a beginning. 2. It lies open to the second of the objections which apply to the word *statute*.

12. *Institution*

(13) Of all the words that have been mentioned that which

13. *Mandate*

[e] In French indeed there is a collection of the laws known by the name of the *Establishments of S. Louis*[1]: but this is a particular case.

[f] Games, festivals, orders of knighthood are spoken of as institutions: and though laws may have been made on the occasion of these institutions yet the institutions were possible and intelligible without the laws.

[1] Compiled probably before 1273, this collection comprises ordinances of Louis IX (1226–70) and laws and customs of Anjou, Maine, and Orléans.

seems the best adapted to express in all its amplitude and under all its modification the large and comprehensive idea to which from necessity I have ventured to appropriate the term *law*, is the word *mandate*. It is not confined by any of those peculiarities which limit the extent of the word *order*, any more than by those which limit that of the word *law* considered as the emanation of legislative power: it is equally applicable to the laws of the sovereign as to the orders of the judge, of the general, or the master of a private family: it may even be applicable without distinction to the will which is expressed, and to the material instrument made use of to express it: perhaps too it might even without much violence be extended to signify a countermand as well as a command itself.

In short it might with great advantage have been made use of as the *genus generalissimum* in the room of the word *law* had it not been for two objections, the latter of which arises out of the former: In the first place it is upon no better a footing than the words *command, order*, and *injunction* in respect to its not conveying any intimation that the expression of will to which it is applied has the sovereign for its source: it is as natural to speak of an illegal, as of a legal, mandate. In the next place it does not, upon the face of it, appear to mean that sort of thing which forms the contents of the sort of book which is called a book of law: so that had I taken for the subject of the definition the word *mandate* instead of the word *law*, the reader would have been apt to have asked himself what the former had to do here, and how it came that no mention was made of the latter. Indeed who could have endured that in a book professing to treat of laws, the leading term should be other than the word *law*? [g]

[g] For the difference between a law or mandate and a piece of advice see supra 1. n.[1] For the import of the words *invitation, requisition*, see infra § 12.3. n.[2]

[1] Bentham's reference is apparently to a page of the Ms. (U.C. lxxxviii.101) which he later struck out. This explains the difference between a law and a piece of exhortation or advice as follows:
'The concluding part of the definition [of law] which runs in these words: "the party of whose will it is the expression trusting for its accomplishment to the expectation of certain events the prospect of which he intends should act as a motive and which he intends the declaration in question should upon occasion be a means of bringing to pass"—this part, I say, was inserted for the sake of distinguishing *law* from *exhortation* and *advice* or *counsel*, or to speak more precisely, of distinguishing a law from a piece of advice or exhortation. Advice and exhortation administer neither of them any new motives. Advice, the only sort of advice from which instruction is to be gained, is the language of the understanding: advice is either motived or unmotived. Exhortation is the language of the will adding a motive to advice. He who advises

[2] [See next page.]

Although not qualified to stand as the leading term, the word *mandate* is however so much more extensive and unrestricted in its import than the word *law*, that it may be substituted in the room of it with advantage in an occasional analytical sketch the object of which is to give an analytical view of the principal distinctions which obtain between the objects to which the definition has given the name of *laws* considered in respect of their *source*; by which means the conformities and disconformities that subsist between the expressions of the will to which men are wont in common to refuse the name of laws and those which they are accustomed to characterize by that name, may be exhibited. This however must in course be deferred to the next section.

Thus much however it will be convenient to observe before a period is put to the present section. In such an analysis the first partition would be into *legal* and *illegal*. By a legal mandate is to be understood such an one and such only as in a manner more or less immediate (a distinction which will be explained at large in the next section), [is] emanable from the sovereign; by an illegal mandate, every other mandate whatsoever. These are distinctions which bear reference to the *source*: in that point a legal and illegal mandate differ. But in all other points they will be found to agree: so that under every other head what is predicated of the one may with equal truth be predicated of the other.[h] In future then it will be sufficient to make use of the word *mandate* simply, without prefixing to it the epithet *legal*; more especially as the mandates with which our

[h] In so far as the source of the mandate comes in question, what is predicated of it belongs exclusively to jurisprudence: but every thing else that is said of it belongs equally to the hitherto undenominated branch of logic above spoken of, which may be called the *logic of imperation* or more generally and exactly, the *logic of the will*; in contradistinction to the logic which may be termed the *logic of the judgement*, see supra [1].

applies no new motives: all he does is to suggest and bring to view the probability of such interesting events as seem likely to come to pass from other sources: he who exhorts expresses a wish that the party exhorted would be determined to pursue the conduct in question, but without furnishing any fresh motives, except in as far as the desire of gratifying the party exhorting may operate in that character.
Note
Between advice and exhortation it is difficult to draw the line. Many people when they pretend to give advice give nothing but exhortation; what they call advice, instead of bringing latent facts or probabilities under review, is nothing more than the unmotived expression of their own wishes.'

[2] The reference is to the latter part of the long footnote subjoined to the part of the early draft of Ch. x below which in this edition is relegated to Appendix D: cf. 298–9 n. a.

[1] Bentham's uncompleted reference here was probably to the note to Ch. xvii of *An Introduction to the Principles* (in *CW*, 299–300) printed by Everett, ed. cit., pp. 93–5.

business is at present, are such and such only, as come under this description. The word *mandate* then, if the sense of it be strained so as to make it include the import of the word *countermandate*, may be taken for the *genus generalissimum* of that class of things of which the most material species are known by the name of laws, and from whence by abstraction is drawn the fictitious entity called *law*.

Concessions of sovereign are not laws

8. In the definition that hath just been given of a legal mandate it follows that the mandate of the sovereign be it what it will, cannot be illegal: it may be cruel; it may be impolitic; it may even be unconstitutional: but it cannot be illegal. It may be unconstitutional, for instance by being repugnant to any privileges that may have been conceded to the people whom it affects: but it would be perverting language and confounding ideas to call it *illegal*: for concessions of privileges are not mandates: they are neither commands nor countermands: in short they are not *laws*. They are only promises from the sovereign to the people that he will not issue any law, any mandate, any command or countermand but to such or such an effect, or perhaps with the concurrence of such or such persons. In this respect they are upon the footing of treaties with foreign powers. They are a sort of treaties with the people. It is not the people who are bound by it, it is not the people whose conduct is concerned in it, but the sovereign himself; in as far as a party can be bound who has the whole force of the political sanction at his disposal. The force then which these treaties have to depend upon for their efficacy is what other treaties have to depend upon, the force of the moral and religious sanctions. The effect of such a concession is to weaken on the part of the people, in the event of its being violated, that disposition to submission and obedience, by which the power of the sovereign, in point of fact, is constituted: as the effect of a treaty is to weaken in the event of its being violated that disposition on the part of the other sovereign by which a state of amity on his part is constituted; I mean the disposition to restrain his subjects from hostility.

No more are treaties between sovereigns

9. It may be observed here for the sake of regularity, though after what has been said in the last article it is but repetition, that a treaty made by one sovereign with another is not itself a law; from which indeed it is plainly distinguished by the definition we set out with giving of the word *law*. It has an intimate connection however with the body of the laws, in virtue of its being apt to be converted by construction into an actual law or set of laws, and at any rate from the expectation it affords of the establishment of express laws conformable to stipulations of which it is composed.

10. The above seem to be the principal terms whose import it can *Local names* be of any use to compare in the present stage of our inquiries with *of statutes* *dismissed* that of the word *law*: I mean in a book of which though the language is local, yet the plan, as far as is consistent with the locality of the language, is universal. I omit therefore all those expressions which, whatever footing they may happen to have got in the English language, are in their respective originals neither more nor less than so many synonyms to the word *statute*. Of this stamp are *act* (meaning act of Parliament) in Great Britain, *declaration* (meaning a declaration of the King) in France, *Bull* in the German empire and the ecclesiastical state, *Recess* (meaning a statute made at the recess of the Diet) and *Capitulation*[1] in the German Empire. *Pragmatic Sanction* in the Byzantine and German Empire, *placard* in the Low Countries, and the like.

[1] The principal contents of the Imperial capitulations are either concessions of privileges or treaties according to the relation which the Emperor is considered as bearing at the several periods to the other states. I would not, without examining them in this particular view, be sure of their containing any matter of the mandative kind.

CHAPTER II

SOURCE OF A LAW

A law must come from a sovereign   **1.** First then with respect to its *source*. Considered in this point of view, the will of which it is the expression must, as the definition intimates, be the will of the sovereign in *a* state. Now by a sovereign I mean any person or assemblage of persons to whose will a whole political community are (no matter on what account) supposed to be in a disposition to pay obedience[a]: and that in preference to the will of any other person.[b] Suppose the will in question not to be

[a] I do not say in all cases: cases in which the sovereign shall not make any law, acts which he shall neither command nor prohibit, laws already subsisting which he shall not alter, *may* be settled in a variety of ways: by the original compact where any such thing has taken place (See Fragm. on Govt. Ch. IV para. 34) by subsequent compacts and engagements such as we see entered into by sovereigns every day: as in the cases of conquest, capitulation, cession, exchange, succession, and so on. I speak all along as to what is practicable: as to the matter of expediency, that is not in question here (Ibid., para. 37).[1]

[b] It may happen that one person or set of persons shall be sovereign in some cases while another is completely so in other cases. (See Ch. XVI (Division) 17*n*).[2] On this supposition they may be considered as composing all together but one sovereign. The truth of these propositions, which may perhaps be found not very conformable to the most current notions, may presently appear. Power over persons, is either power over their passive faculties merely, or power over their active faculties: which latter may be termed *power of imperation*. Now in point of fact not to meddle at present with the point of right (or to speak more intelligibly with the point of utility or expediency, since right independently of law and of utility is unintelligible) in point of fact, I say, the ultimate efficient cause of all power of imperation over persons is a disposition on the part of those persons to obey: the efficient cause then of the power of the sovereign is neither more nor less than the disposition to obedience on the part of the people. Now this disposition it is obvious may admit of innumerable modifications—and that even while it is constant; besides that it may change from day to day. The people may be disposed to obey the commands of one man against all the world in relation to one sort of act, those of another man in relation to another sort of act, else what are we to think of the

[1] These paragraphs of *A Fragment on Government* (Bowring, i, 289–90) deal critically with Blackstone's claim that in every political society there must be an absolute authority which even express conventions cannot bind. In the second of the paragraphs cited Bentham is concerned particularly to argue that the binding force of conventions entered into by governments need not operate as a barrier to improvement and reform.

[2] *An Introduction to the Principles*, Ch. XVI: Bentham's reference is apparently to the last footnote to para. 17 of that chapter (in *CW*, 200)

the will of *a* sovereign, that is of some sovereign or other; in such case, if it come backed with motives of a coercive nature, it is not a law, but an illegal mandate: and the act of issuing it is an offence.[c]

constitutional laws of the Germanic body: those of one man in one place, those of another man in another place, as we see all the world over: those of one man (for instance the dictator at Rome) at one time, those of another man or set of men (for instance the assembly of the governing part of the Roman people) at another: they may be disposed to obey a man if he *commands* a given sort of act: they may not be disposed to obey him if he *forbids* it and vice versa. In some of these cases, sharp, one should think, must be the eye that can detect encroachments, and resolute the hand that can bear up against them, and that can say to the torrent of sovereign power, thus far shalt thou go and no farther. But there is nothing of this sort which religion cannot do at any time: in the purest monarchies as well as in the freest commonwealths. The Jews would have done anything else for Antiochus, but they would not eat his pork. The exiled Protestants would have done anything else for Lewis, but they would not go to mass. The Catholics of Great Britain would obey any other law of the Parliament of Great Britain but they will not stay away from mass. In all other points they will obey the temporal sovereign for the time being: in this point alone they choose to obey the commands of departed sovereigns or of the Pope, or what comes to the same thing, what to them appear to be the dictates of the religious sanction. Why might not this, (in point of practicability I mean) be settled by law, as well as by an inward determination which bids defiance to the law? Does not the Briton when in France obey the sovereign of France? Does not the Frenchman when in Great Britain obey the sovereign of Great Britain? and do not the Briton and the Frenchman both when at Rome do as they do at Rome? Let it be observed once more I consider here not what is most eligible, but only what is possible.

One great difficulty is to draw the boundary line betwixt act and act, betwixt such classes of acts as the sovereign may, and such as he may not, take for the objects of his law, and to distinguish it by marks so clear as not to be in danger of being mistaken: especially where religion and the *acumen* and pertinacity which that principle inspires, are out of the question. The plainest marks are those which are made by *place* and *time*. By place: for this is all that there is to distinguish the power of any one sovereign from that of another. By time: accordingly at Rome, even in a rude age, a man would be absolute for six months without any hope or chance of protracting his power a day longer: so in regencies, as we see every day, though the minority be ever so long. As to *place*, where that circumstance is the mark, the line is the stronger, in as much as the physical power terminates in great measure with the political. But to examine these matters in detail belongs to the particular head of constitutional law.

[c] If the mandate (being a command) comes to be obeyed, the act of issuing it is an act of *simple injurious restrainment,* or *simple injurious compulsion,* according as the command is positive or negative (see *infra,* Ch. x); if not obeyed, it is an attempt to commit the one or the other of those offences: at any rate, as also if it be a countermand, it is a *disturbance,* or if on pretence of

2. If the person of whose will it is the expression be a sovereign, but a sovereign to whose power in the case in question a person of the description in question happens not to be subject, it is a law, which as to that person indeed has no force, yet still it is a law.[d] The law having no force, the not obeying it is either no offence or an offence which cannot be punished. Yet still it cannot here be said that the issuing it is an offence: because the person from whom it issues is one whose act, as such, cannot be invested with the character of an offence. Were the Lord High Treasurer of Great Britain to issue of his own authority an order for laying a tax on all the inhabitants of Great Britain the issuing of that order would indeed be an offence: since the Lord High Treasurer of Great Britain is no more a sovereign in Great Britain than he is anywhere else. But were the King of France to issue an order to the same effect addressed to the same persons, such law would indeed be of no force, but yet it would hardly be looked upon as coming under the name of an offence: why?—because the King of France, though not sovereign in Great Britain is sovereign elsewhere; to wit in France: on his part then it would be an act not of delinquency but of hostility.

title an *usurpation*, of some branch of power beneficial or fiduciary, private or public. See Ch. xvi (Division) liv n., p. cclxxxvii.[1]

[d] It is evident that in point of fact (for to that point I still exclusively adhere) sovereignty over any given individual is a matter which is liable to much diversity and continual fluctuation. Subjection depends for its commencement upon birth: but for its continuance it depends upon a thousand accidents. In point of fact a man is subject to any and to every sovereign who can make him suffer: whether it be in person (that is in body or in mind) in reputation, in property, or in condition. (See Ch. xvi. (Division) 11[2] and B. I tit. (Persons subject).)[3] In body he can be subject to but one at a time: but in mind in reputation and in property he may be subject to multitudes at once. Every Catholic for example, or if there be any difference, every Papist who is so at heart, whatever nation he belong to, is in a certain sense subject to the Pope, in virtue of those pains of the religious sanction (See Ch. v, Pleasures and Pains 9)[4] which the head of the Catholic church has it in his power to inflict upon minds whose religious biases (Ch. vi (Sensibility) 19)[5] prepare them for such impressions: pains the infliction of which, were it an offence, would come under the head of simple mental injuries (Ch. xvi (Division) 33).[6]

[1] *An Introduction to the Principles*, Ch. xvi, para. 54 n. (in *CW*, 260 ff.). Bentham's page-reference is of course to the edition published in 1789 (printed 1780).

[2] *An Introduction to the Principles*, Ch. xvi, para. 11 (in *CW*, 191 ff.).

[3] A reference to one of the 'titles' of Book I of Bentham's *Plan of a Penal Code* (cf. *An Introduction to the Principles* in *CW*, Introduction, xxxviii–xxxix).

[4] *An Introduction to the Principles*, Ch. v, para. 9 (in *CW*, 44).

[5] Ibid., Ch. vi, para. 19 (in *CW*, 37).

[6] Ibid., Ch. xvi, para. 33 (in *CW*, 222–4).

3. Now a given will or mandate may be the will or mandate of a given person in either of two ways: in the way of *conception* as it may be called (that is of original conception) or 2. in the way of *adoption*. A will or mandate may be said to belong to a sovereign in the way of conception when it was he himself who issued it and who first issued it, in the words or other signs in which it stands expressed: it may be said to belong to him by adoption when the person from whom it immediately emanes is not the sovereign himself (meaning the sovereign for the time being) but some other person: insomuch that all the concern which he to whom it belongs by adoption has in the matter is the being known to entertain a will that in case such or such another person should have expressed or should come to have expressed a will concerning the act or sort of act in question, such will should be observed and looked upon as his.[e]

This it may do 1. in the way of conception or 2. of adoption

4. Where a mandate appertains to the sovereign only by adoption, such adoption may be distinguished in several respects: 1. in respect of the *time* in which the mandate adopted appears with reference to that of the adopting mandate: 2. in respect of the persons whose mandates are thus adopted. 3. in respect of the *degree* in which the adoption is performed: fourthly in respect of the *form* of expression by which it may be performed.

Adoption is either 1. susception: or 2. pre-adoption

(1) First then, with regard to *time*, the mandate which the sovereign in question is supposed to adopt may be either already issued, or not: in the former case it may be said to be his by *susception*; in the latter by *pre-adoption*. Where the sovereign holds himself thus in readiness to adopt the mandates of another person whensoever they shall happen to have been issued, he may thereby be said to invest that person with a certain species of power, which may be termed a *power of imperation*. Examples of this distinction we shall see immediately.

5. (2) As to the *persons* whose mandates the sovereign may have occasion to adopt, it would be to little purpose here, and indeed it would be premature, to attempt reducing the enumeration of them to an analytic method. In the way of susception, the sovereign for

Persons whose mandates he adopts – 1. Former sovereigns

[e] In this there is no mystery: the names perhaps are new, but the distinction itself is continually exemplified, and that in the most ordinary concerns of life. You are giving orders to your servant: this it is plain you may do in either of two ways: by saying to him, 'Go and do so and so', mentioning what: or by saying to him, 'Go and do what Mr such-an-one bids you'. One of these ways is just as familiar as the other: the order you yourself give in the former case, is yours by conception: the order Mr such-an-one gives in the latter case is yours by adoption.

the time being adopts as well the mandates of former sovereigns as those of subordinate *power-holders*ᶠ: in the way of pre-adoption, he can adopt the last mentioned mandates only: for to pre-adopt the mandates of subsequent sovereigns would be nugatory, since whatever actual force there is in sovereignty rests in the sovereign for the time being: in the living, not in the dead. As the propensity to obedience may admit of every imaginable modification, it is just conceivable indeed that the people should in certain points obey the mandates of a deceased sovereign in preference to those of his living successor. Lycurgus, if the story be a true one, found means by a trick, thus to reign after his death: but it is a trick that would hardly succeed a second time: and the necessity he found himself under of having recourse to that expedient would be a sufficient proof, if there required any, how little need the sovereign who is recognized as such for the time being has to be beholden for his power to his departed predecessors.[1]

2. *Sub-ordinate power-holders*

6. As to the subordinate power-holders whose mandates the sovereign pre-adopts, these are of course as many and as various as the classes of persons to whom the law gives either powers of *imperation* or the contrary powers of *de-imperation*, if such is the name that may be given to the power of undoing what by imperation has been done. These powers it may give to the power-holder on his own account, in which case the power is beneficial, or on that of another; in which case it is fiduciary: and in this latter case, on account of an individual, or on account of the public at large; in which latter case again the power is of the public or constitutional kind. It is thus that every mandate that is issued within the limits of the sovereignty and that is not illegal, is in one sense or the other the mandate of the sovereign. Take any mandate whatsoever, either it is of the number of those which he allows or it is not: there is no medium: if it is, it is his; by adoption at least, if not by original conception: if not, it is illegal, and the issuing it an offence. Trivial or important makes no difference: if the former are not his, then neither are the latter. The mandates of the master, the father, the husband, the guardian, are all of them the mandates of the sovereign: if not, then neither are those of the general nor of the judge. Not a cook is bid to dress a dinner, a nurse to feed a child, an

ᶠ (*Power-holders*) So I will take leave to term those who stand invested with a power: the term is analogous in its formation to the words *landowner, freeholder, householder.*

[1] This refers to the story that Lycurgus, after inducing the Spartans to promise not to alter his laws in his absence, then went into exile (or, according to Plutarch, committed suicide) so that the promise should bind the people in perpetuity.

usher to whip a school boy, an executioner to hang a thief, an officer to drive the enemy from a post, but it is by his orders. If anyone should find a difficulty in conceiving this, he has only to suppose the several mandates in question to meet with resistance: in one case as well as in another the business of enforcing them must rest ultimately with the sovereign. Nor is there anything of fiction in all this: if there were, this is the last place in which it should be found.

To continue the laws of preceding sovereigns, and the powers of the various classes of magistrates, domestic as well as civil, is (in every tolerably well settled commonwealth at least) a matter of course. To suffer either of those systems of institutions to perish, and not to establish anything in their stead, would be to suffer the whole machine of government to drop to pieces. The one course no sovereign was ever yet mad enough, the other none was ever yet industrious enough, to pursue. If the adoption be not declared in words, it is because the fact is so notorious, that any express form of words to signify it would be unnecessary. It is manifested by means not less significant than words, by every act of government, by which the enforcement of the mandates in question is provided for. If it be alleged that the trivial transactions that pass in the interior of a family are not specifically in the contemplation of the sovereign: (trivial as they may be termed when individually considered, though in their totality they are the stuff that human life is made of) the same may be said of the transactions of fleets and armies: of those which become the objects of the mandates issued by the general or the judge. The same may even be said of those laws which emane directly from the very presence of the sovereign. It is only by the general tenor of their effects and not by any direct specification that individual acts of any kind can be comprised under extensive and general descriptions.

7. It is in this very way that conveyances and covenants[g] *Concern which the Sovereign has in giving legality to conveyances and covenants*

[g] This is another of the many occasions that occur in a work of general jurisprudence in which it is difficult to find a proper term to make use of. The word *promise* would have been too extensive: since even of such promises as it is lawful to make it is not every one that the law will oblige a man to observe: and the same thing may be said of the words *agreement*, and *engagement*. The word *stipulation* is liable to objections which it would take up too much room to discuss here. The word *pact* is not in common use, and it has no conjugates belonging to it. The word *compact* might seem to exclude the case of a *nudum pactum*, where there is but one pact, one promise, between the parties: without any promise or anything else to which English lawyers give the name of a *consideration* given on the other side. The word *contract* (though at first sight it might seem more apposite than any that have been mentioned) is too extensive. In the Roman law it is applied to various sorts of mixed transactions:

to transactions consisting of a conveyance on each side as in *emptio-venditio:* to transactions consisting of a perpetual conveyance on one side and a covenant or covenants on the other, as in *mutuum:* to transactions consisting of a temporary conveyance on one side, and a covenant or covenants on the other, as in *depositum* and *commodatum:* of a conveyance which might be temporary or perpetual according to contingencies, and a covenant or covenants on the other: as in *pignus:* not to mention cases in which there is neither conveyance nor covenant between the parties, but only certain obligations imposed upon them in consequence of some community of interest by the law itself: as might be the case in *societas* where for instance [a][1] thing had accrued to the *socii,* the partners, by the gift of a third person. In the English law there is a similar confusion, though not the same. The name of *contract* is given to some transactions in which there is nothing but pure conveyance, as in sale and exchange: to others in which there is conveyance and covenant both as in *bailment,* and in *hiring* and *borrowing:* to other cases in which there is neither conveyance nor covenant, but an obligation to convey, arising from some other source; as in several cases of *debt.* It is not a place here to enter into any further discussions concerning the Roman *contractus* or the English *contracts,* or to draw any parallel between them. The ideas respectively annexed to these terms are compound ideas, consisting of conveyances, covenants and other sources of obligation made up in various mixtures. To understand these mixtures, a man must understand the elements of which they are composed; that is, he must know in what respects those elements are distinct not only from other things but from one another. Among those elements are conveyances and covenants. But of the difference between a conveyance and a covenant no lawyer that has ever written seems yet to have entertained a clear idea. This is at least must be said of all those who have acquiesced in this part of the nomenclature either of the Roman or of the English Law. The Roman jurisprudence on this subject is a perfect chaos: the English jurisprudence is as perfect an one in another way: and one may venture to affirm that there is no other system of jurisprudence anywhere that is in any better case. To infuse order into this chaos, to throw light upon the darkness is impossible to a man who has not some such analysis as the following before his eyes. Let any obligation, to which one man can be subjected in favour of another, be conceived. Such obligation either is incumbent upon you or is not: if not, and the case is that it was imposed upon you, it must have been taken off. Whether it remains incumbent on you or has been taken off, the imposition or removal must have been performed either directly by the law itself, without the intervention of any other will either on your own part or on that of any other person, or else by an individual or individuals in virtue of powers conferred on them by the law. In the first case there is neither covenant nor conveyance. In the other case if the obligation is imposed upon yourself alone by yourself alone, (I mean in the first instance) the expression of will which it is imposed by is a covenant: in all other cases whether it be that an obligation is taken off in the first instance or imposed, the expression of will whereby such effect is produced is a conveyance: conveyance of a right to him from whom an obligation is taken off, or in whose favour an obligation is imposed on some one else. (I say in the first instance: for whatever further operations may be necessary either to *corroborate* a right and give it that degree of force which in most systems of law it possesses, or to turn the possession of it to the account of a third person, these

[1] Ms. 'the'   24

acquire all the validity they can possess, all the connection they have with the System of the laws: adopted by the sovereign, they are converted into mandates. (See Ch. xvi (Division) 35 n.).[1] If

ᵍ cont.
of themselves may be looked upon as sufficient to create it. Concerning the corroborative provisions attended to see the next paragraph in the text.) It appears then that in a large view of the subject a covenant may be regarded as a species of conveyance: it is a conveyance of a right to certain services: but it can never be a conveyance of anything but a right to services; nor of any other services than those of the conveyor or covenantor himself. Saving this exception as on the one hand, a man may always covenant without conveying; or on the other hand may he always convey without covenanting: and though it often happens that the operations of covenanting and conveying are performed together, yet this does not render them in themselves the less distinguishable. The case in which the effect of a covenant comes nearest to that of a conveyance, is that of a covenant to convey: but even in this the difference is manifestly discernible. Every one knows that a person in whose favour a covenant to convey, a piece of land for instance, has been made, which covenant has not been performed, is not yet in the case of one in whose favour that covenant has been performed: a conveyance has been made accordingly. In this first case, the occupation of the land on his part would as yet be wrongful, whatever wrong there may be in the behaviour of the other who *withholds* from him the sort of *service* which consists in the making such conveyance as would render the occupation lawful; in the other case such service having been rendered the occupation is not wrongful any longer. It perhaps may be thought superfluous to observe, that by *covenant* I mean all along what people at large are in use to mean by it: viz: a promise, any promise whatsoever, which is rendered binding by the law, and not such promises only, for the breach of which the remedy given by the English law is called, in the technical language of that law, *an action of covenant*. Superfluous it would indeed be were it certain that no lawyer would ever look into this book, or none but what was superior to the prejudices of his profession. But it must often have been observed, that when a man gets the habit of using words in the technical sense, to which the use of them is confined by lawyers, he is apt to lose the memory of the more extensive sense which is given to them by other men.

As the word *contract* is applied to transactions where there is conveyance and to transactions where there is covenant, one might be tempted at first sight to look upon it as a term that might be made use of as a common name for conveyances and covenants in all cases. But this would not by any means agree with the nomenclature either of the English or of the Roman Jurisprudence. To covenants the word contracts might perhaps be applied in every case without any great apparent harshness; although there are some cases in which it is not usually thus applied. But in regard to conveyances it could not without great violence be applied to any others than those to which it has usually been applied: because the particular usage of lawyers, which seems in this instance to have grown up in repugnancy to common usage, will not bear a man out in such repugnancy any further.

[1] *An Introduction to the Principles*, Ch. xvi, para. 35. It is not clear that any of the notes to this paragraph fits the description in the reference. Possibly n. g3, which mentions contracts (in *CW*, 227) was intended.

you give your coat to a man, and the gift is valid, and nobody else has a right to meddle with your coat, it is because a mandate subsists on the part of the sovereign, commanding all persons whatever to refrain from meddling with it, he to whom you gave it alone excepted, upon the event of your declaring such to be your pleasure. If a man engages or covenants to mend your coat for you, and such an engagement is valid, it is because on the part of the sovereign a mandate hath been issued, commanding any person upon the event of his entering into any engagement, (exceptions excepted) and thereby that particular person in consequence of his having entered into that particular engagement, (it not being within the exceptions) to perform it: in other words to render you that particular service which is rendered to you by performance of the act which he has engaged for.

Thus then in all cases stands the distinction between the laws which belong to the legislator in the way of conception, and those which belong to him in the way of pre-adoption. The former are the work of the legislator solely: the latter that of the legislator and the subordinate power-holder conjunctively, the legislator sketching out a sort of imperfect mandate which he leaves it to the subordinate power-holder to fill up.[h] In the first case there are no other mandates in the case than those which emane from the legislator *immediate*: in the latter case whatever mandates there are emane from the subordinate power-holder *immediate*, and whenever they happen to be issued can only be said to emane *potestative* from the legislator. In the former case there are mandates from the first that exist *in actu*: in the latter until issued by the subordinate power-holder, whatever mandates there may be conceived to be exist only *in potentia*. In the former case the law will more readily than in the other be perceived to be occupied in issuing or repeating commands: In the other case it will be apt to appear as if it were employed solely in giving descriptions: for example of the *persons* by whom powers shall be possessed: of the *things* over which, or persons over whom, such powers shall be possessed: of the *acts* to which such power shall extend; that is of which the performance shall be deemed an exercise of such power: of the *place* in which and the *time* during which such powers shall be exercised, and so on. Yet still such descriptions have so much in them of the nature of a command or what stands opposed to it, that whenever the power which they confer or limit comes to be

[h] This is one way among innumerable others in which as will be seen hereafter, the complete power of imperation or de-imperation may be broken into shares, see infra Ch. ix (Generality).

exercised, the expression of will whereby it is exercised may, without any alteration made in the import of it, be translated into the form and language of a mandate: of a mandate issuing from the mouth of the lawgiver himself.[1]

8. Next as to the degree in which the mandate of a subordinate power-holder may be adopted by the sovereign: or in other words the degree of force which such mandate acquires by the adoption. *Degrees of adoption* Take any single manifestation of the sovereign's will, and all the assistance that the mandate of a subordinate power-holder can receive from it consists in a bare permission: this is the first step that the sovereign takes towards the giving validity to subordinate mandates: the first and least degree of assistance or rather countenance that the inferior can receive from the superior: the not being made the subject of a law commanding him not to issue the subordinate mandate which is in question. The part thus far taken by the sovereign is, we see, merely a negative one. Nor would it be worthwhile, or indeed proper, to notice him as taking any part at all, since it is no more than what is taken by every the merest stranger, were it not for its lying so much in his way to take the contrary part; a part which he actually does take in relation to the greater number of the other members of the community. If any further degree of countenance is shewn it must be by another law or set of laws: a law permitting the subordinate power-holder to punish with his own hand the party who is made subject to the mandate in case of disobedience, by a law permitting others to assist in the administering such punishment, by a law commanding others to assist; and so on. Such ulterior corroborative laws however are not to be reckoned as exclusively necessary to the particular business of adoption: for a set of subsidiary laws like these are equally necessary, as will be seen hereafter, to the giving *force* and efficacy to such laws as emane from the sovereign himself in the most immediate manner.[j]

9. Next as to the form or manner in which the adoption may be performed. We have already intimated that it may be done by *Forms of adoption* permission: that is by a legislative permission: but it may also be done by mandate, by a legislative mandate: by a permission

---

[1] The fundamental law of those by which conveyances of property in things corporeal are adopted is that which corresponds to and prohibits the offence of wrongful occupation of property: that by which covenants are adopted, is that which corresponds to and prohibits the offence of wrongful withholding of services. See Ch. xvi (Division).[1]

See infra, Ch. xi (Force).

[1] Ch. xvi of *An Introduction to the Principles*. The reference intended is presumably the same as that discussed above, 25, n. 1.

addressed in the first instance to the power-holder; a permission to issue the mandates which it is proposed to adopt; or by a mandate addressed immediately to those whom it is meant to subject to his power; a mandate commanding them to obey such and such mandates whensoever, if at all, he shall have thought fit to issue them. In the former case the mandate of the subordinate power-holder whenever it comes to be issued, is a *primordial* one: in the latter case it is *superventitious*, the mandate of the sovereign being the primordial one, of which this which is superventitious is *reiterative*. These terms should they appear obscure, will hereafter be explained.[k] Whichever be the form, it comes exactly to the same thing: and the difference lies rather in the manner in which we may conceive the inclination of the sovereign to be expressed, than in the inclination itself. In both cases the mandate depends for its force upon a further set of mandates, as hath been already intimated and will be shewn more particularly further on. Whether these subsidiary mandates be annexed to a mandate on the part of the sovereign *ab initio,* or to the mandates of the subsidiary power holder when they arise, is a matter of indifference.

By-laws, what

10. The mandate of a subordinate powerholder, when it has the requisite degree of permanency and generality, to constitute it according to common speech *a law* is in the language of the English jurisprudence in many cases termed a *by-law.* It was first applied to the laws made by the governing body in corporate towns, being so much as to say a *town-law.* In process of time it has been extended to laws made by any other bodies corporate; although they had nothing to do with the government of particular towns: such as the trading, banking and insurance companies. It might with equal propriety and convenience be extended to any subordinate laws whatever. In Great Britain, King's proclamations, wherever they are anything more than admonitions to observe the already established laws are *by-laws*: King's Charters inasmuch as they confer new powers of legislation are by-laws: the articles of war which it is the custom for the King to establish for the government of the army are by-laws: treaties entered into by the King, inasfar as they contain anything that binds the subject *ipso facto* are by-laws: the ordinances established by James when Duke of York and Lord High Admiral for the government of the Dock-Yards[1] are by-laws:

[k] Infra, Ch. x (Aspect).

[1] James, Duke of York, later James II, was Lord High Admiral from 1660 to 1672, during which period a number of royal proclamations were issued to regulate naval affairs.

Standing Regulations which the Justices of the Peace are allowed in certain cases to make in their judicial capacity or otherwise for the government of their respective counties are by-laws: standing rules of Court made *mero motu* by judges of all sorts are by-laws. So in France many of the *arrêts* of their parliaments though ranked without distinction under the same name with their judicial mandates, will be found upon examination to be by-laws; as in short are all other permanent mandates whatever which bear not the signature of the King. General ordinances established by the several states of the German Empire within their respective dominions, are, in as far as they hold themselves subject to the dominion of the Diet, no more than by-laws. Ordinances issued by the assembly of the States general of the Dutch United Provinces for the government of the provinces of the generality (*pays de la généralité*) are no more than by-laws, the sovereignty over the States general being considered as residing in the collective or aggregate body composed of the several sovereignties of the seven provinces or perhaps of the several independent townships; who for this purpose must be understood as constituting all together but one sovereign. This aggregate sovereign, if the ordinances of their delegates, the States general, require to be ratified by the several component sovereignties before they receive their binding force, imperates so far, in the way of original conception; if no such ratification is necessary, in the way of adoption: being the same way and the only way in which the Electors[1] of the British House of Commons and their electors imperate, in virtue of the share which is exercised by the House of Commons in the sovereignty of the British Empire.

11. I shall conclude this section with the analytical recapitulation promised in the last. A mandate is either referable to the sovereign or it is not: in the latter case it is illegal, and what we have nothing to do with here.

Analytical sketch of the different sorts of mandates distinguished according to their source

A legal mandate then is either private or domestic, or public or civil: a domestic mandate is one that emanes from a person having power in virtue of his being invested with a condition of the domestic kind, and is addressed to the person who stands invested with the correlative condition: a civil or public mandate is either sovereign or subordinate. If sovereign either it is *suâ naturâ* permanent or it is not: in the former case it is a sovereign law at any rate: in the latter, if it proceeds from a number of persons possessing the sovereignty in conjunction, it is still a sovereign law as before; if from a single

[1] Thus Ms., though 'Members' is presumably what Bentham intended.

person possessing the sovereignty in severalty, it is a sovereign order. If the authority from which it immediately emanes be subordinate, it is issued either on the occasion of a suit, or independently of any such occasion: in the former case it is a judicial order or mandate, and may be styled an order *litis causa* or *propter quid*: in the latter case it may be styled a subordinate legislative mandate *ex mero motu*. In this latter case again if it is susceptible of perpetuity it may be styled a *subordinate law* or *by-law*: if not, it may be styled an *executive order*.

In this analysis conveyances and covenants are not included. This is owing to the multitude of different species there are of them which could not here be brought all of them under the same head, nor yet distinguished without engaging in discussions for which we are not as yet prepared. Of the general nature of a suit at law and of the distinction of suits into civil and penal more will be said hereafter.[1]

[1] See infra, Ch. xii, xiii, xxi.

CHAPTER III

ENDS WHICH A LAW MAY HAVE IN VIEW

1. Secondly, with regard to the *end* which the law may have in view. Now by *end* is here meant not the eventual end, which is a matter of chance, but the intended end, which is a matter of design. But the intended end of any act in general, and therefore of the particular sort of act or measure which consists in the issuing of a law is one of those objects which we have already had occasion to speak of under the appellation of a *motive*, to wit, the external motive in prospect.[a]

The end of a law is the external motive which he whose law it is had in prospect

2. It is to be remembered that law may belong to the sovereign either in the way of conception or in the way of adoption: in the latter case there are necessarily two persons whose law in these two different senses it may be said to be. These two persons it may happen may in regard to the parts they have necessarily taken in the establishment of the law, have been actuated by two different motives: they may have had in view two different ends.

This end may in certain cases be the private interest of him from whom the law immediately emanes

As to the sovereign, the end or external motive[b] he can have had in view in adopting the law, can upon the principle of utility, have been no other than the greatest good of the community[c]: which end we suppose his measures to be directed to of course: since it is only in as far as that is the case that these enquiries are calculated or designed to be of any use to him. But with regard to the party to whom the law appertains in the way of conception and from whom it immediately emanes, the case is different. In many instances it may happen, and that properly enough, that the end which he has in view is no other than his own particular benefit or satisfaction: which is the case with all those mandates which are issued in virtue of a power of the beneficiary kind: in this case are all the mandates for instance of the master acting as such, as also those of the parent

[a] See Ch. x (Motives) 5.[1]

[b] As to the internal motive, whether it be the purely social motive of benevolence or as in this case it is called public spirit, or the semi-social motive of love of reputation, or the self-regarding motives of love of power, love of wealth and so forth, or, what is commonly the case, a mixture of all these together, these are points which as in most cases they are undiscoverable, so in all cases they are immaterial.

[c] See Ch. i (Utility).[2]

[1] Ch. x of *An Introduction to the Principles*, para. 5 (in *CW*, 97–8).
[2] Ch. i of *An Introduction to the Principles* (in *CW*, 11–16).

and of the husband in as far as the parent and the husband are allowed to act in the capacity of a master. To the same head may also be referred even such mandates as persons possessed of fiduciary power are allowed to issue, in as far as that allowance is given them in the way of salary: though indeed wherever that is the case the power may be and, to consider it in an accurate point of view must be, looked upon as being *pro tanto* of the beneficial kind, and the *power-holder* as being invested *pro tanto* with the authority of a master. To the same head indeed may also be referred even such mandates as are issued in the exercise of such power of the beneficial kind as the sovereign himself is allowed and upon the principle of utility may be allowed to exercise: either in the way of salary like any other trustee of the public, or as a member of the community whose interest there is just as much reason for consulting as any other's, and no more. In this as in so many other particulars he stands exactly upon a footing with the parent, in whose hands the beneficial power is blended with the fiduciary, and who is allowed to exercise over his children the authority of a master, partly for their sakes, and partly for his own.

But the most conspicuous cases are those in which it ought to be the public at large

3. But the more conspicuous case and the more common with such mandates as in consideration of their generality and their permanency are usually distinguished by the name of *laws* is that in which the proper end of the sovereign who adopts, and that of the subordinate magistrate who issues the mandate, coincide: being each of them not the particular good of the author of the mandate but the general good of the community at large. This good may be considered either in respect of the parties it more immediately affects, or in respect of what it is in its own nature. In the former point of view it will be particularly considered by and by.[d] In the latter point of view it hath already in some measure been considered in a preceding chapter, though not in any great detail.[e] The sketch then which has been already given for the purpose of that chapter will likewise be made to answer the present purpose, by changing only the position in which it presents itself.

Analysis of this common or general end into the specific ends that are subordinate to it

4. The common end of all laws as prescribed by the principle of utility is the promotion of the public good. But since good and evil are opposites, the promoting of good where the good is negative is but another name for the averting of mischief when the mischief is

[d] See infra, Ch. VI.
[e] See Ch. XVI (Division).[1]

[1] Ch. XVI of *An Introduction to the Principles.*

positive[f]: as the averting of negative good is for the promoting of positive mischief. Now in the chapter alluded to, offences (that is acts which appear to be of such a nature as to require their being made offences) are classed according to the nature of the mischiefs, negative as well as positive, which it is their tendency to produce. But to create an offence is to make a law: the offence being given, the law is thereby given. Moreover the mischief of the offence exhibits the end of the law, not in its natural situation indeed but as it were in an inverted posture, by the rule of contraries: the end of the law being not the mischief itself, but the good which consists in the prevention of that mischief. By classing offences then according to their mischiefs, laws have already been classed according to their ends: so that in giving an analysis of offences, we have given, as far as it has gone, an analysis of legal *ends*.

[f] For the offences that stand opposed to the promotion of positive good see Ch. xvi (Division) liv n. (m).[1]

[1] Ibid., loc. cit., para. 54 n. r2 (in *CW*, 262).

CHAPTER IV

SUBJECTS OF A LAW

Subjects of a law, persons, things—as agents or patients

1. Thirdly, with regard to the *subjects*, that is the persons and things to which the law may have relation.[a] Either may come under the notice of the law in each of two capacities: as *agents* or as *patients*: as beings in which the act or motion which is the *object* of the law in question may have its commencement, or as those through which it makes its progress or in which it has its termination.[b] In the former case they may be termed the *agible*, in the latter, the *possible* subjects of the law.[c] A person for example may be the striker or the party struck: a thing may be the thing destroyed or the instrument of destruction.

Persons may be subjects of a law in a physical or in a pathological way

2. The words *possible subject* we may observe as well as the correspondent word *termination* apply as naturally to a person as to a thing: and there will be at least as much occasion for applying

[a] The distinction between the *subject* of a thing and the *object* is, it must be confessed, by no means an explicit one: nor does it seem possible to settle it by any general rule: since there are few cases perhaps in which, if the one of those appellations be proper, the other may not also be employed. Even in the present case the articles to which I have appropriated the former might perhaps with equal propriety have been characterized by the latter. A person or thing may as well be considered in the light of one which has been *thrown* and *stands* in the way of the law (*ob, jactum*) as in the light of one that has been thrown and *lies underneath* it (*sub, jactum*): and so *vice versa* with regard to acts. What determined me to apply the substantive *subjects* to persons and things rather than to acts is that its conjugate adjective *subject* seems to be more frequently applied to persons and things, but more particularly to persons than to acts. To speak of persons as subject to the law, of countries as subject to the law are expressions perfectly familiar. When all is done, the distinction can scarcely be kept up with any degree of pertinence beyond the particular occasion in which it is noticed: since on other occasions it will be scarcely possible to avoid applying the terms *subject* and *object* both to persons and to things as well as to acts.

If the appellation of *objects* is applied to persons and things as well as to acts, the two former may for distinction's sake be termed the *material*, or rather to save ambiguity the *substantial* objects of the law, while the latter are termed its *modal* objects.

[b] See Ch. VII (Actions) 14.[1]

[c] The word *possible*, though not familiar, is already in the language. (See Johnson's Dict.) The word *agible*, for aught I can find is new to it, though exactly correspondent to the other.

[1] *An Introduction to the Principles*, Ch. VII, para. 14 (in *CW*, 77).

them to the former as to the latter. The parallelism may be carried on still further. The persons and the things that are the passible subjects of the act which is the object of the law, and thence also of the law itself, it may be equally said that they are the persons *in* whom and the things *in* which that act hath its termination, and that they are the persons *upon* whom and the things *upon* which the act is exercised. From this identity in point of expression one would naturally be apt to conclude that the ideas signified were also the same: that the meaning of the word *termination* were the same when applied to persons as when applied to things; and so with regard to the word *upon*. But this is far from being the case: so that if the idea raised in a man's mind by either of these words when applied to things, were to be transferred without alteration or addition to persons, it would be found very defective. This depends upon the different properties of the classes of beings which are respectively indicated by the terms: in virtue of which properties, an act may have serious effects upon persons which it cannot have upon things. Things considered as such have none but physical properties: persons have mental as well as physical:[d] that is they have the faculty of sensation (I mean that of experiencing pain and pleasure), that of perception (I mean perception as distinct from pain and pleasure), and volition: the two former of which come under the head of merely passive, the last under that of active, faculties. In a thing then in which an act is considered as having its termination, it can only have produced physical effects, viz: motions or quiescent situations: but in a person it may have produced volitions, perceptions or sensations. With regard to such of the effects of an act as consist of volitions or indifferent perceptions we have not at present any concern: but those which consist of sensations may be termed its *pathological effects*. On a thing then, an act can have only physical effects: on a person it may have not only physical effects but (amongst others) pathological.

3. As to the pathological effects or consequences of an act, they may be either of the pleasurable, beneficial, or of the painful kind; and each again may be considered either as certain or as contingent.[e] Be they of which of these kinds they may, the act by which they are

Pathological termination of an act—its various modifications

---

[d] Of the inferior animals I omit for shortness' sake to make any particular mention: in as far as their mental faculties are taken into the account, they stand upon a footing with persons: in as far as they are not taken into the account, they stand on a footing with inanimate things.

[e] See Ch. xii (Consequences).[1]

[1] *An Introduction to the Principles*, Ch. xii.

produced will have been either according to law or not according to law: in which latter case it is called an offence. For an analysis of the possible modifications of which the pathological termination of an act which is *not* according to law are susceptible we have therefore only to turn to the division of offences: or if that be not particular enough, to the catalogue of pains and pleasures.[f] The same analysis will serve equally well for the case where the act *is* according to law, for instance where it is an act of punishment.[g]

4. It will appear then that an act may have a physical termination and no pathological: or a pathological termination and no physical one: and that where it has both, the *locus* of its physical termination may be in one subject and that of its pathological termination in another.

1. An act may have a physical termination and not a pathological

(1) An act may have a physical and no pathological termination. This is the case with every act that is not in some way or other a *material* one. This appears sufficiently from the definitions of the two words.[h] In this case indeed it is not of the number of those which upon the principle of utility it can be proper to take for the object of a law. Still however it must be taken notice of as a case which at any rate is possible, and which in fact is every where but too frequent.

2.–or a pathological and no physical

5. (2) An act may have a pathological termination and no physical one. This is the case where the act is merely of the negative kind[i]: for example that of a mother who should suffer her infant to starve for want of being suckled.

3. or a physical and a pathological in distinct subjects

6. (3) Where an act has a physical termination as well as a pathological one the *locus* of the physical termination may be in one subject while that of the pathological termination is in another. Indeed there is but one case in which these two *loci* coincide: this is where the pleasure or pain which constitutes the material part of the effects of the act is of the corporeal kind. In all other cases, if the act be of the physical kind the physical effects of it stop short before they reach the person whose mind is the *locus* of the pathological termination. A thief steals your household-goods: or the judge causes them to be seized in satisfaction of a fine. The physical termination of the act is in both cases in the goods themselves; and

[f] Ch. v.[1]
[g] See infra, Ch. vi, p. 55.
[h] See Ch. vii (Actions) 3.[2]
[i] Ibid. 6 etc.[3]

[1] Ibid., Ch. v, entitled 'Pleasures and Pains, Their Kinds'.
[2] Ibid., Ch. vii, para. 3 (in *CW*, 74).
[3] Ibid., Ch. vii, paras. 6 ff. In fact the distinction between positive and negative acts is first mentioned in para. 8 (in *CW*, 75).

takes place perhaps as soon as the goods are set down out of your reach or knowledge: it reaches not to your person, which perhaps is at a hundred miles from the scene of action. At this period the act considered with respect to its pathological effects must be considered as suspended or (as lawyers say) resting in *abeyance*: nor in respect of such of them as concern you does it come to its termination, till it produces in your mind the pain of privation resulting from the consciousness of having lost the goods; or at least deprives you of some satisfaction you might otherwise have had in using them.

7. The necessity of this distinction will be still more apparent where the influence of the act is considered as extending itself to the community at large: insomuch that the community at large is considered (that is strictly speaking some individually unassignable members of it are considered) as constituting the passible subjects of the act: as where the act being an offence, and that a private one, is considered with respect to its semi-public and public mischief: or being an offence is purely of a public or of a semi-public nature.[j] In these cases after the physical termination of the act has taken place, the pathological termination of it may be considered as resting not only in abeyance but in contingency: that is, to speak strictly, as being more particularly uncertain, since in strictness every event is contingent while it is future.[k]

In as far as the consequences are of a public or semi-public nature the pathological termination of the act is contingent

[j] Ch. xvi (Division) 1 and 5.[1]

[k] It may be said that as no act any more than any other event which takes place without the limits of a man's person can reach his mind but by means of sensible signs, these signs must be looked upon as continuations of the physical act: that therefore the physical act is not at an end till these signs have had their effect, and as thereupon the pathological effects immediately take place, the *locus* as well as the period of these two terminations are still in effect the same: that for example in the instance above produced the pain you suffer by the loss of your goods, you yourself being at a distance, does not take place till you come to be informed of it, for example by the verbal relation of somebody, or by a letter. Thus far the objection. It may be answered, that every termination that is assigned to an act must at any rate be an arbitrary one: since it seems impossible for us to say where the chain of causes and effects ends anymore than where it begun in any part of it. That therefore the best period which can be assigned for the physical termination of an act is that which can be easiest described: and that there can be no period so easily and certainly described, described in a manner so little liable to mistake, as that in which the progress or course it takes changes from a purely physical act to an act of so disparate a nature as an intelligible sign, or an act of discourse. While the thief or the minister of justice is carrying away your goods to the place where they are to rest, the act or course of events is uniform and homogeneous: it changes

[1] *An Introduction to the Principles*, Ch. xvi, paras. 1 and 5 (in *CW*, 187, 188).

*Different
senses of the
word* upon *as
applied to a
person who is
a possible
subject of the
law*

8. Without calling to mind these distinctions it will hardly be possible (at least in my own case I found it was not possible) to find any clear ideas, any distinct images, to annex to the phrases in which a man is mentioned as one *upon* whom an act of punishment is exercised: one *upon* whom a punishment is inflicted. To this one expression correspond in the three different cases that have been stated three perfectly different ideas or pictures in the mind: In one case, the idea that that of an act of the positive kind terminating physically in the body of the person punished: in another it is an act still of the positive kind but never by its ordinary physical effects extending to his body: in a third case, it is not so much as any positive act at all: it is nothing more than a mere negative act which has neither a termination nor a commencement anywhere. This negative act may indeed be preceded by judicial opinions, judicial orders, and the like: but these are acts of the positive kind, and as distinct from that in question as the province of the judge is from that of the executioner.

9. But further, for perspicuity's sake, the articles which a given law takes for its subjects, whether agible or passible and whether things or persons, must, in consideration of the different ways in which they may be regarded by it, be distinguished into such as are its subjects in a *direct* manner, and such as are so in an *indirect* manner only: or, to speak more concisely, into the *direct* subjects of the law and the *indirect*. To the former head belong the examples above given. But the persons and the things whereof the names may happen to occur in the tenor of the law will naturally be looked upon all of them without distinction as being comprised under the appellation of its subjects: and why should they not? Nor can it well be otherwise, for that to all of them the law bears a certain relation cannot be denied: and by what other name can they be

into one of a quite different nature when a letter is written to you informing you of the misfortune, or when upon sending a person for some of the goods, word is brought back to you that they are not to be found. The course of events that intervene between the misfortune and the suffering undergone at such a period suffers as great a change as a road does when having taken its course for miles through a narrow lane it opens into a common, where instead of continuing in one tract it is in a manner lost by being broken into a thousand obscure paths of which the appearance is very different and whose commencements and terminations are oftentimes scarce discernible. The stand which takes place in point of time is another remarkable ground of distinction. A man may be years before a misfortune which has taken place has reached his ear: during which time the action may be not going on slowly and continually, as where the mischief is produced by the application of poison or of a cause of corrosion or putrefaction, but absolutely at a stand.

called in respect of that relation, if not by this? At the same time in comparison of this great multitude of subjects as it may often prove, those which can be included under any of the descriptions above given will commonly be but a very few; these then may be distinguished by the appellation of its *direct* subjects: while the others may be indiscriminately styled the *collateral* or *indirect* subjects of the law. And thus it is that the whole infinitude of material things or persons whereof the names can for any purpose be introduced into any such discourse as is susceptible of the appellation of a law, is circumscribed. The indirect subjects of the law can be styled so only with reference to the law: the direct subjects of it are also subjects of the act, and it is by being subjects of the act which is the object of a law that they become subjects of the law itself. It will be seen hereafter that the persons and things here spoken of in the character of the indirect subjects of the law, are the same whose natures, conditions and changes of conditions form the *circumstances* or collateral objects by means of which the description of the acts which are taken for the direct objects of the law is diversified according to the exigency of the occasion.

10. In separating in our minds the direct subjects of the law from the indirect we must be careful not to be deceived by the irregularities of language. A law lays a tax, suppose, *upon* corn: from this expression we might naturally enough be led to think that corn was among the direct subjects of the law. Upon examination however we shall find the contrary to be the case. The object of such a law is not any act which either in its termination or in any part of its progress has any thing to do with *corn*. The only use which there is in mentioning the word *corn*, is to mark the occasion on which a certain act, an act that has nothing, physically speaking, to do with corn, shall be performed, viz: the act of paying no matter to whom nor how a certain sum of money. Let it be a tax on the exportation of corn: the word *corn* then is one of those which serve to mark the event upon the happening of which you are to pay a sum of money: you are to pay it upon the happening of the event which consists in your exporting a certain quantity of that commodity: such is the act you are commanded to perform whenever the *time* occurs, if ever it should occur, which is characterized by the circumstance just mentioned. On this occasion it happens that the only subjects which there is any occasion to mention by name in the tenor of the law (the person whom it takes for its agible subject, that is the party whom it is addressed to, or in other words the party who is bound by it being excepted) are its individual subjects: viz: the

Example of such as are indirect

corn and what other things or persons there may be occasion to make mention of in the details. The act itself, which is the object of the law, viz: the act of payment, being in respect of its physical character and appearance so various, indeterminate and discretionary, that it would be endless to characterize it in general discourse any otherwise than by a name which has a view to the material part of its effects:[1] viz: the causing him who has been paid to have a right[m] to the disposal of the money or whatever it is in which he has been paid. This is what may be done by any one of an indefinite number of different sets of signs: such as laying down money to such an amount upon a table, giving an order upon a third person to pay so much money, giving credit for so much money in an account, and so on: but as these sets of signs have nothing in them that is material over and above this common circumstance of their aptitude to produce the effects in question, it would be idle to go about to describe them in any other manner than by reference to those effects.

[1] See Ch. xvi (Division) 35n.[1]

[m] To any one who is in this train of thinking it may be easy to perceive that the words commonly exhibited by grammarians to serve as examples of active verbs are many of them but ill calculated to answer that intention. According to their account, the verb should signify the act together with the agible subject, while the substantive which the verb is said to govern should signify the passible subject in which the act hath its termination. This is verified perfectly well by the verb τυπτω, I beat, in the phrase τυπτω σε, I beat you: but *moneo te*, I advise you, does it but obscurely; φιλεω σε, *amo te*, I love you, still more obscurely if at all: and in *audio te*, I hear you, the course taken by the act is the reverse of that which is attributed to it by the grammarian. If I *beat* you, the act proceeds from me and the impression which is a physical one terminates in you: if I *advise* you, the act proceeds from me, and the impression which is a mental one, if any, terminates again in you: but if I *hear* you, the act which is a physical one proceeds from you, and the impression terminates in me: if I *love* you, the act (if any act be necessary in the case) has proceeded from you and the impression which is a mental one terminates again in me. The example to have begun with is that which stands first in order here: in this there is neither fiction nor obscurity. The others might then if it were necessary be explained by means of the analogy which they bear, or by fiction of language are supposed to bear to this.

This note is thrown in, not for its own sake, but in hope that a subject which is familiar may be a means of reflecting light upon remarks which are abstruse.

[1] *An Introduction to the Principles*, Ch. xvi, para. 35: Bentham's reference is to the fourth note to that paragraph (in *CW*, 227 n. c3).

CHAPTER V

OBJECTS OF A LAW

1. Fourthly, with regard to the acts that are the objects of the law. To these also the division into direct and indirect may apply, as well as to persons and to things. *Acts may be directly or indirectly the objects of a law*

2. The mention of the word *act* makes it in a manner necessary to say something of the words *circumstance* and *case*: since these are words which will continually be occurring, and without which one act can scarcely be either described by itself or spoken of as being distinguished from another.[a] *Necessity of introducing the words circumstance and case*

3. The chief use of a circumstance as annexed to the name of an act is to specificate it, that is to distinguish it from acts which in other respects are of the same name. Yet it is not every circumstance that has this effect; or to speak more properly, it is not on every occasion that a group of words expressive of a circumstance has this effect upon the act with the name of which it connects. Circumstances may accordingly be distinguished into *unspecificant,* and *specificant.* The unspecificant are mentioned rather for regularity's sake and lest it should be asked what we are to think of them, than for any occasion there will be to make mention of them hereafter. The distinction between these two ways of introducing a circumstance may be thus made out. *Specificant circumstances in a law, what*

Conceive an assemblage of words put together by which an act of any sort is expressed under the character of the object of a mandate: this done, any other words that purport to have anything to do with the description of the act may be considered as expressive of a circumstance belonging to it. Suppose the act to be that of exporting wheat out of the country; and let it be mentioned in the character of the object of a mandate in this manner—'No man shall export wheat out of the country'. The sentence then as it stands at present may be looked upon as expressive of an act without a circumstance. Add now the words 'that breathes' and let it stand 'No man *that breathes* shall export wheat out of the country': the words *that breathes* are expressive of a circumstance indeed, but of a circumstance which is not specificant: wheat cannot be exported by any man but it must be exported by a man that breathes. So if it be

[a] I could easily write a volume upon it, but the difficulty is to say anything of it that will be of any use in the compass of a few pages.

41

said 'No man shall *in anywise* export wheat out of the country'. But if it be said, 'No man shall export wheat out of the country in any foreign navigable vessel' here a circumstance is introduced which is specificant, because corn may be exported in navigable vessels of the country, or if the country be not an island, by land carriages. So likewise if it be said, 'No man shall export wheat out of the country—*when* the market price at the place from whence it is meant to be exported is more then 44s. a quarter'.[b]

To give one instance more. Suppose the law to say— 'let no man steal anything, knowing that he has no title to it': the words 'knowing that he has no title to it' are expressive of a circumstance; but of a circumstance which is not specificant: a man can not steal anything without knowing that he has no title to it: since if this consciousness be wanting, the taking is not what is meant by stealing. But let the law say 'let no man steal in a dwelling house' or 'by night' (as where it means to impose an extraordinary penalty on account of the intervention of these circumstances) these circumstances it is evident enough are specificant, for the reason that has been given. As to circumstances that are not specificant, it seems pretty evident, that the introduction of them into a law, unless in as far as they answer the purpose of explanation, or some rhetorical purpose, is altogether nugatory.

So much by way of a general direction. As to the framing a set of rules sufficient to point out with accuracy in every case by what assemblages of words an act is described without mention of any such thing as a circumstance, and in what assemblages of words the mention of a separate circumstance is included, this would be a task which if it could be executed at all would take up more room than I believe any reader would bear to see bestowed upon a subject apparently of such small importance: such variety is there in the phrases by which acts of different natures are denoted.

Specificant circumstances are to an act what specificant properties are to a substance

4. If the import of the word *circumstance* should still be obscure, (and difficult indeed it will be found to make it otherwise) it may be made something clearer perhaps by changing it into the word *property*. Not that a circumstance can be said to be a property; they being fictitious entities of a different order. But wherever the word *circumstance* is employed with reference to an act, the phrase in which it stands may be changed into another phrase containing the word *property*. An act is attended with such or such a circumstance: this upon the present occasion will be found (although the identity of the two meanings may perhaps not be perceptible at first sight)

[b] British Stat. 13 Geo. III c. 43. § 5.

to be the same thing as to say, an act is endued with such or such a property. I will that such an act be done in such or such circumstances; that is if attended with such or such circumstances: this is as much as to say, if possessed of such or such a property or set of properties. This brings us into the beaten paths of common logic. In common logic indeed we hear rather more of substances or of fictitious substances than of acts; and therefore the word *property* is more frequently made use of with reference to such substances or pretended substances than with reference to acts: but it is likewise occasionally made use of, at least it is evident that it may be made use of, with reference to acts. In its application to substances it hath passed from the language of the logicians into the language of natural science, and thence into familiar speech: but the word *circumstance* as applied to acts seems to have had its birth originally in familiar speech without passing through the hands of the logicians. While logicians and naturalists made use of the word *property*, people at large made use of the word *circumstance*.

5. Let us take the examples above given, and instead of the word *Example* *circumstance* make use of the word *property*. A certain genus of acts is proposed for consideration: the act of exporting wheat out of the country: out of this a certain species, as distinguished by its being performed in a certain set of circumstances or what comes to the same thing by its possessing a certain property, is taken and rendered the object of a prohibitory mandate: viz: that species which is performed 'in any navigable vessel belonging to a foreign country'. So again in the next case, another species is taken out of the same genus: viz: that species which is performed, (that species which comprehends the individual acts of exportation as above mentioned which are performed) when the market price of the commodity in question is at the rate above mentioned. In the same manner the word *circumstance* may be exchanged for the word *property* in the other examples above proposed.

In the last of the two here given it may seem that the application of the word *property* is not quite so natural as in that which goes before it: because mere *time* is not commonly taken for the differential character of a species. But the establishment of species and genera and so forth are but so many contrivances for throwing individuals into groups or parcels; and the groups may as well be formed upon this principle as upon any other.

6. It may occasion a good deal of perplexity if we are not careful to observe, that the question whether such or such an act as noticed by the law be attended with circumstances, or whether it be

not a mere act free from circumstances, depends altogether upon the wording: insomuch that the same act precisely in one way of expressing it shall be attended with circumstances, in another not. In the few instances in which an act which is the object of a law happens to be characterized by a universal name such as theft, or by a name which though multivocal is simple enough to enter into grammatical construction upon the footing of a univocal one, as wrongful homicide, wrongful occupation of property; in such instances, I say, so long as the name of the act remains in this simple form, there are no circumstances that accompany it: expand it, throw it into the form of a definition, then circumstances appear: specificant circumstances which whenever the definition is in the regular form being annexed to the name of some superior genus, reduce such superior genus to the dimensions of the species expressed by the simple name which is defined.

7. Not that the idea of an act can ever be clothed in any such expression, as the word circumstance will not in some way or other associate with. For here too it is with an act and its circumstances as it is with a substance and its properties: you may strip a substance of its properties one by one till you reduce it to nothing: so you may an act by stripping it of its circumstances: an act being made up of circumstances, as a substance is of properties. Such at least seems to be the way of speaking in these cases. But the plain truth of the matter is that as the description of a substance is performed by the enumeration of particulars which are called properties, so the description of an act is performed by the enumeration of particulars which are called circumstances. The misfortune is that with these very circumstances of which the very texture of the act as it were is made up, it is said (such is the phrase) to be *attended*; as if the act itself were a thing that subsisted without them, and they something separate from and external to it. This makes such a confusion between these *constituent* circumstances, as they may be called, and specificant circumstances, as is scarcely to be remedied or avoided. Although no circumstances are specified in the law against theft when couched in these words, 'thou shalt not steal', or 'let no one steal'; yet no individual act of those that come under the name of theft, can be conceived without the conceiving, or described without the enumerating, of circumstances; which circumstances when mentioned under that name are spoken of as circumstances attending or accompanying the act of theft.

A case, what   8. A word or two, according to promise, concerning the import of the word *case*. The import of this word is nearly allied to that of the word *circumstance*: and perhaps there is no occasion on which if the one may be employed, the other may not be employed instead of it. Yet of a case it cannot be said, that it is a circumstance, these as well as *circumstance* and *property* being fictitious entities of a different order. This will appear by making up the phrase. We speak of an act as being attended or accompanied by or with a circumstance: but we cannot speak of it as being attended or accompanied by or with a case. On the other hand we speak of an act as being performed *in* such or such a case: but we cannot speak of it as being performed *in* such or such a circumstance. We may speak of it indeed as being performed in such or such circumstances: for an assemblage of circumstances may be considered as constituting a case.[c] The relation which the word *case* bears to the word *circumstance* appears to be somewhat of a piece with that which the word *species* bears to the word *property*: since as a substance by being possessed of such or such a property is said to belong to or come under such a species, so an act by being attended with such or such a circumstance is said to be performed in or to come under such or such a case.

9. These disquisitions are of no other use as applied to the explanation of a law, than in as far as they are necessary to ascertain the distinction between a conditional and an unconditional mandate: a distinction which it will be necessary to advert to in considering the different forms which a mandate may assume in respect of the different aspects it may bear to the acts which are its objects. Here then we must leave the subject. *Use of the above disquisition*

The few observations that have been already given may serve to exhibit a slight and general view of the principles to be pursued in investigating the import of these very vague though universal terms, *circumstance* and *case*: to sift the matter to the bottom, so as to guard against all inaccuracies,[d] and to exhibit all the different

[c]What may be called the archetypation of the word *case*, as compared with that of the word *circumstance* is as follows. In the word *circumstance* the image is that of an assemblage of objects *standing round* a given object. In the word *case* it is that of an assemblage of objects *falling* as it were around the given object, and by virtue of their common relation to that object, cemented as it were into one, and forming a ring *in* which the object is said to stand or be.

Case, in Latin *casus*; in French *cas* in Italian and Spanish, *caso*; in German *falle*: the image is in all these languages the same. So in Greek πτωσις; though here the use of it seems to be more confined. In the word *circumstance* the analogy runs in the same manner through all those languages.

[d] It may be observed for example that the word *circumstance* can scarcely according to the usage of the language, be applied to any real entity: it can be applied to nothing but a fictitious entity. Thus in the group of circumstances *'Circumstance' not applied to real entities*

applications that may be made of the two expressions, is a task which I shall probably be very readily dispensed with from fulfilling, and which belongs rather to the subject of general metaphysics, than to that of jurisprudence.

Collateral circumstances

10. Next with regard to the circumstances to which the will of a legislator may apply. These are *modes of being* of the indirect subjects of the law. Now it has already been observed that there is no object whatever but may be spoken of under the appellation of a circumstance.[e] The distinction then between acts and circumstances turns not so much upon the nature of the objects themselves as upon the manner in which they are respectively regarded by the law, or what comes to the same thing, the purpose for which the mention of them is introduced by it. Circumstances as mentioned in a law, are not acts which the legislator wills should be performed or not performed, motions or situations which he wills should take place or not take place in consequence, but objects the names of which are made use of for the purpose of specifying and characterizing those acts, motions and situations. The manner then in which they are regarded by the law may be thus made out. When once a set of words are put together sufficient to characterize and point out an act of any sort as one which is the object of a law, if any other words be added, the objects signified by such other words may with relation to the act so expressed be termed *circumstances*: and the effect of their being mentioned, if they have any, and if nothing is intimated to the contrary, is, (as we shall see more particularly farther on) that of narrowing the description of the act: that is reducing the class (or *genus*) of acts in contemplation from the extent and amplitude of that characterized by the words first made

mentioned upon a former occasion as accompanying the act performed by Felton in the stabbing of the Duke of Buckingham (See Ch. vii (Actions) 25)[1] it is not the bloody knife, the hat found upon the ground, the sentences written in the hat, and so forth that according to common speech are the circumstances, but the bloodiness of the knife (that is the existence of the quality of bloodiness in the knife) the finding of the hat on the ground (that is the happening of the act of finding the hat upon the ground) and the writing of the sentences, (that is the happening of the act consisting in the writing of those sentences).

This particularly in the use of the word *circumstance* is more than I was aware of on a former occasion in which I was endeavouring to give an exposition of that word. (See Ch. vii (Actions) 22 n.)[2]

[e] Circumstances are the modes of being incident to the indirect subjects of the law.

[1] Ch. vii of *An Introduction to the Principles*, para. 25 (in *CW*, 80–1).

[2] Ibid., loc. cit., para. 22 n. 1 (in *CW*, 79–80).

use of, to another class (or *species* as it is now called) coinciding as far as it extends with the former, but of less extent and amplitude, and consequently included under it.

Circumstances of which the mention is thus introduced are styled the circumstances *in* which it is the legislator's will that the act should, or should not be performed. For distinction's sake, in order to mark the purpose for which they are introduced they may be termed *specificant* circumstances with relation to the act: circumstances specificative or characteristic of the act. If there are no particular circumstances mentioned on the occasion, then, for anything that appears on the face of the law, it is the law-giver's will that the act should be performed, or not performed, or that a man should have the choice of performing it or not, *in* or *under* any circumstances whatever: that is in any *case*[f] or, what comes to the same thing, in all cases whatsoever. The *circumstances* then or *cases* or *case* in which it is the intention of the legislator that the act as characterized by a given name should be performed are as material to consider as the act itself.

In every act of the body there must be three particulars at least concerned: a body or portion of matter in which the motion in question is considered as commencing: 1. this is what we called its *agible* subject: 2. a portion of matter in which it is considered as having its termination, i.e. its *passible* subject: 3. the abstract act or motion itself which is considered as having its commencement in one of those portions of matter and its termination in the other.[g] Without these particulars be all of them brought to view in every case no individual act nor consequently any *genus* of acts can be

[f] The connection between the idea belonging to the word *case* as here applied, and the idea belonging to the words *genus, species* or any other significative of a class is this. Any individual act of a certain *genus*, or larger class, every such act or class by having been attended with certain circumstances, by having been performed *in* certain circumstances, or in a certain case, may be said to be of a certain *species*, or smaller class. A circumstance or set of circumstances constitute the case which an individual act has been or may be performed in: a species or class which it is of.

[g] It might seem that acts of belief are capable like any other acts of being made the objects of the law: but this is not the case. Acts declarative of belief may indeed, and that with some effect: but these are always external acts: acts of the body. Whether a fact appears true to me or no, I may be hired or forced to tell an untruth and say I believe it: but if it does not appear true to me, all the force in the universe will not make me believe it in reality. I am speaking of the direct and immediate efficacy of any such force: as to the indirect and gradual influence which the affections may exercise on the judgment that is not to the present purpose.

brought to view: there is no basis formed to which any specificant circumstances can apply: no larger class out of which by the application of such circumstances a smaller specific class can be extracted. Not that it is always necessary that these three particulars should be each of them mentioned by name: all that is absolutely necessary to mention is the name of the abstract act or motion, provided that name be such an one as serves to characterize the material part of its effects. By means of this single name it will then appear that the agible subject intended could be none other than a being which at the same time that it is capable of being influenced by the will of the legislator is capable of contributing to the production of the effects in question: as also with respect to the passible subject that it could be none other than a being of such a class as to be susceptible of effects such as those by which the abstract act or motion as expressed by the above mentioned name is characterized. However it is only in virtue of a mere grammatical ellipsis that the mention of either the one or the other subject can be dispensed with. The ideas that respectively belong to them must at any rate be present to the mind, or no image of any act whatsoever can be formed by it.

Example – a law against killing expressed without the help of any specificant circumstances

11. By means of a few examples these positions abstruse as they are, may perhaps be rendered tolerably clear. Conceive a law to be exhibited in these terms: 'Let no one kill'. Here no subject at all is mentioned by any distinctive name: neither an agible subject nor a passible: all that is mentioned (in conjunction with the will of the legislator) is the act (I mean the class of acts) which that will has taken for its object: to wit the act of killing: that is any physical act or motion, in short any act whatever, the effect of which is to reduce a being to that condition in which when it is in, it is said to be *dead*. By the nature then of this act as characterized by its effects the agible as well as the passible subject is in some sort limited and determined: the latter must be such a sort of being as is susceptible of being killed, viz: a being endued with life: the agible subject such a sort of being as is capable of contributing to the effect of another's being killed, and at the same time such an one on whose acts it is possible that the legislator can expect the expression of his will to have an influence. By virtue then of the word 'to kill' the intention of the legislator is thus far limited and determined, that the passible subject can not be a class of beings more extensive than that which includes all living creatures, nor the agible subject of a class more extensive than that which includes all human creatures.[h] It appears then that the words in question 'Let no *one*

[h] What farther limitations the apparent intention of the legislator may

kill' as coming out of the mouth of a legislator are exactly equivalent to these 'Let no *person* kill any *animal*': and supposing the idea of the animal to stand limited by any other consideration to that of a human creature, they will then be equivalent to these, 'Let no person kill any *person*'.

Now, let the law stand in either of these forms, what specificant circumstances can there be said to be in the case? None, it is plain, while it stood in the narrowest form 'Let no one kill'. Nor yet when the words of it are, 'Let no person kill any animal'. For a passible as well as an agible subject of some class or other the act must have, and there are no words introduced to limit either subject to a narrower class that it otherwise could have been of. Nor even supposing that instead of saying 'Let no person kill any animal' it were to say 'Let no person kill any person'. For a passible subject of some class or other the law must have had in view: and the class it actually has in view it means by the proper *univocal*[1] name of that class without introducing any words importing that class to be a species of any other. A person is indeed a species of animal, viz: a rational animal: but persons are here mentioned under the name of *persons* and not under the name of *rational animals*.

12. On the other hand let the law instead of saying 'Let no person kill any person' say 'Let no person kill any rational animal', or as it would be more natural to say 'any human creature', here there is a specificant circumstance taken for the object of the law. For without the word *rational* there would have been a word to

–with specificant circumstances

receive from the consideration of any other circumstances that may present themselves to view is not to the present purpose. From the practice of most nations and the disposition of most legislators it would indeed be a very natural conclusion to make that the protection afforded by this law was not meant to extend to any more ample class of beings than that which is composed of human creatures. But such a conclusion though a natural would not like the former be a necessary one. Take for instance for your legislator a Pythagoras, and to make him a little more consistent let him be as studious to preserve his friends of the brute creation from being killed as from being eaten[1]: and if this be not enough, tincture him with a spice of Quakerism, and let him be as averse to the destroying of the lives of his fellow-animals as that inoffensive sect are to the shedding of the blood of their fellow-men. Even now, absurd as the opposite conclusion might appear in Europe, it would hardly appear equally so in Hindostan.

[1] By an *univocal* name I mean a name consisting of no more than a single word.

[1] The school of mystical philosophy founded by Pythagoras in the latter part of the 6th century B.C. taught, among other doctrines, the unity of life and the transmigration of souls.

express a class of entities as being the possible subjects of the law: viz: the word *animal*: and the class of beings intended is here denoted by two words, the one expressive of one larger than that intended, and the other serving to express that the class intended is but a species or part of such larger class.

–with cir-
cumstances
that are not
specificant

13. Suppose again that the law were to stand thus: 'Let no person kill any animal having life'. Here also a circumstance would indeed be introduced: but this circumstance would not be a specificant one. Applied to another word it might indeed be specificant: it is not so however, as applied to the word here in question. It would have been specificant if applied to such a word as the word *being*: because there are other classes of beings than those which are endued with life. But as applied to the word *animal* it is not: because of animals there are not any other classes than those which are endued with life.

The law nar-
rowed with or
without add-
ing circum-
stances – e.g.
where the
person killed
is a judge

14. Let the law again instead of saying let no one kill any person, say let no one kill a judge. The act is again reduced to a narrower class than it was before. Still however no specificant circumstance is introduced: the possible subject is characterized, as before in the case of the word *person*, by its own univocal name without the mention of any circumstance. But let it say let no one kill *his* father here there is a specificant circumstance introduced: father, a father, (viz: any person who bears the relation of paternity to any other person) is a genus, whereof the word *his* which being applied to the word *father* determines it to mean the father of the person in question (a person who bears the relation of paternity to that particular person) indicates a species.

So, where the
act is per-
formed by
poison

15. Let the law again stand thus: 'Let no one kill any person by poison'. Here again another circumstance is introduced, which also is specificant as before. A subject in which the act has its commencement, viz: an agible subject, and a subject in which it has its termination, viz: a passible subject being the only circumstances that are indispensably necessary to constitute an external act, stand already expressed without the words 'by poison': the effect of these is to express a circumstance relative to the *progress* of the act[j]: viz: the circumstance of its having been performed by poison: that is of poison's having been of the number of the bodies concerned in the progress of the act from the agible subject to the passible subject in which the pathological effects of the act were manifested, and in which the act is considered as having its termination.

[j] See Ch. vii (Actions) 14.[1]

[1] Ch. vii of *An Introduction to the Principles*, para. 14 (in *CW*, 77).

16. But let the law stand thus, 'Let no one poison any person'; *– or with pre-* here there are no specificant circumstances introduced: the *meditation* specificant circumstances which before were annexed to the name of the act in such manner as to stand detached from it, are now merged in the new name which is substituted in the room of the former. And yet the species or class of act designed in the two cases is just the same.

Suppose the law again to say: 'Let no one kill another with a premeditated design to kill'. Here again is another specificant circumstance introduced. But let it stand thus 'let no man murder any person'; here again is none. And yet the word 'murder' may include amongst other circumstances that of a premeditated design to kill considered as having subsisted on the part of the person killing.

17. Notwithstanding what has been said the distinction between *Why in some* acts that are not attended with circumstances and acts that are will *cases it may* be very apt to appear to be something more than nominal. Take for *appear to* *have a neces-* example once more the act of killing and the act of poisoning. To *sary respect* come under the notion of an act of the former sort it may be thought *to circum-* that an act need not be attended with any circumstances: but that *stances* to come under the notion of an act of the latter sort it must. The act of killing, it may be thought, is one that need not be attended with any circumstances: but that as to the act of poisoning, there is a circumstance with which it must necessarily be attended: the circumstance of poison's having been employed in the production of the effect. The reason however of such an appearance seems to be neither more nor less than this. A class of acts like a class of any other objects in order to represent itself to the mind with any degree of precision, must represent itself under some name: and the name under which upon any given occasion it will be most apt to represent itself, will be the name which is most in use. According to this position, it can scarcely happen that the word *poisoning* should ever present itself to the mind, without presenting some such word as *killing* or *murdering*, at the same time. The act therefore is recognized to be an act of killing as soon at least as it is recognized to be an act of poisoning: and as poisoning is distinguished from other acts of killing, by certain circumstances, the act in question will be recognized to be an act of killing attended with certain circumstances. In point of fact every act is attended with circumstances innumerable: from every being that exists it derives a group of circumstances. It is not this then that can make any distinction between one class of act and another. The distinction then between acts which are and acts which are not attended with circumstances lies not in the things themselves: if then it lies any-where, it must lie in the words. Accordingly it seems to have no other ground than the manner in which we speak of the matter of fact. Where the act presents itself under no other name than one which, for the purpose of distinguishing the act in question from all others from which it is meant to distinguish it, may be made use of without the mention of any circumstances, there it is apt to appear as if the act were not necessarily attended with any circumstances. But there are two cases where it will appear as if an act, in order to bring it within a certain class must necessarily be attended with certain circumstances: 1. where there is no name at all in use by which the act can be characterized without the mention of certain circumstances, that is where the class in question has no univocal name belonging to it at all: 2. where although it has an univocal name, yet that name whenever it presents itself is apt to bring to view at the same time another name which though it includes the class characterized by the former can not be made to quadrate with it exactly till it has been narrowed down by the applica-tion of certain circumstances. When a definition of a thing that is a definition of a class of objects (for classes of objects are the only things that can be defined) is given, the genus of which it is a species is narrowed down to the extent of that species by the appli-cation of certain circumstances which constitute the specific properties of that species. If then the word to be defined, the name of the act in question, is such as is scarcely to be understood without being defined, the act which it stands for, the act of which it is the name, will be apt to appear as one which whenever performed is attended with certain particular circumstances, and to the notion of which the notion of certain circumstances is essential.

CHAPTER VI

OF THE PARTIES WHICH MAY BE AFFECTED BY A LAW

1. [Fifth]ly[1], with regard to the parties who may be concerned in or affected by a law: and the different ways in which they may be concerned in or affected by it. There are three sorts of ways in which a party may be concerned in or affected by a law: 1. by being *bound* or coerced by it: 2. by being exposed at least to *suffer* by it: 3. by being *favoured* or intended to be favoured by it. Upon examination it will be found that on the one hand there must necessarily be one or more persons concerned in all these three ways, on the other hand that there are no other ways in which any person can be concerned in it.

Different ways in which persons may be affected by the law: viz. by being 1. bound or coerced: 2. made to suffer: or 3. favoured by it

2. Upon a hasty glance it might seem that this source of division had been exhausted, that this topic had been discussed already: for that the parties concerned in or affected by the law could be no other than the persons who are its agible subjects, added to those who are its passible subjects. But upon a closer examination it will be perceived, that it is only part of their respective grounds that the two topics extend over in common. In the first place under the head of the *subjects* (that is the passible subjects) of the law were included *things*. But the consideration of the *things* that are concerned does not here come in question: it is only the consideration of the persons concerned that belongs to the present head. In this respect therefore the extent of the present topic falls short of that of the preceding one above-mentioned. On the other hand, the parties favoured by the law could not without doing a kind of violence to language be comprised under the denomination of the persons who are its subjects: in this respect the extent of the present topic stretches beyond that of the preceding one.[a]

This source of distinction different from that concerning the subjects of a law

---

[a] N.B. Even these are strictly speaking among the number of the persons in whom the act has its pathological termination: though where they are only exempted from a chance of pain this may seem strained.

[1] The Ms. leaves a blank before the last two letters of this word. Here and later Bentham failed to systematise these introductory adverbs for the chapters down to Ch. XIII inclusive, which follow, more or less, the topics listed at the beginning of Ch. I (1 above). In the present edition the sequence of adverbs or adverbial phrases has been brought into line with the order finally adopted.

That there must be 1. a party bound or coerced

3. We may now proceed to shew, that in every law there must be one or more persons concerned in all these ways. First then that there must be some person or persons who are bound or in other words coerced by it, is undeniable. These are the same persons who in other words have been termed the agible subjects of the law: without these a law cannot so much as be conceived. A law by which nobody is bound, a law by which nobody is coerced, a law by which nobody's liberty is curtailed, all these phrases which come to the same thing would be so many contradictions in terms.

2. a party made to suffer

4. In the second place, a condition equally necessary to the existence of a law is, that there should be some person or persons who are exposed at least to suffer by it. This condition is in truth a necessary consequence of the other. It may be laid down as an axiom in pathology, that there is no sort of act assignable which it is at all times a pleasure to a man to perform: and this may even be extended to negative acts. Take even any given time, and at that time let the act itself be pleasant to perform, the idea of coercion intervening may of itself be sufficient to give it an opposite effect. Even were the truth of this position disputable in the latitude here given to it, still it must be admitted with regard to all such acts as it could answer any purpose to take for the objects of a command. Either then the law has no effect, or there is a party who is exposed at least to suffer by it: if no one else, yet at any rate the party whom it binds. It follows that a law, whatever good it may do at the long run, is sure in the first instance to produce mischief. The good it does may compensate the mischief it does a million of times over: but still it begins with doing harm. No law can ever be made but what trenches upon liberty: if it stops there, it is so much *pure* evil[b]: if it is good upon the whole, it must be in virtue of something that comes after. It may be a necessary evil: but still at any rate it is an evil. To make a law is to do evil that good may come.

True it is that the inconvenience a man is exposed to from this cause is in many cases in itself very uncertain and inconsiderable: and that there are some obligations of which the burthen is in general very light: and that of obligations which are even burthensome in themselves the pressure may for the most part be taken off by the operation of other concomitant laws made in favour of the party who before was bound. Still however all the industry of man can not prevent but that upon the intervention of particular

[b] See Ch. iv (Value).[1]

[1] Ch. iv of *An Introduction to the Principles*, the full title of which is 'Value of a Lot of Pleasure or Pain, How to be Measured'.

circumstances the pressure of coercion will get the better of its counterpoise, and make itself sensible in its original and essential form of inconvenience. A man takes upon him the office of a Receiver of public money: receiving money with one hand, he is obliged to pay it with the other. It follows not indeed from hence that he experiences a separate pang for every penny that he parts with: it is his business to part with money in that manner: he takes it in order to part with it, he has no hope of being able to keep with impunity, and he is paid for parting with it. Still however there is not a penny of the money that he would not rather, were he at liberty, dispose of to purposes of his own. Particular circumstances may also render the obligation particularly irksome: he may wish he had the money to repair a casual deficiency in his own private funds: indolence, ill health, or the importunity of other avocations, necessary or pleasurable, may at a particular conjunction render it particularly unpleasant to him to give his time to the fulfilling of the requisite formalities.

That there should be a party who is exposed to suffer by a law any other wise than in virtue of the coercion which it imposes on him, is not essentially necessary: whether there is or no depends upon the particular nature of the law. Where there is, he may be exposed to it either through necessity (that is not purposely) or purposely: if purposely, he is exposed to it for the purpose either of punishment or of vindictive compensation.[c] In all three cases the suffering which he is exposed to may be, as in the two latter it must be, intentional on the part of the legislator: but in the first case it can only be obliquely intentional; in the second case, it is directly intentional, but still not ultimately: it is in the third case only that it is ultimately intentional.[d] In these two last cases the law is of one or other of those species of adjective laws to which we have assigned a particular name: in the second case, of the punitory kind, in the third case, of the compensative. Of these as well as of the case where the suffering is but obliquely intentional, more will be said a little farther on.

5. In the third place, in every law there must also be some person or persons who are favoured by it: meaning a person on whom it is the *intention* at least of the legislator to confer a benefit. To suppose

3. a party favoured

[c] See Ch. XIII (Cases unmeet).[1]
[d] See Ch. [VIII] (Intentionality).[2]

[1] *An Introduction to the Principles*, Ch. XIII.
[2] Ibid., Ch. VIII. Bentham has omitted the number of the chapter. In the Ms. the following note appears at this point: 'Alter this. It is never ultimately intentional but where the legislator proceeds upon the principle of antipathy.'

the contrary is to suppose the legislator to act without a motive. Possibly indeed the party favoured may be one who ought not thus to have been favoured: possibly no other then the legislator himself: still at any rate somebody who is favoured by it there must be. No effect without a cause: no act, no law without a motive. Had the necks of the whole Roman people, according to the wish of Caligula, been consolidated into one; and had his wish been followed up by a law, even to that law there would not have been wanting a party favoured: the law of Caligula would have been made in favour of Caligula.[1]

Whether a party on whom it is the intention of the law to confer a benefit, shall really enjoy that or any other benefit, may depend indeed upon the event. It may design to benefit a man without benefiting him: it may benefit him without designing it: it may design to benefit one man and eventually benefit another. But since in the ordinary train of things the efficacy of laws as far as it goes is conformable to the intention, it will be proper to suppose that such is the case in each particular instance: if then the intention of the law appear to be that such a party be benefited, the presumption is that he is benefited: as on the other hand if it appears that he is benefited, the presumption is that he was intended so to be.

There are no other ways in which a party can be affected than the above

6. It now comes to be shewn that there are no other ways in which a party can be affected by a law than what are comprehended as above. Take any given person for example: the influence of the law either is material to him, or it is not: if not, he is not affected by it in any way: if it is, the tendency of it is either prejudicial, with regard to him or beneficial: in as far then as it is prejudicial, he is exposed to suffer by it: in as far as it is beneficial, he is favoured by it.

It is equally evident that either he is bound by the law or he is not: in which last case he is left at liberty. If he is bound, it has been shewn already, that he is at any rate in the first instance exposed to suffer: and besides that, he may be favoured or not, as the case may be: so may he likewise if he be left free.

N.B. In laws creative of self-regarding offences the same person is coerced, made to suffer, and favoured at the same time.

In what sense a party may be said to be favoured in point of agency

7. As a party who is laid under coercion by a law is thereby exposed to suffer, so a party who is not laid under coercion by it may be said in a negative sort of way to be favoured by it: a party who is favoured in this particular sort of way may, for distinction's

[1] This anecdote is recorded by Suetonius in his life of Caligula.

sake, be said to be *favoured in point of agency*. I say in a negative sort of way: for it is only in consideration of the aspect which the law *might* have borne towards him and of that which it does actually bear to other parties, in short it is only in a negative way and by comparison, that a man can be said to experience any favour from a law of such a nature. The aspect which the law turns to *him* being negative is inefficient: of itself therefore such aspect can do him neither good nor harm: his condition as far as depends upon this part of the law is just the same after the making the law as it was before; and as it would have been if there had been no law made about the matter.[e]

It is only in as far as it is a source of obligation, it is only by means of its coercive influence, that a primordial law can be of any benefit to a man: since in fact it is only by these means that it can produce any effect whatever. Suppose him indeed to be already laid under coercion by a primordial law, then indeed a superventitious law, a counter-mandate, may have an efficient influence in his favour. It is upon this principle that where a mandate is issued by which others in respect of a given act are laid under coercion, an exception made to it in his favour may as such be considered as conferring on him a positive advantage: for every mandate which has an exception to it may be considered as consisting of two laws, the one primordial, the other superventitious, and *pro tanto* revocative of the former.

8. With regard to primordial laws then, it is only by some obligation which they impose, they can either shew a man any favour or indeed produce any other effect whatever.

By favouring one party in point of interest the law gives another a right to services

Now as to the party bound he may either be the same party who in point of interest is favoured or it may be another. In the former case the offence which the law by imposing the obligation creates, the duty which it enjoins, is of the self-regarding kind: in the latter case, of the extra-regarding kind.

Moreover it hath already been observed, that the law, when it imposes on one party a duty of the extra-regarding kind, does thereby confer upon some other party a right to services: a right to services to be rendered by the party on whom the duty is imposed: the doctrine of services therefore extends itself (as there hath already

[e] It follows that an *autocheiristic* power over a person or a thing (that is the power of exercising any physical act which shall have its physical termination in the body of the person or the substance of the thing) is not properly speaking any more than the right of performing acts of an intransitive nature, the work of law. To the law indeed a man must be indebted for any measures that are taken to secure him in the possession of the power in question, but that requires other laws addressed to other persons.

Auto-cheiristic power not originally the work of law

been occasion to observe) over little less than the whole body of the law. Every primordial law that is efficient is a command: every legal command imposes a duty: every legal command by imposing a duty on one party, if the duty be not only of the self-regarding kind, confers a right to services upon another. So in laws of the revocative kind: every law that is revocative of an efficient law is a countermand: every legal countermand takes off a duty: every legal countermand by taking off a duty from one party, if the duty be not merely of the self-regarding kind, takes away a right to services from another. As to the particular nature of such duty and such services, it is to be sought for in the nature of the act which is the object of the command, or which comes to the same thing, in the nature of the opposite act which by prohibiting it the law turns into an offence.

Services are either affirmative or negative: they are of the affirmative stamp, where the duty is affirmative, the mandate which creates it a command, the act which is the object of the law a positive or in other words an affirmative act, consequently the offence which it creates, a negative offence: they are of the negative stamp, where the duty is negative, the mandate a prohibition, the act which is the object of the law a negative act, consequently the offence which it creates, a positive offence.

A party so favoured may be an individual, a subordinate class, or the community

9. Who the party is that is favoured by the law may be seen by observing the nature of the offence. An offence which is extra-regarding may be either a private, a semi-public, or a public one: the party favoured may accordingly be either an individual, a subordinate class of persons, or the whole community at once. It is to be observed however, that as semi-public offences are generally attended with a public mischief, and private offences with a semi-public mischief as well as a public, the public is favoured by every law in virtue of its being injured in one way or other by every offence: the distinction is that in certain cases there is, besides the public at large, a particular individual who is a party favoured, in others none.

This distinction inapplicable to the party bound

This distinction, I mean that which turns upon the question concerning the description of the party, whether an individual, a subordinate class or the whole community, it would be of no use to carry any further. Important as it is[f] where applied to the party favoured, it is of no importance at all or we may say perhaps is not so much as discernible, when applied to the party bound: coercion

[f] See Ch. xvi (Division) 5.[1]

[1] Ch. xvi of *An Introduction to the Principles*, para. 5 (in *CW*, 188).

if it attaches at all can attach only upon individuals.[g] Benefit men may receive from the law in their collective capacity: but it is in their individual capacities that it is addressed to them: if proved to have been transgressed it is by individuals that it must be proved to have been transgressed: if punished it is upon individuals that it must be punished.

10. It is not in every case that the party favoured in point of agency is favoured in point of interest, any otherwise than in the negative way above mentioned. When a man is favoured by a law in point of agency, it may be either for his own sake or for that of another party. In the first case the power or the right of which he is left in possession is of the beneficial kind[h]; in the latter case of the fiduciary kind.[i] In this former case there is but one party favoured, who may be said to be favoured on his account, *causa propria* or *sua*; in the latter case, there are two parties favoured: the one *causa propria*, the beneficiary; the other *causa aliena*, the trustee. And reciprocally a party who by means of a favour shewn to someone in point of agency is favoured in point of interest may be thus favoured either by being himself favoured in point of agency, or by another's being so favoured on his account. *A party may in point of agency be favoured for his own sake or another's*

11. By one and the same law there may one party be favoured in point of agency and another in point of interest: the first left free to act in such or such a manner *in order that* through his acting the other may reap a benefit. But it is not this same law that is sufficient of itself to confer that benefit. It is sufficient to empower the trustee to render the services in question to the beneficiary: but it requires another law to make it his duty so to do. *But to complete the favour designed for such beneficiary requires another law*

To illustrate the observations we have been making concerning the different ways in which different parties may be affected by the same law it may be of use to cast a slight glance over the several classes of laws which there is need of in a state as determined by the several classes of offences to which they apply.

12. First, as to the laws concerning offences against person. Here the parties bound are either all persons whatsoever (those excepted to whom in such and such cases powers over persons of such and such individuals are given, whether the powers be permanent or occa- *Parties affected in laws concerning offences against person and reputation*

[g] This is not true in regard to offences against laws that are universal *ex parte subjecti agibilis*. Coercion here attaches as much as favour in the other case.

[h] See Ch. xvi (Division).[1]

[i] Ibid.

[1] Ibid.   The reference in this and the next footnote is presumably to the discussion of trust in para. 25, including nn. e2 and f2 (in *CW*, 205–8).

sional, exercisable on a private or a public, a beneficial or a fiduciary, account): or in particular cases particular classes of persons from whom offences of the nature in question are particularly apprehended. The parties purposely exposed to suffer, none: the parties favoured in the first instance, each person in particular to whom protection for his person against the mischief in question is thus given. As to the parties favoured in the second and third instances in respect of the mischief of the second and third orders against which they are protected, these have been already noticed, nor will it be necessary to make any farther mention of them.

Secondly, the same observations may be applied to the laws respecting offences against reputation.

–property   Thirdly, as to the laws concerning offences against property. Property is either in things or in the services of persons. Let us begin with property in things; taking for examples those subjects and those rights of which the description is most simple. To understand who are the parties affected by the laws of property, we must conceive as many laws as there are different things that are the subjects of property within the dominion of the state. The statement of the parties who are affected will be different in every such law. In a baker's shop let there be two loaves, one of which you have just bought of him, and one other which being as yet unsold remains the baker's. In a law which gives or secures to you the property of that loaf which is yours the parties bound are all mankind the baker himself included, you excepted: the parties intentionally exposed to suffer, none as before: the party favoured, you and you alone. In a law which gives or secures to the baker the property of the loaf which remains his, the parties bound are all mankind, you included, the baker excepted: the parties intentionally exposed to suffer, none as before: the party favoured the baker and he alone.

So in immovables, which will afford a more convenient example for illustrating the manner in which the interests of the several parties are affected by the pair of laws which are necessary to constitute an article of fiduciary property. In a given district let there be two acres of land contiguous; the one, which shall be called y in your possession, the other which shall be called f, in the possession of another person who shall be called F. In a law which gives or secures to you the exclusive possession of the acre which is yours, the parties bound are all mankind, except you: the party favoured, you and you alone. In a law which gives or secures to F the exclusive possession of the acre f the parties bound are all mankind, except F: the party favoured, F and F alone.

But let the design of the law be that F indeed have the exclusive possession of the field f, but that another person who shall be called B, have all the benefit: F alone gathering the produce of the field, but disposing of it entirely according to the orders, or in any other way for the benefit of B: then is F, while this arrangement lasts, the fiduciary; B, the beneficiary, proprietor. For this purpose a new law is requisite in addition to the former. By the former law, F was permitted to gather the produce of the field; by this latter he is commanded. In the former law mankind in general were the parties bound; and the obligation was of the negative stamp; and F alone was the party favoured: by the latter law, F alone is the party bound; the obligation is an affirmative one, and B alone is the party favoured. It is evident that the operation of gathering in the produce of the field and disposing of it for B's benefit is a complex business not to be achieved perhaps but by a variety of different sorts of acts: to these different acts correspond so many different services: which if the description given of them requires to be different may present matter for so many different laws.

So in regard to services. But of the manner in which the several parties are affected by the laws by which this species of property is created or secured an exemplification has just been given. By the same law which renders B the beneficial possessor of the land cultivated by F, a right to certain services to be performed by F is created, as we have seen, and conferred on B.

Fourthly, as to the laws which concern offences relative to the several conditions in life. A man's condition is made up by clusters of duties, powers, rights, or the negations of those respective objects, variously compounded: to exhibit the ways in which the several parties may be affected by the laws relative to this topic, the condition in question must therefore be resolved into such of the constituent articles just mentioned of which it is compounded. *—condition*

Fifthly, as to the laws relative to semi-public and public offences. Here the party favoured in the first instance is a whole class of persons: in those relative to offences of a public nature, the whole community.[1] *Semi-public and public offences*

Thus far with regard to laws of the substantive stamp. In punitory laws the parties bound are the ministers of justice: the party purposely exposed to suffer, the delinquent: the party favoured, the community at large, i.e., 1st the individual if any, prejudiced by the primary mischief, and so on. In such laws of the compensative kind *Punitory laws*

[1] After this paragraph the Ms. has the following note: 'Insert here self-regarding offences.' But no such insertion has been made.

as have the same object or end in view as those of the punitory kind have, the parties are the same; except that in this case the favourable part of the influence of the law before it reaches the community extends itself in the first instance to a particular individual.

In a remote way many sets of parties may be exposed to suffer or favoured by the same law

13. In considering the different ways in which a party may be affected by a law we have hitherto considered it with regard only to its immediate and obvious effects. But in two of these three ways a party may be affected by a various and remote concatenation of causes and effects. As to the parties that are bound by it, so as the import of the law be clear, they are seen at once: but what other parties if any are exposed to suffer, and the parties who either intentionally or eventually are favoured, are not alike discernible or determinable. As to the parties who are exposed to suffer, a law, how beneficial soever it may be upon the whole, may, over and above the mischief it does by the restraint it lays on liberty, do a deal of mischief which is seen but can not be helped, as well as a good deal which perhaps can be neither helped nor seen. Every body knows for example into what a multitude of remote and sometimes imperceptible branches the mischief produced by a tax will oftentimes divide itself. Nor is the benefit which in some cases may result from it much less various and diffusive. Let the tax payable to the public be laid upon a manufacture: the law then upon the happening of the event from whence the obligation to pay the tax is made to take its rise, commands the manufacturer, suppose, to perform that sort of service which consists in the payment of a certain sum of money, to the person who for the benefit of the public is to receive it: the public then is by this means favoured in a way which is direct and obvious: but in another way which is less obvious, though perhaps when pointed out not less indisputable, so may another party, viz: the proprietor of a rival manufacture: the public is a gainer by what the manufacturer who is taxed works up in spite of the tax: the rival manufacturer by so much as the other is prevented from working up by reason of the tax.

But of the different ways in which by the influence of remote causes a party may reap a benefit from a law, a pretty ample account will be given in a succeeding chapter.[j]

[j] Ch. | | (Indirect Legislation).[1]

[1] Bentham had originally intended to discuss 'indirect legislation' in Ch. xviii of *An Introduction to the Principles* (cf. Ch. xvi, para. 27 n.: in *CW*, 220). When Ch. xvii of the *Introduction* grew into the present work, Bentham's tables of contents show that a chapter on indirect legislation was again envisaged; but by June 1782 it was already being conceived rather as a separate essay (see above, Introduction, xxxiii; and below, Appendix E, 308). The incomplete Mss. for that essay were used by

14. These various relations which may be borne to various parties *Use and* by the same law must all of them be present to a man's mind before *importance of the above* the true nature and influence of it can be understood by him. On the *distinctions* circumstance of there being a party whom it binds, a law depends for its essence: on the circumstance of there being a party whom it is designed at least to favour, it depends for its cause: on both together it depends for the sum total of its efficacy: without the last it never exists; without the first it could not so much as be conceived. To trace out the mischievous part of its tendency we must observe whom it lays under coercion, whom on any other account it exposes to suffer: and observe in what respects and to what amount it exposes them to suffer: to trace out the beneficial part of its tendency, we must observe whom it favours, and in what respects, and to what amount it favours them.

All these several parties, have need to be acquainted with it: and as the benefit which any body can derive from it will be in proportion to the acquaintance which they have with it, [so][1] on the other hand the need they have to be acquainted with it will be in proportion to the amount of the detriment which they may individually incur by it, or the benefit which they may individually derive from it. Both parties have need to be informed of it in order to determine them with respect to the different lines of conduct they have need to observe according to the different aspects which it bears to them: the party bound, that by timely obedience he may save himself from the lash of those laws of which the express business is to make men suffer, and that by timely consideration he may obliterate or palliate at least the inconveniences of obedience: the party who in the event of his disobedience it is designed should suffer, in order that he may consider and take warning from the sufferings that are proposed for him: the party who from necessity is exposed to suffer in order that he as well as the party bound may learn to accommodate himself to his situation: the party favoured in order that he may see what the law has done for him, to what favours it has given him a right, whom he is to resort to for the performance of them, and in case of failure on the part of those from whom they are due, what means are given him of making himself amends and bringing the wrongdoers to repentance. The party bound, and the party where there is one, who is purposely exposed to suffer, will be sure

Dumont for Part III of *Principes du Code Pénal* (*Traités de législation civile et pénale*, Paris, 1802, t. iii, pp. 1–199; and cf. Bowring, ii, 533–80, 'Of Indirect Means of Preventing Crimes'). The *Essay on Indirect Legislation* will form part of a subsequent volume in this section of the present edition.

[1]Ms.'as'.

enough to appear upon the face of the law, by description at least if not by name: but the parties on the other hand who are favoured whether on their own account or that of another will be very apt to be out of sight: and insomuch that it may very well happen that in a long string of laws by which a man is favoured there shall not be a syllable which can serve to give him notice or to point him out to view. It is the business of the legislator for his own instruction to discover these latent interests, and for the information of the parties to announce them.

Constitu-
tional laws in
principem

15. There yet remain a class of laws which stand upon a very different footing from any of those that have hitherto been brought to view. The laws of which we have hitherto been speaking have for their passible subjects not the sovereign himself, but those who are considered as being subject to his power. But there are laws to which no other persons in quality of passible subjects can be envisaged than the sovereign himself. The business of the ordinary sort of laws is to prescribe to the people what *they* shall do: the business of this transcendent class of laws is to prescribe to the sovereign what *he* shall do: what mandates *he* may or may not address to *them*; and in general how he shall or may conduct himself towards them. Laws of this latter description may be termed, in consideration of the party who is their passible subject, laws *in principem*[1]: in contradistinction to the ordinary mass of laws which in this view may be termed laws *in subditos* or *in populum*.

They may be
addressed to
the law-giver,
his successors
or both
together

16. These laws *in principem* may be of either of two sorts according to the party from whom they emane and the party whose conduct they are designed to influence. This latter party may be the individual sovereign himself from whom they emane, or any future sovereign or sovereigns his successor or successors: in the former case they are what are strictly and properly termed pacts or covenants: and to distinguish them from the ordinary covenants entered into by subjects, they may be styled *pacta regalia* or *royal covenants*: in the latter case, they have not as yet acquired any separate denomination. In the common way of speaking these indeed are likewise termed pacts or covenants, one man being considered as having covenanted in virtue of a covenant actually entered into by another: the succeeding sovereign in virtue of the covenant actually entered into by his predecessor. But this way of speaking, familiar as it is, is improper: it is inaccurate, inconsistent and productive of

---

[1] At this point the Ms. has a note, 'Distinction here between *Le Souverain* and *Le Prince*'; but the distinction does not seem to have been followed up.

confusion[k]: to obviate which, acts of this sort may be styled *recommendatory mandates.* When a reigning sovereign then in the tenor of his laws engages for himself and for his successors he does two distinguishable things. By an expression of will which has its own conduct for its object, he enters *himself* into a covenant: by an expression of will which has the conduct of his successors for its object, he addresses to *them* a recommendatory mandate. This mandate the successor whenever the sovereignty devolves to him will probably adopt: and then and not till then it is his covenant.

17. The causes which originally produced the original covenant and the considerations of expediency which justified the engaging in it on the part of the predecessor will in general subsist to produce and justify the adoption of it on the part of the successor. In most instances therefore it will have happened that upon any change taking place in the sovereignty such adoption shall have taken place: it will have become customary for it so to do: the people, influenced partly by the force of habit and partly by the consideration of the expediency of such adoption, will be expecting it as a thing of course: and this expectation will add again to the motives which tend to produce such effect in any given instance. So great in short is the influence of all these causes when taken together, that in any tolerably well settled government the successor is as much expected to abide by the covenants of his predecessor as by any covenants of his own[1]: unless where any change of circumstances

How leges in principem come to be *adopted by* *successors*

[k] I call it inaccurate: for a covenant is an expression of will on the part of the person whose covenant it is said to be: but the successor, who perhaps at the time of the entering into the covenant does not so much as exist, probably has not so much as entertained, certainly has not expressed, any will about the matter. I call it inconsistent: for inconsistent it is to make use of the same expression where an object of any kind does exist to announce the existence of that object, and where no such object exists, to announce the existence of such an object notwithstanding: productive of confusion it will be, when a proposition which at one time is strictly true, and in order to a right understanding of the subject must be understood to be so, must for the same purpose at another time be understood not to be true, at the same time that there is nothing to give warning when it is to be regarded in the one of those lights and when in the other.

[1] An uniform and universal expectation of this sort is not of such long standing in society as at first sight might be imagined. Even history will carry us back to times at which the notion of the unity of the sovereign in different reigns was far from being perfectly established. An act or power is exercised, a declaration of will is issued on the part of the sovereign authority: is it or is it not to be understood to have continuance, to possess a binding force, after the decease of the individual sovereign whose pleasure it declared? This is a question which in every state must for a time have remained unsettled.

has made a manifest and indisputable change in the utility of such adherence. This expectation may even become so strong, as to equal the expectation which is entertained of the prevalence of that disposition to obedience on the part of the people by which the sovereignty *de facto* is constituted: insomuch that the observance of the covenant on the one part shall be looked upon as a condition *sine qua non* to the obedience that is to be paid on the other. Things are most apt to be upon this footing in those governments in which the sovereignty is ascribed nominally to a single person, who in reality possesses only a part, though perhaps the most conspicuous part, in it. But in all governments where either the whole or a principal part of the sovereignty is in the hands of a single person, the exercise of the sovereignty and the observance of the covenants entered into by preceding sovereigns are looked upon as being in such a degree connected that upon taking upon him the former a man is universally understood to have taken upon him the latter: understood, not only by the people, but by the sovereign himself. This notion is so universal and deep-rooted that if by accident a sovereign should in fact come to the throne with a determination not to adopt the covenants of his predecessors, he would be told that he had adopted them notwithstanding: adopting them tacitly by taking upon him those powers to the exercise of which the obliga-

---

[1] cont.
Applied to acts of legislation it would be settled first with regard to laws *in populum*, not till latterly with regard to laws *in principem*. Under the English constitution instances are yet extant of its being subject to doubt with regard to this latter kind of laws: see Barrington's Observations on the ancient Statutes.[1] (N.B. Coronation Oath.) Who can wonder at this, when with regard to such acts of power as consist in the appointing men to offices,* the general rule is to this hour in the negative? By the original rule of the common law upon the demise of the crown, most of the offices in the appointment of the crown become vacant. All military, all judicial power is at an end. The laws themselves, though not expressly are virtually repealed, by the extinction of every power that can give them force. The bonds of society are broken forever, unless it should please this or that man to make them whole. Whose interests, by the bye, were most considered in this maxim and for whose sake society was proposed to be maintained, the prince's or the people's, is easy enough to perceive.

* These there will hereafter be occasion to distinguish by a particular name, viz. acts of endynamistic[2] power.

[1] Daines Barrington (1727–1800), lawyer, antiquary and naturalist, published in 1766 *Observations on the Statutes, chiefly the more ancient from Magna Charta to 21st. James I, cap. 27, with an appendix being a proposal for new-modelling the Statutes.* This was one of the books which Bentham first read in the 'most interesting year' of 1769 (cf. Bowring, x, 54).   [2] See below, 84–5 n. n.

tion of adopting those covenants, stood annexed. Nor would this way of speaking, how untrue soever it may be by the very supposition, seem mis-applied: since it has become the habit among men of law to speak of the matter of right in the same terms in which they would speak of the matter of fact: that which, according to the general opinion, *ought* to be done being spoken as if it *were* done.[m]

18. It appears then that there are two distinct sorts of laws, very different from each other in their nature and effect: both originating indeed from the sovereign, (from whom mediately or immediately all ordinances in order to be legal must issue) but addressed to parties of different descriptions: the one addressed to the sovereign, imposing an obligation on the sovereign: the other addressed to the people, imposing an obligation on the people. Those of the first sort may again be addressed either to the sovereign himself who issues them, (the sovereign for the time being) or to his successors, or (what is most common) to the one as well as to the other. It is evident then that in the distinction between these two classes of laws it is the quality of the parties who are respectively bound by them that is the essential and characteristic feature.

In what sense the sovereign may be said to bind himself

Here it may naturally enough be asked what sense there is in a man's addressing a law to himself? and how it is a man can impose an obligation upon himself? such an obligation to wit as can to any purpose be effectual. Admit indeed we must that for a man to address a law to himself, is what indeed there would be little sense in, were there no other *force* in the world but his: nor can a man by his own single unassisted force impose upon himself any effectual obligation: for granting him to have bound himself, what should hinder him on any occasion from setting himself free? On the other hand, take into the account an exterior force, and by the help of such force it is as easy for a sovereign to bind himself as to bind another. It is thus, as was seen in a former chapter, that in transactions between subject and subject a man binds himself by the assistance of that force which is at the disposal of the sovereign. Nor is the assertion we make in speaking of a man's binding himself

[m] It is thus that upon a thousand occasions the question of right and the question of fact get confounded: insomuch that men pass backwards and forwards from the one to the other without perceiving it.

See Fragm. on Govt. Ch. | |.[1]

[1] Bentham's uncompleted reference is to Ch. v of his *Fragment on Government*, and perhaps especially to para. 10, where he says this among other things of Blackstone: 'Between these two points, indeed, the *is*, and the *ought to be*, so opposite as they frequently are in the eyes of other men, that spirit of obsequious *quietism* that seems constitutional in our Author, will scarce ever let him recognise a difference.'

so wide from the literal truth as at first sight might appear. The force which binds, depends indeed upon the will of a third person: but that will itself waits to receive its determination from the person who is said to bind, from the person who is the promulgator of the law. Without the covenantor, there would be no law at all: without the *guarantee*, as he is called, none that can be effectual. The law then may in strictness be considered as the work of both: and therefore in part, of either: but the share which the covenantor takes in it is by much the more conspicuous. It is this at all events that is taken first: it is seen to be taken while the other perhaps is expected only: it is certain; while the other perhaps is but contingent. In short the part which the sovereign for the time being has in the establishment of a *pactum regium* whereby he binds himself and his successors may be as considerable, and as independent of the part which may come to be taken by those to whom belongs the enforcement of such covenant, as the part which is taken by the legislator in the case of a law of the ordinary stamp *in populum* is of the part which may come to be taken by the judge.

–by what means

19. By what means then can a law *in principem* be enforced and rendered efficacious: what force is there in the nature of things that is applicable to this purpose? To answer this question, we have nothing to do but to resort to the enumeration, that has been already given on a former occasion, of the several sorts of forces by which the human will is liable to be influenced. The forces and the only forces by which the human will is influenced are *motives*: these, when considered in the mass, may be distinguished according to the sources from whence they issue: to these sources we set out with giving the name of *sanctions*. Of these sanctions that which we termed the *physical* is out of the question: for the force in the case in question is supposed to be directed *by design*. There remain the political, the religious and the moral. The force of the political sanction is inapplicable to this purpose: by the supposition within the dominion of the sovereign there is no one who while the sovereignty subsists can judge so as to coerce the sovereign: to maintain the affirmative would be to maintain a contradiction.[n] But the force of

[n] See supra.

This proposition stands in need of explanation: the truth of it depends upon the idea annexed to the word *sovereign*. The case is, that supposing the powers in the state to be thus distributed, there is no one person or body of persons in whose hands the sovereignty is reposed. Suppose two bodies of men, or for shortness' sake two men, the one possessing every power of the state, except that the other in case of a public accusation, preferred in such or such forms, has the power of judging him; including such power as may be

68

necessary to carry the judgment into execution. It is plain the sovereignty would not be exclusively in either: it would be conjunctively in both. Yet in common speech it is probable that the first man would be styled *the* sovereign, or at least *a* sovereign: because his power would be constantly in exercise: the other's only occasionally, or perhaps never. Now then if the narrow sense were to be given to the word *sovereign*, it is plain that the proposition above mentioned concerning the impossibility of the sovereign's being judged by anyone, would not be true. A logician of the ordinary stamp (for nothing is more common than to be versed in the forms of dialectics without any clear notions of terminology) would find no difficulty in maintaining the contrary, and proving it by what to him might seem a demonstration. Taking advantage of the inexplicit notions annexed to the words *superior* and *inferior*, he would perhaps assume for his medium this proposition, that it is impossible for a man to be superior and inferior to another at the same time: or perhaps in different propositions he would use the same word *sovereign* in two different senses: at one time in its strict and proper sense; at another time in its popular and improper sense, according to the distinction above taken. Till men are sufficiently aware of the ambiguity of words, political discussions may be carried on continually, without profit and without end. It may occur, that the distribution of power above supposed is not an expedient one, or that it cannot be a lasting one. This may or may not be the case: but the expediency or the durability of such an arrangement are points with which we have nothing to do here. I consider here only what is possible: now it is possible: for every distribution as well as every limitation of power is possible that is conceivable. The power of the governor is constituted by the obedience of the governed: but the obedience of the governed is susceptible of every modification of which human conduct is susceptible: and the rules which mark it out, of every diversity which can be clearly described by words. Wheresoever one case can be distinguished from another, the same distinction may obtain in the disposition to obedience which may have established itself among the people. In the former case they may be disposed to pay it to one magistrate, in the latter to another: or in the former case they may be disposed to obey one of those magistrates, and in the latter nobody. Many are the commonplace phrases in use which would seem to assert the contrary: that an *imperium in imperio* is a monster in politics: that no man can serve two masters: that a house divided against itself cannot stand: and these phrases are made to pass for arguments. There is indeed something specious in them at first sight: and without due examination a man may be easily misled by them. Thus much is indeed true, that the same individual branch of power cannot be possessed, and that exclusively, by two persons at the same time. But any two branches of power may that are distinguishable: and any one branch of power may be shared amongst ever so many. What gives rise to the internal contests by which states are agitated or destroyed, is that two different men or bodies of men claim exclusively the same individual branch: which in governments that are not purely monarchical may ever be the case, and that on all sides with the best faith imaginable, while laws are wanting to decide the matter, or those which there are are ambiguous or obscure. The minuteness and refinement of which the distribution of powers in a state is susceptible depends upon the proficiency that is made in the anatomy of language, and the use that is made of the proficiency in the body of the laws.

the religious sanction is as applicable to this purpose as to any other: and this is one of the great and beneficial purposes to which the religious sanction, where it happens to have an influence, is wont to be applied. The same may be said of the force of the moral sanction. Now the force of the moral sanction as applied to the purpose in question may be distinguished into two great branches: that which may be exerted by the subjects of the state in question acting without, and perhaps even against, the sanction of political obligations, acting in short as in a state of nature; and that which may be exerted by foreign states. When a foreign state stands engaged by express covenant to take such a part in the enforcement of such a law as that in question, this is one of the cases in which such foreign state is said to stand with reference to such law in the capacity of a guarantee.° Of a covenant of this sort many examples are to be met with in the history of international jurisprudence.

To all or any of these forces may a law *in principem* stand indebted for its efficacy. Of all these forces even when put together the efficacy it must be confessed is seldom so great as that of the political. How should it? when it is in the nature of the political sanction to draw with it in most instances a great part if not the whole of the force of the other two? But to deny them all efficacy would be to go too far on the other side. It would be as much as to say that no privileges were ever respected, no capitulation ever observed.ᵖ It would be as much as to say, that there is no such

° Berne and France guarantees to Geneva. France to Westphalia and all the German Princes.[1]

ᵖ It is a trite and idle observation that the engagements of sovereigns are kept no longer than suits their convenience. This is in no other sense true, than in that in which it is also true of the engagements of private men. If it means that the engagements of sovereigns have never any effect, and that, after an engagement of that sort entered into, things are in precisely the same situation as if no such event had taken place, it is notoriously false: if it means anything else than this it is nugatory. No man acts without a motive: no man acts against a preponderant mass of motives: but, to the sum of motives which may tend to withold a sovereign from pursuing a certain line of conduct, does a solemn engagement not to pursue it make no addition? Let experience decide.

This observation is of a piece with another observation equally trite concerning man in general, that he is never governed by any thing but his own interest. This observation in a large and extensive sense of the word interest (as comprehending all sorts of motives) is indubitably true: but as indubitably false in any of the confined senses in which upon such an occasion the word *interest* is wont to be made use of. These levelling notions are in point of tendency as pernicious as in point of fact they are ill-grounded: the tendency of them being

[1] Bentham's references here are probably to the guarantees contained in, respectively, the Treaty of Ryswick (1697) and the Peace of Westphalia (1648).

system in Europe as the Germanic body: that the inhabitants of Austrian Flanders are upon no other footing than the inhabitants of Prussia: those of the *pays d'états* in France than those of the *pays d'élection*: that no regard was ever paid to the American charters by the British Parliament: and that the Act of Union has never been anything but a dead letter.

Necessity of promulgation

20. *The notoriety of every law ought to be as extensive as its binding force.* It ought indeed to be much more extensive: since the parties whom it binds are in every case one set of persons out of two and in many cases but one out of three who may be equally concerned to be apprised of it.[q] No axiom can be more self-evident: none more important: none more universally disregarded. Considering how obvious it is a man may be ashamed even to mention it: and to think how little chance there is that the mention that is made of it will be attended to. Yet till it is attended to and the grievance remedied, the business of legislation is from the beginning to the end of it a cruel mockery, and every legislator without thinking of it a Caligula, or rather in this respect even worse than a Caligula. Caligula published his laws in small characters, but still he published them: he hung them up high but still he hung them up.[1] How many laws in this enlightened age that are neither hung up nor published!

Not to put in practice the only means of remedying this grievance out of tenderness to the lawyers would be like bringing up half the people in the state for the sake of the undertakers. Every law which is productive of no material benefit is sure to be to the highest degree pernicious were it on this account alone: and in a nation where the voluminousness of the laws is got to a certain pitch (let the French and English serve for examples) it may almost be doubted whether the benefit of which even the best law is productive in virtue of its particular excellence can be compensated by the mischief it does to the subsisting stock by worming them insensibly out of the memory and notice of the people, and thrusting them into obscurity and oblivion. For this crying grievance there is a remedy, and there is but one. I have pointed it out; it is for others to apply it.

constantly, and the design frequently, to cover and to cherish the very immorality which they represent as being already at the extreme: the existence of which they maintain and pretend perhaps to deplore.

[q] See Ch. | | (Limits) § 6.[2]

[1] Another anecdote recorded by Suetonius.

[2] The form of Bentham's reference here is explained by the fact that this passage was originally written for the chapter on 'Corpus Juris' (see above, Introduction, xxxiii): it bears the deleted heading 'Corpus' replaced by 'Limits'. The reference is thus to what was then conceived as § vi of Ch. XVII of *An Introduction to the Principles*, i.e. to Ch. IV of the present work.

CHAPTER VII

OF THE LOCAL EXTENT WHICH A LAW MAY HAVE

Local extent of a law may be direct or indirect

1. [Sixth]ly, with respect to the local extent or extension of a law; the extent of which it is susceptible in point of place.

The local extent of a law may be distinguished into direct and indirect. The former may be understood to depend upon the situation and magnitude of the territory or tract of land with the space above and below it[a] which is of the number of the things that are the passible subjects of the law: that is of the acts which are its objects. A law then in point of direct local extent extends or applies itself to such portion of land on which the acts which it takes for its objects come to have their termination: the fields which, among the persons who are the agible subjects of the law, some are permitted, others forbidden, to cultivate: the roads on which some are permitted, others perhaps forbidden, to travel: the waters (that is the grounds covered with waters) on which some are permitted, others perhaps forbidden to travel, or to fish.

As to what may be termed the indirect local extent of a law, it is determined by some relation or other which the persons who are the agible subjects of the law are looked upon as bearing to the land: such as the being on it at the time of performing the act in question, although those acts have no material influence on the condition of the land: the having been born upon it: the being of the number of those who are looked upon as being in the habit of paying obedience to persons, who are in the habit of issuing laws, of which the land in question is a passible subject. Accordingly a law may in point of indirect local extension be said to apply to any tract of land which is so situated, that the relation of any kind which a person bears thereto is a circumstance which aggregates him to the agible subjects[b] and his acts to the objects of the law.

Thus the law which forbids the planting of tobacco anywhere in England is a law which extends in a direct manner to the country called England, and a law of which the local extent is determined in

---

[a] Each man's estate a quasi-pyramid.

[b] I.e., the parties who are looked upon as bound by it.

a direct manner by the situation and extent of the country so denominated.

Thus on the other hand in that species of treason which consists of the English laws against treason in as far as they include within the punishment appointed for that crime an attempt made upon the life of the King of England by the subject of any other country so as the attempt be made in England, or an attempt made abroad, so as the offender were a native or adopted subject of the British crown, may be said to apply in point of indirect local extent to England.

2. This head it may be observed can scarcely be said to be a distinct one of itself: it being always reducible to one or other of the topics already noticed. The idea of the tract of land over which a law extends in a direct manner is included under the idea of the *things* that are its passible subjects: that over which it extends in an indirect way in the manner above mentioned is only a specificant circumstance made use of to characterize the *persons* who are its agible or its passible subjects. Deference however to usage and to the general common bent of men's notions on the subject seemed to dictate the propriety of mentioning it apart. The questions concerning the dominion of the sovereign and the jurisdiction of the judge are questions that seem to point to the local extent of the law without reference to any other circumstance.

This head reducible to the preceding

CHAPTER VIII

OF THE DURATION OF A LAW

Extent in point of time is also reducible to the preceding heads

1. [Seventh]ly, with regard to the extent which a law may have in point of *time*. This topic seems also to be reducible to within the bounds of those already mentioned. To determine the time during which a given individual is commanded or forbidden to perform acts of a certain class, is to determine the multitude of those acts, and thereby the amplitude or logical extent as it might be called of the class which they compose. To determine the time during which the individuals of a given class are commanded or forbidden to perform acts of a certain class is to determine the multitude of the individuals which by entering into that class may have become the agible subjects of the law. Time then is but one out of an indefinite multitude of specificant circumstances which may be made use of to mark out the assemblage of individuals whom it is proposed to take for the subjects of the law.

Why mentioned separately

2. For mentioning this as a separate topic there is the same reason, and seems to be the same necessity, as for mentioning the former in the same light. Space and time though nothing of themselves are the inseparable and yet distinguishable accompaniments of everything that is. The wider the space, and the greater the length of time, over which a law extends, the greater the number of acts of persons and of things, of objects therefore and of agible as well as passible subjects, it will be apt upon an average to extend to.

A law temporary by nature, by institution

3. A law to the duration of which no express limits are set, such a law, provided it be general throughout, general in respect as well of its objects as of all its subjects, will of course, if nothing appears to the contrary, be looked upon as perpetual: such at least is the mode of interpretation in every settled government. In such case however the duration of it may be contracted to any length by the express will of the legislator. On the other hand, where the law is in any respect particular, a necessary period is thereby put to its duration: it expires the instant that the article (whatever it be) in respect of which it is particular is no more. If it be particular in respect of more articles then one, it then expires along with that article which first goes off the stage.[1] In this latter case it may be said to be

---

[1] The Ms. at this point has an illegible footnote consisting of two (probably Latin) words.

temporary in its own nature: in the former, if it be temporary at all, it may be styled *temporary by institution*.

This line of distinction, however, is not so clear an one as at first sight it might be thought to be. It is indeed in general true that classes are longer lived than individuals: and in particular with regard to persons, individuals must die though classes may be, and some of them, so long as any of the human race are left upon the globe, must be, immortal. But even classes die or sleep at least when the individuals which used to fill them are no more: and of individuals, when we come to speak of things, there are some to the existence of which it would not be easy to set a term. The laws concerning the killing of wolves in England expired along with the last wolf many centuries ago. The laws made in England against Jesuits have in our days been laid asleep, by the dissolution of that formidable order. But should a fresh colony of wolves be ever imported, and should the order of Jesuits be ever re-established, the laws against wolves and Jesuits would revive. The laws concerning regents sleep everywhere during the majority of the prince but awake upon the succession of a minor. The laws concerning enemies are dead in time of peace, but revive upon declaration of a war. The great bridge at Westminster[a] is an individual object: but should the zeal for constitutional reformation which from time to time hath been observed to break forth in the neighbourhood of that magnificent structure gather strength, perishable as it is, it may chance to outlive many a class of useless or supposed useless placemen.

In short wherever the continuance of a class of entities of any kind depends in any manner upon human will, that class, it is evident, can never have any other than a precarious existence.

Laws which are temporary by institution must be revived by institution: laws temporary by nature expire and revive again with their subjects without the aid of institution.

[a] There are particular laws made for the preservation of this bridge by stat. 9. Geo. 2. ch. 29.

There are likewise in different parts of the statute book other sets of laws relative to so many other bridges.

CHAPTER IX

THE GENERALITY OF A LAW

A law may be particular, general, or both in one

1. [Eighth]ly, with regard to the *generality* or *particularity* of a law. This results from the generality or particularity of the persons things and acts, of the subjects of all kinds [and] of the objects to which it relates. Considered in this point of view a law is either particular throughout or general throughout or partly particular and partly general: and it is evident enough that in one or other of these predicaments every law must be. A law may be said to be particular throughout when its subjects of every class [and] its objects are all of them individuals: partly particular and partly general if any one or more of those articles are individual: general throughout, if they are none of them individual, but are each of them a class.[a]

Imperfection of the language with relation to this topic

[a] For expressing the distinctions relative to this head the current language is very indifferently provided.

In the first place there is no neutral term which can be applied in common to the ideas denoted by the words general and particular, so as to bring to view the one without putting an exclusion upon the other. To profess to consider laws in respect to their generality and then to distinguish them into such as are general and such as are not so, is a sort of verbal contradiction which however it seemed impossible to avoid. Instead of *generality*, I might perhaps have said *logical extent*: but who would have conjectured what I meant by *logical extent* before the expression had been explained? Words which are made use of in expressing the heads of an arrangement should if possible be to such a degree familiar, that of the import of them some idea however loose might be caught up at the first glance.

In the next place the terms *particular* and *general* are both of them extremely vague and uncharacteristic. Had I the liberty of coining words without control, I would distinguish the former by some such name as *atomoprosectic* the latter by some such name as *eidoprosectic*: *atomos* an individual object, *eidos* a species or class, *prosectic* from *prosecho* to concern or reach to: upon this plan a law which was *atomoprosectic* in all points might be further termed a law *atomoprosectic simpliciter*; one that was *eidoprosectic* in all points, *eidoprosectic simpliciter*: one that was atomoprosectic in some parts and eidoprosectic in others might be termed indifferently *atomoprosectic secundum quid* or *eidoprosectic secundum quid*, according to the exigency of the case. Or if it should seem less uncouth instead of atomoprosectic we might say *atomoscopous*; instead of *eidoprosectic, eidoscopous*: *scopo* to regard, or relate to. Thus much may perhaps be pardoned in a note: but my heart failed me at the thoughts of introducing into the text words so uncouth and formidable as these, although fashioned out of the most pleasing of all languages, must appear to anyone to whom they are altogether new. The word *atomos*, an atom

A law I say may be particular in any one point, and at the same time general in any other: the truth of this when once announced will be immediately perceived. Hitherto however the common way of dividing laws in relation to this head has been into general and particular only, as if nothing more were ever worth considering in a law than merely the *persons* it related to, and as if it could relate to but one set of persons at a time. Thus inaccurate must every speculation be that relates to law, so long as any part of the field belonging to this branch of science remains unsurveyed.

2. Upon the same inaccurate idea such laws as appeared to come under the notion of particular laws have been termed in Latin *privilegia*: and these have been distinguished into unfavourable (*odiosa*) and favourable (*favorabilia*). By an unfavourable *privilegium* has been meant a law in which the party made to suffer in the first instance is an individual: by a favourable *privilegium*, one in which the party favoured in the first instance was an individual[b]: it is in the latter only of the two senses that the word *privilege* or what corresponds to it is used in the languages of modern Europe.

Privilegia, what

3. If we look for examples, we shall find none of any mandates that are particular in every point except those transient ones which emane from private power-holders, and of which the influence is confined within the circle of a private family. Even the *lettres de cachet*, those *privilegia odiosa* which are so much felt and so much heard of in one country in Europe, and whatever may answer to them in any other countries, can not be deemed particular in all points, upon the supposition of their emaning from a sovereign acting as such and for the benefit of his people; since upon this supposition the whole community is the party whom they are meant to *favour*. To look upon them as being particular in respect of the party favoured (except in the very few cases mentioned in a former section) is to look upon them as emaning from a despot, the master of an immense family of slaves, acting for the gratification of his own particular passions or those of some individual favourite.

Domestic mandates the only ones that are particular throughout

4. Of laws which are particular *ex parte*, examples, as may well be imagined, are not difficult to meet with. Such mandates will hardly

Examples of laws which are particular ex parte. Domestic mandates

or individual, being better known by its physical than its logical sense may here seem misapplied: but it is the very word which is made use of to signify an individual by Aristotle and his commentator Porphyry. Arist. Topic. 1, 1. Porph. Eisag. cap. 2.[1]

[b] In this sense the application of it is frequently enough extended to the case where a class of persons are the objects of the favour.

[1] The reference is to the comment on Aristotle, *Topics*, iv.1 in the *Isagoges* or introduction to logic of Porphyry (*c.* 232–302).

however, be found in great abundance in the number of those laws which emane immediately from the sovereign. The mandates which are of this stamp are most commonly the work of some subordinate class of power-holders: mandates domestic; and among those of a public nature, mandates judicial and military; such in short as in contradistinction to *legislative mandates* or *laws* are termed *executive mandates* or *orders*. Domestic mandates are commonly particular in all points. In respect of the persons who are concerned they will seldom be otherwise than particular, unless where the family is very large: and the frequency of such as may be deemed general in this point, in comparison of such as are evidently but particular, will increase in proportion to the largeness of the family. The boundary-line between the number of persons that composes a private family and the number that composes a public body is by no means fixed. Sometimes we see families so large, and at other times, common-wealths so small, that the former shall be more numerous than the latter.

Military, judicial and other public orders

5. Judicial, military, and other public mandates are in the very essence of them general in respect of the persons who are favoured in the last instance: in other points they are sometimes general, sometimes particular as it may happen. Among military mandates the frequency of such as are general is apt to bear a greater ratio to the frequency of such as are particular than among judicial mandates: although as an army is but a part of the community to which it belongs, the circle out of which the agible subjects of judicial mandates are taken is less limited than that out of which the agible subjects of military mandates are taken. They are devoted to a whole regiment at once, to a whole company at once.

Covenants

6. Among such mandates of subordinate power-holders as are issued *mero motu*, and may have in view the benefit of individuals or the public as it may happen, it may be proper to take a more particular notice of covenants and conveyances. Of covenants it is an essential characteristic that the party covenanting and consequently the party bound *ipso facto* by the very covenant itself is always an individual or determinate assemblage of individuals.[c]

[c] It may be said, no: for that covenant entered into for example, by the governing body in a corporation, an assemblage of determinate individuals, is oftentimes made to bind the community at large, an assemblage of persons indeterminate. And in the same manner the covenant of a single person is made to bind his heirs, executors, administrators and assigns for ever more: an assemblage of persons altogether unascertainable and indeterminate. But the plain truth of the matter is, that these though bound by the covenant, or rather in consequence of the covenant, are not parties to the covenant: it is not

7. In conveyances on the contrary the parties bound, such of the *Conveyances* agible subjects of the law as are bound by it, are almost always *–in what* numerous and indeterminate. This at least is the case of those con- *general, and* veyances of which the passible subjects, the *proprietary subjects* as *in what* they may be called, are *things*. To give a man a property, if it be an *particular* exclusive property, in a thing, there must be two provisions: 1. a mandate prohibiting persons at large from meddling with it: 2. a countermandate operating as an exception to the mandate, and permitting such meddling on the part of him who is made proprietor. The former may be considered as the work of the sovereign alone: as to so much he imperates *immediate*: it is the latter that is the joint work of the sovereign and the individual: the individual issuing a countermandate repealing as far as it goes the mandate, to which countermandate the sovereign by his adoption gives the force of law. If then the imperative part of the law to which a conveyance of this nature appertains be considered in respect of the persons who are bound it is usually general, and that in the

they who enter into it, they are not contracting parties. Persons may be *spoken to* collectively, but if they *speak* it is individually. To lawyers who make no scruple of feigning a covenant whenever they want to justify an obligation, the plain truth of the matter may seem a paradox.

But to understand a subject we must take for true that which *is* true and not that which is false. Now whether a promise is made or no is always a matter of fact: and when it is known to be made by anyone, he by whom it is made is always individually known and ascertainable. Moreover what is clear enough is that at the time a man makes a promise, his heirs who do not exist make no such promise: on his part then there is a covenant, which the sovereign by adopting turns into a law of which he the covenantor is the agible subject: but on the part of his heirs there is no such covenant: if in consequence of the act of their ancestor, they are bound, it is not by a covenant that they are bound, but by a mandate: by a mandate or recommendation or request no matter what it is called, which by being adopted by the sovereign is turned into a law: in other words by a conveyance which the covenantor is allowed to make of a right to such and such services to be rendered in certain contingencies by his heirs to the party in whose favour the covenant is made.

If a man has any power over his assigns as such it is in virtue of a power of conveyance: the power of limiting the interest that anyone in future shall have in a proprietary subject, which at this present time happens to be in his possession or *pro tanto* at his disposal, in such manner that if they acquire that interest, it shall be on condition of their being subjected to such or such an obligation. I covenant for myself and my assigns under a penalty of £5 not to plough up a certain meadow which I am about to rent: that is I promise for my own part that I will not so long as it is in my own possession, and as concerning my power of conveyance I limit it in such manner that were I minded to dispose of the meadow to any person, such person could not acquire it without subjecting himself to the same obligation, sanctioned by the same penalty.

highest degree: if the de-imperative part be considered which is the part in which the force of the conveyance more particularly resides, it may be particular in this respect or general according to the quality of the party or parties who are favoured by it: that is, to whom the right in question is conveyed.[d] In other points the law may be general or particular as it may happen.

When the corporeal proprietary subject is of the class of persons, insomuch that the right conveyed is a right to the service or services of a person or a class of persons, no regard being paid to any particular subject of the class of things, the conveyance is a mandate which in respect of the party bound may be general or particular as it may happen. Instances where it is general are a right of toll; a title of honour; a copy-right; or any other kind of monopoly.[e] Instances where it is particular are a pecuniary debt, a right to the services of an apprentice.

Use of the distinction between general laws and particular

8. The distinction between a general law or mandate and a particular law or mandate, as here explained, is more material than at first sight might be imagined. Developed and applied it will afford us a clue without which it would be scarce possible for us to find our way through the labyrinth of constitutional jurisprudence. Correspondent to the distinction which respects the laws themselves is that which respects the power of making them. The power of enacting particular laws, the power as it may be called of imperating *de singulis* is one sort of power: the power of enacting general laws, that is of imperating *de classibus*, of making laws in general terms is, as we shall see, another and a very different sort of power. The latter power, although it be susceptible of a degree of extent of which the former is not susceptible, is on the other hand liable to peculiar limitations by which its force may be diminished or even utterly destroyed. These limitations give room for other powers, which in many cases form a necessary complement as it were to the imperative power when modified as here supposed. Adding to these the autocheiristic power and dividing each into the shares into which any lot of political power upon being distributed among several hands is liable to be divided, we have the sum total of all the powers whatever, constitutional as well as private, that can have existence in a state. Of the complemental powers above alluded to it will be necessary to give a variety of examples, without

[d] They may be an individual or a body corporate.

[e] Speaking according to the current language, we should hardly look upon a law conferring upon a man any of these possessions as coming in any respect under the notion of a general law.

which the peculiar nature of a general law in contradistinction to a particular one could hardly be understood. If the several powers thus introduced for example's sake should themselves receive illustration from the occasion on which they are brought to view, the information thence derived will be a kind of collateral acquisition. In this way a sort of side glance will be given, as it were by anticipation, of the structure of the constitutional branch of law: some glimpses will be afforded, however incomplete, of the connections and dependencies of some of the principal parts of that complicated whole: and those oppressive ideas of immensity and incommensurability which have hitherto hung over the subject will even at this early period have been in some measure dispelled.

9. To the words *power of legislation* we naturally annex the idea of the power of enacting general laws: laws that shall be general in all points: such laws of which the bulk of the statutes, by whatever name termed, which emaning from the sovereign authority and being consigned to the press are handed down from age to age, appear to be composed. The power of issuing such laws in all cases, in such sort that no man has authority to render them invalid, and every man is bound to submit to them or obey them would naturally upon first mention of it appear to be the same thing with absolute uncontrolled power. Such power one would naturally suppose must involve in its texture, must absorb as it were into its substance, every other power that could have existence in a state: insomuch that he who had this power would have everything, and that no one without his appointment could have any thing. The possible powers in a state are reducible to two: the power of contrectation or impressive power[f] as we have termed it, and the power of imperation: which latter again may be distinguished into the power of *imperation properly so called,* and the power of *de-imperation.*

Power of legislation is but a part of the whole power of imperation in any given case

But so far from being equivalent to or coextensive with both these powers it does not include so much as what is contained in the power of imperation properly so called. This we shall presently perceive. Let a field of dominion be conceived of given amplitude embracing a given tract of land, a given number of persons, and a given assemblage of valuable things which have become or are capable of becoming proprietary subjects. It might naturally enough be supposed that there were two ways in either of which a person might have all the power which it would be possible for a man to exercise over this land, these persons and these things: by taking the persons in classes, commanding them or setting them at liberty to perform

[f] Autocheiristic.

81

such and such acts in classes with or without relation to such and such things taken in classes, or by taking them individually and commanding each person to do so and so, (the particularity will hardly bear to be carried any further) as it shall be thought proper: in a word that the power of imperating *de classibus*, and the power of imperating *de singulis* were but two different ways of exercising the same power. But upon examination this will be found not to be the case. Neither of them of itself includes the power of doing every thing that is to be done by commanding and countermanding. Let a man possess either of them in the complete extent there will always be something which he cannot do without the other. To form the complete power of imperation there needs the union of both these powers. The power of imperating *de classibus* at any rate: to which must be added either the power of imperating *de singulis* or what is equivalent to it. To demonstrate this we shall first state what it is that the power of general legislation *de classibus* or the power of legislation ordinarily so called wants of being complete: and what it is that is wanted by the power of particular legislation or the power of issuing the sort of mandates which are commonly called *orders*.

To begin with the deficiencies to which the power of general legislation or legislation *de classibus* is exposed.

The power of aggregation or accensitive power is the other

10. The commands of a sovereign will like any other communications be liable to receive a tinge from the channel through which they are conveyed. The channel through which alone the bulk of a sovereign's commands can be conveyed is that assemblage of conventional signs which taken collectively are called *language*. A legislator in uttering a law which shall be general must in as far as it is intended to be general make use of general terms or names. By these general terms or names, things and persons, acts, and so forth are brought to view in parcels; which parcels are the larger and the more comprehensive in proportion as the extent or logical amplitude (if so it may be called) of such names is the more considerable. This being the case the legislator in the grouping of the persons things and acts which he takes for the subjects and objects of his laws is limited to such parcels as correspond to the generic names which are furnished by the language.

Conceive him then on any occasion to have taken up any such generic name. By this name a class suppose of subjects (no matter what) is brought to view. This class taken at a given period is composed of a certain number of individuals. As to these individuals then, by what means is it that they have come to be aggregated to this class? to be looked upon as belonging to it? to be the individuals who are deemed to have been had in view upon the mention of this name? By whatever means the event of their belonging to this class has come to pass, such event either depended or did not depend upon the will of a human being: if it did, such person has thereby a power: in the [latter] case, whatever limitation the power of the legislator is subject to on this account, the power which remains to him, whatever it be, is still so far his own, that no other person is a sharer in it. In the other case, the power of imperation does not belong to him alone; he has a sharer or partner in it: and this partner is the person on whose will the event above mentioned has a dependence. Thus by giving a power to a man and his assigns the sovereign may give it to his mortal enemy. The share which this person has in the entire power of imperation may be termed the *accensitive power*[g] or power or right of *aggregation* with regard to the class in question.

11. This power according to the different applications that may be made of it, according to the nature of the subjects or objects to which it may be applied, will admit of so many modifications or specific subdivisions. It may be applied to persons, to things, to acts, to places, or to times. It may accordingly be distinguished in the first place according to these several applications: and may accordingly be termed accensitive power *in personam, in rem, in actum, in locum,* or *in tempus.* Of each of these several branches of accensitive power examples will be given further on. But first it will be proper to trace the division of accensitive power *in personam* a little further. *[margin: Accensitive power—its five branches]*

12. To begin with accensitive power *in personam.* To every class of persons who in any manner stand affected by a law a certain condition or station in life is attributed by the fashion of language[h]: a person being said to be of such or such a condition in virtue of his belonging to such or such a class. To aggregate a man then to a class is the same thing as to invest him with a condition: the accensitive power *in personam* has therefore the same effect as the power we have already had occasion to allude to in speaking of investment and non-investment.[i] *[margin: Accensitive power in personam has the effect of investitive]*

[g] From *accenseo*, to aggregate to a class; whence the word Censor.
[h] See Ch. xvi (Division).[1]
[i] See Ch. xvi (Division).[2]   [i] [cont.]

[1] Ch. xvi of *An Introduction to the Principles.* Bentham's reference is probably to the discussion of offences against condition in paras. 38 ff. (in *CW*, 234 ff.).

[2] Ibid. Bentham's reference is probably once again to the discussion of offences against condition (see n. 1 above); but the terms *investment* and *non-investment* also occur in the discussion of offences against trust in paras. 25 ff. (in *CW*, 205 ff.).

Modification of the accensitive power in personam

13. Now we have seen what the possible ways are in which a man or any class of men may be affected by the law[j]: by any given law, and thence by the sum total of the laws put together: if affected by it at all, he must be either favoured by it, bound by it, or exposed by it to suffer: in the first case the condition that belongs to him in consequence may *pro tanto* be spoken of as an advantageous one, in the two others as a disadvantageous one: in the first case he stands invested with a *right*, which in certain circumstances may be also termed a *power*: in virtue of which right or power other men owe *services* to him: in the second case an *obligation* is incumbent on him, and he owes services to other men; in the third case no obligation is incumbent on him on this score, but he may be said to be *obnoxious to impressions* which other persons have the right and perhaps are under the obligation of causing him to undergo.

Now in all these cases the power of aggregating a man to the class to which the condition in question belongs, may, as we set out with observing, be styled a power of investment, or an investitive power. But in some of these cases owing to the particular figure it is apt to make in those particular instances, it may be worth while to give it a particular name. Accordingly where the condition is accompanied with a right, it may be of use to distinguish the power of investing a man with it by some such name as that of *juris-dative*[k] or *dicaiodotic*[l] power: and where that right amounts to a power the power of investing a man with it may again be distinguished by some such name as *potis-dative, dosidynamic*[m] or *endynamistic*.[n]

[i] cont.

Difference between accensitive power in personam and investitive power

Notwithstanding what is said in the text we are not to conclude that accensitive power *in personam* and investitive power are precisely the same thing; that is that the two expressions may in all cases be used interconvertibly for each other. True it is, that he who exercises this branch of accensitive power may in all cases be said thereby to exercise investitive power. But it is not in every case that accensitive power is exercised by the exercise of investitive. The exercise of this latter power includes not that of the former, in any other case than where the person who is invested with the condition does in virtue of that condition acquire a particular denomination such as on a similar account either hath been applied or is about to be applied to other individuals. A particular commission of an unprecedented nature, unaccompanied with any official name, whatever powers it may invest a man with does not aggregate him to any known class of persons unless it be some such vague and general one as that of *commissioner* or *power-holder*.

[j] Supra, Ch. vi (Parties).

[k] In Latin *juris* is already used in composition with *dictio* subjoined to it; or *datio* with *satis* prefixed to it.

[l] From δικαιοδοτηρ compounded of δικαιον, right, and δοτηρ, a giver.

[m] This form of composition is exemplified in the words δοσιδικης, Δωροθεα.

[n] From ενδυναμιζω, to confer power on a man or as we say *empower* him to

This *jurisdative* power (if the term may be allowed) is neither more nor less than the power of making conveyances when the word *conveyance* is taken in the largest sense which it will admit of: a power which when the rights conferred are powers of a public or constitutional nature, comprehends one of the grand divisions of the powers of government.

14. As to the accensitive power *in rem* this though different in its name and in its first appearance, comes when examined to the same thing as the accensitive power *in personam*: inasmuch as the things in question are in the number of the subjects of some law by which the persons in question are affected. *The other branches of accensitive power are productive ultimately of the same effects*

Now it hath been shewn, that there is no way in which a thing can be mentioned but what it is in some way or other the subject of the law: indirectly° at least if not directly. To cause a thing that before appertained to a class of things which did not belong to a man to appertain to a class of things that does belong to him is in effect to invest him with a power over that thing. The case is the same with all the other branches of accensitive power: with accensitive power *in actum, in locum,* and *in tempus.* This will be rendered sufficiently apparent by the examples which will be found a little farther on.

15. Opposite in a certain sense to accensitive power is a power that may be termed *disaccensitive*: of this it will be convenient to give some explanation before we proceed to give examples. Conceive a person to belong to a certain class of persons, characterized by a certain name: either then there is a power in some other person or persons to cause him to belong no longer to that class, or there is not: if there is the power possessed by such person or persons may be termed *disaccensitive* power. This then is an accidental concomitant which may exist in regard to any class, or not exist, and which when it exists, may exist in the same hands with the accensitive or in different hands, as it may happen. In like manner the power which is opposed to investitive may be termed *divestitive* or *dis-investitive*, and more particularly, that which is opposed to juris-dative, *juris-ademptive*, that which is opposed to endynamistic, disendynamistic power. *Disaccensitive power, what*

16. It appears then, that these three expressions, *Investitive power* when it regards a right (that is, when it is the power of invest- *Correspon-dency between investitive power, power of conveyance, power of jurisdation and en-dynamistic power*

do so and so: a word that may be made from εν and δυναμαι to possess power: as πλουτιζω to enrich or confer riches is made from πλουτεω, to possess riches. In the same manner βαδιζω to cause to go, is derived from βαινω, to go.

° See supra, Ch. ɪv (Subjects).

ing a man with a right), *power of conveyance*, and *power of jurisdation* are but three names for the same thing: they each of them consist in the power of *accensing* if we so say for a moment, or aggregating a man to some division or other in the wide-extending class of *right-holders*. In particular cases which are so various that it is impossible to comprise them under any concise description, the right is also termed a *power*; in these cases the power of investing a man with it, the power of conveying it to a man, may be styled *endynamistic power, dosidynamic power*, or *power of potisdation* When the right or power which is conveyed is one that is exercisable on a private account, that is for the benefit either of him alone who exercises it or of some other individual or subordinate class of individuals, the power of conveyance is a private proprietary power: when the right or power which is conveyed is one that is exercisable only on a public account, that is for the benefit of the public at large, the power of conveyance is a *constitutional* power, for public powers differ no otherwise from private fiduciary powers than in respect of the scale on which they are exercisable: they are the same powers exercisable on a greater scale. Correspondent then to the rights and powers which may be conveyed, are so many branches of the power of conveyance: as also of that branch of disinvestitive power which may be styled *juris-ademptive*.

Now of the several rights and powers which may be conveyed a pretty detailed enumeration was given in a former chapter,[p] in which it became necessary to mention them as capable of giving occasion to so many species of delinquency. It should seem therefore that to the exemplifying of the several branches of the power of conveyance nothing more can be requisite than to give a brief indication of the hands in which in certain instances they are lodged.

Instances of the exercise of accensitive and dis-accensitive power: 1. as applied to the matrimonial condition

17. The matrimonial contract, whatever covenants may be annexed to it, is at any rate a conveyance, if it were only in virtue of the autocheiristic or contrectative powers it conveys to the husband commonly over the property of the wife and necessarily over her person. The power of conveying these powers belongs to the several parties whose concurrence collectively or disjunctively is necessary and sufficient to the validity of the marriage: such as the parties, the parents or guardians, the priest or magistrate who performs the ceremony, the magistrate who grants the license, and so on. The divestitive or potis-ademptive power belongs to the several persons whose concurrence is necessary and sufficient to the validity of a

[p] Ch. xvi (Division). [1]

[1] Ch. xvi of *An Introduction to the Principles*.

divorce: such as the parties or one of them, and the judge or judges having cognizance in that behalf. To the former set of parties then belongs the *accensitive* power with regard to the class of persons who are styled husbands: to the latter, the *disaccensitive*. It would be easy enough but can hardly be necessary to apply the same method of exemplification to the powers belonging to the other conditions of the domestic kind. In virtue of the obligations or other burthens which may stand annexed to any of those conditions, the same example may also serve for such branches of investitive power the exercise of which has the effect of subjecting a man to obligations and of rendering him obnoxious to the exercise of powers of contrectation or as they may be otherwise termed *impressive* powers.

18. Let us pass on to constitutional powers. Taking examples from that country alone in which I write I shall lessen the trouble of citations, and the danger of mistakes. In Great Britain the King possesses with respect to the chief of the great offices to which judicial power is annexed the investitive or endynamistic, and with respect to some of them the divestitive or disendynamistic power. With respect of the offices of Chancellor, [and] Privy-Councillor, in both of which the judicial power forms a considerable part of the authority that belongs to them, as also with respect to the humbler office of Justice of the Peace, he has the divestitive power as well as the investitive: with respect to the offices of Member of the House of Lords, the 16 Scotch Peers excepted, and with respect to the magistrates included under the collective appellation of the twelve Judges as also with respect to some other judges of inferior note, he has the investitive power only. In regard to military offices he possesses the investitive and divestitive power both: though in the former there are other persons who by custom have in some instances a share[q] at the same time. The divestitive power belongs to him to exercise *mero motu*: at the same time there are other persons, I mean the members of Court Martials, who have the power of doing the same thing *propter quid*, that is for delinquency. *2.–to various constitutional powers, such as that of appointing and displacing officers of various sorts*

19. To him alone belongs the power of declaring war: that is of aggregating large denominations of men to the disadvantageous condition of enemies: a condition, which depriving them of a variety of rights and laying them under a variety of disabilities, subjects them and the things which otherwise would be their properties to various applications of contrectative or impressive power: and the converse of this account will serve for the power of making peace. *–declaring war and making peace*

q The Lord Lieutenants of counties sign all the commissions in the militia.

Convicting
delinquents

20. To juries, in most cases belongs in conjunction with the regular judges as also with prosecutors, witnesses and individual officers of justice, and other persons whose share in this power however inconspicuous is not the less real, the power of aggregating persons in most cases to the disadvantageous class of delinquents, a class which is branched out into the various classes we have seen.[r] They thence become the persons from whom the legislator has taken such and such rights, whom he has subjected to such and such obligations, and rendered obnoxious in the way of punishment or for other purposes to such and such applications of the *impressive* power. This branch of the accensitive power is a distinct power from that of issuing judicial mandates, at least in as far as a part is distinct from the whole. Take the instance where a man is to be hanged for robbery or any other crime. To authorize any person to perform such an act of violence on the body of another a warrant or order issued by a magistrate of a certain description is made necessary. In the issuing of this warrant or order no juryman has any direct participation. The order is signed not by the jury but by certain other magistrates who are called judges. But to the validity of such order or at least to the indemnity of those who issue it a variety of conditions are made requisite: among which are a previous declaration made on the part of a certain number of the above mentioned occasional magistrates called jurymen, importing that such or such a person, the person who afterwards is taken for the passible subject of such an order, belongs to one of those classes of persons out of which and which alone the judges are allowed to select the individuals on whom such violence shall in pursuance of their orders be committed.

All these are instances of accensitive power *in personam.*

Regulating
the coin—an
instance of
the accensi-
tive power in
rem

21. An instance of accensitive power *in rem* is the power of assigning value and giving currency to coin. This power applies itself to and modifies the effect of that part of the body of the laws which relates to the offence of wrongful non-investment of property in the case where the proprietary subject in question consists in money, or in goods which require to be marked out by weights or measures. On the 1st of Jan. 1780 Peter enters into a covenant which obliges him to pay to Paul on the 1st of Jan. 1781 the sum of twenty s. On the 1st of Jan. 1780 a shilling contains 93 grains of silver. The King has the power of determining what pieces of money shall be understood to belong to the class of things called

---

[r] Ch. xvi (Division).[1]

[1] Ch. xvi of *An Introduction to the Principles.*

shillings.[1] Before the 1st of January 1781 he issues a number of pieces of money which he calls shillings, but which in fact contain each of them but half the quantity of silver that was contained in any of the pieces of money which on the 1st of January 1780 went by the name of shillings. What is the consequence? that Peter is exempted from so much of the obligation as concerns ten out of the twenty shillings he had covenanted for. A covenant to pay twenty shillings may be considered as consisting of two covenants each for the payment of ten shillings. Each of the covenants by means of the standing declaration made by the sovereign concerning the validity which he gives to covenants is turned into a law. What then is the influence of the act of accensitive power in question upon these two laws? The one of them indeed it leaves standing: but the other it repeals. So mighty is the force of this single branch of the accensitive power. Supposing it exercisable without control, and the force of the legislative power in all money matters may be reduced to nothing. Pecuniary engagements may be annihilated at pleasure: taxes may be levied upon the creditors of the public to the amount of almost the whole of what is due to them. All laws whatsoever which have no other punishment than what is pecuniary to corroborate them may be rendered of no force. These are but two out of a multitude of revolutions which might be brought about by the exercise of this single power.

Another power of a nature nearly approaching to the former is that of regulating weights and measures. Revolutions similar to those just mentioned may accordingly be made by an alteration in the import of such terms as the words *yard* and *bushel*. This will be easily enough conceived without farther explanation.

22. Of the accensitive power *in actum* no separate examples need be given. One way in which a person may aggregate himself or render himself liable to be aggregated to a class of persons is by performing such or such an act. In this way to aggregate any act which a man has performed to such or such a class of acts is virtually to aggregate him to such or such a class of persons. Thus it is that by pronouncing an act to be an act of robbery, the agent is pronounced a robber: by pronouncing an act to be an act of lunacy the agent is pronounced a lunatic, and so on. Accordingly the instance above given of the power exercised by jurymen might as well have been applied to the illustration of this branch of accensitive power as of the other.

Accensitive power in actum needs no separate exemplification

---

[1] At this point the Ms. has the following note: 'Qu. how this stands by actual law and state it. He certainly had it once.'

Instances of accensitive power in locum

23. Instances of accensitive power *in locum* are the power of consecrating churches and other places of religious worship. Even by this power if exercised without control revolutions might be effected not less extraordinary than any which the preceding branches of accensitive power are capable of producing. By this power we have seen property usurped, debts rendered irrecoverable and crimes dispunishable.[s]

Accensitive power in tempus

24. There remains only that branch of accensitive power which concerns *time*. Of the exercise of this power we have an instance in the regulation of the style. Exercised without reason and without measure even this power might be productive of revolutions as extensive as any which we have seen produced by an abuse of the right of coinage. Interest of money might be diminished or increased, bonds forfeited, proprietary terms protracted or curtailed, minors emancipated, adults subjected to the disadvantages of minority, and the effect of an infinite variety of covenants, conveyances and other legal dispositions perverted or destroyed: and that without the designation of the legislator or the intention or expectation of the parties. As great changes might be made by it, and as much mis-

---

[s] In the reign of Rich 2d of England, an ecclesiastic if he happened to see any land that lay convenient for him used to turn it into a churchyard: an act of Parliament became necessary to put a stop to these metamorphoses.[1] The abuses that have been introduced by the establishment of asylums are known to every body. Asylums are mostly of a religious origin, but in some instances they have owed their establishment to the secular authority. In some places it has been thought for the honour of God that crimes should go unpunished: in others for the honour of the King that debts should go unpaid. In England the verge of the court as it is called, together with certain other privileged places are a sort of imperfect asylum for insolvent debtors.

Long before the clergy had begun to possess themselves of the estates of individuals by turning them into churchyards, the King had been used to swallow them up in much larger masses by turning them into forests. Had it not been for the successful struggles of the other estates, the kingdom might by this time have consisted of nothing but forests and churchyards. See the history of England during the 12th and 13th centuries, *passim*; particularly the reigns of William Rufus, John, and Henry 3d. See also among the statutes that called *Carta de Foresta*.[2]

---

[1] The reference is to an act of 1391 (15 Ric. II cap. 7) which declared that converting land to a churchyard came within the scope and penalties of the Statute of Mortmain (1279).

[2] The royal forests were essentially the creation of the Norman kings. Magna Carta has three clauses dealing with the burden of the forest laws, and two years later, in 1217, the separate Charter of the Forest was issued: it was confirmed with some revisions in 1225 and remained the basis of the forest laws until, in the 16th century, they finally became obsolete.

chief done as by a general abolition of debts, or an agrarian law:[t]
These general illustrations will I suppose be thought sufficient:
demonstrations more particular it were easy enough, but can hardly
be necessary, to bring to view.

25. It is by this time, I suppose, sufficiently manifest that the
legislative power ordinarily so called, I mean the power of legislat-
ing *de classibus* even though it be supreme, can never of itself be
absolute and unlimited. It can never so much as amount to the
entire power of imperation: it will fall short of being equal to that
power by so much as is contained in whatever powers of aggregation
or disaggregation are established in the state. We have seen what
the points are in respect of which a law may be general or particular:
in whatever of these points it happens to be general there may be
room for the intervention of those other powers.

Imperfection of the power of imperation de singulis

It now remains to shew that the power of imperation in particular
terms, the power of imperating as we may say *de singulis*, how extensive and unlimited it may be in itself, can never possess all the
efficacy that is capable of being exerted by this and the preceding
power put together. The principal article to be considered in this
view is that of the person or persons whom the law has principally
in prospect, whichever be the purpose of the sovereign concerning
them; whether to favour them, to coerce them, or to make them
suffer. Whichever then be his purpose, the intercourse he has with
particular persons can never comparatively speaking be very
extensive. Few will be the individuals whom he can find motives for
selecting or the means of describing. We even see families so large
as to include more servants than come individually under the
master's notice: in how much greater a degree must this be the case
in empires? Thus limited by the nature of things is the power of the
despot (to use the term in the indifferent sense which first belonged
to it) in comparison with the power of the legislator. I mean even
with relation to their contemporaries: and in regard to posterity the
difference is still more conspicuous. With posterity the despot, as
such, has no means whatever of communication. He has no names
to call them by; he has no language in which to converse with
them. But to the power of the legislator time has no barrier to
oppose: the *nati natorum et qui nascuntur ab illis* form but a small

---

[t] Care was accordingly taken to obviate these inconveniences in the British
act (24 G. 2 c. 23) for the adoption of the new style.[1]

[1] The act of 1751 providing for the adoption from 1752 of the Gregorian Calendar in
Great Britain.

part of the multitude he has under his care[u]: so that in this line alone the power of the latter is to that of the former as infinity to one. Were power indeed to be considered in no other light than that of an instrument of private satisfaction to the possessor, and the measure of its magnitude were the tendency it has to contribute to that end, further discussions might perhaps be requisite; but in this quality it does not concern us here.

At any rate it appears that the power of the legislator and the power of the despot are not even when put together equal to the whole power of imperation in a state: that a chasm is still left, to supply which requires the addition of the several modifications of power which may be included under the names of accensitive and disaccensitive.

[u] In the act above referred to express and separate provision is made for the concerns of the years 2[000] and 2[800].[1] It is curious and not unpleasing to observe this evidence of the legislator taking so large a stride.

[1] In the act providing for the adoption of the Gregorian calendar in Great Britain, the years 2000, 2400 and 2800 A.D. are mentioned in connection with the provision that every fourth hundredth year shall have 366 days, whereas other hundredth years shall have 365 only.

CHAPTER X

ASPECTS OF A LAW[1]

§ i. *Plan of this Chapter*

1. We come in the ninth place to consider what may be termed the *aspects* of a law: the aspects of which it is susceptible with relation to the articles which it is capable of taking for its *objects*: the aspects or *phases* which the will of a legislator may be considered as presenting to those objects in virtue of the different volitions, inclinations, or wishes which he may entertain concerning them, and the different names which may be given in consequence to the expression of such will.

In examining the law with relation to this head, perspicuity requires that we should begin with viewing it in the simplest form in which it can appear. There are two things essential to every law: an act of some sort or other, being the object of a wish or volition on the part of the legislator; and a wish or volition of which such act is the object. When an act of any sort is marked out, as also on the part of a legislator an aspect of any kind, as turned or directed as we may say, towards that act, a law is expressed; let either of these requisites be wanting, the supposed law wants something without which it cannot be a law: nothing is enacted; no distinguishable volition is expressed. But to the making up of a law there are no other essential requisites than these; so that if to a given law anything else be added, such additament is accidental and unessential to its nature. Laws however are things which are generally found in multitudes: insomuch that there is no state in which, if there be found one law there are not found a multitude of others at the same time. Conceive then a given law no matter to what purport to be established in any state: in the same state there are also other laws. Of these other laws take any one at pleasure, this second law either has something, or has not anything, in common with the law first supposed. If it has not anything, the two laws are entirely distinct from and independent of one another: each may as well be conceived without the other as with it. On the other hand if it have anything, it will be necessary in order to form any conception

A law may take for its objects either acts alone, or other laws as well as acts

---

[1] For the special textual problems connected with the Mss. of this chapter see above Introduction, XXXIX–XL.

of either, so long as they stand thus connected, to consider them together. Now the essential ingredients in the idea of a single or simple law are, as we have seen, the *act*, and the *aspect*. If then the second law have anything in common with the first, it must be one of these: and it is evident that it may have both or either.

Four heads under which what concerns the aspect of a law may be arranged 2. This being the case, what we shall have to say with relation to the aspects of a law may naturally arrange itself under four heads, which may be taken for the subjects of so many ensuing sections. Accordingly in examining the modifications of which a law considered in this point of view is susceptible, we shall consider in the first place the case where there is only one mandate applying itself to one act: in the second place where there is a mandate applying itself to an act to which another mandate of the same aspect has applied already: in the third place, where there is a mandate applying itself to an act to which another mandate of a different aspect has applied already: in the fourth place where there is a mandate applying to one act an aspect which is spoken of as having been applied already to another.

For these purposes, it may be sometimes necessary that not only acts but laws themselves should be spoken of under the name of *objects* of a law. Between these very disparate classes of objects there will always however be this conspicuous difference: acts are essentially objects of a law, for without them it could not have existence: laws only incidentally so; since it is not a matter of course for any one law to apply itself to any other.

Throughout this analysis there will be four particulars, the consideration of which will go hand in hand; but which on account of the different terms in which there may be occasion from time to time to speak of them will need to be distinguished. These are 1. the will or inclination which the legislator bears towards the act or the law which is the object of it. 2. The law or assemblage of words by which such will or inclination may stand expressed. 3. The act which is the object of such will or inclination. 4. the precedent law, where there is one, towards which the law in question bears a reference. These objects will all of them require to be kept in view: and each of them may in conformity to the changes of which the aspect of the law or laws in question is susceptible, admit of and require a different appellative. In the catalogue of these appellatives it will be necessary to exhibit the leading articles: but it would be tedious, and in some measure superfluous to pursue the enumeration through every article: where this catalogue is defective, analogy will fill up the gap.

§ ii. *Primordial*

1. To begin with considering a mandate in its simplest form: viz: that which it wears when it hath *acts* alone for its objects, not applying itself to other mandates. Wherever this is the case, the aspect which the will of the magistrate bears to the act which is its object may, with reference to other aspects which it might have borne, be termed *primordial*: in the opposite case, *supervening* or *superventitious*. At present we are to suppose the aspect of the law to be primordial: laying out of the question all other laws or expressions of will with respect to which it might be superventitious.

Aspect primordial, superventitious

2. Conceive then, any act at pleasure: with regard to this act it is either the wish of the magistrate to influence the conduct of the party in question or it is not: in the former case the aspect of the magistrate may be said to be decided, in the latter *neutral* or *undecided*: and as to any mandate whereby such aspect is expressed, it may in the former case be termed a *decisive, operative, influencing,* or *directive*; in the latter, an *indecisive, inoperative, neutral, uninfluencing,* or *undirective,* mandate.

Aspect decisive or neutral: mandate decisive or indecisive

3. To begin with the case where the will is decided. The wish must either be that the act should be performed, or that it should not be performed: in the former case the mandate is what in the most confined sense of the word is termed a *command*: in the latter, a *prohibition*. The will being undecided, there is no wish, that can be operative or efficient, to express: all that the mandate can express is the negation of one or other of the two operative kinds of mandates: it is accordingly either what may be termed a *non-command*, or else a *non-prohibition*, that is to use the common language a *permission*. 'Every householder shall carry arms': this is an example of a command: 'No householder shall carry arms': this of a prohibition: 'Any householder may forbear to carry arms': this, of a non-command: 'Any householder may carry arms': this, of a non-prohibition or permission.

A command– prohibition– non-command–non- prohibition or permission

4. In the first and last of the above cases the aspect may be termed *affirmative* with relation to the act: in the second and third, negative: and the same distinction may be applied to the mandates by which those aspects are respectively expressed.

Aspect and mandate affirmative– negative

5. In the above definitions, the act is supposed, as of course, to be of the positive kind: let it be of the negative kind they will of course change places. A negative aspect towards a positive act is equipollent to an affirmative aspect towards the correspondent

A negative aspect towards an affirmative act equipollent to an affirmative towards a negative

negative act. To will that during a given period the act of not carrying arms shall be performed is to will that throughout that period
the *continued act* or *habit* of not carrying arms should be persevered
in. It is in this way that a command may wear the form of a prohibition: and a prohibition that of a command. The law which
prohibits the mother from starving her child commands her to take
care that it be fed. The one may be at pleasure translated or *converted* into the other.[a] Of these two species of mandates then, an
affirmative and a negative, each one may at pleasure be translated
or converted into the other. A mandate prohibiting drunkenness
may without any change in its import be converted into a law
commanding sobriety: a mandate commanding chastity into a
mandate prohibiting incontinence. But amongst names of acts
those of the affirmative class are much more abundant than those of
the negative. Accordingly, of the two forms into either of which a
mandate may be thrown the most natural will generally be that in
which the name of the act is of the affirmative stamp. In the
particular instances however where there happens to be a particular name for the negative act, the affirmative and negative form
of imperation will appear equally natural in both cases. To command sobriety is as natural as to prohibit drunkenness: to prohibit
drunkenness as to command sobriety. It would make little difference
although the substance of the mandate were to be changed. A
mandate commanding drunkenness, if a mandate to such a purport
were conceivable would in point of expression be neither more nor
less natural than a law prohibiting sobriety. These remarks in order
to be perfectly exact would need to be pushed to a further degree of
minuteness: it would be necessary that examples of laws should be
exhibited *in terminis*: and that a variety of grammatical and other
metaphysical discussions should be travelled through. But what has
been said already is probably at least as much as will be generally
endured.

Mandate im-
perative,
obligative,
coercive, or
unimperative
etc.

6. When the aspect is *decided* the mandate which contains the
expression of it may be termed an *imperative, obligative,* or *coercive*
mandate: in the opposite case, *unimperative, unobligative,* or
uncoercive.

Of imperative mandates as well as of unimperative there are

---

[a] Refer to Sanderson's Logic[1] for *conversion.*

[1] Robert Sanderson (1587–1663), *Logicae Artis Compendium,* 1618 and many later
editions. This was the 'Logic Compend' which Bentham had studied as an Oxford
undergraduate: see his letter to his father of 12 June 1761 (*Correspondence,* in *CW,*
i, 47).

affirmative as well as negative: and of affirmative mandates as well as of negative, there are imperative as well as unimperative.

7. Of the mandates then which are capable of being delivered with relation to any given act there are never either more or less than four: expressive each of them of a different aspect: a command; a non-command; a prohibition; and a permission. Among these mandates there subsists such a relation, that with respect to one another some of them are necessarily repugnant and exclusive; others as necessarily concomitant. Examine them in this view and we shall find that there are upon all occasions two of those aspects, and upon none more than two, presented to the act at the same time: the aspects going together constantly in pairs. To represent this the more clearly, let us advert at present to the act: and let us state the condition into which it may be said to be put, the manner in which it may be said to be affected, by being taken for the object of the mandates corresponding respectively to those aspects. First, it may be commanded: it is then left unprohibited: and it is not prohibited nor left uncommanded. 2. It may be prohibited: it is then left uncommanded: and it is not commanded nor permitted (that is left unprohibited). 3. It may be left uncommanded: it is then not commanded: but it may be either prohibited or permitted: yet so as that if it be in the one case it is not in the other. 4. It may be permitted: it is then not prohibited: but it may be either commanded or left uncommanded: yet so as that if it be in the one case, it is not in the other, as before.

Opposition and concomitancy among mandates

A command then includes a permission: it excludes both a prohibition and a non-command. A prohibition includes a non-command: and it excludes both a command and a permission. A non-command of itself does not necessarily include either a prohibition or a permission: but it excludes a command: and, as a prohibition and a permission exclude one another, it can only be accompanied with one of them at a time: and as they are contradictory to each other, it must be accompanied with one or other of them.

8. In comparing the distinctions here laid down with respect to the mandates by which different aspects of the will may be expressed, it may be observed that they do not in every direction descend so far as to embrace every distinction of which the internal state of the will itself is susceptible. To speak particularly, this is the case with regard to the uncoercive sort of mandates. When a legislator takes up the pen and says in so many words that any householder for instance may carry arms, or that any house-

Aspects for which there are no corresponding mandates

holder may forbear to carry arms, it is out of question that he has taken the matter into contemplation, that he has made up his mind about it, and that he has formed a decided wish that the subject shall enjoy the liberties which in the two cases are respectively allowed him. Suppose either to be established, and the condition of the subject in respect of the act in question is free as far as they respectively go: and suppose them both to be established, it is completely free. But these mandates take them together are expressive of but one of three states which the will of the legislator may be in, and the condition of the subject alike free in all of them. It may be in the first place, that the legislator has never so much as taken the act into contemplation: it may be in the second place, that having taken it into contemplation, yet he has made no choice with regard to the question whether the subject shall or shall not have *his* choice as to the performing it: or thirdly it may be as in the case above supposed, that having taken it into contemplation he has positively chosen that the subject shall have his choice. But of these three states of the legislator's will there is but one which there can ever be occasion to express: which one is the same which is here last mentioned. The first supposing it to take place is what in the nature of things it is impossible for the legislator to express: since a declaration of its existence would carry the proof of its own falsity upon the face of it. The second may indeed be expressed without contradiction: but if expressed in such manner as to distinguish it from the third, the distinction would be of no use. The use of a mandate is determined by the nature of the act or mode of conduct which is the object of it: and where there can be no difference in the conduct of the subject, it is to no purpose to mark out any difference in the mind of the legislator.

The state of the mind may be expressed partly by words and partly by silence

9. It has already been observed that of the various aspects of which the will is susceptible with relation to an act, there can never be either more or less than two presented to it at a time. Accordingly where the law is silent with reference to any act, insomuch that there is no mandate that applies to it, it is not of one aspect only that such silence is expressive, but of two, viz: the undecided ones both together: so that there are two sorts of mandates, viz; the two undecisive ones, neither of which taken by itself is so expressive as mere silence. Of course where one only of these mandates is visible upon the face of the law, and at the same time neither of the decisive ones, the state of the legislator's mind with respect to the act is but half-expressed: that is to say, in words. It is not however the less effectually determined: the aspect that is wanting being made known, in the manner in which without the mandate in question both the undecided aspects would have been made known, by silence.

10. Here it may be asked,—since the undecisive mandates taken together express no more than silence, that is than what is expressed without them, and neither of them by itself even so much, of what use then can they be made? and to what purpose can it be to take any sort of notice of them?—The question is natural: but the answers that may be given to it, will be found to be satisfactory. *Use of the undecisive mandates*

1. In the first place, they are possible and conceivable: which of itself would be a sufficient reason for the mentioning of them: since without them the view of the possible aspects of a legislator's will with the mandates by which they may respectively be expressed would be incomplete.

2. More than this they are actually in use, and that frequently. Instances it is not worthwhile to exhibit here on purpose: enough will make their appearance of course as we advance. This would of itself be an additional reason why the mention of them ought not to be omitted; although no good reason were to be given for the using them. But the fact is that they have their use, and that on more occasions than one.

3. They may be of use, for the purpose of removing doubts: where the subject, having seen his liberty infringed in any point or seen cause to apprehend its being infringed, stands in need of an express declaration, an assurance on the part of the law to ease him of his fears. In this case indeed the effect is produced not so much from the literal import of the mandate itself, as from another mandate which is so connected with it that if not expressed it may of course be looked upon as implied. I mean a mandate which in the form of a prohibition is addressed to subordinate power-holders in general restraining them from breaking in upon the liberty of the party whom the uncoercive mandate in question is meant to favour. Thus much must be inferred of course: to which may be added in some cases a law of a particular kind[b] including the sovereign himself under the same restriction.[c] It is easy to see that some of the most important laws that can enter into the code, laws in which the people found what are called their liberties, may be of this description.[1]

[b] See supra Ch. vi (Parties affected).
[c] This may be distinguished by the appellation of a law *in principem*.

[1] At this point the Ms. has the following note: 'A note instancing Mag. Charta &c.'; but Bentham seems not to have followed up this hint.

4. A mandate of this stamp may be of use in the way of introduction. Though the purport of it be of no significance, and the legislator would have done nothing had he stopped there, yet for the purpose of expression there may be a convenience in setting out with a mandate of this stamp, in order to express in a more easy or pointed manner a mandate of the opposite or coercive stamp. Examples will be found a little further on.

§ iii. *Reiterative*

Mandates reiterative, what

1. So much for the different sorts of mandates as distinguished by the aspect; no account being taken of their applying to any other mandate. We come now to the different sorts of mandates as distinguished by the manner in which they apply to other mandates: and in the first place to that sort of mandate which not only applies itself to the same act as does the mandate it applies to, but is expressive of the same aspect. A superventitious mandate of this description may, with relation to the primordial mandate it applies to, be styled *re-iterative*. With relation to the act which is their common object it requires no particular denomination. Such as the primordial mandate was, such is the superventitious: if a command, a command; if a prohibition, a prohibition: and so on.

Subalternation of acts

2. On this occasion it will be requisite to bring to view the doctrine of *subalternation*: that is (to denominate it more fully and precisely) *logical subalternation*. Acts which are the objects of mandates, acts like any other entities, that is the names of acts like names of any other entities may be said to stand in subalternation: meaning with relation one to another, when they are species one of another: when the ideal compartments which they respectively denominate are included one within another, in the manner that a *species* is within a *genus*. Now it is evident that so long as language serves, this sort of connection may subsist amongst any number of acts, that is separate sorts and denominations of acts, forming a *chain of subalternation*, as it may be termed, of any length. As A is a species of B, so may B be of C and C of D and so on indefinitely: or conversely as it is a genus with respect to Y so may Y be with respect to X, and X with respect to W.

Reiteration in genere or in specie

3. Acts, or rather the ideas that are derived from them, and the names that are given to those ideas, standing in this relation one to another, it is evident that a mandate, which with respect to another mandate is reiterative may be so either *in genere* or *in specie*: *in genere* when the superventitious mandate applies to the whole of the

division or compartment of acts which the primordial mandate has taken for its object: *in specie,* when it applies to but a part of that division.

4. It is evident that on this occasion instead of saying *in genere* –in toto *or* and *in specie* one might with equal propriety say *in toto* and *pro* pro tanto *tanto*: but this nomenclature it will be convenient to reserve for a purpose somewhat different. As language is constituted, the same sense may almost in every instance be expressed either in the same or in a different set of words: in whichever way then the business of reiteration be performed, the distinction of reiterative *in genere* and reiterative *in specie* may equally apply. But as those expressions point more naturally to the very words or tenor of the law it may be of use to appropriate them to the case where the superventitious provision coincides as well in terms with the primordial one as in effect; using the expressions *in genere* and *in specie* where no account is taken of the words.

5. As it seemed with regard to the undecisive mandates in the *Purposes to* case where in point of date they are primordial, so may it seem with *which* *reiterative* all superventitious mandates in general in the case where they are *mandates* reiterative. Judging of them upon a hasty view, it might seem that *may be ap-* the issuing of any such mandates were but a nugatory sort of *mation—* business: that it were but *actum agere*: and therefore carried a kind of *continuation* confession of its own inutility upon the face of it: to what purpose *–admonition* then, it may be said can the issuing of any such mandate be ap- *–exposition* plied?—It may be answered—To several.

1. To the purpose of *confirmation*: where the title of the lawgiver from whom the primordial law emaned is looked upon as liable to dispute.[d]

2. To the purpose of *continuation*. To this purpose it may be applied in two cases: where the primordial law was by institution temporary[e]: and where although the duration of it, as far as de-pended upon the legislator from whom it originally emaned were designed perhaps to be indefinite, a doubt comes afterwards to be entertained, whether it be the intention of a succeeding sovereign to

---

[d] See Ch. [ɪɪ] (Source). Restoration and Convention Parliaments.[1]
[e] See Ch. [ᴠɪɪɪ] (Durability).[2]

[1] The two parts of this note are not connected. The first part like n. g below, refers to the earlier discussion of the 'adoption' of laws by a sovereign (21–9). The second part is an unexpanded reference to the irregular parliaments which met in April 1660 and January 1689 respectively.
[2] By 'Durability' Bentham evidently intends his earlier chapter 'Of the Duration of a Law' (Ch. ᴠɪɪɪ above).

adopt it.[f] All the cases hitherto mentioned, and particularly the first, may be considered as cases of adoption.[g]

3. To the purpose of *admonition*: where an apprehension appears to be entertained, that the primordial law, though the validity of it be out of question, should remain unheeded.

4. To the purpose of *explanation*: where the terms of the primordial law are looked upon as deficient in any of the three essential points in which a discourse as such is capable of being deficient; viz: perspicuity, explicitness and precision.[h] In this case the reiterative mandate may be termed explanatory, expository or expositive with relation to the primordial one.

An ex-
pository
mandate,
what

When it is for this latter purpose that the reiterative provision is issued, it may be said to be *explanatory* or *expository* with respect to the primordial one. In the other cases the two provisions may for anything that hinders, be conceived both of them in the same terms. but in this last the terms in which they are conceived must necessarily in some point or other at least, be different: since it is the supposed unsuitableness of some term or terms of the one that is the very reason for issuing the other.

An expository
mandate the
only one that
must vary in
tenor from
the pri-
mordial one

Here then we may note the distinction between a provision which is reiterative in *tenor* or as we may say *in terminis*, as well as in *import*, and one that is reiterative in *import* or, as we say, in *purport* only. A provision which is reiterative for any of the three first of the above four purposes may be reiterative in both these points with relation to the primordial one: in other words may agree with it in both these respects: a provision which is reiterative for the last of these purposes can not agree with it completely in any other wise than in purport. As far as particular words are concerned the one may be reiterative of the other *pro tanto*, but not *in toto*.

The reitera-
tion may be
with or with-
out notice
taken of the
primordial

6. For whichever of the three abovementioned purposes the superventitious mandate is designed, it may take notice or not of the primordial mandate of which it is reiterative. Now the primordial mandate if any such thing was ever actually issued is probably already extant in a certain assemblage of words: which assemblage of words it is strange if there be not some way or other

[f] See Barrington.[1]

[g] Ch. [II] (Source).

[h] See App. tit. (Composition).[2]

[1] Cf. 66 n. 1 above.

[2] Bentham's early Mss. contain a good deal of material on the subject of 'Composition'—i.e. the text of laws. Everett (ed. cit., 193–5) prints one fragment from this material. But the projected Appendix to the *Plan of a Penal Code* referred to here by Bentham seems not to have been completed in that form.

of describing, shorter than by repeating them. This being the case
either the words are such as the legislator is satisfied with, or they
are not: if they are, to what purpose express the proposed import
required in any other way, than by referring to the words by which
it has been expressed already? By expressing them over again in
other words there can be no good, and there is this obvious inconvenience: an addition is made *pro tanto* to the voluminousness
of the body of the laws. Nor is the inconvenience removed by taking
for the words of the reiterative mandate the same terms precisely
that were made use of for the primordial.[1] This precaution, though it

[1] It is evident that in order for a law to be reiterated in the way of reference
and not in the way of repetition, by reference to a title which has been given to
it and not by repetition of its detail, it must at the time of its first conception
have been distinguished by some mark whereby on any subsequent occasion it
may be described. This is effected by furnishing the body of the laws in its
totality as likewise the several constituent parts of it, with the ordinary
apparatus of divisions and subdivisions, entitled by some such denominations as
book, chapter, section, paragraph, article, number, and the like: expedients
which in didactic works of inferior importance it would be thought a mark of
ignorance or negligence to omit: which accordingly in the codes of perhaps
every civilized nation but one are carefully turned to account; but which in the
written law of a nation, which in matters of jurisprudence arrogates to itself
the pre-eminence over every other, is unaccountably neglected: as if every
thing that savours of method ought to be studiously excluded from a work
which stands more in need than any other of such assistance to render it
intelligible.

In the acts of the British legislature as much legal matter as is enacted in the
course of one session of Parliament, be it ever so much or ever so little forms
what is called in the technical language one *Statute*. Of this again so much as
hath happened to go through the forms of authentication at one and the same
time, so as to have been couched in one and the same instrument is in the same
technical language termed one *chapter*; viz: one chapter of the statute. Such a
chapter when spoken of by itself, and without reference to the statute of which
it forms a part is termed *an act*: the words '*of parliament*' being understood.
Thus the technical title of the famous act commonly called the *Habeas Corpus*
act is the statute of the [31st] year of the reign of Charles 2d, chapter [2]. But in
common speech a single *act* when spoken of by itself is also termed a *statute*.
There is no lower division than this into *acts* which is authentic: so that an act
or chapter is the least integrant part of the whole body of statute law for which
the care of the legislators has provided a name: an act then in English jurisprudence is like the *point* in mathematics, a thing which has no parts. The
editors of the printed copies of these acts do indeed of their own authority
break them into subdivisions which are termed *sections*. But these subdivisions
are not marked upon the original written instrument: it is one entire undivided
chaos: accordingly the penner of a superventitious act takes no notice of any
such thing as a section in the primordial. These acts in point of bulk are
frequently so large, that the matter contained in them is sufficient to fill a
moderate duodecimo or even octavo volume: sometimes a single section, or

were taken, would not be sufficient to obviate any of the ill effects which a superfluity of this sort must necessarily be attended with: neither those which apply to the whole body of the law taken together, nor those which apply to the particular part which is thus unnecessarily repeated. Being as much law as the primordial, there is the same occasion for its being inserted. It must be inserted then for the second time, that people may be sure it is the same that was issued before: which done, it contributes as largely to the bulk and terrific appearance of the whole, as if it were ever so diverse.

How in an expository mandate the style of imperation is dropped

7. When exposition is the object, a remarkable change in the style of the mandate naturally and almost constantly takes place. The language of imperation is insensibly dropt, and the discourse slips aside into the ordinary didactic or assertive style. This change is too important, and without explanation too perplexing to be permitted to pass unheeded. A large portion, commonly even much the largest portion of the whole mass of law in a complete code must remain a riddle, without the connection which there is between that part of it which happens to be couched in the one of those forms and that which happens to be couched in the other be laid open, and the equipollency which there may be between them be made appear.

even such a part of a section as still falls short of concluding the sense or completing the grammatical sentence shall contain a quantity of matter equal to what is commonly alloted to a shilling or eighteen-penny pamphlet. In the printed copy of so much as is published of the stat. | | Geo. | | ch. | | in Ruffhead's edition[1] in which neither the first section nor the first sentence is finished, that first section occupies thirteen pages and a fraction. These thirteen pages and a fraction I have had cast, as the term is with people of the art. The quantity of letterpress they contain is such as if printed in the form in which the novel of Tristram Shandy is printed would occupy | | pages. In a volume of Tristram Shandy the number of pages which in the several editions that have hitherto (1781) been printed is upon an average of the six volumes | |. This fragment of a section then contains within $\frac{x}{y}$th's as much as a volume of the size of those in which books of entertainment are frequently printed.

In point of diversity, in the same act are frequently contained eight or ten sets of provisions of which the purport is as various as that of any eight or ten portions that could be picked out of the whole code. There is a familiar name for such of these acts in which the variety is most remarkably conspicuous: they are termed *hodge-podge* acts. I mention these particulars, lest such readers, if any such there be, as have never happened to turn over a collection of the British acts of parliament, should look upon the supposition of a mass of law which has no name that it can be cited by, as an impossible one.

[1] Owen Ruffhead, *The Statutes at large, from Magna Carta to the end of the last Parliament*, 1761. It is not possible to identify the statute Bentham had in mind.

That there should be such a connection and such an equipollency might at first view seem a paradox. The property and very essence of law, it may be said, is to command: the language of the law then should be the language of command. For expressing command there is in all languages a particular *mood*, which is styled the *imperative*. Of what other mood should a law-giver make use? To this it may be answered, in the first place, that the only mood to which grammarians have thought fit to give the name *imperative* is by no means the only one which is calculated to perform the office of *imperation*: the name so far indeed belongs to it with propriety, that being capable of performing that office, it is not capable of performing any other: but it is far from being the only one which possesses this capacity. The future tense of what is called the indicative mood is in truth a stronger imperative than the imperative itself. By way of example, let us take a law or mandate against stealing. How strong soever be the phrase 'steal not'; 'thou shalt not steal', is stronger still. By the former set of words, all I do is simply to make known my will: in the latter I not only make known my will as perspicuously as in the former case, but I go further: I give the party to understand that the motive I trust to for producing the effect I aim at is of such strength as to warrant me in foretelling to the very person I am commanding, that in spite of his free agency my command will be followed by his obedience. 'Thou *shalt* not steal' is as much as to say thou *wilt* not steal; but with this addition: that it is the intimation I give thee of my will, and of the motive which makes it thy interest to obey it, that will be the cause of thy not doing so.[j]

Still it is the language of imperation that is employed; though not that particular sort of word to which among grammarians the appellation of a *verb of the imperative mood* has been confined. Still there are *words of volition*: words by which a will on the part of him whose words they are is plainly and palpably expressed. Whatsoever therefore be the name which grammarians are in the habit of giving to the verb which is employed, the style of the discourse, to judge of the matter independently of accidental denominations, must be confessed to be essentially and visibly imperative. There is still enough that serves, and that as effectually as in the other case, to distinguish the imperative from the ordinary didactic, narrative, informative, or assertive style: the language of the will from the language of the understanding.

[j] In this respect the English has the advantage over the Greek, Latin, French, and probably most other languages.

But in many instances it will be found that the style of imperation is altogether dropped: no intimation being given in the sentence in question nor perhaps in the course of many sentences, or even pages, in short or even volumes, that the will of the legislator or of anybody else, has any concern in what is delivered: and this may be said of every system of law that has ever yet appeared, or is ever likely to appear. Many are the cases in which this change is apt to take place: and in that which is now before us, the case in which exposition is the object, such change is in a manner necessary. This will be manifest enough, as soon as ever an example of an expository mandate in the imperative form is exhibited. By the verbosity and uncouthness of such a mode of expression it will immediately be perceived that nothing could be more unnatural or ineligible than to adhere to it. It is not necessary that that part of the discourse by which the concern that the will has in the matter is made known be constantly expressed: it is sufficient if on the part of the reader it be perceived, and to that end, if on the part of the writer it be made perceptible. Let us now proceed with the investigation whereby the manner in which the concern which the will of the legislator has with everything that comes under the head of law may be developed and ascertained.

In an expository mandate then there must be some term or terms at least, as hath been observed, different from some term or terms at least in the primordial one: some term or terms at least of the primordial one must be changed. This may be the case either with all or with less than all. In either case the reiteration may be *in genere* or *in specie*. If *in genere*, it may be performed either by one single mandate as in the primordial, or it may take more mandates than one. If it be reiterative *in specie*, it may be either accompanied with other mandates sufficient to complete the reiteration *in genere*, or not. In the latter case the number of expository mandates need not be greater than that of the primordial: for the case may be that there shall be but one such superventitious mandate. But in the other case it is evident that there must be more superventitious mandates than one: for there cannot be fewer than two specific terms necessary to express the import of one generic one. Where the exposition is performed by a multitude of mandates, which taken separately are but so many mandates reiterative *in specie*, it is plain the number of these mandates may be multiplied as often as in the primordial one there are generic terms: as will presently be seen by an example.

Now in the description given of the act it is possible then that there may be no more than two terms (names of two different sorts of entities) employed: viz: the name of the agible subject and the name of the abstract act itself: as in this mandate, 'let no one steal'. In this instance it is even possible that there shall be but one such term employed: viz: the name of the act: as if the mandate were to run thus: 'steal not': or 'let not theft be committed'. But in most cases they are much more numerous: nor indeed in the present instance would the number be so small, were it not for an ellipsis or ellipses: which must be supplied before the logical proposition, before the grammatical sentence, is complete; in short, before anything is expressed. In one case the passible subject must be supplied, viz: 'any thing': 'let no man steal any thing': in another case not only the passible subject but the agible: 'steal not': that is 'do thou not steal any thing': 'let not theft be committed', that is 'let not theft of any thing be committed by any persons'. For other examples of similar simplicity take the following: 'let no person carry arms':—'let no person export corn'.

It is manifest that where a name or title of any kind has once been given to a mandate in such case, in order to reiterate it, if the reiteration is to be performed *in toto*, there needs no mention whatever of anything else belonging to it but the name: there needs no mention of the contents. In this case how voluminous soever be the mandate, the reiteration of it is performed in a few words: as thus 'let such or such a law' (naming it) 'stand confirmed': or 'let it be continued for such or such a time' or 'take heed and let it be observed' according to the purpose for which, as above mentioned, the reiteration is performed.

As to the question, which is the most convenient form for giving title to a mandate, this is a question of no mean importance: but the discussion of it does not belong to the present subject. It depends as anyone may see [upon][1] the method in which the whole body of the law of which the mandate in question forms a part, shall have been disposed, upon the bulk and shape of the divisions into which it is cast.

8. Here is the place to speak of what is meant by a declaratory law or mandate: an expression which in certain systems of jurisprudence is apt frequently to occur. For this purpose it will be necessary to anticipate a little in order to introduce for a moment the mention of the customary or unwritten law. The term *declaratory* may perhaps in some instances be employed in the cases where the

A declaratory mandate, what

[1] Ms. 'with': Bentham substituted 'depends' for 'is connected', and failed to adjust the sentence consistently.

primordial law exists in the form in which we all along suppose it to exist, the form of written as it is called or statute law: in these instances it is synonymous to *explanatory* or *expository*. But the cases in which it is most frequently employed are those in which the primordial law (or pretended primordial law) is supposed or pretended to exist in no other form than that of customary law. As the former have an appellation of their own, I shall confine the use of the term *declaratory* to these.

–its uses   It may here be asked, as on former occasions, what use can there be in a mandate of this stamp? For without entering into any discussion concerning the particular nature of a customary as distinguished from a statutory mandate, either the mandate which is given for a declaratory mandate exists or it does not. In the former case the statutory mandate is useless; in the latter it is not declaratory but primordial. Let its existence be even a matter of doubt (a case by the bye which can only occur where the supposed mandate is an article of customary law) what use can there be in the solving of any such doubt; a business which consists in assertion not in volition, and which is therefore foreign to the nature of a mandate? Over acts which have happened already the legislator has no power: and over such as have not yet happened his power is the same whatever may have happened before: granting him to have power to command an act to be done in future, what use can there be in his declaring whether such a command has or has not been issued heretofore?—Thus far the objection. The truth is, that in this case the discourse in question answers a double purpose. It commands or otherwise expresses volition: and merely by so doing it is not indeed declaratory. But besides that it asserts a matter of fact; viz: the existence of a mandate of the like purport in time past: by the former part of its import it is a mandate, by the latter part, it is declaratory.

As to the use that there may be in coupling the declaration with the imperation, this stands upon a somewhat different footing, according to the quality of the party who is the agible subject of it; according as it is a mandate *in principem*, or *in populum*. What use it has is indeed in both cases of the same nature: but in the former case it is much the most considerable. Where the question is between subject and subject, his rights on the one hand and his obligations on the other may as to their immediate foundation be grounded wholly on the statute law; on the sum total of the mandates of the sovereign. This might be the case at any time, and would be the case if anywhere the whole body of the law were reduced (which hitherto it never has been any where) into the statutory form, in a word if an entire code of law were any where established. But when the question is between the subject and the sovereign this can only be the case where he has become such by an original contract between him and his subjects actually and expressly established. Now of this state of things the instances are but few. In other cases the authority of the sovereign is founded or at least in a great degree influenced by custom and disposition: on a habit of commanding on one side, accompanied by a habit of obeying on the other: and more immediately on the one part in a disposition on the one part to expect obedience, on the other part in the disposition to pay it, according to the course of that custom from whence the disposition takes its rise. In such cases the force and efficacy of the law may depend in a considerable degree on the existence, real or supposed, of some customs to which it is or pretends to be conformable. When therefore a law *in principem* is established having custom for its foundation, the appealing to that custom is a sort of step taken towards the ensuring the observance of it.

Let us take by way of example two celebrated acts of the British government: the Bill of Rights in the time of William the third, and the American Declaratory Act of George the third: the former an obligative act of the whole sovereignty, the English Parliament, limiting the authority of one constituent part of it, the King[k]: the other an unobligative act of the English, now by the union with Scotland become the British Parliament, taking away all limits from the authority of the whole sovereignty over a part of its subjects, the natives of the British Colonies in North America. By the Bill of Rights the Lords and Commons after asserting that the then 'late King James the second' had amongst other things 'assumed and exercised a power of dispensing with and suspending of laws, and the execution of laws without consent of Parliament' aver that that act of authority amongst others is 'contrary to the known Laws (meaning maxims of customary law) as well as Statutes of the Realm': they then pray the King and Queen that the right in question: viz: the right of seeing him and his successors restrain themselves from the exercise of the power so condemned may be '*declared*' amongst others to be the '*ancient* right of the people of the kingdom' and concerning all which rights 'their Majesties with the consent of the same Lords and Commons are pleased that the same shall be declared enacted and established:

[k] 1. W. and M. Stat. 2. C. 2.

and the same are by their said Majesties, by the advice and consent of the same Lords and Commons, declared enacted and established accordingly'. I palliate as much as is consistent with the fidelity of quotation the verbosity and perplexity of the English legislative style.

By the American Declaratory Act[1] the British Parliament '*declares*' that it had, hath and of right ought to have full power and authority to make laws and statutes of sufficient force and validity to bind the colonies and people of America, subjects of the crown of Great Britain, *in all cases whatsoever*.[1]

§ iv. *Alterative*

Superven-titious aspect unconfor-mable, super-ventitious provision contradictive – contrariant

1. Next, let the superventitious aspect be unconformable to the primordial. Now it may be unconformable in either of two ways: in the way of simple *contradiction*: or in the way of *contrariety*:[m] in this latter way in certain cases only as we shall presently perceive.[n] Accordingly, in the former case the superventitious provision may be said to be *simply contradictive* or *revocative* of the primordial one; in the latter case, *contrariant* or *reversive*.

Primordial aspect active, superven-titious pro-vision if contradictive, deobligative – a counter-mandate

2. Let us begin then with the case where it is simply contra-dictive or revocative: and first let the primordial aspect have been active. If then it was affirmative, the expression of it was a com-mand: the expression of the superventitious aspect then being revocative of such command may be styled a *countermand*: and the act may be said to be countermanded: it is accordingly left uncom-manded and made free again.

A counter-mand – a re-permission

3. Next, let the primordial aspect (being active still) have been negative: the expression of it then was a prohibition: the expression then of the superventitious aspect being contradictive of the other, is what is styled a *permission*; and the act is said to be permitted: it is accordingly left unprohibited and made free again. Moreover the permission, wherever there is occasion to distinguish it from the inactive original permission above spoken of, may be termed a *superventitious permission* or it may likewise be said to be *active*: and the act may be said to be repermitted. Also, whether the pro-vision be a countermand or a repermission, it may in either case be termed a *countermandate* or a *de-obligative* provision.

[1] 6 Geo. III c. 12.

[m] Sanderson's Logic Lib. II cap. 5.[2]   [n] Infra, 111.

[1] At this point what appears to be Bentham's revised version of this chapter (cf. Introduction, XXXIX) breaks off abruptly.

[2] Cf. 96 n. 1 above.

4. Again, let the primordial aspect have been inactive. The expression of it then was either a non-command, or an inactive permission. The expression then of the superventitious aspect will accordingly be either a command or a prohibition.

Primordial aspect inactive, superventitious provision if contradictive a command or a prohibition

5. We come now to the case where the expression of the superventitious aspect is doubly alterative or reversive of that of the primordial. And first let the primordial have been active. The superventitious then will be active likewise: only on the opposite side. If then the primordial aspect was affirmative, and consequently the expression of it a command, then the superventitious aspect is negative and the expression of it, a prohibition; if the primordial aspect was negative and the expression of it a prohibition, the superventitious aspect is affirmative, and the expression of it a command. Between command on the one hand and prohibition on the other, inactivity lies midway. The superventitious provision then takes in either case two steps instead of one: one from command or prohibition down to inactivity: another from inactivity up to prohibition or command. A reversive provision may accordingly be resolved into two provisions, both having for their object the same act: the one destroying the obligation imposed by the primordial provision, the other imposing a new obligation, but of the opposite nature.

Primordial aspect active, superventitious provision if contrariant, a prohibition or a command

6. Lastly, let the primordial aspect have been inactive. In this case, the superventitious aspect can not be opposite to it in the way of contrariety: it is only in the way of simple contradiction that it can be so. Let it take one step and it becomes unconformable: but let it take another, and it falls back again into conformity. The expression therefore of the one can not be reversive of that of the other. Contradict a non-command and you have a command: but contradict the command, and you have a non-command as before. Contradict a permission and you have a prohibition: but contradict the prohibition, and you have a permission as before.°

Primordial aspect inactive, superventitious provision can not be contrariant

---

° The correspondence here observable between the word *countermand* and the word *permission* does not hold throughout: it does not hold good with respect to all their conjugates: nor even throughout all the phrases into which the words themselves may be introduced. A man may be said to *be permitted* to do a thing; to have a *permission given him* to do it: but he can not be said to *be countermanded* not to do it, to have a *countermand given him* not to do it. The word *permission* again as we have seen is used as well where the aspect is primordial as where it is superventitious: the word countermand can not be used where the aspect is primordial: it necessarily supposes a command preceding. This want of symmetry is not confined to the English language. It will be found I believe to prevail in most other languages that deal largely with the

Countermand –does not match in every case with permission

We come now to speak of the appellations that a provision may receive in consideration of the relation it bears to the specificant circumstances which may be made use of for the purpose of determining and characterizing the act.

Command etc. conditional—unconditional

7. Let the aspect be active, and that primordial. If an act then is commanded either it is commanded purely and absolutely, without the insertion of any specificant circumstances, or it is commanded *in* such or such circumstances; or in other words when accompanied by such and such circumstances: in the former case it may be styled an *unconditional* command; in the latter, a *conditional* one. And so in the case of a prohibition.

'Every man shall maintain his children': this may serve as an example of an unconditional command.[p] 'No man shall export wheat out of the country': this may serve for an example of an unconditional prohibition. 'Every man shall maintain his children, *so long as* they are unable to maintain themselves:' this may serve

Cause of this want of symmetry in language

Latin. Perhaps the cause is of a more extensive nature: and is grounded in the nature of the acts themselves that are in question. The case seems to be that in general there are more acts which men have need to be restrained from doing, than there are which they have need to be constrained to do. I mean more sorts of acts. Moreover let the sort of act be in the main ever so innocent, beneficial, or even necessary, it is only at certain seasons that it is so. The moments which give a man the opportunity of performing any positive service to the community are separated by long and frequent intervals: but mischief a man may do almost at any time. The great crimes such as murder, robbery, incendiarism, perjury and so forth are almost always committed by acts of the positive stamp. Mankind then, take the sum of their conduct throughout life have much greater need of a bridle than of a spur. Since prohibitions then come oftener in question than commands there will be more frequent occasion to grant re-permissions, that is to countermand prohibition (I mean in particular cases that are excepted) than to countermand affirmative commands.

Dispensation, what

The word *dispensation* may be used in some cases either instead of the word countermand or instead of the word re-permission: but it is scarcely used where the description of the persons whose acts are the objects of the superventitious provision is co-extensive with that of the persons whose acts are the objects of the primordial provision. It is most commonly applied only to individuals. This word too is very imperfectly supplied with conjugates.

[p] It must be confessed that the idea belonging to the word *maintain* as applied to children is very changeable and vague: it includes a vast variety of different acts to be performed upon different occasions. But there was no finding any such thing as one unvaried physical act that could pass even for a moment as a proper object for an unconditional command. The reason is that there is no positive physical act of any sort the performance of which could in all circumstances be of a beneficial nature to any one: nor on the other hand if there were, would there be any act which it could ever be expedient that any person should be obliged under all circumstances to perform.

as an example of a conditional command. 'No man shall export wheat out of the country *when* the market-price at the place from whence it is meant to be exported is more than 44s. a quarter':[q] this may serve as an example of a conditional prohibition. 'No man is obliged to maintain his children':[r] this may serve as an example of an unconditional non-command. 'Any man may export corn out of the country': this may serve as an example of an unconditional permission. 'No man is obliged to maintain his children, if they are weakly or deformed':[s] this may serve as an example of a conditional non-command. 'Any man may export wheat out of the country when the market-price etc. is under 44s. a quarter': this may serve as an example of a conditional permission.

When a command is unconditional, that is when the act which is commanded is mentioned by itself without the mention of any circumstances, the intention of the legislator (at least for anything that is expressed) is that it shall be performed, whatever circumstances it be attended with, that is in any circumstances or cases whatsoever: in other words that every individual act of the class of acts signified by the generical words in question shall without exception be performed.

Limitative circumstances –words– clause– proposition

8. So likewise, *mutatis mutandis*, where the act is prohibited or left free. Let the command now be conditional; let certain circumstances be mentioned as those in which it is his will that the act should be performed: what is his intention now? what is the effect which the mention of those circumstances may be attended with?[t] Either it has none at all, and then the import of the command is neither more nor less than what it would have been if no such circumstances had been mentioned, or it has the effect of intimating that in these circumstances indeed it is his intention the act should be performed, but in these *only*: and that in cases where the act is not accompanied by these circumstances, he means not to express any such will about the matter: that where the act is not of the class to which the genus is reduced by the specificant terms in question, it is not the object of his will. The effect then of introducing

[q] British Statutes 13 Geo III c. 43 § 5.

[r] A liberty allowed by the law of Athens and many other Grecian states. Potter's Antiq. B. IV—Ch. 14.[1]

[s] A liberty allowed by a law of Sparta. *Ib.*[2]

[t] A new offence is made by the addition of specific circumstances. A command in this case extends only to this species.

[1] John Potter, *Antiquities of Greece* (first published 1697–9), 1775, vol. ii, part iv, ch. xiv, pp. 318–35: 'Of their Customs in Child-bearing and managing infants'.

[2] Potter, op. cit., ii, 359.

a specificant circumstance, is to set *limits* to the case in which it is his will that the act should be performed. These circumstances then may, with reference to the case in which the act is commanded to be performed, be styled *limitative circumstances*: the words by which they are made to have that effect, *limitative words* or *words of limitation*: the assemblage of those words, a limitative clause: and that clause if it be in such a manner detached from the rest of the words in the law as to form an entire proposition, may be termed a limitative proposition, or provision.

Exceptive circumstances

9. By the same operation every case which does *not* lie within the case composed of the same circumstances is *excepted* and thrown out as it were of the case in which it is his will the act should be performed: the same circumstance may therefore with reference to the case in which the act is commanded to be performed, and all the cases in which it is not commanded to be performed, be styled *exceptive* circumstances; to wit as taking these last cases out of the limits of the former. The words then are virtually words of exception: the clause, an exceptive clause: the proposition, an exceptive proposition.

In what cases the words are limitative; in what, exceptive

10. There are other words however by means of which the same effect may be produced in a more explicit and conspicuous manner. This is done by describing in positive terms the case which it is meant should *not* be regarded as included within that to which the expression of will has already been applied, at the same time mentioning the former as meant to be taken out of the latter. This is commonly what is done where such words as the words *exceptive clause* and *exceptive proposition* may be made use of. It is one and the same import which may be couched in either of the two forms of expression. In both ways the general and unlimited case which is constituted by the entire assemblage of all the circumstances with which the performance of the act can by possibility be attended is divided into two subordinate and more particular cases: one of which *is* that which the act must be in so as to be of the sort which the legislator commands to be performed; the other, *not*. Of these two subordinate cases it is the one or the other that is expressly mentioned according as the clause is in the limitative form, or in the exceptive: if in the limitative form, the former: if in the exceptive form, the latter. A limitation then is an indirect exception: an exception, an indirect limitation.

Example of a conditional law reduced to the unconditional form

11. To give an example: suppose a prohibitive law to this effect:[u]

[u] The difficulty of finding an example of an unconditional law of the affirmative kind has been already noticed (supra, 112 n.). It was scarce possible to find a

No man shall export corn out of the country, when the market-price (at
the place from whence it is meant to be exported) *is more than 44s.
a quarter.* This is a conditional prohibition: the act is that of exporting corn out of the country. This act then is capable of taking
place in either of two cases: in the case where the market price at
the place in question is greater than the sum specified: and in the
case where it is not greater than that sum. When the act then is in
the first of these cases, it *is* the lawgiver's intention that the prohibition should take place and that the act should *not* be done: he
accordingly subjoins the words 'where the market-price etc.' and
by so doing he narrows the unlimited extent which the prohibition
had while it was general, so as to confine or limit its application to
that particular case. Where the act is in the other particular case, it
is *not* his intention that the prohibition should take place: the act,
for any intention that he has to the contrary, may be performed or
not performed as a man pleases: narrowing then the general case to
the above particular and *limited* one, the other case is tacitly excepted and thrown out. Here then it is the limitation that is expressed; the exception being only implied. But the same provision
might have been expressed in the opposite way; so that the exception should have been expressed, and the limitation only implied.
'Any man may export corn out of the country: except where the
market-price is so and so.'

12. It appears then that the same species of act, the same com- *Circum-*
partment of the logical or generic whole may be expressed in either *stances etc.*
of the two ways; viz: by words of limitation or by words of excep- *tative or ex-*
tion. But although words of either import may by a particular mode *ceptive may*
of application be made to produce the same effect, yet in themselves *qualificative*
those words are different. As therefore on some occasions it may be
requisite to distinguish them, so on other occasions there may be a
conveniency in characterizing them indifferently by one common
name: accordingly whether it be by words of the one kind or of the
other that the sort of act denoted by the generic name is narrowed
and the species in question extracted out of it, the words may in
either case be termed words of *qualification*: the circumstances
denoted by them, qualificative circumstances: the clause composed
of them, a *qualifying* or *qualificative clause.*

13. It also appears that a conditional provision (a conditional *Provisions*
prohibition to keep to the same example) is convertible into two *unconditional*
provisions: a general unconditional permission, and a particular *tional inter-*
convertible
clear specimen but what if totally divested of all limitative as well as exceptive
clauses would appear too absurd to pass even in the way of supposition.

exceptive clause which stands opposed to it: and it is the exceptive clause that wears the aspect of which the provision, when in the conditional form, is expressive. Thus in the example above put— '*No man shall export corn*' etc. is a prohibition: accordingly the general clause '*Any man may export corn*' being a permission, the particular exceptive clause, '*except where the market-price is so and so*' operates as a prohibition likewise. In other words, a permission with an exception, is equipollent to a prohibition with a limitation.

In like manner a conditional command may be converted into a general non-command and a particular command in exception to it: so that a non-command with an exception is equipollent to a command with a limitation: a conditional non-command into a general command and a particular countermand in exception to it; so that a command with an exception is equipollent to a non-command with a limitation: a conditional permission into a general prohibition and a particular permission in exception to it: so that a prohibition with an exception is equipollent to a permission with a limitation.[v]

Qualificative matter may be placed all of it on either side

14. It may also happen that a law, although it be conditional, and thereby provided with limitations, may be provided with exceptions likewise: which indeed is most commonly the case. Even when in this form it may be converted into either of the simple forms above-mentioned: viz: that of an unconditional law with exceptions, or that of a conditional law without any. In short the qualificative matter may be placed either on both sides, or on one side only: and when on one side only, on either side indifferently. All this, as may easily be imagined from the examples already given, depends upon the turn and phraseology of the sentence. In some cases one of these forms is the most natural and commodious: in other cases another. This may be easily enough imagined: further details and distinctions would take up more room than can be allotted to them here.

An un-qualified law to be explicit must be translated into a qualified one

Words of limitation and exception various

15. It has been observed already that in the unconditional form specimens of affirmative laws are hardly to be found[w]: with laws of a negative aspect this is not altogether the case. Of laws of this kind

[v] As to the words and turns of expression by which a clause may be made to have the effect of a limitative or that of an exceptive clause, they are too numerous and too various to be here enumerated. Among words of limitation are, *where, when, only, if, so that, provided that*: among words of exception are *except, without, unless, except where, except when, but, yet, but not, but not if, if not, nevertheless, however, notwithstanding*; and the like. The way in which they may respectively be made productive of these effects depends upon the turn and fashion of the sentence.

[w] Supra, 112n, 114–15n.

a number of specimens such as they are might be produced: specimens in which the mandate is apparently not only unconditional, but altogether unqualified; to appearance at least[x] having neither limitations nor exceptions. Take for example the cases of murder, theft, embezzlement, extortion, peculation, rape, robbery, adultery, and so on.[y] Offences however which are characterizable in this manner bear but a very small proportion to the whole number of the acts which might be or of those which ought to be, created offences. Moreover even in these few while the prohibition continues in this simple and inexplicit form it can hardly answer the purposes of a law. Expressions of this kind may be compared to those literal symbols which in order to expedite the business of calculation are substituted by algebraists in the place of a long line of figures. Of themselves they signify nothing; they present no determinate idea any otherwise than through the medium of some other signs which they serve to bring to view. A proposition thus scantily expressed is rather an index to a law than a law itself. To render it explicit enough to be understood by those who are to obey or execute it, it must be taken to pieces as it were and made up again according to a fuller pattern. The short name given to the act must be laid aside and a definition substituted in its stead. Now when a definition is

[x] I say to appearance: for strictly speaking even the laws here alluded to, concisely as they are expressed must be acknowledged to be accompanied with limitations. Take for instance this law: 'Let no person commit theft.' The expression is grammatically speaking an elliptical one: to render it complete instead of *theft* we must say *act of theft*: 'let no man commit, i.e. perform an act of theft.' It is not here as in the case of the law against exporting corn where *corn* was the passible subject of the act signified by the verb *export*. (Supra, 115.) Here no passible subject is expressed at all: which is one cause of the obscurity of the law. All that is expressed is the agible subject '*person*' and the abstract act or motion, which in the first instance is here no otherwise characterized than by the *genus generalissimum* '*act*': to specificate which and reduce it within the intended compass the words '*of theft*' are immediately subjoined: No person shall perform any act of that sort which is known by the name of an *act of theft*. In this particular instance indeed and a few others the law may be expressed in a form which is strictly unconditional: 'let no person steal': so likewise 'let no person murder: let no person rob'. But among the laws here alluded to there are others with which this is not the case; for instance those against adultery and treason. This depends upon the idiom of the language. In English we cannot say let no man adulterize but in Latin we may say *non moechaberis*: and in Greek μη μοιχευσεις.

[y] Among the laws made against these offences there are a few which in certain cases, the appellation of the act remaining still the same, may apply to positive offences as well as negative. Thus the law against murder will include the law against starving to death, which may be performed without any positive act as in the case of a mother leaving her infant child to perish.

given in such case instead of the term to be defined, another term, the name of some superior genus is exhibited: and this superior genus in order to be narrowed down to the dimensions of the act in question, must be diminished by the application of a certain assemblage of qualifying clauses, applied to it in the shape either of limitations or of exceptions. To take for example the law against theft. 'Thou shalt not steal': or 'let no man commit theft.' This may be taken for a law against theft exhibited *in terminis*. It is expressed without any sort of qualification[z]: and so without any impeachment on the score of integrity it may be: for whatever circumstances relative to it may be brought to view, may be considered as included under the word *theft*. But what after all is theft? it is an idea the composition of which is so far from being determinate, that to this hour no tolerable definition of the word seems ever to have been given.[a2] It is the taking (that is the beginning to

[z] I mean taking the law to be framed, as here, according to the simplest pattern: so as to stand in the shape of a mere directive law, without any punitory law to give it force. It therefore needs no inculpative nor exculpative clauses but apply a punitive law to it together with a comminative clause and then as to exemptive clauses it will stand upon the same footing as every other law.

[a2] I do not mean to say but that the idea entertained of this offence by the generality of the people is in most cases clear enough for use: but for this idea, whatever it may be, they are indebted to their own observation, not to any explanation that has been ever given them of it by men of law.

Furtum is defined by Justinian (Inst. de oblig ex delict) *contrectatio fraudulosa* etc.[1] But what is meant by '*fraudulosa*'? this is shifting off the difficulty, not explaining it: he might as well have said *furtiva*.

English Lawyers to make the matter clearer add to the word *fraudulent* the word *felonious*: (Hawk. 89.[2] Burn, Larceny.[3]) but this again is only a roundabout way of saying *furtive*: Theft is the taking of a thing in circumstances in which the taking of it is punished by a certain punishment, which is the punishment inflicted on the act of taking when accompanied with circumstances which make it theft. Ld. Hale is honest enough to confess he does not know what those circumstances are. (H.H. 509).[4] This however was no hindrance to his hanging men for theft. It is one thing to conceive an idea, it is another thing to express it: it is one thing to form a particular idea on a particular occasion, it is another thing to abstract from it a general idea for all occasions.

[1] Inst. iv.i.1: 'Furtum est contrectatio rei fraudulosa vel ipsius rei vel etiam usus eius possessionisve quod lege naturali prohibitum est admittere.'

[2] William Hawkins, Serjeant-at-law, *A Treatise of the Pleas of the Crown*, 1739. Book I, ch. xxxiii, p. 89: 'Of Simple Larceny'.

[3] Richard Burn (ed.), *The Justice of the Peace and Parish Officer*, 1755, ii, 98–108.

[4] Matthew Hale (1609–76) was Lord Chief Justice from 1671 to 1676. His *History of the Pleas of the Crown* was published posthumously in 1713. Bentham's reference is to p. 509 of vol. i of the 1739 edition: ch. xliii, 'Of Larceny and its kinds' runs from p. 503 to p. 516.

occupy) a thing under certain circumstances. To make the law against theft intelligible enough to exhibit an idea of the offence it must accordingly be translated into a law that forbids the taking under certain circumstances; which circumstances when specified will constitute so many limitations or exceptions to the general prohibition against taking.

16. We are now in a condition to apprehend the use and effect of non-commanding and originally-permissive provisions. Of themselves, it is manifest, they can have none. A law of either kind, if that were all of it, would be nugatory and inoperative[b2]: since after the establishment of such a law the condition of the subject would be not a whit altered from what it was before. 'Any man may export corn out of Attica'—To what purpose would such a law have been to the Athenians? So might any man have done so soon as Triptolemus had taught them the arts of husbandry[1] and before ever they had learnt from Theseus to bear the bonds of government.[2] It might indeed have happened that Theseus or some of the intervening powers had previously to this allowance considered the traffic in question an object of prohibition: but then the law would have been not an unobligative, but a de-obligative one. The only use of a provision of either of the unobligative kinds is to introduce some provision of a more active and efficient nature: the former serving as a basis to which the latter in the shape of a limitation or an exception may adhere. When regarded in this point of view every efficient law whatever may be considered as a limitation or exception, grafted on a pre-established universal law of liberty: and thus a kind of medium of connection may be established in the mind, whereby the idea of every law that can be conceived may be confronted with, and rendered as it were commensurable to that of every other. Under the single term *acts* are included all the possible modifications of human conduct: add the several possible aspects or phases of the will, and you have the whole possible assemblage of laws as well as of autocratic ordinances. The will of the legislator like that of any other person is a uniform unvaried surface: susceptible indeed of as many different colours as it may have aspects: but in other respects deriving its distinctive character no otherwise than from the various images, which are reflected upon it

Use of non-commanding and originally-permissive provisions

[b2] Provisions of either kind might accordingly be termed provisions *inefficient per se*: in contradiction to which, provisions expressive of any of the other aspects may be termed *efficient per se*.

[1] Triptolemus was the legendary first priest of Demeter (cf. the *Hymn to Demeter* formerly attributed to Homer) and inventor of the plough (Virgil, *Georgics*, i.19).

[2] Theseus was credited with the union of Attica into a single state.

as it were from the several modes of conduct towards which it turns itself. The non-commanding and permissive phases of the law placed side by side and turned towards the universal system of human actions are expressed by the before-mentioned universal law of liberty: a boundless expanse in which the several efficient laws appear as so many spots; like islands and continents projecting out of the ocean: or like material bodies scattered over the immensity of space.

Limitations and exceptions to preceding limitations and exceptions

17. As any kind of provision which happens to take the lead, whether it be obligative, unobligative or de-obligative, may have its limitations and exceptions, so again may any of those limitations and exceptions have *their* limitations and exceptions; and so on through any number of alternations. In such case every such limitative or exceptive provision having the effect of narrowing the dominion as it were of that which stands next above it, widens in the same proportion that of the next but one: a qualification to a limitation widens the provision first limited: a qualification to an exception widens the provision first excepted from, just as in arithmetic, subtraction from a subtrahend is an addition to the minuend. Let the following chain of provisions serve for an example. 1. Leading provision in the form of a general permission: or 'any man may export corn out of the country'. 2. Exceptive clause having the effect of a particular prohibition: '*unless* the market-price be above 44s. a quarter': 3. Exceptive clause of the 2d order having the effect of a re-permission: 'and even then, if it be for the subsistence of the King's armies'. 4. Clause limitative of the last mentioned exceptive clause, and thereby re-extensive of the first prohibition: 'and provided a license from the first magistrate of the place have been previously obtained'.

Here the chain of provisions has four links in it. Convert the law into the conditional form and it has but three. 1. Leading provision in the form of a conditional prohibition—'no man shall export wheat out of the country where the market-price is above 44s. a quarter'. Exceptive clause having the effect of a particular permission—'unless it be for the subsistence of the King's armies'. Limitation to the above exception—'*and* the license from the first magistrate of the place have been previously obtained'.

The same limitation converted into an exception to the same exceptive clause: 'nor then, without a license from the first magistrate *of the place* have been previously obtained'.

An offence, what. Circumstances and clauses justificative, exculpative or de-obligative

18. When an act is taken for the object of a legislator's will, and that will is declared, the opposite act (in the case where such

120

declaration is meant to be enforced by motives of the coercive kind) is thereby rendered an offence: if the object of such will be an act of the positive stamp, then it is the opposite negative act that is converted into an offence: if that object were an act of the negative stamp, then the offence so created is the opposite positive act. In other words where the provision of the law is a command or a prohibition, it creates an offence: if a command, it is the non-performance of the act that is the offence: if a prohibition, the performance. The effect then which a limitative clause has upon such a provision is to take all other particular cases but the one marked out by the limitation out of that general one in which the performance of the act is an offence: as the effect of an exceptive clause is to take out of the general case the particular case itself to which the exception is applied. In either way then a circumstance is introduced which has the effect of taking the act in some particular case or other out of the general case in which the non-performance or the performance of it is an offence. Such circumstance may therefore be termed an *exculpative* or *justificative* circumstance: a circumstance *of exculpation* or *justification*: and the clause or provision which invests it with that character an *exculpative* or *justificative provision or clause*.[c2] Moreover the law, in constituting any act an offence, is said to impose thereby an *obligation* on the persons in question not to perform it: which obligation, upon the act's ceasing to be an offence, is taken away. The same circumstance may therefore be termed also upon occasion a *de-obligative circumstance*, and the clause a *de-obligative clause*: that is, provided the exception in taking the act out of the case in which it is commanded or prohibited stops there, and does not go on to place it in the case in which it is forbidden, and so *vice versa* in the case of a prohibition: in short provided the exception be simply contradictory and not contrariant to the clause to which it is applied: in this latter case the provision might with reference to the proceeding one, be termed *reversely-obligative*.

19. So on the other hand when the leading provision of the law is a non-command or a permission, (which is the case where the command or prohibition is conditional) there is no offence created by it:

Circumstances and clauses etc. inculpative and criminative

The word 'exemptive', why not used

[c2] It might also be termed *exemptive*. But this word we shall have occasion for by and by for the purpose of expressing an idea which is different from that which it is here intended to bring to view by the word *exculpative*; and to which this latter word would not be applicable: I mean the idea of a circumstance which takes an act out of the case in which it is thought proper to punish it, without taking it out of the case in which it is wished it were not done.

the effect then which a limitative clause has upon such a provision is to take all other particular cases but the one marked out by the limitation out of that general one in which neither the non-performance nor the performance of the act is an offence: as the effect of an exceptive clause is to take out of the general case the particular case itself to which the exception is applied. In either way then a circumstance is introduced which has the effect of taking the act in some particular case or other out of the general case in which the non-performance or the performance of the act is *not* an offence. Such circumstance may therefore be termed an *inculpative* and in some cases a *criminative* or *criminalizing* circumstance[d2]: and the clause which contains it, an inculpative, criminative, or criminalizing clause.[e2]

In what cases exculpative circumstances come first; in what, inculpative

20. According then as the mandate of the law is unconditional or conditional, the circumstances which make their appearance first are of the exculpative kind, or of the inculpative: if it be unconditional, of the exculpative kind; there being no room in the first instance for any that are inculpative: if conditional, of the inculpative kind: for the offence must first of all be created, before any limitations or exceptions can be applied to it: a *genus* of acts must first be expressed, before any species can be excluded or taken out of it.

The word criminative not applicable to all cases

[d2] Of these three words the words *criminative* or *criminalizing* would in all cases be the clearest were it not for the appearance they have of excluding all offences of inferior magnitude. This forms such an objection to the applying it to those offences as seems to be insurmountable.

Objection to the term inculpative

The objection to the word *inculpative* is that owing to the uncertain and ambiguous signification of the particle *in*, in the language from which it is taken, it may appear doubtful whether the idea meant to be annexed to it is that which it is here put to signify, or the opposite idea which is here denoted by the term *exculpative*. But this objection vanishes as soon as it is perceived that the former word is put in opposition to the latter. It must be confessed indeed that the sense here attributed to the word does not seem to be warranted by any Latin writer: it is made use of however in this sense by the French law. See Dict. de Trevoux verbo *Inculpation*.[1]

The word delinquefying or delinquefactive proposed

The term that would point in the clearest manner to the idea in question would be some such word as *delinquefying* or *delinquefactive*, if a term so novel and uncouth could be endured.

[e2] It may be worth while just to mention, that the absence of an exculpative circumstance is equipollent to the presence of one that is inculpative: and *vice versa*. This proceeds from the interconvertibility of limitations and exceptions.

[1] *Dictionnaire Universel François et Latin vulgairement appellé Dictionnaire de Trevoux*, 1752, vol. iv: 'Inculpation . . . Terme de Palais, qui s'emploie lorsqu'on attribue quelque faute à quelqu'un, qu'on l'accuse d'avoir fait quelque action reprehensible . . .'

21. Now the case is as hath already been observed[f2] that by far the greater part of the mandates that occur in a body of laws will be in the conditional form. In general then the circumstances that stand first in order in the texture of a law will be of the inculpative kind: there will come a certain number of circumstances of this nature before there come any that are exculpative.

Inculpative circumstances to be found in most laws

22. Exculpative circumstances then are limitations or exceptions to an obligatory or inculpative clause: inculpative circumstances, to a de-obligatory or exculpative one. If in an unconditional law after the first set of exculpative circumstances there come any that are inculpative, they are so many limitations or exceptions to preceding limitations and exceptions: so likewise if in a conditional law any that are exculpative come after the first set of inculpative ones. In this way then it is plain that sets of exculpative and sets of inculpative clauses may like any other limitations and exceptions[g2] follow each other alternately without end. To distinguish then a clause of any such sort from another clause of the same denomination, they might be numbered according to the order in which they make their appearance. Upon this plan they will stand thus: Where the mandate is unconditional; 1. exculpative circumstances of the first order: 2. inculpative circumstances of the first order: 3. exculpative circumstances of the 2d order: 4. inculpative circumstances of the 2d order: and so on: Where the mandate is conditional; 1. inculpative circumstances of the 1st order: 2. exculpative circumstances of the 1st order: 3. inculpative circumstances of the 2d order: 4. exculpative circumstances of the 2d order: and so on.[h2]

Exculpative and inculpative circumstances of the 1st, 2nd, etc. etc. orders

---

[f2] Supra, 116.

[g2] By way of illustration the cases constituted by the above circumstances might in conformity to the archetypation above suggested be represented under the similitude of a nest of boxes of opposite colours enclosed one within another: where the law is unconditional, first a black box; within that a white box; then a black one again; and so on: where it is conditional, first a white box; within that a black one; and then a white one again; and so on.

[h2] In the mutual allegation of circumstances thus militating one against another (that is of the existence of such or such a circumstance in the case in which the individual act in question was performed) consists what are called the *pleadings* in a cause: the *actionis instantia, exceptio, replicatio, duplicatio,* etc. of the ancient Roman Law: the *declaration, plea, replication, rejoinder,* etc. of the English Law. This is to be understood of the cases in which the plaintiff alleges a wrong to have been already done to him. In the cases where there is no complaint of that sort, the cause being of a purely civil nature, there it is plain the words *inculpative* and *exculpative* do not apply. Thus it is where the plaintiff does no more than claim to be invested with a right as yet not created

Pleadings in a cause explained

In uncondi-tional man-dates in-culpative circumstances may be termed re-inculpative

23. Where the mandate is unconditional the offence is created without the help of any inculpative circumstances: the effect then of the first set of inculpative circumstances that occur is not to place the act for the first time in the case in which it is an offence, but to bring it back into that case after it has been taken out of it by circumstances of the exculpative kind. In this case then the inculpative circumstances may all of them, even those of the 1st order, be termed *re-inculpative*. This will serve to show all along that the mandate is unconditional, and thereby distinguish the case from that in which the mandate is of the opposite complexion.

Principal or leading pro-vision, what

24. A legislative provision either contains a law of itself, or only goes towards the making up of a law by the help of others. Now of every group of legislative provisions making all together a law, one at least must be so expressed as to present the name of the act which is the object of the will in conjunction with words expressive of the aspect of the will towards that act: a provision so expressed may be termed the *principal* provision. If there are several so expressed then the appellation of principal provision may be given to that in which the name of the act is of the greatest amplitude: and of which what other provisions there are in the law are but so many qualificative or expository clauses. This to be understood of the case where the provision of the greatest amplitude is of the obligative or efficient kind[12]: where it is not, there the amplest of those that are obligative may be considered as the principal provision. These rules may easily be illustrated by turning to the examples already given.[12] In this latter case it is not the principal provision that stands first, but an un-obligative one, which, were it not for the use it may be of in serving as an introduction to some obligative provision, would be inefficient, and, in the way of original imperation at least, whatever purpose it might answer in the way of instruction or information, nugatory. But in other cases the principal provision will commonly stand first, and may on that account be also styled the *leading* one.

or not liquidated: or what comes to the same thing, demands that others shall be subjected to the obligation of doing or forbearing to do something or other for his benefit. In this case the terms *inculpative* and *exculpative* must be changed for some such words as *investitive* and *divestitive*. See Ch. xix (Corpus Juris).[1]

[12] Supra, 119.
[12] Supra, 120.

[1] This reference reflects an early stage in the evolution of the present work, when the chapter on 'Corpus Juris' was still conceived of as Ch. xix of *An Introduction to the Principles*, with 'Indirect Legislation' forming Ch. xviii, and the present work an extension of Ch. xvii.

§ v. *Extensive*

1. We set out with supposing the superventitious provision to *Provision extensive*
regard all along such a class of acts as is included within the same
bounds which limit the primordial. But it may happen, that the
primordial aspect may regard one act, and the superventitious
another not comprehended by the primordial: and yet, either on
account of the identity of the two aspects themselves, or on account
of some circumstance which enters in common into the description
of the acts which are respectively the objects of them, the provision
expressive of the latter will may be considered as connecting with
and exercising a sort of an influence over the provision expressive of
the former will. As to the acts, there are three descriptive circumstances any two of which they may have in common without belonging to the same genus, viz: the agible subject, the passible subject,
and the bare act which is the object. Hence it happens that when
upon the back of a provision which has already been expressed
there comes another relating to a distinct act in the description of
which some of the circumstances are made use of that served to give
the description of the former act, the two acts may be considered
as being both of them comprised under the first provision: which
however, as of itself it comprised only the first of them, is now
considered as having been altered and *extended* for the purpose;
by the operation of the second provision. This second provision
may in such case be spoken of as *extensive* with reference to the
former. To recur to the old example. Let the primordial provision
be—'No merchant shall export barley'. A provision extensive
of this might stand thus:—'The same provision which was made
concerning the non-exportation of barley by merchants shall extend to the growers'. In like manner importation might be added
to exportation: or wheat to barley.

It is evident that the extension in all those cases might more
clearly as well as more concisely be expressed by a distinct superventitious provision unconnected with the primordial. As thus:
'No merchant shall export barley':—'no grower of barley shall
export barley':—'no merchant shall import barley':—'no merchant
shall export wheat.' A circumstance however that may render it
convenient sometimes to make use of an extensive provision rather
than of an independent law is that by this means the qualifying
provisions and subsidiary laws belonging to one law may be taken
up as they stand and applied all together to another law: and thus a
considerable saving may be made in point of words.

It is evident that an extensive provision may apply to one provision of a law as well as to another: to any qualificative clause as well as to the principal: if it applies to a qualificative clause of the first order, it joins with it in narrowing the amplitude of the principal; if to one of the second order, in extending it: and so on through any number of alternations.[k2]

Provisions indirectly or virtually extensive

2. There is also another way in which a provision becomes entitled to the appellation of an extensive one. This is the case wherever there is a qualification of the second order narrowing one of the first: that which narrowed the principal provision being itself narrowed, the principal provision is thereby of course extended. In this way all qualificative clauses after those of the first order are extensive: extensive according to the order they are of, either of the principal provision, or else of the qualification of the first order by which the principal provision is narrowed: in which latter case they are restrictive of the principal provision. But in this way the extension that is applied to the principal provision is not applied in a direct way nor by such formulary as carries the idea of extension upon the face of it. They may therefore for distinctions sake be termed *indirectly* or *virtually* extensive.

Provisions may be issued uno or diverso flatu – difference between a provision, a law and a statute

3. Provisions, considered with respect to the relative time of their enactment may have been issued *uno flatu* or *diverso*. This distinction it may on various occasions be of use to bear in mind. Two or more provisions may be said to be issued *uno flatu* when they are authenticated[12] at one and the same time: *diverso flatu*, when at different times. Upon this distinction turns the difference between the object to which it is all along proposed to appropriate the term *law*, and that which is commonly known by some such names as *edict, ordinance*, or *statute*. A legislative provision as we have seen[m2] is by possibility the whole, but generally a constituent part only, of a law: a statute is either one or any other number of provisions which with respect to one another are issued *flatu uno*, with respect to all other provisions, *diverso*.

We have frequently had occasion to bring to view the distinction between the primordial aspect of the will and the superventitious. Where of two provisions that stand in connection with one another

---

[k2] See supra, 120.

[12] Any ceremonies employed as signs for the purpose of making known to the people that such or such a discourse is expressive of the will of the legislator may be styled *ceremonies of authentication*: and a legislative provision upon the fulfillment of such ceremonies may be said to be *authenticated*.

[m2] Supra, 124.

the aspect expressed by the one is superventitious with respect to that of which the other is expressive, this does not necessarily imply that they were issued *diverso flatu*; that they are provisions of different statutes. They must indeed if they are repugnant *in toto* and are both allowed to have a meaning: otherwise the legislator must be supposed to have been willing contradictions: willing that the same act shall be performed and not performed at the same time. But if repugnant *ex parte* or *pro tanto* only, that is, if they be qualificative one of another; in short, if they be anything but repugnant *in toto*, no such consequence follows: a repugnancy thus limited may as naturally take place within the limits of one single statute as within the compass of ever so many different statutes. Indeed without going into such a repugnancy as this there are in general no means of making the dimensions given to the act upon paper quadrate with those under which it presents itself to the will. There are few cases, as hath been observed, in which there are any single phrases by which the act (I mean always the class of acts) can be expressed exactly of its proper shape and size: in all other cases, the only expedient is to begin with a class that is too large and then reduce it to the requisite degree of amplitude, by a number of different provisions, which though in the order of conception they may perhaps have been contemporary and thereby all of them equally primordial, must in the order of enunciation be successive, and thereby one after another superventitious.

4. As to qualificative provisions, and such expositive ones as apply only to single words, from the account that has been given of them it will appear that so long as they possess the precise form from which they take their names they cannot by themselves convey any intimation of the legislator's will. Yet some share in the expression of that will it is evident they must have. To estimate the amount of this share it must be extracted from the rest, and delivered in separate propositions. Now a superventitious provision, we may remember, if not re-iterative of the primordial must be alterative. Being re-iterative, if it is not re-iterative *in toto*, it is re-iterative *pro tanto*: being alterative, if it is not revocative *in toto* it must be revocative in part. Accordingly a provision of the expositive kind may be rendered into an independent provision, re-iterative as far as it goes with respect to the primordial one of which it is expositive: this is but the converse of what has been shewn already. So on the other hand, a provision which is qualificative may be rendered into an independent provision, revocative, that is destructive as far as it goes, of the primordial one which it qualifies. This with respect to

Provisions expositive and qualificative, how reducible to independent provisions

an exceptive provision is seen immediately: and it is equally true of
a limitative provision; since there is no limitation as we have seen,[n2]
but may be rendered into an exception.[o2]

'No man shall export wheat when the market-price etc. is more
than 44s. a quarter—*except* it be for the use of the King's armies':—
Here the leading provision (which is a conditional one) is obligative:
the exception therefore being revocative *pro tanto* of the principal
provision is not obligative. 'Any person may export corn for the use
of the King's armies.'

It may be observed that in passing from the dependent to the
independent form, the provision is changed from a de-obligative one
into one that is simply un-obligative, by which means the reference
it bears to the principal provision which it was employed to qualify
is no longer apparent upon the face of it. In this case it would
appear an absurdity, were two provisions that were thus related to
be placed close together in the same statute, without the insertion
of some adversative particle or other (such as *but, nevertheless, provided always,* and the like) for the purpose of giving notice of such
relation: it would look as if the legislator himself could not see what
he was doing.

*Recapitula-
tion*
5. Thus much concerning the several aspects of which the will of
a legislator is susceptible, and the several sorts of provisions in
which they may display themselves when expressed in words. In
order to present a summary view of their mutual relations and
dependencies, their several agreements and diversities, the following analytic sketches, framed according to the exhaustive method,
may be not without their use.

First then with regard to the aspects of which any single provision
may be expressive, no regard being had to the connection it may
have with any other provisions.

A provision is either significant (as such) of itself, or not but by

---

[n2] Supra, 115.

[o2] Accordingly what has been said of qualificative provisions lying one within
another in alternation (Supra, 123 and n. g2), may be said of provisions of the
same purport when thrown into the independent form. Independent provisions
of one and the same aspect respecting acts standing in logical subalternation
under one and the same *genus generalissimum* are boxes of the same colour
enclosed one within another: independent provisions of different aspects
respecting acts that are in like manner subalternate to one another are boxes of
opposite colours enclosed one within another in the same manner: the general
law of liberty which for its object has the *genus generalissimum* indicated by
the word *act* without addition, being as it were the outside box which encloses
all the rest (supra, 123 n. g2).

reference to others. A legislative provision that is significant of itself stands either insulated or in connection with others: if insulated, it makes a whole law: if in connection with others, it makes a part only of a law.

Provisions that are significant of themselves are either unobligative or obligative, otherwise termed imperative. Provisions that are significant only by reference to others are provisions extensive, expositive, de-obligative, limitative, and exceptive.

Secondly, to consider a provision with relation to the differences of aspect and the connection it may have with other provisions, both at once.

A legislative provision then is either *primordial* or superventitious.

A primordial provision is either obligative or unobligative.

A primordial provision when obligative is either an original command or an original prohibition.

A primordial provision when unobligative is either a non-command or an original permission.

A superventitious provision is either un-alterative of the primordial one, or alterative.

If unalterative, it is either re-iterative of it (viz: *in toto*) or expositive, viz: reiterative (*pro tanto*).

If alterative, it is either unextensive of it or extensive.

If unextensive, it is either destructive (viz: *in toto*); or qualificative; (i.e. destructive *pro tanto*).

If destructive, it is either revocative or reversive.

If revocative, it is in itself either de-obligative or obligative.

If de-obligative, it is a countermand or a re-permission.

If obligative, it is either a command as before, or a prohibition, as before.

If reversive, it is either a prohibition or a command: a prohibition instead of a command: or a command instead of a prohibition.

If qualificative, it is either limitative or exceptive.

§ vi. *Repugnancy*

When two laws appear to disagree in their terms, a great question is often made whether they are or are not repugnant. The occasion on which it is brought upon the carpet is generally where the two laws in question emane the one of them from a superior the other from an inferior legislature. The question then is in truth a great question of constitutional law: but since the word which is the subject of it is one of those which appears to be expressive of the *Repugnancy, what aspect* of a superventitious law to a primordial one, it seems to have some claim to be considered here.

Hitherto the primordial provision and the superventitious have been considered as emaning from the same source: so long as this is the case the word repugnant may be looked upon as synonymous to alterative. Repugnancy may accordingly be simply revocative or reversive: and in either case either *in toto* or *pro tanto*. In this case the superventitious law then which upon the words of it is either *in toto* or *pro tanto* reversive or revocative of the primordial one is repugnant to it. But this is not the meaning that is commonly annexed to the word repugnant: repugnancy as between laws is not commonly judged of from the words of them. The laws of different states how different soever from each other are not commonly spoken of as repugnant. For repugnance carries with it the idea of incompatibility, and intimates that the laws of which it is predicated cannot both of them have their effect. But the laws of Great Britain have in the main all the effect they are designed to have notwithstanding the laws of France: the laws of France all the effect they are designed to have, notwithstanding the laws of Great Britain. The laws therefore of Great Britain and those of France are not spoken of as repugnant to each other—Why? because they have not the same persons nor consequently the same individual acts for their objects. The laws of Great Britain forbid the saying of mass: the laws of France not only permit it but enjoin it. Does that make any repugnancy? by no means: and why? because the former laws have one set of persons, the latter another set of persons in view, they move in different orbits. They are not at odds—they do not clash nor interfere: they are disparates, and among disparates there is no repugnancy.

Yet in words they shall be as opposite as any can be: at least if they are not so in any point it is only by accident: owing to some accidental mention which is made of the territory or the persons to which the operation of them is respectively meant to be confined. The reason is that the species of acts to which they respectively apply, these species I say howsoever identical they may appear to judge of them by the words of the law, are in truth altogether different and distinct. It has been already observed that differences between objects in point of time make differences in species, although such differences do not appear upon the face of any names by which those objects are characterized. For species are but groups of individuals: and any one group so as the limits of it can be marked out by general description has as good pretensions to be reckoned a species as another. The English soldiery subsisting in the year 1780 form a group as distinct from that of the English soldiery of 1680, or the French soldiery of either 1780 or 1680, as that of the clergy of either of those nations at either of those periods: yet upon the face of the laws those different groups of soldiers might chance to be all characterized by the same name.

There is no repugnancy then, according to the import commonly given to the word in the English language (for unfortunately there is no writing in more than one language at a time) there is no repugnancy I say between laws made by independent sovereignties, each moving within their proper sphere. There is no repugnancy between laws which have not the same individual persons and things for their subjects, the same individual acts for their objects.

Is there then a repugnancy in all cases where the tenor of the laws being contradictory or contrary, the individual subjects and objects are the same? Nor here neither in all cases.

The occasion on which in the nation of whose language I am writing the word *repugnancy* has been the most frequently made use of is that where powers of legislation have been delegated from a superior to a subordinate authority; and to speak more particularly from the sovereignty or representative of the sovereignty of a mother country to a body of subjects colonizing in a distant region: although it is equally applicable to every case where there is a delegation of legislative power. Power has been granted for instance by the representative of the English sovereignty to persons of a limited description among a tribe of settlers in Virginia to make laws for the government of themselves and the rest of the settlers in that country, with this proviso that such laws shall not be repugnant to the laws of England: at the same time it is declared that those settlers carry with them the whole body of English laws then subsisting. If all laws whatever are repugnant that contain opposite provisions, (I mean either contrariant or simply contradictory) even with relation to the same individual acts of the same individual persons, these two provisions are in fact contradictory and incompatible. For in a settled commonwealth how can any new law that is not being a merely reiterative one be made that is not as far as it goes either contrary or at least contradictory to the old. If it repeals a mandate whether *in toto* or *pro tanto* the case is clear upon the first stating: nor will it after a little reflection be found otherwise where a coercive mandate is established, in a case where the subject was at liberty before. For whatever the law permits a man to perform or to abstain from, it inhibits all others from compelling him to abstain from or to perform. The latter prohibition indeed is not the work of the same law as the former permission but it is the work of a law which never fails to be annexed to the former by the customary if not by the statute law.

The restriction then literally taken is destructive of the power. To reconcile them I know of no other way of interpreting them than by putting the following restrained sense upon the restriction. The subordinate authority has power to enact within the provincial territory all laws whatsoever which the metropolitan legislature within the limits of the metropolitan territory has power to enact; that is, unless any particular reason can be given to the contrary, any laws whatsoever. This being the general rule, there are two exceptions to it. 1. where the provincial law is contrariant either *in toto* or *pro tanto* to any of the reservations of superiority that are made already in the charter: 2. where it is contrariant to any subsequent laws of the metropolitan legislature made with the express intention of their extending to the province. These then are the two only cases of repugnancy: and thus it is that the meaning of the word repugnant as applied to a superventitious law differs from that of the word alterative and those which are synonymous to or included under it. Where the superventitious law emanes from the same authority as the primordial did, there is no distinction; if alterative it is as far as it goes repugnant. But where the primordial having emaned from a superordinate authority the superventitious law emanes from an authority deriving its powers from that from which the primordial law emaned, in such cases how ample soever the alteration be which it introduces, there are only two sets of laws of those established by the superordinate authority, by the repeal or reversal of which the system of legislation established by the subordinate authority can be repugnant to that of the superordinate: 1. those which are specially established at the very time of the concession: 2. such others as from time to time are established by the superordinate authority under the declared intention of their extending over the territorial or other field of dominion conceded to the subordinate.

The above may serve for a general sketch of the principles upon which the import of the word *repugnancy* as applied to the acts of a subordinate legislature as such is to be determined. To apply them in detail is a task that belongs to the particular department of public or constitutional jurisprudence.

CHAPTER XI

FORCE OF A LAW

1. [Tenthly,] with respect to the *force* of the law: that is, with respect to the motives it relies upon for enabling it to produce the effects it aims at. Motives of some sort or other to trust to it evidently must have: for without a cause, no such thing as an effect: without a motive, no such thing as action. What then are motives? We have seen that they are but the expectations of so many lots of pain and pleasure, as connected in a particular manner in the way of causality[a] with the actions with reference to which they are termed *motives*.[b] When it is in the shape of pleasure they apply, they may be termed *alluring* motives: when in the shape of pain, *coercive*.[c] It is when those of the alluring kind are held up as being connected with an act, that a *reward* is said to be offered: it is when those of the coercive kind are thus held up, that a *punishment* is said to be denounced.

Motives a law relies on, alluring or coercive— reward or punishment

2. The next question is from what source these motives may issue. Now it has already been observed, that of the four sources from whence pain and pleasure may be said to take their rise, there are three which are under the influence of intelligent and voluntary agents; viz: the political, the moral, and the religious sanctions. The legislator then may, in the view of giving efficacy to his laws take either of two courses: he may trust altogether to the auxiliary force of the two foreign sanctions, or he may have recourse to motives drawn from that fund which is of his own creation. The former of these courses is what has sometimes been taken with success[d]: there seem even to be cases in which it is to be preferred to any other. These cases however are in comparison but rare. For the most part it is to some pleasure or some pain drawn from the political sanction itself, but more particularly, as we shall see presently, to pain that the legislator trusts for the effectuation of his will.

Sources from whence they may issue— the moral, religious, or political sanctions

---

[a] Ch. vii (Actions).[1]
[b] Ch. x (Motives).[2]
[c] Ch. xvi (Division).[3]
[d] See Ch. xviii (Indirect Legislation).[4]

[1] *An Introduction to the Principles*, Ch. vii.
[2] Ibid., Ch. x.
[3] Ibid., Ch. xvi.
[4] Cf. 62 above, n. l.

12—I.G.   **133**

3. This punishment then, or this reward, whichever it be, in order to produce its effect must in some manner or other be announced: notice of it must in some way or other be given, in order to produce an expectation of it, on the part of the people whose conduct it is meant to influence. This notice may either be given by the legislator himself in the text of the law itself, or it may be left to be given, in the way of customary law by the judge: the legislator, commanding you for example to do an act: the judge in his own way and according to his own measure punishing you in case of your not doing it, or, what is much less frequent, rewarding you in case of your doing it. As to the particular nature of customary law, more will be said of it by and by.

4. But the most eligible and indeed the most common method of giving notice is by inserting a clause on purpose: by subjoining to that part of the law which is expressive of the legislator's will, another part of the office of which is to indicate the motive he furnishes you with for complying with such will.

In this case the law may plainly enough be distinguished into two parts: the one serving to make known to you what the inclination of the legislator is: the other serving to make known to you what motive the legislator has furnished you with for complying with that inclination: the one addressed more particularly to your understanding; the other, to your will. The former of these parts may be termed the *directive*: the other, the *sanctional* or *incitative*.

5. As to the incitative this it is evident may be of two kinds: when the motive furnished is of the nature of punishment, it may be termed the *comminative* part, or *commination*: when it is of the nature of reward, the *invitative* part, or *invitation*.

6. Of the above two methods of influencing the will that in which punishment is employed is that with which we are chiefly concerned at present. It is that indeed of which we hear the most and of which the greatest use is made. So great indeed is the use that is made of it, and so little in comparison is that which is made of reward, that the only names which are in current use for expressing the different aspects of which a will is susceptible are such as suppose punishment the motive. Command, prohibition, and permission, all of them point at punishment: hence the impropriety we were obliged to set out with, for want of words to remedy it.

7. The case is that for ordinary use punishment is beyond com-

[1] Bentham in fact reversed the order of these two headings in his marginal heading, which makes the use of 'former' and 'latter' in the next heading a source of confusion.

parison the most efficacious upon the whole. By punishment alone it seems not impossible but that the whole business of government might be carried on: though certainly not so well carried on as by a mixture of that and reward together. But by reward alone it is most certain that no material part of that business could ever be carried on for half an hour.[e]

[e] The reasons why the principal part of the business of government cannot be carried on any otherwise than by punishment are various: among which there are several which would each of them be abundantly sufficient of itself.

Why government cannot be carried on by reward alone

1. In the first place, any man can at any time be much surer of administering pain than pleasure.

2. The law (that is, the set of persons employed for this purpose by the legislator) has it still less in its power to make sure of administering pleasure than particular persons have: since the power of administering pleasure depends upon the particular and ever-changing circumstances of the individual to whom it is to be applied: (See Ch. (Sensibility)[1] of which circumstances the law is not in any way of being apprised. In short the law seems to have no means of administering pleasure to any man by its own immediate operation: all it can do is to put the instrument in his way, and leave him at liberty to apply it himself for that purpose if he thinks proper: this is accordingly what the law does when it is said to give a man a pecuniary reward.

3. The scale of pleasure supposing it actually applied is very short and limited: the scale of pain is in comparison unlimited.

4. The sources of pleasure are few and soon exhausted: the sources of pain are innumerable and inexhaustible. It has already been observed that the only means the law has of administering pleasure to a man is by placing the instruments of it within his reach. But the number and value of these instruments is extremely limited. Any object in nature may be converted into an instrument of pain: few in comparison and rare are those which are calculated to serve as instruments of pleasure.

5. The law has no means of producing pleasure without producing pain at the same time: which pleasure and which pain being considered by themselves apart from their effects, the pain is more than equivalent to the pleasure. For, an instrument of pleasure before it can be given to one man must have been taken from another: and since *ceteris paribus* it is more painful to lose a given sum than it is pleasurable to gain it, the pain produced by the *taking* is upon an average always more than equivalent to the pleasure produced by the *giving*.

6. The insufficiency of rewards is more particularly conspicuous when applied to acts of the negative kind. The acts of a positive kind of which it is necessary to enjoin the performance are always made referable to some definite possible subject, and included within a definite portion of time: such as to pay money on a certain occasion to a certain person: to lend a hand to the repair of a certain road for such a number of days; and so forth. But acts of a negative kind are commonly comprised under no such limitations. Take for instance the not stealing, and the not doing damage to the roads. Now by not stealing is meant the not stealing from any person any stealable articles at any time: but

---

[1] *An Introduction to the Principles*, Ch. vi. Bentham's note omits the number of the chapter.

Hence the idea of punishment is with difficulty separable from that of law

8. The sense of mankind on this head is so strong and general, however confused and ill developed, that where the motives presented to the inclination of him whose conduct it is proposed to influence are of no other than the alluring kind, it might appear doubtful perhaps whether the expression of the will of which such conduct is the object could properly be styled a law. The motives which the law trusts to are in most cases of a coercive nature: hence the idea of coercion shall in their minds have become inseparably connected with that of a law. Being then an invitation, that is an expression of will trusting for its efficacy to motives not coercive, they will conclude that it can not with propriety be styled a law.[f]

An invitative or praemiary law

9. The conclusion however seems not to be a necessary one. For as these invitations are as much the expressions of the will of a lawgiver as commands themselves are, as they issue from the same source, tend to the same ends, are susceptible of the same aspects, applicable to the same objects, and recorded indiscriminately in the same volumes with those expressions of will which beyond dispute are entitled to the appellation of a law, it should seem that without any great incongruity, they might be established in the possession of the same name. To distinguish, however, a law of this particular kind from the other, it should never be mentioned but under some particular name, such as that of an *invitative* or *praemiary* law; or it might be styled a *legislative invitation*, or a *bounty*.

A law with an alternative sanction

10. As a law may have sometimes a penal sanction to back it, sometimes a sanction of the praemiary kind, so may it, (as is obvious) be provided with two opposite sanctions, one of the one

persons are numerous, stealable articles still more so, and time indefinitely divisible. If then Paul for example were to be rewarded for not stealing it must be in some such way as this: for not stealing from Peter a farthing at 12 o'clock, one shilling: for not stealing another farthing from the same Peter at the same time, another shilling: for not stealing another farthing from the same Peter at a moment after 12, another shilling: for not stealing from John a farthing at such a place at 12 o'clock, another shilling: the same sums to be given also to Peter and John for not stealing from Paul: and so on for everlasting.

[f] In the nomenclature as well as in the practice of the law, it is upon punishment that every thing turns: nothing upon reward. Try, for instance, the words *obligation, duty, right, power, title, possession,* and *conveyance.* Take away the idea of punishment, and you deprive them of all meaning. A set of fictitious entities analogous to these might indeed be conceived to be generated by reward. But they would evidently be of a very flimsy consistence in comparison of the objects men have hitherto been accustomed to call to mind upon the mention of those names. The obligation would be a cobweb; the duty, a feather; the right, power, title, possession, conveyance not worth a straw.

kind, the other of the other. A law thus provided may be styled *a law with an alternative sanction.* In this case the mode of conduct with which the one of these sanctions is connected is the opposite to that with which the other is connected. If the one sanction is connected with the positive act, the other sanction is connected with the correspondent negative act. Take the following example. Whosoever comes to know that a robbery has been committed, let him declare it to the judge: if he declares it accordingly, he shall receive such or such a reward: if he fails to declare it, he shall suffer such or such a punishment.

11. We are now arrived at the notion of an object which might in a certain sense admit of the appellation of a law. It may even be looked upon as constituting a law and something more: since there are to be found in it two distinguishable parts: the directive part, which must of itself be a complete expression of will, and an article of a different nature, a *prediction.*[g] But nothing hath as yet been brought to view by which the efficacy of the directive part, or the verity of the predictive can have been established upon any solid footing. Let the law stop here, and let the influence of the two auxiliary sanctions be for a moment set aside, what has been done by the law as yet amounts to nothing: as an expression of will, it is impotent; as a prediction, it is false. The will of the legislator concerning the matter in question has indeed been declared: and punishment has been threatened in the case of non-compliance with such will: but as to the means of carrying such threats into execution, nothing of this sort hath as yet been made appear. *[margin note: Law principal– subsidiary]*

What course then can the legislator take? There is but one, which is to go on commanding as before: for as to taking upon himself the infliction of the punishment with his own hands, this, were it practicable in every case which it manifestly can not be, would be overstepping the bounds of his own function and exercising a different sort of power.[h] All he can do then in his capacity of legis-

[g] A prediction is the expression of an act of the understanding, whereby a man declares it to be his opinion or belief that such or such an event is certain or more or less likely to happen in time future.

[h] What then is this unnamed sort of power, which is different from, and the necessary complement to the imperative? This we must see presently: for without it our notions of dominion whether private or public, beneficial or fiduciary, in short all our notions about government and property would be imperfect. Meantime, whatever it be, it is plain that if it be anything, the power of legislation, though it be supreme and unlimited legislation, nay, even the entire power of imperation, though that too be supreme and unlimited imperation, is not self-sufficient and complete. It is in fact but half the power which *[margin note: Of perfect dominion power of imperation is but one half; power of contrectation being the other]*

137

^h cont.

those by whose submission and obedience dominion is constituted are capable of conferring, and which must be exercised ere property can be enjoyed or government carried on.

Dominion consists in the exercise of power. The faculties by which a being of any kind, rational or irrational, animated or inanimate, is capable of being the subject of power are all reducible to two classes, those which are merely passive, and those which are active or self-moving: the former are common to beings animated and inanimate, the latter belong to such as are animated alone; that is to such only as are endued with the faculty of volition. Power which is exercised over the passive faculties may be styled in a large sense *power of contrectation*; that which is exercised over the active or self-moving faculties, *power of imperation*. Power of contrectation, (for by this name I am reduced to call it for want of one more apposite and comprehensive) must be distinguished into that which is properly, and that which is improperly, so called: the former might be termed the power of *physical* contrectation; the latter, the power of *hyperphysical* (that is *superphysical*) contrectation. The former is that which is exercised over the body of the subject, and may be exercised as well over inanimate as over animated subjects: the latter that which is exercised over the faculties, meaning here the passive faculties, of the mind; and can of course be exercised over animated beings alone. As to the inferior animals, their pathological faculties being commonly disregarded more than is consistent with humanity, and their intellectual faculties than is consistent with just reasoning, they are commonly spoken of as being subject to no other power than that of contrectation; and stand accordingly degraded into the class of things. Instead of the *power of contrectation*, we might say, making use of a term more familiar but less apposite, the *power of action*: or making use of a term more apposite, but altogether new and unfamiliar, epergastic power, ἐπι, upon, εργαζομαι to act.

Power of contrectation is in private dominion, the power which a man exercises over the land he walks over or cultivates: the bread he bakes or eats: the coat he wears or brushes: the child or the servant he feeds, beats or reprimands: in public dominion, the power of the soldier over the persons, and occasionally over the property, of those whom he is commanded or allowed to treat as enemies: of the executioner or other inferior ministers of justice over the persons and properties of those who come under the control or censure of the law: and indirectly the power of the public gunsmith, the public gunpowder maker, the public storekeeper, and so forth, over the things they make or keep or use for the benefit of the public.

Power of imperation is in private dominion the power which the master exercises over the will of his servant, the parent over that of his child, the husband over that of his wife, the guardian over that of his ward: in public dominion that which the sovereign exercises over the will of his subjects, the general over that of his soldiers and occasionally over that of other persons who come within the sphere of his command, the judge over that of the persons who are subject to his jurisdiction.

Power of contrectation is most apt to be the power of the many: power of imperation, to be the power of the few.

Power of imperation, as we have seen already, may in an infinite variety of ways be broken into shares: in the same manner may the power of contrectation: the latter however is not so apt to be thus broken, as the former.

lator is to issue a second law, requiring some person to verify the prediction that accompanied the first. This secondary law being issued in aid of the primary may with reference thereto be termed the *subsidiary* law: with reference to which the primary law may on the other hand be termed the *principal*.

12. To whom is it then that this subsidiary law should be addressed? It can never be the same person to whom the principal law was addressed: for a man *can* not reward himself; nor *will* he punish himself. It must therefore be to some other person: a circumstance which of itself is sufficient to shew that the principal and subsidiary are two distinct laws, and not parts of one and the same law. It may be any other person indefinitely. Commonly however it is to some particular class of persons, who, occupying some particular station or civil condition instituted for the purpose, such as that of judge, are presumed on the one hand to be properly qualified, on the other hand to be previously disposed, to execute or cause to be executed any such commands when issued by the legislature.

The subsidiary law addressed commonly to the judge

13. But neither can the hand nor the eye of the judge reach every-

Who must have assistants—hence more subsidiary laws

ʰ cont.

Power of imperation as we have seen in the text, rests ultimately upon the power of contrectation; since all punishment is an exercise of the power of contrectation; those punishments excepted which apply themselves to the active faculty, such as banishment; and even these depend for their efficacy upon those which apply to the passive faculty.

Finally, in an established commonwealth, of the power of all subordinate power-holders the ultimate efficient cause is the command or allowance of the sovereign: of the power of the sovereign himself the constituent cause is the submission and obedience of the people.

As to rights, they are either rights of dominion, or mere liberties, rights of exemption from dominion: rights of dominion are either entire powers (for every power is a right) or shares of powers: for every right is not a power. See supra, Ch. IX.

The plan of arrangement in which *powers* and *rights* are the leading terms is more particularly adapted to the civil branch of the law; and more especially to that subordinate branch of it which may be termed the constitutional: as that in which the laws and offences are the leading terms is more particularly adapted to the penal. By what is here said of the power of contrectation, added to what has been said in Ch. IX of the power of imperation, the limits of the private part of the civil branch and more clearly those of the constitutional part are marked out, and the possible modifications of constitutional power, and the possible combinations of those modifications, viz: the possible forms of government, brought within our grasp.

As to the two plans just mentioned: the power of imperation being the same thing with the power of creating offences; it is thus that the two plans above mentioned coincide: the power of contrectation is the power of doing those acts which are necessary, amongst other purposes, for that of punishing offences, and which where this power is wanting, are offences of themselves.

where: to be in a condition to discharge his functions he must be provided with a variety of assistants: which assistants must for certain purposes be of various ranks, occupations and descriptions: witnesses, registers, court-keepers, jail-keepers, bailiffs, executioners, and so forth. Of these there are many who must begin to act in their respective characters even before the matter is submitted to his cognizance: consequently before they can be in a way to receive any commands from him. On this and other accounts they too must have their duties prescribed to them by the law itself: and hence the occasion for so many more subsidiary laws or sets of subsidiary laws, of which they are respectively the agible subjects, and their acts the objects.

On what circumstances the number of these depends

14. It is evident that the number and nature of the subsidiary laws of this stamp will be determined by the number and nature of the different sorts of acts which on the part either of the same person or of different persons it is thought proper should be performed or abstained from in the course of the *procedure*. Now by the procedure is meant on the present occasion[1] the suite of steps which are required to be taken in the view of ascertaining whether a man has or has not done an act of the number of those which stand prohibited by some principal law: and thereby of ascertaining whether he is or is not of the number of those persons, on whom a punishment of the sort denounced by the principal law in question is required to be inflicted.

Subsidiary laws proximate–remote: the proximate punitory or remunerative

15. Amidst this various train of laws subsidiary, that which is addressed to the judge and contains the command to punish, may for distinction's sake be termed the punitive or *punitory* law: and with reference to the rest the *proximate* subsidiary law: the rest may indiscriminately be termed *remote*. Where the principal law is of the praemiary kind, the proximate subsidiary law may be termed *remunerative*.

Laws substantive –adjective

16. Now it is evident that in like manner as a principal law must have its subsidiary laws, so also must each of those subsidiary laws have a train of subsidiary laws to itself, and that for the same reason. This is a circumstance that belongs alike to every law which takes its support from the political sanction. *A* commits an offence:

[1] All judiciary or contentious procedure as there will be occasion to shew hereafter (infra, Ch. xviii)[1] is divisible into procedure *delicti causâ* and procedure *petitionis causâ*. The former comes nearest to what is commonly meant by penal procedure, the latter to what is meant by civil procedure. The former is that with which we are concerned at present.

[1] Ms., '§ 19 or 20'.

it is thereupon rendered the duty of *B* to contribute in such or such
a way to the bringing of him to punishment in the event of his
proving guilty: and a particular process is appointed to be carried
on for ascertaining whether he be or no. In the course of that process
such and such steps are required to be taken by *C* in such and such
contingencies: such and such others by *D* and *E* and *F*: and so on
indefinitely. But what if *B* also proved refractory? a similar process must thereupon be carried on and a similar provision made by
the law for the bringing of him also to punishment: and so on if any
failure should arise on the part of *D* or *E* or *F*. In this way must
commands follow upon commands: if the first person called does
not obey, the second may: if the second should not, yet a third may:
if even the third should fail, yet there may be hopes of a fourth. If it
is not expected that anyone will obey, the law is plainly impotent
and falls to the ground: but let obedience be but expected from
any one of the persons addressed, at whatever distance he stands
from him who was addressed first, this expectation may prove
sufficient to keep all the intermediate persons to their duty. If an
offence then be committed, until obedience takes place on the part
of some one person or other of the persons thus connected, the law
is as it were asleep, and the whole machine of government is at a
stand: but let any one law in the whole penal train meet with
obedience, let punishment take place in any quarter, the law awa-
kens out of its trance, and the whole machine is set agoing again:
the influence of that law which has met with obedience flows back as
it were through all the intermediate laws till it comes to that principal one to which they are all alike subsidiary.[1]

To every law then, subsidiary ones as well as others, there must
be others which with reference to it are subsidiary: so far all laws
which for their support depend solely on the political sanction
are upon a footing. There are however certain laws in particular
which and which alone although like the rest they have their set of
subsidiary laws belonging to them, do not themselves stand in that
relation to any other laws. In this predicament stand those which
we set out with mentioning under the appellation of principal ones.
There are then two sorts of laws: one of which are altogether
principal without being subsidiary to any: the other subsidiary and
principal at the same time. As to these latter however the subsidiary
character is that in which they cannot but appear in the first

---

[1] Bentham has made the following notes at this point: 'Take notice that this not a
certain consequence. State here the instance of the Sheriff, Coroner and [*last word
illegible*]'.

instance. They not only could not have any effect, but they could not be understood, nor even have existence, without having a principal law to refer to: the idea of such a law being included in their very essence. 'Punish him who refuses to bear his part in bringing to punishment those who commit murder,' is the law which supposes the existence of a law against committing murder. On the other hand a law which forbids the committing of murder is not only possible and intelligible, but may even possess a certain degree of efficacy, although there were no such thing as any other law in the world: to wit by the help of the two auxiliary sanctions. Those laws then which cannot stand alone, but require to be preceded by some other to which they may adhere, may on that account be styled *adjective* or *enclitic* laws[j]: those of the opposite description, *substantive* or *self-subsisting*. To the adjective class belong all laws relative to the course of judiciary procedure.[k]

Connection between the principal law and its proximate subsidiary

17. To consider the proximate subsidiary law, it is evident that between that and the principal, distinguishable as they are, there cannot but be a very intimate connection and dependence. On the one hand the principal law by its comminative part has an essential reference to the subsidiary; of the contents of which if that reference be expressed it must necessarily give some general intimation. The business of the former being to predict that same evil which it is the business of the latter to endeavour to produce.

On the other hand the description and texture of the subsidiary law must of course be determined in great measure by that of the principal. There is always one person who is concerned in both: the person whose obedience is required by the principal law, and for whose punishment in case of his not obeying provision is made by the subsidiary law. This person after having been considered in the light of an agent in the one is considered in that of a patient by the other. Or to speak more exactly the class composed of the persons who are the passible subjects of the subsidiary law is taken out of the class composed of those who are the agible subjects of the principal: for the persons on whom the punishment is to be inflicted,

---

[j] (Enclitic) By the Greek and Latin grammarians certain particles such as τε, δε, *que, ve*, which never stand alone, but are always tacked on to the end of some other word are termed *enclitic* particles.

[k] In the language of the English law the word *procedure* is not much in use: questions which arise in the courts with relation to laws of this stamp are styled *questions of practice*: cases which give rise to such questions *cases of practice*: and the subordinate laws which are made by judges with relation to this head, *rules of practice*. The word *procedure*, though not so familiar, seems more characteristic and determinate.

are not all such persons to whom the mandate of the principal law has been addressed, but such of them only by whom it has been transgressed: nor in fact even all these, but such of them only against whom such and such persons on such and such appearances shall have deposed; or more generally, in the proceedings against whom such and such formalities can have been, and actually shall have been, observed.[1]

By this dependency the nature and description of the subsidiary law is limited in divers manners. The aspect which the legislator's will bears upon the occasion can scarcely be other than affirmative: the act which it commands, of course a positive one: the expression given to it, an affirmative command: moreover as hath already been observed in other words, the act is in respect to its pathological termination[m] confined to the particular sorts of persons who shall have appeared to be delinquents as against the principal law. In this respect then the description of the subsidiary law is influenced and narrowed by all the circumstances which contribute to narrow the description of the act commanded by the principal law: the definition of the former is determined by the definition of the latter.

18. The unity of the law, it is to be observed, is not to be determined by the unity of the proposition or grammatical sentence which expresses it. So close is the union between a principal law and the subsidiary law which stands next to it, that one proposition is frequently enough to hold them both. Indeed the principal law is commonly thought sufficient of itself to answer the purpose of the first subsidiary law that belongs to it: that part which is incitative to the one set of persons being directive to the other. Let it be once known that there is a judge appointed for trying such and such offences and murder among the rest, a law which says 'who so commits murder shall be put to death' is sufficient intimation to the judge that in case of a man's being convicted before him of that crime it is the will of the lawgiver that the judge should cause that man to be put to death. So on the other hand were a law to say 'Let the judge cause every man that commits murder to be put to death', the prohibition thereby given would be not a whit less intelligible than if it were to say, 'let no man on pain of death, commit murder'. The ways of expressing a will are infinitely various, many of them such that nothing can be more indirect. The versatility of language is endless, and its variety inexhaustible.

One expression may serve for both the principal law and the subsidiary

[1] See infra, para. 23.
[m] Supra, Ch. iv, para. 4.

There is no trusting therefore to mere words. To understand any subject, but more particularly that of law, to have a clear perception of the ideas that belong to it, we must strip them of their fallacious covering and judge of them by themselves.

It is to be observed that the principal law which is here comprised in the same sentence with the subsidiary consists itself of two distinguishable parts, the directive and the incitative (see *supra*) and which are so distinguishable that the former is frequently to be found without the latter. In the same manner where the law has no assistance from the political sanction, a particular turn of the phrase or alteration of a single word may be sufficient to give it one sometime from the moral. (See indirect legislation.)[1] It should be remembered once for all, that there is no judging of the logical division of a law from the grammatical divisions of the discourse in which it happens to be contained.

The principal most commonly serves for both

19. These two methods of abbreviation are both of them perfectly natural and intelligible, so much so that not to make use of one or the other of them would be such an instance of unnecessary diffusion as is perhaps scarce anywhere to be found exemplified. The first however of the two is by much the more natural and the more eligible: since the party whose conduct it is the first and principal design of the law to regulate, and against whom in case of disobedience the punishment is denounced, is the person who of all others has the first and greatest occasion to be informed of it. That done, one general notice to the judge will serve for as many principal laws as there are in the whole code. A very short one will suffice. The various punishments which stand denounced against the various classes of offenders, 'let such and such judges see inflicted': or in a less explicit though more usual way, 'let such and such judges have cognizance of such and such offences'.[2]

To a praemiary law when principal, the next subsidiary must be penal

20. It has just been observed that instances are now and then to be met with of laws in which the sanction, if such it can be called, is purely of the remunerative kind. But laws of this kind can not be strung together one upon the back of another like laws of the

[1] Cf. 62 above, n. 1.

[2] Bentham has inserted the following undeveloped hints at this point: 'Show how a whole system of penal law is indirectly contained in a system of constitutional law through the medium of a system of procedure. v. Russian Code. British India regulating act.'

The projected code for which Catherine the Great had issued her *Instructions* in 1767 had long interested Bentham: cf. his letter to the Rev. John Forster, April/May 1778 (*Correspondence*, ii, in *CW*, 99 and n. 4). The second reference is to the Regulating Act of 1773.

ordinary penal mould. If the principal law is of the former kind, the very next subsidiary law that is applied to it, or at farthest the next but one, must be of the latter. You are a legislator; you wish to have the longitude discovered: you offer a reward suppose in money for the discovery. So far all is right: the course you take is not only a proper one, but the only one that could be so. Here however you are obliged immediately to change the sanction, to proceed further in the remunerative track, and as a means of getting the judge to pay the money, to offer him a reward for paying it, without appointing any punishment in case of his omitting to do so, would be but an indifferent expedient. To pay for the trouble of receiving and telling the money is again no more than right: but if this were all, the money would be received indeed, but when it came to be told, it would be rather extraordinary if none of it were told into the wrong purse. There are cases then in which the law may not without advantage step aside into the remunerative path: but it can scarce ever take more than a single step at a time. Although the principal law be of the praemiary kind, the proximate subsidiary law though styled remunerative[n] will commonly have something in it that is of a penal nature.[o]

21. It is this notion of the distinction between the principal law and its subsidiary that must lead us to the notion of those circumstances belonging to a law which may be styled *exemptive*. Exemptive circumstances are circumstances which limit the application of the punishment without limiting the description of the offence. We have seen already that the connection between delinquency and the demand for punishment, however close, is not inseparable: but that there are cases in which though guilt even in the highest degree be indubitable, yet punishment would be improper.[p] Where ever there is a circumstance which, over and above any influence it may have on the mischief of the act, has the effect of taking it out of the case in which it would be expedient to punish it, such circumstance is fit to be invested with the character of an exemptive circumstance: and at any rate, however the matter may stand in point of expediency, if in fact a circumstance of any sort is made to operate in

Exemptive circumstances

[n] Supra.

[o] It might indeed consist in a mere exemption. But even a law of this kind has a necessary reference to punishment: it consists in abrogating the punishment he would otherwise be liable to in case of his not doing what he is exempted from.

[p] Ch. XIII (Cases unmeet).[1]

[1] *An Introduction to the Principles*, Ch. XIII.

that manner without obliterating or outweighing the mischief of the offence, such circumstance may with equal propriety be characterized by that name.

Difference between exculpative and exemptive

22. Exemptive circumstances are distinguished in several particulars from exculpative. The latter must have had their existence at or before the time of the performance of the act which had it not been for them, would have been an offence: among the former are such as cannot take place till a long time afterwards.[q] Exculpative circumstances apply as well to laws which have no other force than what they derive from the two auxiliary sanctions as to those which are armed in the ordinary way from the political sanction: exemptive circumstances apply only to the laws last mentioned.

It hath already been observed[r] that the principal law and the punitory law which is subsidiary to it, are two essentially distinct laws: exculpative provisions then are qualifications to the principal: exemptive ones, to the punitory.

How laws of procedure apply exemptions to substantive laws

23. To ascertain what circumstances are in point of utility proper to be invested with the character of exemptive circumstances, comes not within the design of the present chapter: our business here is to represent the mere matter of fact: in what manner a circumstance which has this effect, is made to have it. For this purpose it is to be observed, that where ever in the course of the procedure a person is required to perform such or such an act, upon the non-performance of which the party accused is acquitted or the process put an end to so as not to begin again, such non-performance is thereby constituted with regard to the principal law an exemptive circumstance; and the person by whom the act in question is required to be performed is thereby virtually invested with a power of dispensing with the principal law, upon the terms of running the chance of the punishment annexed to the violation of the subsidiary law. This is the case for instance, where in order to warrant a conviction an instrument of accusation couched in a certain form is rendered necessary. In such case, the person invested with this power is the officer or other person to whom it belongs to draw the instrument: in order to exercise such power he has nothing to do but to draw the instrument in a form different from that required. So where the appearance of a witness within a certain time, or his taking a certain oath within a certain time are rendered necessary, he has but to keep out of the way or to refuse the taking oaths

q Not so e.g. in insanity.
r Supra, para. 12.

during that time, and upon those terms he may save whom he will from punishment.

24. As there may be circumstances to which the legislator has given the effect of taking an offence out of the case in which it is punishable, so there may be others which are attended with the effect of reinstating it in that case, after its having been taken out of it as above. Circumstances of this stamp if any should occur may be termed disexemptive circumstances. *Disexemptive circumstances*

As exemptive provisions are qualifications of the punitory law,[s] so disexemptive are qualifications of the aforesaid original qualifications: re-enlarging the law after the defalcations which by virtue of such original qualifications have been made in it.

25. Upon considering the matter with a little attention it will be evident that providing any tolerable regard be paid to justice, there are a certain string of exemptions by which every punitory law will of course be qualified: I mean those which antecedently to the infliction of the punishment require the fact of the delinquency to be ascertained by the result of a particular process to be instituted for that purpose. The form in which a qualifying clause to this effect presents itself will naturally be that of a limitation rather than an exception; expressing at first in general terms the sort of process which is in question: of course by means of some word of limitation,[t] the connection which is meant to be established in point of causality[u] between the event of such process and the act of punishment. 'Who soever' (let the imperative provision say) 'has been a thief, let the judge cause him to be hanged.' Thus far the imperative provision: provided, says the limitative provision, that he have been duly convicted and sentenced in course of law. *Limitations which are annexed of course to a punitory law*

This very general provision in order to be expressive of all the effects which the institutions of a system of procedure can have upon a punitory law to which it is annexed, must be considered as including in its bosom an extensive string of qualificative clauses, some indeed after the manner of the general one, narrowing the extent of the imperative provision, but others again, re-extending it. Exemptive clause: 'provided he be convicted upon trial':—disexemptive clause: 'unless upon non-appearance he be outlawed':—exemptive clause of the 2d order: 'and the outlawry shall not have been reversed.'

[s] Supra, para. 22.
[t] Supra, 116 n.
[u] See Ch. VII (Actions).[1]

[1] *An Introduction to the Principles,* Ch. VII.

– and which are made obligative on the other side

26. But a limitation, as hath been observed, is always convertible into an exception[v]: and that exception is again convertible into an independent provision,[w] destructive *pro tanto* of the imperative provision which is excepted from. Being destructive then, it may be either simply revocative or reversive. In the present case it is always as of course reversive. Leading provision a command 'Whosoever is a thief the judge shall cause him to be hanged': exemptive in form of a limitation: 'provided he have been duly convicted and sentenced in course of law.' The same turned into an exception: 'except he have not been duly convicted and sentenced in course of law.' This exception turned into an independent provision simply revocative of the imperative: 'The judge need not cause a thief to be hanged when he has not been duly convicted and sentenced in course of law.' This were it to stand thus would leave it to the judge's option altogether, whether when a thief (that is a person whom he believed to be a thief, for the judge's belief is what the question must always turn upon) when a thief I say is not duly convicted and sentenced, whether he shall be hanged or not: the judge is not obliged to cause him to be hanged: he may however if he pleases, for anything that the law says to the contrary. This option however is what it is never thought fit to leave to the judge: accordingly the provision goes a step further and becomes imperative on the opposite side: 'The judge shall not cause a thief to be hanged unless he have been duly convicted and sentenced in course of law.'

Law anaetio-sostic, the antagonist to the punitory

27. If this be everywhere the case, it follows that wherever there is a punitory law established on the one side, there is another law established to control it on the other. For this other law, the standing antagonist[x] of the punitory, there is as much need to find a name as for the punitory itself. It may be termed the *anaetiosostic*.[y] The punishment of guilt is the object of the former one: the preservation of innocence that of the latter. The provisions that have been styled exemptive may be considered as clauses expository of the anaetiosostic law: those which have been styled disexemptive, as clauses expository of the punitory law.

[v] Supra, 114–16.

[w] Supra, 127.

[x] In anatomy muscles which counteract each other are spoken of as antagonists to each other, and termed antagonizing muscles.

[y] From αναιτιος, one who is innocent, and σωστικος, having the property of saving.

CHAPTER XII

APPENDAGES OF A LAW

1. [Eleventhly,] with respect to the occasional appendages of a law: by which I mean certain subsidiary laws of a less essential nature than the *punitory*, which may or may not be subjoined, in the view of contributing still further to obviate the mischief which it is the object of the principal law to provide against: the laws I am speaking of may be termed *remedial*.

Appendages or remedial laws—another species of subsidiary

It has indeed been shewn already that against political mischiefs the only remedy that is of universal efficacy is punishment; a stock of which from some source or other[a] every law must be provided with in order to be effectual. But by punishment as such all that can be attained is the preventing, by the dread of a suffering similar to one which in one instance hath already been inflicted, such similar mischievous acts as might otherwise have been committed subsequently to some given individual instance of delinquency. In some cases however, not only those indeterminate, uncertain mischiefs may be guarded against as above, but measures may even be taken for obviating the mischiefs actual and contingent, which in the way of causality are particularly connected with the individual offence. Let an offence of any kind then have been committed: a certain quantity of mischief is connected with it. Take then any parcel of that quantity, and consider it at any given instant, posterior to that of the commencement of the offence: such parcel must at that instant be either past, present or to come. There are accordingly three courses which the law may take in obviating the mischief: to make *compensation* for what is past, to cure, that is to put a stop to, what is present, and to guard against what might otherwise be to come. Now the course which it may be necessary the law should take for these purposes respectively, that is the acts which it may have occasion to command to be performed and the persons by whom they must be performed will not always be the same. The laws therefore will not always be the same: neither with regard to the punitory, nor yet with regard to one another. In some cases the three purposes may require three different laws, having perhaps as many different sets of persons, for their immediate subjects. A law then if it has the first of these purposes for its

[a] Supra, Ch. XI, para. 2 ff.

object may be styled *compensative*; if the second, *therapeutic*[b] or *catapaustic*[c]; if the third, *metaphylactic*.[d]

Nor is it in every case of delinquency that the attainment of every one of these objects is either requisite or possible. As to compensation, what cases do and what do not admit of it have been already shewn[e]: the cases that require and at the same time admit of any special precautionary measures to be taken for the purpose of guarding the individual injured against future injuries of the same kind on the part of the same offender[f] will be found to be confined within still narrower bounds: those which require and admit of any

[b] From θεραπευω, to cure.

[c] From καταπαυω, to put a stop to. *Catapaustic*, when once understood has the advantage of being more literal and precise: *therapeutic*, that of being less unfamiliar, being in use already among physicians.

[d] From μετα, subsequently and φυλαττω, to keep guard: i.e. to guard against certain future parcels of the mischief which might otherwise ensue from the individual offence which is supposed to have been committed. Provisions of this nature are here styled *metaphylactic*, in order to distinguish them from those which belong to the head of the preventive or prophylactic (Ch. xvi (Division) 17, 54 n.)[1] branch of the police. A provision of the metaphylactic kind necessarily supposes some individual offence to have been actually committed, before the occasion which calls for obedience can take place: some individual offence, though perhaps not precisely of the same species as those which it undertakes to guard against: for example a threat to kill (a species of wrongful menacement) or an attempt to set fire to a house (an accessory offence preliminary to the principal offence of incendiarism) whereas the offences it undertakes to guard against are *wrongful homicide* and *incendiarism*. As to provisions of the prophylactic kind (such for instance as those for the keeping of watch and ward) they do not necessarily suppose the committing of any offence whatever.

[e] Ch. xvi (Division) § 5.[2]

[f] As in case of offences against person or against person and reputation together, for instance by exacting security for good behaviour, or even by banishing the offender from the presence of the party injured. Provisions of this nature however are applicable, wherever the magnitude of the danger requires them, to semi-public, public, and even to self-regarding offences. To this latter head may be referred the provisions made against prodigality by the Roman law and adopted in the laws of several of the modern nations of Europe.

Positive mischief consists either of actual pain or danger. Private offences produce pain as well as danger; semi-public and public offences as such, danger only. It is therefore only the mischief of private offences that can be or requires to be compensated for: but in semi-public and public offences as well as in private, danger which is present may be put a stop to, and that which is future guarded against.

[1] *An Introduction to the Principles*, Ch. xvi, para. 17 (in *CW*, 197 ff.). The second reference is apparently to the section on 'OFFENCES against the PREVENTIVE branch of the POLICE' in the long footnote (n. r4) at the end of para. 54 (in *CW*, 262 n.).

[2] Ibid., § v (=paras. 61–66: in *CW*, 274–80).

special measures to be taken for putting a stop to the mischief of the offence, are fewer still.[g]

2. These then in the cases in which they apply form another class of subsidiary laws with which any one of a certain number of principal laws may be attended: and which in like manner as those of the punitory class may be distinguished into proximate and remote. Moreover to each of these series and combinations of laws correspond so many distinguishable tracks or courses of procedure. Procedure against offences may accordingly be distinguished into procedure *ad puniendum* and procedure *ad satisfaciendum*: and this again into procedure *ad compensandum*, procedure *ad compescendum*, and procedure *ad avertendum*. All these several courses will sometimes run separate for a considerable way: at other times they will coincide: so that one and the same proceeding and one and the same law enjoining it shall answer all those purposes.

Procedure in compensandum – compescendum – avertendum

3. In the same manner also this additional apparatus of adjective laws will require a correspondent prediction to be annexed to the directive part of the substantive law: the clause containing such prediction may be termed *the satisfactive clause*. As the business of the comminative clause of a substantive law is to give notice of the punitory law, so is it of the satisfactive clause to give notice what is done by any or all of the three above-mentioned species of remedial laws, with the help of several trains of remoter subsidiary laws that come respectively in their suite.

Satisfactive clauses added to the substantive law

---

[g] As in the case of wrongful confinement; by deliverance: of wrongful banishment; by recall: of wrongful non-investment, interception or divestment of trust property or condition; by investment. These are among the cases in which the offence is a *continued* act (Ch. VII (Actions) 16)[1]: and the *therapeutic* law requires to be executed before the *punitory*.

In regard to public offences, the provisions contained in the British Statute commonly called the Riot Act (1 Geo. 1 Stat. 2. Ch. 5) (provisions for the suppression of riots upon the spot) are of the catapaustic kind. In the case of wrongful confinement, the provisions in the English Statute commonly called the Habeas Corpus Act (31 Car. 2. c. 2) are also of a catapaustic nature. There are provisions of the same nature in the same case in the Code of Constitutional Law established by Catherine 2d. for the Government of certain provinces of the Russian Empire. See Reglements de Cath. 2. Liège. 1777.[2]

[1] *An Introduction to the Principles*, Ch. VII, para. 16 (in *CW*, 78).

[2] In a letter to his brother dated 28 May 1780 from St Petersburg Samuel Bentham refers to an edition of these *Règlements* published in French at St Petersburg in 1778, and asks whether he shall send this (*Correspondence*, in *CW*, ii, 468). The present reference seems to indicate that Bentham had acquired the earlier edition.

151

CHAPTER XIII

SIGNS OF A LAW

Signs by which a law may stand expressed. Law written –traditionary –customary

1. [Twelfthly,] with regard to *expression*. A law is an *expression* of will: that is an assemblage of signs expressive of an act of the will. These signs then may by possibility be any signs whatever which are capable of expressing such a will: the behaviour of him who instead of saying, put to death the chief leaders of the people, smote off the tallest heads among a parcel of poppies,[1] might instead of being an advice, have been a command. But the only signs which can answer this purpose in a manner tolerably commodious are those conventional signs the assemblage of which forms what is called *discourse*. Now the signs of which discourse is composed may either be of the *transient* kind, of which those most in use are articulate sounds: or they may be a sort of secondary symbols, permanent signs of the before mentioned transient ones, composing what is commonly called *written*, and what by a more comprehensive mode of appellation might be styled *graphical* discourse. Of the last description of all are what are commonly called statute or written laws. Of the first kind, if laws they are to be called, are what in the English language are usually styled *common* or *unwritten*, but which might more aptly be styled *customary* laws. For the second, it being for so many ages out of date among civilized nations, no distinct denomination seems to ever have been in common use: they might be styled *traditional* statute laws: or more shortly *traditionary* laws.

Customary laws are expressed by acts only, not by words

2. When the nature of those laws which are here called customary comes to be precisely understood, which it seems hardly to have been hitherto, the doubt above expressed will not be wondered at. These laws are nothing but so many particular autocratic acts or orders, which in virtue of the more extensive interpretation which the people are disposed to put upon them, have somewhat of the effect of general laws. Here it is to be observed that all verbal discourse is out of the question. Perhaps there shall have been no verbal discourse made use of on the occasion: but if there be, it is not this verbal discourse that makes the law. For the verbal dis-

---

[1] Cf. Herodotus, v.92; Aristotle, *Politics*, 1284a, 26–34. Both refer to ears of corn, not poppies. In Aristotle's account, the gesture was Periander's reply to the tyrant Thrasybulus, who had asked how to deal with the great men of his kingdom.

course containing the mandate of the judge is in point of extent
particular, being confined to the assignable individuals to whom it
is addressed: whereas what there is of law in the case must be
general, applicable to an indefinite multitude of individuals not then
assignable. A magistrate exercises some act of power over a particular individual: the assemblage of acts by which this is done
serves as a sign to the people at large expressing that the like act of
power will probably be exercised in future in a like case. A Cadi[1]
comes by a baker's shop, and finds the bread short of weight: the
baker is hanged in consequence. This, if it be part of the design that
other bakers should take notice of it, is a sort of law forbidding the
selling of bread short of weight under the pain of hanging. Whether
the Cadi makes a record in writing attesting that the baker has sold
bread short of weight, and issues an order to a public executioner
to strangle him, or whether the Cadi himself without saying a word
strangles him on the spot with his own hands, is what to this
purpose makes no difference. The silent act of hanging when thus
made a consequence of the offence has as good a title in point of
extent to the appellation of a law as anything that could be made
out of a whole shelf full of pleadings put together. Written law then
is the law of those who can both speak and write: traditionary law,
of those who can speak but can not write: customary law, of those
who neither know how to write, nor how to speak. Written law is
the law for civilized nations: traditionary law, for barbarians:
customary law, for brutes.

3. Not but that there are plenty of books purporting to be books
of customary or as it is more frequently called *unwritten* law: for if
the written law is written, so is the unwritten too. But what are
they? Books written not by the legislator but by private individuals:
Books not of authoritative but of unauthoritative jurisprudence. In
none of all these books is there so much as a single article which can
with propriety receive the appellation of *a* law. It is owing rather to
an imperfection which as we have seen is peculiar to the English
tongue, if in that language they can with any degree of propriety be
termed books of law: They contain *jus* indeed but not *leges*: *le droit*,
but not *des loix*.

No assignable laws to be found in books of customary law

If in all that has been ever written of this nature there be a
single paragraph which (not being a passage copied from some
statute) is seriously meant to pass for a paragraph of *a* law, I mean
in the sense in which the word *law* is used in contradistinction to the
word *order*, it is a forgery. Whether there be anything in it or not

---

[1] A magistrate among the Turks, Arabs, etc.

that has been marked with the stamp of authority, makes no difference: if authoritative, it is particular[a]; and therefore no law: if general, it is unauthoritative: and therefore again no law. But of this a little farther on.

Various modes of expression that may be given to the same written law

4. Where words are the signs made use of to give expression to a will, the form of words in which this may be done admits of a great variety of modification. A slight sketch of the principal distinctions observable among them is all that can be afforded here: to give a regular display of them in all the formalities of the exhaustive method would take up more room than can consistently be allotted to such a purpose. Taking for a thesis the old example of a law against the exportation of corn, I shall exhibit some of the principal forms of which a command to that purpose is susceptible, arranging them in such manner that the mode of expression grows gradually more and more unexplicit or oblique in proportion as each formulary is more distant from the first.

1. The command expressed at full length—the party to whom it is addressed (the agible subject) spoken to in the 2d person. 'It is my pleasure that you do not export any corn'.

2. The command in the ordinary elliptical form: the verb expressive of the act being put in the imperative mood'. 'Export no corn.'

3. The verb, in the future tense. 'Ye shall not export corn.'

4. The party, spoken of in the 3d person. 'Let no man export corn.' 'No man shall export corn.'

5. The idea of the passible subject put foremost. 'Let no corn be exported.'

6. The command, expressed in the way of commination. 'All persons who export corn shall be punished.' 'Every person, any person exporting corn shall be punished.' 'If any person export corn he shall be punished.' 'Whoever exports corn shall be punished.'

7. The legislator speaking as it were in the person of another man who is considered as explaining the state which things are in, in consequence of the arrangements taken by the legislator. 'It is not permitted to any man to export corn.' 'It is unlawful for any man to export corn.' 'No man has a *right* to export corn. Why? because the legislator has forbidden it.' 'The exportation of corn is forbidden.'

The first five of the above forms of imperation may be styled directly imperative; the sixth and seventh indirectly imperative: and for distinction's sake the sixth, comminative; the seventh declarative.

---

[a] It is an act of punishment or other act of censure exercised not upon a class of persons, but upon a particular individual.

Thus much may suffice for the present concerning the different manners in which the connection between the will of a legislator and the act which is the object of that will may be expressed. I pass by a multitude of observations which, however necessary to the complete explanation of the subject, would be thought misplaced, as belonging to the head rather of grammar than of legislation.

I pass over also for the sake of brevity the explanation of the different ways in which the other aspects of the will may be represented in connection with the same act.

As to limitative and exceptive clauses, those as hath been shown already[b] may all be reduced to the form of independent obligative or de-obligative provisions. With regard to the words and phrases that may be made use of for expressing the particular relation they bear as such to the leading provision to which they are subjoined, enough has also been said already.[c]

[b] Supra, Ch. x, § v, para. 4, 127–8
[c] Supra, Ch. x, n. v, 116.

CHAPTER XIV

IDEA OF A COMPLETE LAW

*The defini-
tion of a
complete law
varies accord-
ing to the
fullness of
the pattern*

1. We are now prepared for endeavouring to fix what may be called the *individuality* of a law. Now the individuality of a law results from the *integrality* and the *unity* of it laid together. To fix the individuality of a law then is to ascertain what a portion of legislative matter must amount to in order on the one hand not to contain less, on the other hand not to contain more than one whole law. And first with regard to the integrality or completeness of it.

It may have been observed already that there are laws of different patterns which are of different degrees of fullness: the description of a complete law will therefore depend upon the pattern it is of. 1. It may consist merely of a directive part without an incitative: which is the case where having no subsidiary laws belonging to it, all the force it has depends upon what it derives from the auxiliary sanctions. 2. It may have an incitative part as well as a directive: which incitative part again may consist as we have seen either of a comminative part alone, or of an invitative part alone, or of both together. 3. It may have temperative clauses annexed to it; which again as hath been shown may be either extenuative or aggravative. 4. It may in certain cases have satisfactive clauses annexed to it; which is the case when it has a set of remedial laws for its appendages: which laws again may, as hath been shown, be any of them either of a compensative, catapaustic or metaphylactic nature. Of all these parts the only essential one is the directive: as to the rest it may be provided either with all of them together or with any one or more of them, as it may happen.

*A law of the
first or
narrowest
pattern—in
what respects
it may be
complete or
incomplete*

2. To begin then with a law of the first and narrowest pattern; a law which consists solely of a directive part: when is it that such a law can be pronounced complete? A law is either obligative or deobligative. These must be considered separately: since what is said of the one will not apply exactly to the other.

A law may be considered as capable of being complete or incomplete in either of these respects: in point of expression, in point of connection, and in point of design: it may be completely or incompletely expressed, put together, or imagined. Now completeness is a word of reference: it supposes a standard of reference: This standard then may be either what actually was the will entertained by the legislator relative to the matters in question, or what on a certain contingency it is supposed, *would* have been his will: his *actual* will as it may be styled, or his *hypothetical* will. In the first and second cases, the standard referred to is of the former kind: in the third case, of the latter.

3. First then, with regard to the completeness of a law in point of *expression*: the standard of reference being what is supposed to be the actual will of the legislator. When is it that that will with respect to any act is to be deemed to be completely expressed? how much of the matter contained in the whole code goes to make up the expression of that one will? Now in every obligative law there must be an imperative provision: if with respect to any act there be no such provision in the code, there is no law concerning it. But this provision may stand unqualified or qualified: unexpounded or expounded. If it be unexpounded as well as unqualified it is a complete law of itself: if it has expositions, it is not complete without those expositions: if qualifications, without those qualifications. As to any such expository or qualificative provision, it is plain it cannot, so long as it continues in that form, be a complete law. It may indeed be thrown, as we have seen, into the form of an independent provision: and then if it be of the obligative stamp it is imperative, and as such is capable of being a complete law; yet then not without leaving out of the code all such provisions, if any, as are sub-alternately or *pro tanto* contradictive with regard to it: that is, without leaving out all other provisions in the code, if any, which may apply to it in the shape of a qualification.

To return to the old example. 'It is to be deemed exportation whether the conveyance be by water or by land.' This it is plain could never be a complete law. Nor this, 'when the market price is above 44s. a quarter'. Nor yet this, 'unless it be exported for the use of the King's armies'. Nor in short this, 'provided a licence from the first magistrate of the place have been previously obtained'. Indeed the first of these provisions which above applied to the clause 'no man shall export wheat' as a limitation, may be converted into an exception. 'Any man may export wheat when the price is not above 44s. a quarter.' But this provision is not of the imperative stamp, and on that account can not in the nature of things constitute an independent law: It supposes some other provision which is imperative and with which it is connected in the capacity either of an introduction or a qualification. For the same reason neither can the provision 'unless it be exported for the use of the King's armies' appear in the character of a complete law. The only one of

1. *in point of expression*

157

the above provisions which can appear in that shape is the last of all—'provided a licence from the first magistrate of the place be previously obtained.' This being a limitation to a former provision which was de-obligative may be thrown into the form of an exception, which when placed upon an independent footing will turn out to be obligative, that is imperative. 'No man who has not obtained a licence etc. shall export wheat, where the market price etc. is more than 44s. a quarter.' This is capable of standing in the capacity of a complete law. So likewise is the leading unqualified provision: 'no man shall export wheat': and it will actually be a complete law, however improvident and inexpedient, if in the whole code there be no other provision respecting the exportation of that commodity.

In a complete code there can be no law that is not complete

4. It follows that were a legislator to take a book of any size whatever, containing any quantity of imperative matter whatsoever, and exhibit it as comprehending a complete collection of all the laws he thinks proper should be looked upon as being in force, as many imperative provisions as it contained would, with the help of such qualifications as were to be found, be all and every of them complete laws: I mean always in point of expression: in this point the laws in a complete code, such as they are, cannot be otherwise than complete. For from what other sources can his will be collected, than from the signs and those the only ones which he has made choice of to express it? In searching after his will there may be occasion indeed to travel from one passage of this instrument to another: but out of this instrument so long as the words of it are intelligible, there can be no pretence for travelling. If indeed there should be any words in it which notwithstanding everything that can be done in view of collecting the import of them from the instrument itself, still continue ambiguous or unintelligible, in such case, as a means of finding out the sense of them it may indeed be necessary to have recourse to some other instrument. But such explanatory instrument can not be said to detract from the completeness of the principal one considered as a book of law. If it could, then a common dictionary might be considered as a book of law. The evidence derived from any such foreign source being only presumptive evidence can never be considered as outweighing any direct intrinsic evidence that may be to be had from the body of the code itself. To recur to the old instance of a law against the exportation of corn. A doubt arises what sort of articles are to be understood under the name of corn: whether *maize* for example is to be looked upon as included in the number. The opinions of persons conversant in the trade being doubtful or divided, a dictionary of commerce or a

dictionary of botany is recurred to; and it there appears that maize is looked upon as a species of the commodity in question. The law being totally silent, the interpretation thus obtained may be considered as conclusive, without any disparagement to the completeness of the law. This however could never be the case if the contrary sense could justly be collected from any passage contained in the law itself. In such case to decide according to the dictionary would be to deny the completeness of the code, and recognizing the author of the dictionary as being *pro tanto* the superior legislator.

5. Secondly, in regard to the completeness of a law in point of *2. in point* *connection.* A single law, even of the narrowest pattern, may consist *of connection* and as we shall see more particularly hereafter will usually consist of a great multitude of provisions: a greater multitude by far than from anything that has hitherto been observed would easily be suspected. These provisions in order to have the effect they are designed to have, it is necessary that the influence they are meant to have on one another should by some means or other be made appear. This there are two ways of doing. The one is by making them follow one another in the same instrument without interruption: this may be styled connection by juxtaposition. The other is by sending the reader from the place at which the chain of provisions is broken off, to the place where it is resumed again: this may be styled connection by reference.[a] In the first case the order in which it is meant the ideas should occur is pointed out by the order of the signs: in the latter case, by instructions given on purpose. The first is neither usual, nor in general, for reasons that will appear hereafter, is it practicable: to the other method there can be no objection. A law then how complete soever in itself is never completely adapted to its purpose, whatsoever that purpose be, until it be completely put together. This operation which ought so evidently to be practised upon all laws, has never yet been performed perhaps upon any: why? because the idea of such a body must first have been formed, before the members of it can have been put together. At present open what code you will, pitch upon what law you will, the parts of it lie scattered up and down at random, some under one head, some under another, with little or no notice taken of their mutual relations and dependencies.

[a] I say nothing here of the connection that may be established by use of the particles called conjunctions, as mentioned above (supra, 116 n.), between a leading provision and a limitative or exceptive clause that qualifies it: these will not answer the purpose unless the principal and the qualificative clause be contiguous.

3. in point of design: which may happen through want (1) of discrimination, (2) of amplitude, original or residuary

6. Thirdly, with regard to the completeness of the law in point of *design*: that is with reference to what would, it is supposed, have been the will of the legislator had such or such a case been present to his view. Every law that is made may be said to have been made upon the consideration of some mischief[b]: of a sort of mischief regarded as being apt to ensue from the sort of act which the legislator is thereby induced to prohibit: which general idea of mischief must originally have been suggested by the idea of some particular mischief which appeared to result from some particular act of the sort in question.[c] In as far then as the general idea which (to judge from the act as described in the prohibition) he appears to have formed to himself of the mischief of the case deviates from that which from the view of that case it is thought he should and might have formed to himself, in so far the law may be looked upon as incomplete in point of design. If then the law be considered as deviating from the standard thus assigned, it must be considered as deviating from it in one or other of two ways: as falling short of it, or as stretching beyond it: in the former case it may be said to be

[b] I say of some *mischief*: for on whatever principle he acts, something or other which to him at least presents itself in the light of a mischief it must be his design to obviate: else he would be acting without a motive. This motive if he abuses his trust may be a merely selfish one: still however it is the view of something which with reference to himself at least appears in the character of a mischief that is his motive.

To avoid embarrassment, I forbear making any separate mention of a law of the *agatho-poieutic* stamp (See Ch. xvi (Division)[1]); I mean a law of which the sole object is to make an addition in some way or other to the quantity of positive good there is in the community: in this case the absence of the good as yet unattained may be considered as the mischief.

[c] All ideas originate all of them from the senses: our ideas of mischief and the causes of it, as well as any other. Imagination may do something: but it must always have experience or observation or report, that is it must have sense as a ground to work upon. It follows then that there never can have been such a thing as a law which did not owe its establishment originally to the view of some particular mischief: the mischief resulting from some individual occurrence. In a nation of Struldbruggs (Gulliver's Voyage to Laputa) there would be no such thing, we may presume, as a law against homicide[2]: in a republic of angels, against angelicide; nor in one of devils against diabolicide. The laws which are to be found in the Jewish code against certain impurities are a conclusive proof, as hath been observed, of the prevalence of them among that people, or else, it should have been added, among some of the nations they were acquainted with.

[1] *An Introduction to the Principles*, Ch. xvi, para. 54 n. r 4, § v (in *CW*, 262 n.).

[2] Cf. Jonathan Swift, *Gulliver's Travels*, Bk. III ('Voyage to Laputa'), Ch. 10, which deals with the kingdom of Luggnag: the Struldbruggs being immortal, homicide would be impossible in a nation exclusively composed of them.

deficient or incomplete in point of *amplitude*: in the latter, in point of *discrimination*. Now the amplitude of a law depends jointly upon the several constituent parts of it: that is upon the imperative provision, and upon the qualifying clauses. If then in point of amplitude the law is deficient it may be so from either of two causes: because the class of acts which is taken for the object of the imperative provision is originally too narrow; or because, although originally it was perhaps wide enough, it has been rendered too narrow by the improper bearing and extent of some qualifying clause or clauses. In the former case the law may be said to fall short in point of original amplitude: in the latter case, in point of residuary amplitude.

7. 'Whoso draweth blood in the streets shall be severely punished.'[d] This is a law that may serve at the same time as an example of every fault in point of extent of which a law is susceptible: want of original amplitude: want of proper discrimination: and want of residuary amplitude through improper discrimination. 1. Want of original amplitude: for drawing blood is but one out of a great variety of ways in which a mischief the same in substance may be produced: a bruise, a scald, a burn, and so forth may be as hurtful as a wound. 2. Want of proper discrimination: for how many disorders are there with which a man is as liable to be seized in the streets as anywhere else for which instant bleeding is the only remedy?[e] And what if a man has no other way of defending or otherwise saving his life or limbs, or a woman her chastity. 3. Want of residuary amplitude through improper discrimination: for why must the act be confined to the streets in order to come within the censure of the law? Is it less mischievous if committed in the market-place, or in a church? These cases are but a few out of a multitude which might be alleged under every one of the above heads of imperfection.[f] This instance I chose not as an uncommon but as a simple one: for the difficulty (I might have said the impossibility) is

Example of a law incomplete in point of design

[d] It is given as a law of Bologna, by Puffendorf, B. v. Ch. 12 § 8. who quotes for it Everhard. *loc. legal.* 8. *ab absurdo*.[1]

[e] In the case quoted by Puffendorf a passenger being taken ill in the streets, a surgeon bled him: and for so doing was prosecuted upon that statute. Under the same statute the good Samaritan had he made use of bleeding might have met with the same fate.

[f] For cases that call for provisions of an exemptive nature see Ch. XIII (Cases Unmeet).[2]

[1] Samuel Puffendorf, *De Jure Naturae et Gentium*, 1672, loc. cit., citing Nicolaus Everard, *Topicorum seu locorum legalium Liber*, 1516: cf. edn. of 1544, pp. 77–82, esp. p. 79.

[2] *An Introduction to the Principles*, Ch. XIII.

not to find laws that are incomplete in this point, but to find such as
are complete.

Interpreta-
tion strict–
liberal;
liberal–ex-
tensive–
restrictive

8. These distinctions may enable us to form an idea somewhat
more precise perhaps than has ever yet been given hitherto of what
is commonly meant by interpretation: of the real nature and proper
limits of that practice, of the necessity of it, of the mischief of it,
and of the method to be taken for obviating the mischief by super-
seding the necessity.[g]

If the will which a legislator manifests with relation to a given
act fails of being what it ought to be, such failure (want of power
being here out of the question) must arise from one or other of two
causes: the state of his understanding, or the state of his affections.[h]
In the former case it must be owing either to inadvertency, or to
wrong judgment: the facts which may go to constitute or those
which may serve to control the mischief may not have been, all of
them, present to his *apprehension*: or being present, the judgment
formed by him concerning their existence or their tendency may
have been a wrong one.

Interpretation may be distinguished into *strict* and *liberal*. It may
be styled strict where you attribute to the legislator the will which
at the time of making the law, as you suppose, he really entertained.
It may be styled liberal where the will you attribute to him is not
that which you suppose he really entertained, but a will which as
you suppose he failed of entertaining only through inadvertency:
insomuch that had the individual case which calls for interpretation
been present to his view, he would have entertained that will, which
by the interpretation put upon his law you act up to, as if it had
been his in reality.

I say through inadvertency: for to attribute to the legislator a
will which you suppose him to have failed of entertaining through
any other cause than inadvertency, that is from wrong judgment or
perverse affections, and to act accordingly, is not to interpret the law,
but to act against it: which in a judge or other officer invested with
powers of a public nature is as much as to over-rule it.[i]

[g] See infra, § 8.[1]

[h] See Ch. xvi (Division), Ch. xviii (Indirect Legislation).[2]

[i] It is a common thing among lawyers to speak of the power of interpretation as a power that may be exercised by some persons and not by others *cujus*

[1] The Mss. for this chapter were written at a time when the discussion of the 'idea of
a complete law' was envisaged as § 4 of Ch. xvii of *An Introduction to the Principles*:
this reference to '§ 8' seems to be intended to indicate the discussion of interpretation
in what is Ch. xix of the present edition: cf. 239–41 below.

[2] *An Introduction to the Principles*, Ch. xvi. For the second reference see above, 62
n. 1.

It appears then that to interpret law according to the liberal mode of interpretation is *pro tanto* to apply to the imperative provision either an extensive or a qualificative clause: interpretation when liberal may accordingly be distinguished into extensive and restrictive. To interpret it liberally is accordingly to charge it with being deficient either in point of amplitude, or in point of discrimination: in point of amplitude, if the interpretation be extensive; in point of discrimination if restrictive.

In either case thus to interpret a law is to alter it: *interpretation* being put by a sort of euphemism for *alteration*. Now to extend an old law is in fact to establish a new law: as on the other hand to qualify the old law is *pro tanto* to destroy it. The only circumstance that can serve to distinguish the alteration itself, when made in this way, from alteration at large is, that the alteration goes no farther than from what it appears was the legislator's will to what, it is supposed, would have been his will had the case in question been present to his view: from his actual to his hypothetical will. If then

est condere ejus est interpretari: or that ought to be exercised in some cases but not in others. Esp. des loix L. vi. ch. 3.[1] The persons they had in view must have been persons in authority: persons invested with the judiciary, or some other branch of public power. The mode of interpretation they had in view must also have been that which is here distinguished by the name of liberal: for that which is here called strict is no more than what every man must put upon a law in order to obey it.

A liberal interpretation built on any other ground than that of inadvertency, approaches very near to an act of autocratic power and thence also in some measure to an act of legislation: to an act of autocratic power in virtue of the effects of any particular order which in consequence of the interpretation comes to be issued in the particular cause in the course of which the law supposed to be interpreted came to be referred to: to an act of legislation, in as far as the decision grounded on such particular interpretation is likely to be adopted as a standard of decision in succeeding causes. By what restrictions an order thus irregularly grounded would be distinguished from a perfectly autocratic order, is a point that could not be settled without entering into details that belong to the head of constitutional law. These restraints whatever they were would be very apt to be removed by artifice and collusion: such for instance as was practiced by the Decemvir Appius in order to get possession of Virginia.[2]

The executive power thus exercised approaches to the nature of autocratic power in as far as the effects of it when exercised are confined to the individual case in which it is exercised: to that of legislative power in as far as the exercise of it in that instance comes to serve as a rule of decision in subsequent cases which are deemed of the same sort. It thereby gives birth to a rule of customary law, which in order to be conceived must be represented in the form of a statutory provision connecting in some way or other with the law interpreted.

[1] Montesquieu, *De l'esprit des lois*, VI, iii.
[2] Livy, iii.44–58.

there is a new law made, it is made however upon the pattern, and with some of the materials of the old: if there is part of the old law destroyed, it is such part only as he himself it is supposed would have destroyed, had the particular case in question come before him.

A law takes more words to complete it than an ordinary command – why

9. From what has been said it appears that with regard to completeness whether in point of expression, in point of connection, or in point of design, a law of the pattern here in question, viz: the narrowest pattern, stands on precisely the same footing as any ordinary command: whatever is necessary to give completeness to any such command, just so much and no more is necessary to give completeness to a law.

If this were the case, it might be objected that any trifling command whatever which any private person in consequence of any of the most trivial incidents of private life have occasion to give, for example, to his servant might stand as a model of a complete law: and that such phrases as 'light the fire' or 'put the fire out', or 'open the window', might be as proper as any other: but what similarity, it will be said, between commands so simple and the long winded and voluminous expressions of will which there will hereinafter be occasion to allude to in the character of laws? The case is that with regard to the extreme simplicity observable in the commands just specified, it is to their individuality that they are indebted for it: the act which they seek to have performed is the act of a determinate individual performable on a given and determinate occasion. Now the individual occasion on which you command an individual act to be performed being given, the circumstances (I mean the material circumstances) with which it is attended may be all of them before your eyes: seeing what they are you have no need to particularise them: seeing that whatever other circumstances there might be which if present might give a different turn to your inclination, there are none however that in fact *are* present; you give command accordingly, and that without saying anything about the circumstances: to say what it might have been your pleasure should have been done in a case which you see does not exist would be idle and superfluous. But legislative command can not do less than extend to a class of persons[j]: it therefore extends to a class of acts not individually assignable and therefore to be performed if at all in circumstances, that is on occasions, not individually assignable. Being then a legislator, you can not tell what individual circumstances, what individual incidents every individual act of the number of those which you command to be performed it actually

[j] Supra, 81–2.

will be accompanied with: you must therefore consider what incidents it *may* be accompanied with, and if you find any upon the happening of which you would not think proper to have the act performed, you must set them down in the character of exceptive circumstances.

History affords two examples, the one of a particular command, the other of a general law to the same effect, which when laid together will be well enough suited to show why. Philip III of Spain, sitting one day by the fire side and finding himself too hot, called to one of his Lords in waiting and said to him, 'Put out the fire'.[k] Here there is a command which might very well have been uttered in the same concise and unqualified form of words in which it is here exhibited: and that without affording the least proof of any want of circumspection. But if it be true what is related of William the Conqueror, that in the same peremptory and unqualified manner and with the same silence with regard to exceptions he commanded all his English subjects without distinction at a certain time at night to do the like,[1] a law to that effect would hardly be produced as an example of one complete in point of design. What if a man be sick in the house and fire be necessary to prepare physic for his relief? what if money be coining at the mint, what if arms be forging at the arsenal, and the exigencies of the state admit of no interruption in the process? These and a variety of other exceptions that might be imagined serve to show how great a difference there must be in point of simplicity between a general law and any individual command of the number of those which might be included under it, before the former in point of design can be as complete and perfect as the latter.

10. So much with regard to the completeness or integrality of a law of the pattern in question: the unity of it is a matter that follows of course. Let a certain quantity of discourse be recognized as constituting one complete law, if anything more be added it makes it a *Unity of a law of the foregoing pattern*

---

[k] The Marquis de Pobar. Upon the Marquis's excusing himself on the score of the etiquette which did not admit of his interfering in a business of that sort, Philip, thinking it beneath his dignity to stir, sat on until he contracted a disorder of which he died. Bielfeld Instit. Politique iv. Ch. 3. § 47.[1]

[1] Spelmann's Gloss'y *verbo Curfew*.[2]

[1] Jacob Friedrich von Bielfeld, *Institutions Politiques*, 1760. Bentham is evidently referring to the four-volume edition of that year, or a reprint: in the three-volume revised edition of 1767 the passage in question occurs on p. 490 of vol. ii, in the course of part ii, ch. xiii ('Du Cérémonial'), § 47 ('De l'Etiquette de la Cour').

[2] Sir Henry Spelman (1564?–1641) published his *Glossarium archaeologicum* in 1626: in the edition of 1674 the reference to *Curfew* is on p. 156.

law and something more. This something more will either be of the nature of law or not: if it be, it admits of the following variations

1. It may amount to one other entire law, and no more.

2. It may amount to a certain part or parts of one other entire law and no more.

3. It may amount to several laws all of them entire.

4. It may amount to several parts of laws without including any entire one.

5. It may amount to one entire law, and a part or parts of one other entire law.

6. It may amount to one entire law and a part or parts of many other laws together.

7. It may amount to several entire laws together with a part of some one entire law.

8. It may amount to several entire laws, together with a part or parts of so many other laws together.

Language on this head unsteady

11. This detail may be of use to advert to on occasion as a clue to the process of analyzing the contents of any given quantity of legal matter. A consideration however which must never be lost sight of is that the integrality and unity of a law is dependent in a great measure on the choice of the words that are made use of to express it: that the unity of the law will depend upon the unity of the species of act which is the object of it: consequently that the description of the process will be liable to all the unsteadiness to which that of the latter has been shown already to be liable.[m] According, for example, to the words that are employed, the several articles in a cluster of offences whereof one or more are considered as principal and the rest as accessory, might be spoken of as coming under one and the same law or under so many different laws, and that whether they be offences of one and the same person or of so many different persons. Assassination is forbidden: the hiring of assassins is forbidden also: is it by one and the same law that these offences are forbidden or by two? In like manner fabrication of spurious deeds and the publication of them: perjury and the subornation of that crime. No genus of offence however narrow but may be distinguished into species: the genus was comprised under one law; do the species come under one law or under several? Frauds are forbidden in the lump: among frauds are distinguished defraudment by short weight or measure, defraudment by bad corn, defraudment by forgery of deeds, defraudment by imposture in the

[m] See Ch. vii (Actions).[1]

[1] *An Introduction to the Principles*, Ch. vii.

way of begging, defraudment in the way of gaming, defraudment in the way of insurance and so on; is it by one law that this is done or by several? The instability of language is a source of doubt and controversy against which the legislator can not be too much upon his guard.

12. Let us now consider the laws which are made upon the second of the patterns above mentioned: where the directive part is armed as it were by a commination. As the directive part is an expression of will: a declaration of what it is the wish of the legislator should take place: so the comminative part is an expression of an act of the understanding, an expression of belief; a declaration of what according to the belief of the legislator will take place, in consequence of certain measures which if he says true he himself has taken. As the former then in order to be complete, must be a full and faithful picture of the legislator's mind, so the latter must be a full and faithful picture of the future state of things, of future exterior events: as to what regards the probability of the event predicted in as far as futurity can be the subject of a picture. The commination is a prediction of an event which it is designed should take place in consequence of a man's committing the offence: of an event which is to happen not at any rate, but only, in case such and such other events do, and such and such others again do not, take place: that is in case all the several regulations of procedure are complied with, the observance of which is necessary to the legality of the sentence and the execution of the punishment: in case none of these events happens to take place, the happening of which is invested by the law with the character of an exemptive circumstance: and so on with respect to circumstances dis-exemptive and re-exemptive through as many alternations as there shall be found occasion to establish.

A law with a comminative part when complete in point of connection

The directive part of the law forbids a man to steal: the comminative part says if he does he shall be hanged. The punitory subsidiary law goes on and says, that such or such a kind of judge shall cause him so to die. What then, is a thief sure to be hanged *at any rate*? No, says the comminative part as applying to a law of procedure, he shall *not, if* a clerk in drawing the instrument of accusation chances or chooses to write one word instead of another: *unless,* says another law, the court chooses to let the wrong word be struck out and a proper one inserted in the room of it. The directive part of the law forbids a man to commit perjury: the comminative part says if he does he shall be pilloried. Yes, says a law of procedure, and so too shall a man who is innocent of theft, if being charged with it and sent for in order to answer he does not appear: unless, says another law of procedure, the King's advocate will let him put himself upon his trial.

So many exemptive circumstances as are established, so many incidents there are that may fall out between the cup of punishment and the lip of the offender. Say then that an offender will be punished at all events, and you say what is not true. He will not be punished, not a grain of punishment will ever reach him, if any of those events take place the happening of which is invested by the law with the quality of an exemptive circumstance. It follows that the prediction which the comminative clause consists of, that this prediction, I say, if uttered absolutely is not true: to bring it within the pale of truth, qualifications limiting in a proper manner the generality of it, qualifications holding up to view the events in question in the exemptive character which they are invested with must in some way or other be subjoined to it. One way of doing this and that as natural as any is by making references to the several laws of procedure by which they stand invested with that character.

In point of design

13. To be complete in point of design all the exemptive clauses expressive of all the grounds of exemption (cases unmeet etc.) should be set down.

Unity of an obligative law of the second pattern

14. So much with regard to the integrality of a law made according to this second pattern. As to the unity it may be sufficiently made out from what has been said already.

Integrality and unity of obligative laws of the two remaining patterns

15. With regard to the integrality or the unity of a law made upon either of the two last of the four patterns above specified nothing in particular need be remarked. A law if it has temperative provisions annexed to it, to be complete must exhibit those provisions: if it has remedial appendages, it must contain a satisfactive clause or clauses referring to those appendages.

–of a de-obligative law

16. We come now to the case where the law is of the de-obligative kind; that is either a countermand or a repermission. Where the law bears either of these aspects it is evident enough that the first of the four patterns above mentioned is the only one to which it can be made conformable. In this case the integrality and unity of it are so intimately connected that it will be sufficient to speak of them together. A law of this sort presupposing the existence of a preceding law, the amplitude of it is of course determined by the amplitude of that which it presupposes.

If the superventitious law is not de-obligative in toto, it is only quali-

17. The application then of a superventitious de-obligatory law to the primordial obligative one in respect of unity is susceptible of the four following cases: either

1. The former covers the latter exactly: or

2. It covers it in part only, and without anywhere over-hanging it: or

3. It covers it throughout, over-hanging it at the same time: or

4. It over-hangs it in one quarter, while it falls short of it in another.

ficative: if it is, then by destroying the mandate the qualifications fall to the ground with it

In the first case the act which before was commanded or prohibited being now left free, all the apparatus of qualifying clauses, of punitory and remedial laws and the laws that are respectively subsidiary to them, and consequently of comminative, exemptive, etc., and of satisfactive clauses belonging to the substantive law, as also whatever temperative clauses may belong to it, fall to the ground of course.

In the second case the de-obligatory law in question operates only in the light of a qualification to the primordial, investing some circumstance or other with the character of a limitative or exceptive circumstance with reference to the act commanded or prohibited by the primordial mandate: and consequently with the character of an exculpative circumstance with reference to the offence constituted by that mandate: As to its effects upon the punitory and remedial laws that may be subsidiary to the substantive law in question, they may be analysed in the same manner by considering them as so many distinct laws: and so likewise with regard to any imperative clauses.

In the third case to analyse the effect of the de-obligatory law it must be resolved into two: the one destructive of the primordial mandatory law in question as in the first case: the other either destructive or qualificative of some other mandate or mandates.

In the fourth case the effect of it is the same as in the third: with only this difference that it is qualificative only of the primordial law in question instead of being destructive.

18. Thus much with regard to the case of a de-obligative law, that nothing might appear to be left unnoticed. To have a clear conception however of the state of the whole system of legislation at any period it is upon the obligative laws alone that the spectator should fix his eye: it is by them that he should measure the number and extent, of the laws that are in force during a given period in a given state, and thereby of the obligations to which the members of that state are subject. It is owing merely to the changes which the will of the legislator is liable to undergo with respect to the same act at different periods that laws of the de-obligative kind are susceptible of any separate consideration: were it not for this, the effect

Obligative laws the only standards to measure by

produced by them might be produced in a better manner by more simple methods: where the primordial law or any determinate part of it is destroyed, declare it repealed and throw it out of the code[n]: where the former is made to receive a qualifying clause, insert the clause in the same manner as if that and the rest of the law so qualified had from the very beginning made but one.

This is not only the most eligible method but the most simple: the most common however is to let the old and the new lie all in a confused heap together, the de-obligative and the obligative, the slaying and the slain. To what causes then is so slovenly a practice to be ascribed? to the nature of the things themselves? By no means; but to causes more accidental and less irremediable: to the want of exertion or skill on the part of the legislator, where there is but one: to the same causes added to the want of concert where there are many. Now for supplying the second of these deficiencies there can not be a more effectual expedient than the laying down if possible a precise idea of the integrality and unity of a law. This done, the legislator's task will be comparatively a light one. He may then with care penetrate to the bottom of the whole mass of law, distinguish the several laws which enter into its composition, extricate them from their mutual entanglements, and determine at any time by a glance which are and which are not affected by any new provision that presents itself.

Unity of a law to be determined by the occasions for distinguishing offences

19. By what circumstance determine the unity of the law? By the unity of the class of acts which it takes for its object: by the unity of the offence. That system of provisions is one law which marks out one offence: that system of provisions is more than one law which does more than mark out one offence. But classes of offences like any other classes of acts may be distinguished from one another *ad infinitum*: take one class of offences however narrow and it may be

---

[n] I pass over the temporary provisions that may be requisite to be established, in order to prevent the abolition from having the effect of an *ex post facto* law, upon acts done under the authority of that which is abolished. For these see Append. tit. (Digestion) and (Conservation)[1]. Meantime lest it should be found too difficult to apprehend how any danger should result from a law which of itself does no more than leave a man at liberty, it may be proper just to hint, that in many cases there are obligative laws which are commonly looked upon as annexed of course to de-obligative: thus a law exempting a man from punishment is understood to include as it were a law forbidding all other persons from inflicting on him the punishment he is excepted from. There is no punishment, the infliction of which, were it not for the law which expressly commands it to be inflicted, would not be an offence.

[1] These projected appendices are not extant, but see infra, 235, on Digestion.

made to contain any number of subordinate classes of offences at pleasure: taking this unity of the offence for the standard of unity in the law, the unity of a law is not naturally determinable. If determined then at all, it must be determined by some positive rule: and from whence should this rule be taken but from convenience. So many offences then, so many *species infimae* of delinquency, there may be said to be provided against in the code, as there happens to be thought occasion to distinguish: to distinguish in any manner whatsoever, for any purpose whatsoever. Fewer there can not be: more there need not be.

The next question is for what purposes is it likely that occasion should be taken by the law for making such distinctions? The general answer is, for the purpose of making a distinction in the treatment it gives to some person or other on account of the acts in question. This rule will require to be developed. Acts then which might by the occasions of mentioning them be considered as one have need to be distinguished from one another in the following cases.

1. Where a difference is thought proper to be made with respect either to the quality or the quantity of the punishment. 'He who exports barley is to forfeit 5s. a quarter: he who exports wheat 10s.': it is not enough then for both purposes to forbid the exportation of corn in general: the offence of exporting wheat must be distinguished from that of exporting barley. 'He who exports wheat by daytime is to forfeit 10s. a quarter: he who exports wheat at night is to forfeit all his goods.'

2. Where any difference is thought proper to be made in any part of the system of subsidiary laws. 'If a man is found exporting corn in a waggon the waggon may be seized: if in a ship, the ship shall not be seized.'

It is needless to multiply examples any further. In short take any act whatsoever that has a place in the catalogue of offences. If in any one instance of that act's being performed anything is commanded or permitted to be performed or not to be performed which is not commanded or not permitted to be performed or not to be performed in any such instance, the act is thereby divided into two separate species of delinquency, which for the purpose in question must be distinguished: and the law is thereby divided into so many distinguishable laws. And here we see the difference between the unity of a law and its integrality: a law which was originally one may be divided in this manner into two laws, and yet both of them may be complete.

171

A complete code being given, the number of laws in it is given

20. The principle of unity in a law being hereby given, it follows that a complete code being given, the number of the laws there are in it, so long as it continues what it is, is likewise given. Not the general purport only but the precise number: they might be counted, were it to answer any purpose. The number of the laws will indeed upon this as well as upon any method of computing be liable to incessant changes, owing to the continual occasion there will ever be for new laws: still however take any one period, at that one period the number is determinable. By this means then we may come at the *monades*, of which the vast universe of jurisprudence is composed: the idea of infinitude is consequently removed; and the cloud in which that idea never fails to envelop every subject to which it attaches itself, dispelled.

Genera infima of offences

21. To the *monadic* laws above mentioned, if such for a moment they may be called, or narrowest assignable laws, correspond what may be termed the *species infimae* in speaking of offences. There is another principle of distinction with the help of which we might mark out, though by a line rather abstract and like the former not exempt from change, what may be considered as the *genera infima* with reference to those species. The *genera infima* of offences may be reckoned such and so many classes of offences as are the narrowest in their respective lines of those which happen each of them to be provided with a name: by which I mean not only such names as are strictly univocal, such as theft, murder, adultery and the like, but also any other names which though compounded are like univocal names capable of entering into constructions and occupying the place of a substantive in a sentence. Of this kind are the greater part of those which for the purpose of the analysis attempted in the last preceding chapter[1] I found myself obliged to coin or fix the sense of: such as simple corporal injuries, wrongful confinement, usurpation of the condition of a husband, and so on. Thus then the *species infimae* and the *genera infima* of offences may stand distinguished: the *species infimae* are the narrowest classes which the law has taken for the separate objects of its notice: the *genera infima* are the narrowest of those which can be made to stand as links in an analytic chain.

To apply this then to the laws. A law of which the *genus infimum* of offences is the object may be considered as a cluster of laws having for their objects the several *species infimae* comprehended within that genus.

Species infimae constituted by circumstances of aggravation

22. Of the abovementioned sources or grounds of distinction one

[1] The reference intended is to Ch. XVI of *An Introduction to the Principles.*

172

of the most material is a difference in respect for the demand of *and extenua-* punishment. Conceive an act of any sort to have been constituted *tion applied* an offence and that offence characterized by a generic name: as for *to the above* instance theft, or wrongful homicide. This offence upon first con- *genera* sideration is punished in all cases with one and the same in-variable punishment, for instance death. In process of time divers circumstances occur the intervention of which appears to make a difference in the demand for punishment: the act (that is the class of acts as determined by its generic name) remaining in every case the same. Now the punishment if varied at all must be varied either in quality or in quantity: and if it is varied in quality it can seldom happen but that some variation shall happen in point of quantity. When it varies in quantity, this it may do in either of two ways: in the way of increase, or in the way of diminution.° In the former case the circumstance in consideration of the effect thus given to it may be styled a circumstance of *aggravation*: in the latter, a circumstance of *extenuation*. Thus for instance in theft, grounds of aggravation may be, the irreplaceability of the thing stolen, or the circumstance of its having been committed under favour of a calamity, such as fire or shipwreck: grounds of extenuation, the offender's having acted through compulsion, or through necessity for the sake of preserving himself or a person dear to him, from the immediate danger of starving: in the case of wrongful homicide, on the aggravation side, the circumstance of its having been committed with premeditation: in a manner that indicated deliberate cruelty; in a clandestine manner; by poison; upon the father of the offender; for hire; for the sake of succeeding to an estate; in prosecution of a scheme of robbery; in order to stifle evidence; in revenge for something done in execution of justice; and so on: on the side of extenuation, the circumstances of its having been committed without intention to kill; in a fit of intoxication; through compulsion or deference to authority; upon high provocation; and the like.

° The article of quantity, it is to be observed, includes that of intensity and that of duration. It does not indeed strictly speaking include that of certitude or that of propinquity. These however are of little account on the present occasion. In these respects punishment ought in every instance to be kept at its *maximum* as of course: and it must be through some palpable error in judgment, if ever the legislator should think of making use of intention or remission in these points as a means of producing an intention or remission in point of *value*. See Ch.[1] (Value). Unhappily such errors are by no means unexampled.

[1] *An Introduction to the Principles*, Ch. iv. Bentham has omitted the number of the chapter. The expression 'intention or remission' remains obscure.

Now then, let [us] take any such *infimum genus*, wrongful homicide for example, and add to it any such circumstance of aggravation, premeditation for example, the genus is thereby divided into two species: the one consisting of such individual acts of wrongful homicide as are accompanied with that circumstance, the other of all such as are not accompanied with it: which species being made punishable with two different species or degrees of punishment become thereby the objects of two different laws.

Necessity of mixing with genera infima those which have others under them

23. It is evident that the length of any line of *genera*, if one may so say, in the system of offences, and thereby the station in which the *infimum genus* is to be found must be dependent in great measure upon the accidental differences of language: insomuch that an offence which stands upon a level with a number of *genera* each of which are *infima* in their respective lines, shall however in its own line have some other *genus* or *genera* of offences that stand below it. This may be seen for example in the instance of wrongful occupation; which though it stand upon much the same level as that of extortion, has another *genus* that stands below it; viz: theft. For theft is but a species of wrongful occupation: whereas no such *genus*, as it should seem, would be easily to be found under the article of extortion.

The establishment of genera liable to vary in different languages

24. This will depend likewise a good deal upon the idiom of each particular language. Thus for instance in English under the genus *theft*, we have the genus *robbery*: an offence which it seemed requisite to dismiss to another division; viz: that comprized of offences against person and property together[p]: whereas there seems to be no universal appellative that seems exactly to correspond to it in French: in French to express the idea which in English is characterized by the word *robbery*, people would probably make use of some such phrase as *vol avec force*, theft with force.[q]

Necessity of such establishment for the purposes of discourse

25. These *genera infima* of offences how precarious soever their title to that denomination may appear, it was necessary to establish, otherwise there would have been no such thing as treating to any

[p] Supra, Ch. xvi (Division) 35.[1]

[q] The term *brigandage* may perhaps in some cases convey the same idea: but the sense of it seems not to be very determinate: nor does it seem to be employed in books of law: indeed the distinction itself between theft and robbery does not seem in that law to have been very explicitly recognized. See Code penal pp. c. 99. Jousse Nouv. Comment. sur l'ordonn. crim. de 1670 I 56, 34.[2]

[1] *An Introduction to the Principles*, Ch. xvi, para. 37. Bentham's reference to paragraph 35 is inaccurate.

[2] The second reference is to Daniel Jousse, *Nouveau commentaire sur l'ordonnance criminelle de 1670*, 1763. The preceding reference to 'Code penal' remains obscure.

purpose of the several acts which are taken or appear fit to be taken for the objects of a law: no such thing in short as creating a book of the nature of the present work. Were no other appellatives to be made use of than those which have been given to the head classes and their immediate divisions, the distinctions that could thus have been expressed would never have been particular enough for the purpose. Were none to be made use of but what would result from the enumeration of all the circumstances necessary to constitute the description of the *species infimae* there would be no such thing as carrying on any discourse upon the subject whatsoever: since, as will be stated more particularly a little farther on, for even one of the generic names now employed it would be necessary to substitute a little volume: so that if half a dozen of them came upon any occasion to be included in one sentence, into that one sentence it might be necessary to put words enough to fill half a dozen volumes.

26. It is in short by means of these alone that we are enabled to speak of any act by name under the character of an offence. It is moreover to these names that we refer when we speak of any circumstances under the appellation of inculpative and exculpative circumstances. These terms suppose a class of acts of a certain description to stand invested with a name importing it to be an offence: those which are styled inculpative serve to bring certain species of acts under the genus characterized by that name: those which are styled exculpative serve to exclude others out of it. Were it not for this resource we should have no means of speaking of any act by name in the character of an offence. All that we could say upon the subject would be confined to the law by which the offence was made: instead of speaking of clauses inculpative and exculpative and re-inculpative clauses we could only speak of clauses limitative, exceptive and re-extensive.

References of inculpative and exculpative circumstances to such generic names

27. Thus much concerning the completeness or integrality of a law of the narrowest pattern, as well in point of expression as in point of development, connection and design. As to the completeness of the laws framed according to the other patterns, it is a matter soon determined. Completely expressed a law made upon either of these patterns cannot but be if the code of which they severally make a part is given for a complete one, wherever it professes to exhibit any law according to these respective patterns. Completely developed it will be if there be such and so many words employed as are sufficient to make them readily intelligible. Complete in point of connection they must be if they refer to the several parts of the subsidiary laws whose existence they announce.

Integrality of the laws of the three remaining patterns

But though in a code which by being given as complete is therefore in a certain sense complete, they must be completely expressed, as many as are expressed in it at all, yet it follows not that they are all or any of them completely developed.[1]

First conception of the laws of property to be taken from the offence of wrongful occupation

28. The laws relative to property may be considered in various points of view. To apprehend the nature of them, the relation they bear to the rest of the system, and how they are reducible to the nature of a mandate or its opposite, we must call back to mind what was said of the offences relative to property in the preceding chapter.[2] Let us begin with that sort of property which is the most simple: the principles observed in the explanation of this case will serve with little variation for the explanation of the cases where it is the most complex. The most simple case is where the proprietary subject as we may call it is corporeal, determinate and single. This case I will now endeavour to explain.

To understand the nature of the laws of property it will be requisite to recur to the enumeration we had occasion to make in the last chapter of the possible offences relative to property.[3] It will also be necessary to recollect that an offence and the law whereby that offence is created are a sort of correlatives; so that for every offence there is a law: viz: a law of the mandative or imperative kind, and for every law of the imperative kind there is an offence: and that accordingly the offence being given the law is given also, or the law being given, the offence. Now in the list of the offences against property the radical one seems to be that which we have styled *wrongful occupation of property*: it is to that offence that the law, by which the most simple and elementary species of proprietary right is created, corresponds. This is the leading offence by reference to which the nature of those other offences may most commodiously be explained.

Example where the proprietary subject is a particular field

29. But without the idea of some particular sort of corporeal object before our eyes it will be difficult to reason clearly. Let the proprietary subject then be a certain piece of land, a field, the offence which consists in the wrongful occupation of this property will be any act[r] in virtue of which the agent may be said to meddle with this

---

[r] Such extraordinary cases excepted in which the law may think fit to allow one man to trespass upon the property of another and which though alluded to for the sake of exactness, may then be laid out of the question.

[1] Cf. para. 4, p. 158 above. The final form and placing of paras. 27–38 seems not to have been decided by Bentham.

[2] The reference intended is to Ch. xvi, para. 35 of *An Introduction to the Principles* (in *CW*, 226–32).

[3] Ibid. In the next sentence, at the word 'recollect' Bentham has inserted the following note: 'Supra. This depends upon the place where this article is inserted.'

field. But the name of the offence reflects the act which is the object of the law: now the offence is that of meddling with the field. But that object when represented by the name of the offence is represented just as natural objects are represented in certain mirrors, in an inverted position. The offence then being the act of meddling with the field, the act which is the object of the law, the act commanded is the negative act of not meddling with the field. Annexing then the expression of will to the act thus expressed, we have the whole substance of the law; which amounts to this, 'Let no one, Rusticus excepted', (so we will call the proprietor) 'and those whom he allows meddle with such or such a field'. Here then we have an example of one form in which the substance of a law of property creating property may be expressed.

30. But in this law we see there is an exceptive clause. Now every law in which there is an exceptive clause may be resolved into two provisions. These provisions where the law is, as it is here, of the negative or prohibitive kind are 1. a primordial mandate of the prohibitive kind, the more extensive of the two: 2. a superventitious mandate of the permissive kind which is the least extensive of the two, being revocative but revocative *pro tanto* only and not *pro toto* of the former. No man shall meddle with the field (describing it): Praetextatus[1] and such other persons as he allows may meddle with the field.

This law may be resolved into 1. a general prohibition, and 2. a particular permission taken out of it

31. Viewing the matter in this light it is not to be wondered if a man should be alarmed at first at the multitude of the laws to which the head of property may give occasion. To that multitude it must be acknowledged there are no bounds. In the first place we have a different law for every distinct proprietary subject: and matter is infinitely divisible. In the next place we have a new law every time the subject changes hands, and that may happen fifty times a day. But we are as yet got but a very little way in the enumeration of the circumstances which may give occasion to different laws relative to the same individual subject. In the example above exhibited it is taken for granted that the subject belongs solely to one person, that it is his not only for a certainty but at present, and not only for the present but for ever, that when he chooses to make use of it, he may make what use of it he pleases, and that he may make use of one part of it as well as of another, and that to warrant him in making

Infinitude of the laws of property upon this plan

[1] Bentham originally took as an instance of a 'proprietary subject', in paragraph 29, a coat. Having first altered this to a garment, and finally to a field, he at this point omitted the consequential change in the proprietor's name, which should read 'Rusticus'.

use of it he has no need to wait for any particular event or for the consent of any other person. But a piece of land may belong, part of it to Rusticus, part of it to another person or any other number of persons: it may be his not till a year hence or any number of years hence: nor then unless such a person have died first, or unless such a person have died without issue, or have married, and so on through any number of imaginable contingencies: it may be his for a year only or two years, or any other determinate number of years and not for ever: or, whether certain or contingent, perpetual (if nothing prevent) or temporary, it may be liable to pass from him upon the happening of any event in his power or out of his power, such as the death of another person, or his own marriage, or the failure to pay money on account of rent or taxes, or in short any other account that can be imagined: he may have a right only to feed his cattle upon it or only such and such particular cattle, or only to cut wood from it, or only to dig ore out of it, or only to build upon it or only to pass over it: he alone may have a right to dig ore out of the bowels of it, while another man alone has the right of cultivating the surface of it: or the case may be that neither he nor any body else may have the right of making use of it without the consent of one or two or any other number of persons, as may happen where the land is vested in a corporation the members of which, possessing the right they have in it in trust, have no right of making any use of it individually. In many of these cases for every different modification of the right there will require a different law; and in all of them there will require either a different law or a different clause to be added to the unconditional standard law. I have taken the example from the immovable class of subjects: because those are the subjects which afford room for the greatest variety of modifications on the part of the proprietary right: but there are some movable subjects likewise which perhaps give room for all these modifications: and there are none but what give room to some of them.

That infinitude may be reduced by translating the laws out of the imperative into the assertive form

32. The laws then to which any one single proprietary subject may give occasion being infinite, how is it possible, it may be asked, to comprise the collection of the whole body of the laws relative to property within the limited compass of a code? Certainly to draw them out at length and conceived in the imperative form is not possible. But the modes of expressing imperation as there hath already been occasion to observe are indefinitely numerous.[s] Of these many are indirect and have nothing of imperation upon the

[s] Supra, Ch. xiii (Signs) and Ch. x (Aspect).

face of them; bearing the form not of imperative but of common assertive propositions: as if they were the words not of the lawgiver but of some one else who was giving an account of what the lawgiver had done. Now as in the imperative form the laws relative to this head would swell to an infinite degree of expansion: so in the narrative or assertive form they may be reduced to an almost infinite degree of compression. To describe and distinguish the several contrivances by which in different cases this concentration may be effected, would require a volume.[t] All that can be done here is to give notice to the reader: inasmuch that being aware of the metamorphoses, he may be master of a thread which will conduct him at any time from the artificial and super-induced, to the native and primeval form of the several provisions of the law. To exhibit in this latter form all these provisions collectively is impossible, but it is no more than what a man must be able to do with regard to each of them taken separately, ere he can possess any accurate comprehension either of the nature and operation of such provision taken by itself, or of the relation it bears towards the other parts of the system. For a law of any kind or any part of the law of any kind to have any effect, a man must be punishable in case of his disobeying it: but to have an idea of a case in which a man is punishable for any act is to have the idea of an offence: and to have the idea of an offence, the signification of the will of him who makes it such being added, is to have the idea of a command.

33. It hath already been observed on a former occasion that private conveyances in as far as they are legal, that is adopted by the legislator, are so many laws or assemblages of laws. This being

Among the laws which create property con-

[t] In general it may be observed that where the texture of a law is dilated, or a number of laws are compacted into one, it will generally happen that the greatest part of the matter will be translated out of the imperative into the assertive form. In the former case expositions are subjoined to the words made use of in the expression of the mandate. In the case of consolidation the first process is to reduce the multitude of mandatory phrases into one. But it will seldom happen that this general provision shall be exactly commensurate in point of amplitude to the sum of the several specific provisions which it is meant to include and at the same time equal to them in point of precision and perspicuity. Two sorts of matter then will one or both of them require to be annexed to it: qualificative matter to reduce it to the proper standard in point of amplitude: expositive matter to give it the requisite degree of precision and perspicuity. But whether the matter be of the one sort or the other it will in both cases make its appearance most naturally and advantageously in the assertive form. Thus it is that in consolidation every step after the first is the same as in dilatation: and in both cases the great bulk of the discourse is in the assertive form, the part which points to imperation being nothing but a sort of *punctum saliens* as it were, a mere microscopic object, in comparison of the rest.

Expansion and consolidation both throw a law out of the imperative into the assertive form

veyances are included in which the imperation is performed by the law and the right-giver conjointly

admitted, a body of the laws to be complete must be understood as including *inter alia* the whole body of conveyances: a complete body of the laws taken at any given period will therefore include a complete collection of the several conveyances which within the dominion of the state are in force at the instant of that period. Not that conveyances are on this account to be reckoned laws in any other sense than that in which any other commands issued in the exercise of powers are laws; those not excepted which are issued by parents, masters and other domestic power-holders for any the most trivial purposes of a private family. For the legislator then to take any separate notice of them is impossible. All that he can do, and all that it is requisite he should do is to describe in general terms such as he thinks proper to adopt, and thereupon explicitly or implicitly such others as he thinks proper not to adopt: in other words such as are deemed *good* or *valid*, and such as are to be deemed *void*. Now those are good or valid which are made in such *form* as it is thought proper to acknowledge for good form, by him who has a good title, or to speak shortly a title to convey, in favour of him who has a good title to take or receive: those bad or void which are made in such form as it is thought proper to hold for bad, by one who has no good title, or as the phrase is no title to convey, or in favour of one who has no good title or no title to take or receive. But an event which is allowed to give a man a title to one sort of proprietary subject may not perhaps be allowed to give him a title to a proprietary subject of another sort: and an individual event which gives a man title to an individual proprietary subject does not thereby give him a title to another individual proprietary subject. Moreover an event which is allowed to give to a person one sort of proprietary subject, may not be allowed to give a title to a proprietary subject of that sort to a man of another sort. Also as to events that depend upon the act of man, an event which if it resulted from the act of a person of one sort would be allowed to give to a person of a given sort a title as to a proprietary subject of a given sort, may not be allowed to produce that effect where it results from the act of a person of another sort, as in the case of minors, prodigals, trust-holders and the like. Hence the whole branch of the law relative to conveyances may be comprised in the exposition of a few such words as proprietary, proprietary subject, proprietary rights, proprietor or right-holder, title, conveyance, and the like: of which exposition every distinguishable clause by being applied to any particular conveyance that came into controversy might be translated into a command.

34. It is thus that by being applied to and combined in a manner with the expression of the wills of individual power-holders that branch of the law which concerns conveyances is transformable into and carries the effect of a command. But there is another branch of the law, still referable to the offence of wrongful occupation in which the matter of the command is furnished by the legislator solely and immediately without needing to be applied to the mandate of any private power-holder. This includes the cases where the title of him in whose favour the law is made is constituted either by an event which is altogether in his own power or by an event of any other kind in which, in as far at least as concerns the effect thus given to it, no other person's will has any participation: as is the case for instance with the title derived from occupancy, improvement, natural increment and succession *ab intestato*. In this latter sort of case the connection between the assertive matter of the law and the idea of a command emaning from the legislator will not be quite so remote as in the former. In the one case we may have a complete law, in the other case we can not without descending to that degree of minuteness and particularity as to take in the mandates of individuals. Thus it is that in one or other of these ways a good part of the matter of law is naturally and in a manner necessarily thrown into the assertive form constituting a kind of exposition of some such word as the word *title*.

Cases in which the property is established by the law alone in the first instance

35. This word then we see is a word that will be wanted to make part of the definition of the offence entitled wrongful occupation of property. But this same word or what is equivalent to it will be equally stood in need of for completing the several definitions of the several other acts which are ranked under the head of offences concerning property. Thus wrongful non-investment of property is the forbearing to render a man that sort of service which consists in the conveying to him or investing him with a title to a certain proprietary subject, he having a title to such service: wrongful investment of property, in the doing of any of those acts which are deemed by the law to divest a man of such a title, the wrongdoer having no title so to do: and so on in a manner that may be easily imagined.

Of the expositive matter belonging to the law against wrongful occupation a great part belongs in common to the law correlative to the other offences against property

36. We have shewn how it is that to the single offence of wrongful occupation, considering the matter in a certain point of view, there may belong an infinite multitude of laws. But such as the offence is such is the law: therefore if the offence is *one*, the law considered in a certain point of view, must be *one* also. Considered in this point of view the law when expressed in the imperative form will run

The laws relative to the offence of wrongful occupation are to one—1. in the conditional form

in this wise, 'Let no man perform' or 'let no man commit wrongful occupation, that is an act of wrongful occupation understood of property'. This law then as we have shewn already will in order to be explicit enough stand in need of ample, and those very ample, expositions: out of which expositions and the several distinguishable clauses in them may be constructed, by a proper method of translation, as many laws as there may be occasion for to match with the several individual offences that may come under this title.

2. in the un-conditional form with exceptions   **37.** In the formulary just exhibited the law may be considered as being couched in the conditional form; the epithet *wrongful* prefixed to the term occupation being expressive of a significant circumstance: viz: the *wrongfulness* of the act of occupation. But a law in the conditional form may always be converted into an unconditional provision with exceptive clauses and with exceptions taken out of it.[u] This accordingly is the case with the law in question. Omitting in the first instance the conditionalizing or limitative epithet *wrongful*, the law in the unconditional form will stand thus, 'Let no man perform any act of occupation': or to express the same meaning with less stiffness: 'Let no man occupy any proprietary subject.' After that come the several exceptions, which may be all included under some such single formulary as this, except he have a title so to do: and then in order to accommodate the general proposition to the particular case of each proprietary right-holder, will come the exposition of the word title and of the other leading terms, such as proprietary subject, proprietary right, proprietary right-holder, proprietary right-giver, proprietary right-taker, form of conveyance, and so forth, as above.

The last formulary the plainest   **38.** Of the several forms above-mentioned perhaps this latter is the clearest, and that which places the station which the fundamental law of property occupies in the most satisfactory point of view. Upon this plan the leading provision is one simple mandate: a mandate which is the primordial work of the law itself without needing the co-operation of individuals, which contains what there is universal in the law of property and what must necessarily be applicable to every *corpus juris* whatsoever.

What is necessary to make it appear complete   **39.** Thus much in the way of description: a word or two here may not be amiss in the way of caution. It is not enough that the law be really complete: to have the effect of a complete law it should be made to appear such in the eyes of those who are concerned in it: to the citizen who is to take it, that is to take the whole of it together, for the measure of his conduct; to the judge who is to take

[u] See supra, Ch. x (Aspect).

it for the measure of his decision: and to the legislator, who in order to know whether anything that is requisite remains to be done should be able to see at a moment's glance what it is he hath done. It ought accordingly to be consigned to paper, and that in such a form that anyone who opens a volume of the code may lay his finger upon it and say this is one law: and that is another: here the first of these begins, and there ends: here are all the parts, and these together are what make the whole of it.

40. This being the description of a complete law, where then it may naturally be asked is there a specimen of such a law to be met with? I answer—nowhere. Before any such specimen can be found, a perfect plan of legislation must first have been produced: perfect in point of method at least, whatever it be in point of matter. If in this view we cast an eye over the current systems of legislation, and observe the laws that are contained in them, we shall find them marked, all of them, more or less with the following deficiencies: 1. The inculpative circumstances being in many instances lumped together in one word along with the description of the physical act, have in those instances perhaps never, and in others but seldom, been perfectly developed: this is the case for instance with such words as theft, murder, robbery, fraud, extortion, peculation: words of which no tolerable definition seems ever yet to have been given. *In what respects laws are apt to fail of being complete in this point*

2. Of the circumstances to which the effect of exculpative circumstances ought to have been given, a great part have remained unheeded.

3. Of the punishment instead of its being chosen and fixed by the legislator according to the nature of the offence, it has often happened that no mention has been made: so that the law would have remained impotent had not the judge assumed the place of the legislator.

4. To many circumstances the legislator has given or suffered the judge to give the effect of exemptive or disexemptive or convictive or redintegrative circumstances without placing them formally to that account, and frequently as it would seem without so much as perceiving them to be attended with that effect.

5. For want of observing the many differences which the intervention of so many different circumstances may make in the mischief of the offence, or by other means in the demand for punishment, he has invested few or none with the character of aggravative or extenuative circumstances: so that either no temperament at all has been applied, or none but what has depended upon the casual observation and fluctuating discretion of the judge.

CHAPTER XV

NO CUSTOMARY LAW COMPLETE

A customary law can never be complete **1.** If it be thus with the statute law, how is it, let any one imagine with the customary? A customary law is not expressed in words: now in what words should it present itself? It has no parts: how should it exhibit any? It is one single indivisible act, capable of all manner of constructions. Under the customary law there can scarcely be said to be a right or a wrong in any case. How should there? Right is the conformity to a rule, wrong the deviation from it: but here there is no rule established, no measure to discern by, no standard to appeal to: all is uncertainty, darkness, and confusion.

The original elements of it are acts of autocratico-judicial power **2.** It is evident enough that the mute sign, the act of punishment, which is all there is properly speaking of a customary law, can express nothing of itself to any who have not some other means of informing themselves of the occasion on which it was given: that the act of hanging for example, is no definition of the act of stealing, and that a blow which is given to a dog (for here dogs and men are put upon the same footing) is no lesson to the dog who is in the next yard, or to the whelp that will have been begotten by one of them a year hence. If then it can serve as a rule to any distance or for any length of time, some account of the case must be taken and handed down by somebody: which somebody stands then in the place of a legislator. But of the boundless group of circumstances with which the act punished must necessarily have been attended, how many and which of them were considered as material? what were received as inculpative? what were not suffered to operate in the way of exculpation? to what circumstances was it owing that the punishment was so great? to what others that it was no greater? These and a multitude of other circumstances which it would be needless to repeat must all be taken into the account in the description of the case. But let the case be delineated ever so exactly, it is still but that individual case that is delineated: to make a rule that can serve for cases yet to come, a new process must be carried on: the historian must give place to the metaphysician; and a general rule must be created by abstraction out of this particular proceeding. And by whom then shall the abstraction be performed? by every man for himself, or by some one for all the rest? In the latter case that one man, be he whoever he will, if his rule comes to be adopted and adhered to, that one man becomes in effect the legislator.

3. Under these circumstances the state of the branch of law in question where custom thus bears sway is apt to stand upon some such footing as the following.[a] The judges who perhaps at first did take and are still supposed or rather pretended to be supposed to take an account of every case that came before them never trouble their heads about the matter: the business is left to certain officers who are under them. These officers give what is called the history of the case, which history is termed by some such name as a *record*. This record being copied from precedents of the darkest antiquity instead of being a complete history of the case of which it purports to be the record, is in fact a partial and imperfect history of a different case that was determined upon some hundreds of years before: applied to the case in question it is in consequence, partly imperfect, partly false, partly irrelevant, and partly unintelligible;

Sources of customary law – Records

---

[a] The picture here given of it is local, because it could not well be otherwise. The statute law of a country is upon paper, and may be seen all the world over: the state of the customary law is comparatively a secret, depending in a great degree upon habits which are not perceptible out of the particular circles in which the practice of it is carried on. It was necessary therefore to take up with a single model and to copy from the only system of jurisprudence to the interior history of which I had any opportunity of access. If in the slight sketch here given any of the lines should seem peculiar to the particular original from whence they were copied, the bulk of them will however be found, I believe, to be applicable to all nations, being imprinted on the very essence of this species of law.

Having fixed the idea of a law, shewn what might be its parts, and when it might be looked upon as entire, I perceived what anybody may perceive, that, in the case where the law is of the permanent kind, it was applicable only to a statute law: and that as to a customary law there was no such thing existing. It became necessary therefore to shew how this happened to be the case, and since there were here no laws, (no *leges*) of what sort of materials it is that the aggregate body styled the customary law considered as a body of permanent regulations, is made up.

The picture I am about to give will I trust be found a faithful one. Paint objects in their natural colours, it must appear that a quarry is not a palace, that a lay-stall is not a garden; that a wen or scab is not a beauty. A pleasing one indeed it is not: but who is it that is in fault? I paint things as I find them: if bad, it is in order that they may be made better. Meantime let not my design be mistaken: nor let a picture of the law be misconstrued into a satire against individuals. My business is not with individuals, but with nations: not with the year, but with the age. The dark spots which I am about to exhibit are accordingly inveterate evils, not recent grievances: nor do I believe that the period will be found, at which the constitutional diseases of the law itself have met with so powerful a palliative as they do now in the talents and virtues of its professors.

and is in many instances much the same sort of history of that case as a chapter of Bede[1] or Orosius[2] would be of the present war.[3][b] These documents such as they are are written in a form the most inconvenient for reading or consulting, of any that could have been devised: and being by many a waggon load too bulky for publication they are kept locked up in places where not one in ten thousand of those whose conduct is to be guided by them and whose fate depends on them can know how to find them: much less to make anything of them when found. The trouble of finding them out is so great and the information to be got from them so scanty and indecisive that it is not above one time in a hundred that even the judge who professes to take the decisions, given in the cases of which they purport to be the histories, for the measure of his own, can endure to look at them. Whether they have weight in any case or whether they have none, depends therefore upon accident: if a fit of curiosity happens to take the judge, such an one as shall not take him thrice perhaps in a twelvemonth, they are handed down: if not they are let alone: one out of a thousand becomes a law: the nine hundred and ninety nine others remain waste paper.

*Reports –
their
deficiencies*

4. These documents being become to such a degree useless, another set of documents come gradually into use under the appellation of *Reports*. In these reports taking them all together, about one third or one tenth or one twentieth or one hundredth part of the cases are made public which if they were equally known would be equally entitled to make law. Here you have a little of the history of one court; there of another: sometimes the history of a court goes on pretty well for several years together: then comes a blank for twenty or thirty years during which all is darkness.[c] Sometimes you

[b] More particularly in action of *ejectment*, by which the title to landed property is tried, and which are the causes of the greatest importance of any in the civil line.

[c] Of cases determined in the court of chancery there have been none reported from the year 1755 to the present year 1782: of cases in the Exchequer none from the year 1741, a very few excepted relative to a very narrow branch of practice: and those not published till the last year but one, 1780. The first mentioned court is that which exercises a greater share than all the other tribunals in the nation put together in the disposal of the property of that nation. In matters which are there cognizable the statute law has scarcely anything to do: everything turns upon customary law, which in that court has assumed the particular name of *equity*. Respecting these matters the public has

[1] *Historia Ecclesiastica Gentis Anglorum*, completed *c.* 731.

[2] *Historiarum adversus Paganos libri septem*, written early in the 5th century A.D. as a complement to St Augustine's *De Civitate Dei*.

[3] The American War of Independence.

have the history of the middle of a cause; sometimes of the beginning; sometimes of the conclusion. Sometimes you have the argument without the decision; sometimes the decision without the argument; sometimes the inferior decision of the inferior court without the superior which reverses it.

These reports are published by anybody that pleases, and by as many people as please; and where nobody publishes, nobody cares. If a lawyer who can get no practice happens to think of this method of making money: if the executor of a lawyer happens to find a manuscript among his papers; if either of these or any other such accident happens to throw a copy into the hands of a bookseller: the bookseller without being aware of it and without caring about it, becomes a legislator.

Sometimes by commission from that high authority, a judge who had been dead and forgotten for half a century or for half a dozen centuries, starts up on a sudden out of his tomb, and takes his seat on the throne of legislation, overturning the establishments of the intervening periods, like Justinian brought to life again at Amalfi.[1d]

been six and twenty years, respecting matters cognizable in the other court (which is also a court of equity), it has been forty years, without a guide.

[d] Lord Chancellor Freeman's reports were first published in 1742: there are cases in them as old as the year 1670. Ld. Chanc. William's (the most generally esteemed perhaps of any) were first published in 1740: there are cases in them of the year 1695. Judge Coke's (held also in the highest estimation) in the year 1657: there are decisions in them of the year 1582. Serjeant Maynard's Yearbook was first published in 1679: there are cases in it prior to the year 1306. In the first-mentioned of these books the cases were brought to life many of them 72 years after they were agitated: in the second, 45: in the 3d, 75: in the last, upwards of 370.[2]

In the customary law, a great perhaps the greatest part of the business is done in the way of *ex post facto* law. The decisions, being formed on grounds that were inaccessible to the party previous to the act for which he was made to suffer, carry with them a great part of the mischief of the *privilegia* against which Cicero inveighs with so much justice.[3]

[1] In 1137 a manuscript of the *Corpus Juris Civilis*, lost shortly after the death of Justinian in 565, was discovered in Amalfi following the sack of the town by the Pisans.

[2] Bentham's references are to the following: Richard Freeman, Lord Chancellor of Ireland, *Reports of Cases in Law and Equity*, 1742; William Peere Williams (1664–1736), *Reports of Cases, 1695–1734*, 1740 (Bentham's reference to Williams as Lord Chancellor is mistaken); Sir Edward Coke (1552–1635) whose *Law Reports* were mostly published between 1600 and 1615 in Norman-French and Latin—Bentham is referring to the *Exact Abridgement in English of eleven Books of Reports of the learned Sir Edward Cook*, 1657; Serjeant Sir John Maynard, *Year Books of Edward II*, 1678/79.

[3] See Cicero, *De legibus*, iii.19.44; and *De domo*, 17.43.

–redundancy and confusion   If the series of the cases that are published is broken and interrupted, the deficiency is made up by the multitude of reports there
are of the same case: all perhaps contradicting one another and
contradicting what little there is of truth in the record.

Treatises   5. Meantime out of these scattered atoms, be the collection of
them ever so copious and exact, nothing it is plain so long as they
continue in the order in which they happen to be brought to light
can be made, that shall wear the face I do not say of a law but of any
thing that bears any perceptible relation to any thing that is
entitled to that name. To give them any sort of connection with one
another and with the rest of the matter of which law is made, a set
of general rules must be abstracted from them and worked up into
the form of a treatise. A set of treatises accordingly start up: and
here again the bookseller gets another share in the prerogative of
legislation.

It is plain these general rules can have no foundation in authority
any further than as they are the necessary result of some particular
assignable decisions: if they deviate but a hair's breadth from that
standard, they become laws *suo jure* and the author if they are
adopted and acceded to becomes *pro tanto* as much a legislator as
the sovereign. Accordingly the writer, while living, has no such
independent authority: he has none even so long as his book can be
deemed a modern one. But in proportion as he is more ancient, that
is in proportion as the age he writes in is more barbarous, he stands a
better and a better chance of setting the law: insomuch that at a
certain period his authority shall often prevail not only without the
authority of preceding cases to ground it upon, but even against the
authority of such preceding cases. The treatise is confused and
barbarous: yet less so than the case; so much less, that out of pure
weariness and despair the authority of the treatise is preferred to
that to which alone it stands indebted for all the weight that could
originally have belonged to it. First in point of original authority
comes the record: then comes the report: last of all comes the
treatise: the shadow of the shadow of a shade: and it is this shadow
that is worshipped as the substance.

Manuscript Reports   6. To supply the deficiencies in the reports men of the profession
have a resource: men out of the profession, the people whose lives
and fortunes are at stake upon the decision which ought to have
been or are supposed to be related in the reports, have none: no
matter: the demand for the lawyer rises in proportion to the
ignorance and helplessness of the client. While decisions are yet
young, before any reports of them can have been published and

lest none should be published, such lawyers as happen to be present will naturally be taking notes for their own use. These notes are circulated from hand to hand: and happy is he who has his bookcase full of them. But no one man can be in half a dozen courts at once: nor in any one court before he is born. Every lawyer therefore, if he would make a collection of these recondite treasures, must be beholden to his brethren. By this means two monopolies establish themselves, one within another: a monopoly by the profession itself against the rest of the people: and a monopoly of the illustrious in the profession itself against the obscure: a monopoly of the seniors against the juniors: a monopoly by men of extensive connections against men of small connections.

7. It has already been intimated that the description of the *Formularies* formularies made use of in judging, prosecuting and defending, *of Precedents* enters in a certain manner into the description of every law whatsoever: the invalidity of a formulary exhibited on the part of an accuser or of an order in prejudice of the defendant having the effect of an exemptive circumstance: the invalidity of a formulary exhibited on the part of the defender, or of an order in his favour, that of a condemnative or dis-exemptive circumstance. In a similar manner does the description of the formularies made use of in covenanting or conveying enter into the description of those particular laws which by lending their sanction to such contracts or dispositions convert the several violations of which they are susceptible into so many species of delinquency: the invalidity then of a covenant has the effect of an exculpative or exemptive circumstance to the law which makes the non-performance of the service stipulated for by that covenant an offence: as hath the invalidity of an acquittance from such contract, that of a re-inculpative or of a convictive circumstance. In like manner the invalidity of an investitive conveyance has the effect of an exculpative or exemptive circumstance with regard to the law which makes the invasion of the property or interests disposed of an offence.

Accordingly so long as the validity of these formularies rests upon the customary law, and until a sufficient stock of them has been framed and authenticated by the proper legislator, a collection of such of them as have been drawn into question and confirmed, or passed unquestioned through the scrutiny of lawyers of eminence concerned for parties interested in their downfall, forms another branch of the customary law. The possession of such a collection becomes an object of value: and the access to it like the use of any other object of exclusive property, may form an object of sale.

Hence arise a multitude of little subordinate monopolies, carved out of the great monopoly possessed by the profession at large: the proprietors of each branch having a valuable property in the ignorance of the rest of the profession, as the rest of the profession have in the ignorance of the people.

Preference not settled

8. A report in order to furnish the matter that laws are to be made of, must at least be permitted to be called in debate. But it is not every printed report that is always permitted to be cited: and there is no list of such as are not. The judge A will hear the reporter A: he will not hear the reporter B: the judge B will hear the reporter B: he will not hear the reporter A: the judge A will sometimes hear the reporter A, and sometimes not. Reports become distinguished into citeable and unciteable: and the citeable into good and bad. Those which are citeable to one judge, are not so to another; nor to the same judge at a different time: those which are good to one judge are bad to another. Every judge has his own gauge: and each man's gauge may be set sometimes one way and sometimes another. It is evident that inedited reports must be in a case nearly similar.

In both classes, some are avowed by their authors, some anonymous. Some are the better for having a name: others are the worse: to some the names of the authors add authority: from some they take it away. And the same reporter who mostly reports well, will sometimes report ill: and the same who mostly reports ill will sometimes report well.

Utility – original and derivative

9. But the general rule extracted no matter how, from these particular *data*, and which if there were a law in the case, would be the law, is after all absurd and mischievous: perhaps it was so from the very first, that is the decisions on which it is grounded were so at the first moment of their being made. But at any rate it would be so if applied now to the matter at present in dispute. To decide then according to *this* rule would be mischievous in one way: but to depart from *any* rule which is to be deemed to have been established would be mischievous in another way. It is only in as far as subsequent decisions are rendered conformable to the rules that are fairly to be drawn from prior decisions that such prior decisions can answer, in any even the most imperfect degree, the purpose of a law. Whenever the chain of conformity, such as it is, is broken, the anomalous decision whatever it is, does all the mischief that can be done by an *ex post facto* law. If the question be of a penal nature in the one way it absolves without reason, or the other way it punishes without warning: in a matter of purely civil competition, it subjects

the unsuccessful party to a privation or to a burthen which as far as they go have the effect of a punishment without cause. This it does by its own single efficacy: add to which that in the way of example it gives a shock which from hand to hand is felt by the whole fabric of customary law. Nor is the mischief cured till a strong body of connected decisions either in confirmation of the first anomalous one or in opposition to it have repaired the broken thread of analogy and brought back the current of reputation to its old channel. I speak in metaphors: since in metaphors only on a subject like the present can one speak. This being the case, whenever any past decision, in itself apparently absurd, is brought in the character of a law to govern the proposed decision in the case of litigation, there are two maxims that point different ways and press for opposite determinations. As this dilemma is occurring at every turn, lawyers are of course continually called upon to embrace the one side of it or the other. Accordingly then as the inconveniences on the one side or those on the other have been accustomed to press upon their imaginations with the greatest force they insensibly contract a general propensity to lean on the one side or on the other. They form themselves like the Proculians and the Sabinians of old,[1] though on a ground of much greater extent and importance into different parties: *Stare decisis* is the maxim of the one; *salus reipublicae* or something like it, the motto of the other: both perhaps partisans of utility, though of utility viewed through a different medium: the one of the general utility which results from the adherence to established precedents: the other, of the particular utility which results from the bringing back the current of decision at any rate into the channel of original utility from which the force of precedent they suppose had drawn it aside: the one enamoured of uniformity, the mother of security and peace: the other, of Natural Justice or Equity or Right Reason or by whatever other name the phantom is best known.

10. Given the documents from whence the law that is to govern in a given case is to be abstracted, it is required to find that law. A question arises concerning the title to an article of property. A deed copied from one drawn by a conveyancer of great name and since copied from by a thousand others, but now impeached for the first time; a decision badly reported upon the face of it but taken from a

Competition between documents of different orders

---

[1] The Proculians were a school of lawyers founded in the reign of Augustus by Antistius Labeo, but named after his pupil Sempronius Proculus. The Sabinians, who were founded by Ateius Capito, a jurist in the reigns of Augustus and Tiberius, were named after his pupil Masurius Sabinus, and formed a rival school.

printed book of high authority; a decision well reported upon the face of it but taken from a printed book of low authority; a decision indifferently reported and taken from a book without a name; a corresponding string of unprinted cases; an ancient treatise, and the decisions which it quotes and which when examined make against it; these together with the dictates of utility in the abstract, are all candidates at the same time for the prerogative of legislation: —which of all these outstanding authorities ought to carry it?[e] When the circle has been squared, this problem will be solved.[f]

Uncertainty of this branch of law

11. From a set of *data* like these a law is to be extracted by every man who can fancy that he is able: by each man, perhaps a different law: and these then are the *monades* which meeting together constitute the rules which taken together constitute that inimitable and unimprovable production of enlightened reason, that fruit of concord, pledge of liberty in every country in which it is found, the common or customary law.

[e] There are various other species of authorities, which it would be to no purpose to insist upon: for example

1. Maxims: which are unconnected scraps of general treatises.

2. Opinions of counsel: which are treatises on the particular cases laid before them.

3. Pleadings: (that is formularies of procedure settled by counsel) which carry with them their opinion concerning the validity of these pleadings.

There are also various circumstances which may give different degrees of weight to authorities of the same species.

1. The reputation of the counsel who advised; or of the judge who decided.

2. The rank and fullness of the court: was it before the Master of the Rolls, or before the Chancellor: at a judge's chambers, at Nisi prius, *in Banco*, or at the House of Lords?

3. The solemnity of argumentation—how many times argued? by how many counsel on a side?

4. The solemnity of decision—did the Chief Justice deliver the opinion of the court: or did the judges give their opinion *seriatim*?

5. The number of stages in the cause—was it a decision acquiesced in, or a decision confirmed upon an appeal?

These are a part of the topics which may occasionally be thrown into the scale, all adding to the perplexity of the inquiry, and to the uncertainty of the result.

[f] Mathematicians, when a question presents itself they are not acquainted with, call it x: if there comes another, they call it y: and so they go on investigating the nature of it by means of its relation to other quantities which they are acquainted with. It remains in this state of obscurity for a certain time, but at last out it comes in the intelligible and familiar shape of one, two, three, four, and so forth. Thus it is in mathematics: but in jurisprudence under the customary law, the object is as much unknown at the end as at the first: it is x, y for ever more.

Caligula published his laws in small characters: but still he published them: he hung them up high, but still he hung them up.[1] English judges neither hang up their laws, nor publish them. They go further; they will not suffer it to be done by others: and if there be any dependence to be placed in any rule of common law, whosoever takes upon him to do it, well or ill, he may be punished. The rule is indeed falling into desuetude: but it has lately been recognized; it has never been disclaimed; and it may be enforced at any time. Whosoever takes upon him to do any such service to his country does it, like the Grecian lawgiver, with a halter about his neck.[2]

It appears then, that the customary law is a fiction from beginning to end: and it is in the way of fiction if at all that we must speak of it.

The customary law, you say, punishes theft with hanging: be it so. But by what law is this done? who made it? when was it made? where is it to be found? what are the parts that it contains? by what words is it expressed? Theft, you say, is taking under certain circumstances: but taking by whom? taking of what? under what circumstances? taking by a person of such a sort, taking a thing of such a sort, taking under such and such circumstances. But how know you this?—because so it has been adjudged. What then? Not if it be a taking by any other person, nor if of any other thing, nor if under any other circumstances? O yes, in many other cases: if by whom then? and if of what? and if under what circumstances? if *by* a person of such another sort, if *of* a thing of such another sort, if *under* such and such circumstances? But how do you know this is the case? because I think it ought to be so, because I believe it would be so: because such and such persons believe it ought to be so or would be so. But how *came* you to think so? and how came *they* to think so? and what if I think differently and as many people with me, *quorum ego judicium* (as saith the courtly Cicero, to his friend)[g] *longe antepono tuo*, happen to, tell me, I say, where is your law then?

But for peace sake let your notion be the right one: no matter why nor wherefore. I am content to abide by it, and to acknowledge that

[g] Tuscul. Disput. in principio.[3]

[1] See above, 71 n. 1.

[2] Demosthenes in his speech against Theocrates (139–141) contrasts the incessant legislative changes at Athens with the permanence achieved at Locri in Italy, where anyone proposing a change in the laws of Zeleucus must do so with a halter round his neck, which was removed or tightened till he died according to the approval or disapproval with which the proposal was received.

[3] Cicero, *Tusculan Disputations*, v.4.12: 'A. Non mihi videtur ad beate vivendum satis posse virtutem. M. At hercule Bruto meo videtur, cuius ego iudicium, pace tua dixerim, longe antepono tuo.'

all others ought and are bound to do so, too. Be pleased then to give it words for us to know it by.—And are these then the words? is this paper the standard we are to measure an act by in order to see whether it be an act of theft or no?—Then is this a law, and you the legislator.

Conclusion **12.** In short, if there be still a man who will stand up for the existence and certainty of a rule of customary law, give him everything he asks, he must still have recourse to fiction to produce any such rule: if it appears in any shape it must clothe itself in the similitude of some particular provision of the nature of statute law: it must purport to be, it must pretend to be a provision of statute law, although it be no such thing. To enable ourselves to conceive and express the influence which a rule of this sort may have over the whole system of law and at the same time to distinguish it from the real entity whose semblance it usurps, it may be called after the name of that which it would be if it were anything, with the particle *quasi* prefixed to it; according to the usage of the Roman Law.[h] Upon this plan a rule of customary law describing for example, what is to be looked upon as theft, may be styled a quasi-law against theft: which quasi-law will accordingly have its quasi-imperative, quasi-limitative, quasi-exceptive provisions, and so on.[1]

[h] Fragm. on Govt.[1]

Unaccom-modating-ness of the customary law
[1] This is not the place to enter into a complete detail of the imperfections of the customary law: for such a description the proper place seems to be the title of *Digestion*: since in proportion to the imperfections of such part of the law as is in this form will be the benefits of the salutary operation which consists in reducing it to the form of statutory law. The imperfections which are here brought to view are no others than what transpired, as it were of themselves, in the course of the discussion which seemed necessary in order to give a view of the characteristic nature of this modification of the law. One other capital imperfection may just be hinted in a few words. I mean that which consists in the *unaccommodatingness* of its rules. Every decision that is given is spun out of some vague maxim, conceived in general terms without exceptions, and without any regard to times and circumstances: a maxim conceived in words which whenever put together, were put together, a thousand to one else, by persons who have no such case as the particular one in question present to their view. It admits of no temperaments, no compromises, no compositions: none of these qualifications which a legislator would see the necessity of applying. Even when it aims at utility, which perhaps is now and then, it either falls short of the mark or overshoots it. A sort of testimony in recognition of this truth is contained in the magnificent and well known adage, *fiat justitia ruat coelum.* Though heaven were wrecked, let justice be adhered to. Heaven may always be preserved when the law that governs is the work of the legislator. Hence the hardness of heart which is a sort of endemical disease of

[1] *A Fragment on Government,* Ch. i, para. 12 n., §§ 10 and 11 (Bowring, i, 263 n.).

lawyers where that part of the law which is in the customary form is predominant in the system. Mischief being almost their incessant occupation, and the greatest merits they can attain being the firmness with which they persevere in the task of doing partial evil for the sake of that universal good which consists in a steady adherence to established rules, a judge thus circumstanced is obliged to divest himself of that anxious sensibility, which is one of the most useful as well as amiable qualities of the legislator. An empire shall run to ruin and the lawyer drive on in the same track as if nothing were the matter.

Familiarized with the prospect of all those miseries which are attendant on poverty, disappointment, and disgrace, accustomed even to heap those miseries on the heads of those by whom he knows them to be unmerited, he eases himself by habit of the concern which the prospect of them would produce in an unexperienced mind: the unconcerned spectator of the agonies, just as a man whose trade is in blood becomes insensible to the sufferings which accompany the stroke of death. It must be no common share of humanity that can induce him, nor any common share of wisdom that can enable him to keep this rigour within the bounds presented by utility, and the necessary regard to uniformity of decisions. By men of ordinary mould the dictates of utility in these circumstances may easily be lost sight of altogether: and a precedent the most absurd and mischievous conformed to with as much tranquillity as an equally apposite precedent of a complexion the most reasonable and salutary.

CHAPTER XVI

SEPARATION OF THE CIVIL BRANCH
FROM THE PENAL

The gener-
ality of laws
have each a
penal as well
as a civil
branch

1. We may now perhaps be able to find an answer to the question we set out with[1] concerning the distinction between the penal branch of law and the civil: and we may say at once that in every law (at least in every law that is comparatively speaking of any importance) there is one part which is of a penal, and at the same time another part which is of a civil, nature: and that after the few exceptions which have already been marked out, there is no such thing as an entire law which is penal only and not civil, nor as one which is civil only and not penal. The truth of these propositions if it be not clear already, will presently be made appear. What the cases are in which a law may possess a certain degree of efficacy without having any punishment provided by the legislator for its support have been already stated: they are 1. where the law has for its support the apprehension of a punishment issuable from both or either of the two auxiliary sanctions: 2. where it has no punishment at all to support it, but only reward. In all other cases if it has any support, any efficiency at all, it is to punishment provided by the sovereign that it stands indebted for it: to a subsidiary punitory law or what is equivalent, announced by a comminative clause (or what is equivalent) in the principal law. Now it manifestly is not upon either of the slender pillars above-mentioned that the main parts of the fabric of political society are supported: for example those laws which provide for the preservation and circulation of property. In every one of these therefore, be they what they may, there must be a penal part as well as a civil; so that a law of property which being entire shall have nothing in it of a penal nature is a law which either does not exist or if anywhere it exists is nugatory: nor at any rate is it of a piece with the bulk of those which in speaking of the laws of property men are wont to bear in mind.

Law-books in
which no
mention is
made of
punishment
accounted for

2. All this while it can not but have been observed that nothing is more commonly to be met with [than] not only whole chapters but

---

[1] At this point Bentham has a note which reads 'Supra 29'. The reference intended is evidently to *An Introduction to the Principles*, Ch. xvii, para. 29 (the final paragraph of the text as printed in 1780 and published in 1789), where Bentham asks 'What is a penal code of laws? What a civil code?', etc. (in *CW*, 299).

whole volumes and those authoritative too, in which from the beginning to the end there is not so much as a syllable hinted about punishment, and which notwithstanding are full of assorted matter which is called law. This makes a seeming inconsistency, which it will be well worth our while to endeavour to remove: but which could not however have well been removed upon any other terms than that of travelling through the long and intricate details that have occupied the last chapters.

The cause of it is neither more nor less than this: the want of coincidence or conformity between the typographical arrangement and the logical: between the order of the ideas about which the several laws in question are conversant, and the order of the signs which are made use of to express them.

3. To consider the several laws separately without regard to the exigencies of the whole, without regard to the form into which it might be necessary to cast them, for the sake of the form which is requisite to be given to the whole, the natural course to take would seem to be as follows: to take each law by itself beginning suppose with the law against personal injuries, and under the head of that law to insert all the words whatsoever and how many soever they be which are requisite to give a clear expression of the various ideas that enter into the composition of that law. This plan shews mighty fair upon the first opening: but before a man had got to the end even of this single title he would find, perhaps to his no small surprise, that after a due attention paid to the several limitations and exceptions which the case requires, he would before he had got to the end of this single title have set down matter enough to fill a volume. When after having got thus far he came to consider that the title upon which he had bestowed a volume was but one out of perhaps some hundreds which remain, how great would be his amazement and despondency? 'At this rate', he would say to himself, 'hundreds of such volumes may have been travelled through, and yet the work not done.'

According to the order of the ideas the penal and civil branches would stand together

4. If however after this it would be possible for him to muster up courage enough to go on with the next offence, he might be as much surprised perhaps another way: he would find that with the exception of a page or two he would have that same volume to write over again and insert under this second title. This being the case it would naturally enough occur to him, that there could be no use in inserting those same words twice, either to himself who was to write or to the people who were to read them: but that to both parties it would on the contrary be equally irksome and inconvenient. He would

But must be separated for the convenience of discourse

therefore collect this common matter and set it down in a third title by itself: which third title by the simple expedient of a set of references might be adopted into and made as it were parcel of each of the two others.

Foundation of the penal and civil codes

5. If then with a view to the distinction between the penal and the civil branches of these two laws he were to look over them and examine their contents, he would find that such clauses as were in the imperative or comminative form took up comparatively but a small space: that at the same time these were the clauses which after the separation adhered to the two original titles: that these were in each of those titles different: and that it was the qualificative and expositive matter, as being common to both titles, that took its station under the new one: and in short that in the two first titles thus reduced he had laid the foundation of a *penal* code, as in the third he had of what would be called a *civil* code.[1]

Expository matter

6. Expository matter may therefore relate either: 1. to the description of the act itself: 2. to the circumstances restraining or enlarging[a] the description of the act: 3. to the description of the punishment: 4. to the circumstances restraining or enlarging the description of the punishment: 5. to circumstances influencing the connection in the way of causality between the act and the punishment. Any clause or sentence then of which it is the business to develop the idea of any of the above group of circumstances may be styled a *circumstantiative clause or sentence*: and the contents of any such clause or sentence or of any assemblage of such clauses or sentences broken or entire may be styled *circumstantiative matter*.

Of the expository matter the circumstantiative will be the most copious

7. It has already been observed that the bare act which is commanded or prohibited is always a very simple object: whereas the circumstances belonging to it constitute an immense group of objects which are capable of being infinitely diversified. Now the more diversified they are in their nature, the more diversified of course they will be in their description, wheresoever it is necessary that one should be distinguished from another. The more diversified they are in their description of course the more room will the description that must be given of them occupy in the code. The

---

[a] Show that circumstances (to be material) must do one or t'other.[2]

[1] The remainder of this chapter is taken from what seems from the Mss. to be a much corrected early draft. The material evidently belongs to this phase of the work, but Bentham's failure to complete its final revision accounts for the break in continuity between paras. 5 and 6.

[2] This note is written in pencil in the margin: it is, strictly speaking, not so much a footnote as an undeveloped hint for Bentham's own guidance.

circumstantiative part is accordingly that part of the expository matter which will be much the most voluminous.

8. Now when a parcel of literary matter of any sort is in such a manner connected with another parcel of literary matter that the one cannot properly be understood without the other, the most obvious method of disposing them is to put them together: placing them in the same instrument, and as close together in that instrument as may be. For this reason, if there were no other to the contrary, where there is one parcel of matter connected in the manner above mentioned with a number of other parcels, where a given parcel of matter instead of being connected with one other only is connected with a number, the most obvious as well as commodious method would be to give to the former the same connection in point of contiguity with every one of them. But were this the case the former parcel would come to be repeated as many times as there were parcels to which it was to be applied. Now such repetitions, on account of the enormity of their bulk, would soon become impracticable. Some therefore of these parcels of penalizing matter there must be to which the quantity of circumstantiative matter that belonged to them could not be placed contiguous. Now if this might be the case with some, by the same reason might it be with all. It might therefore and indeed must often happen, that a quantity of circumstantiative matter applying alike to divers parcels of penalizing matter, might instead of being placed contiguous to each, be placed contiguous to none, forming on the contrary a kind of independent parcel of itself. If the parcel were large it might be made to occupy a distinct volume: if larger still, it might be made to occupy even a multitude of volumes.

Circumstantiative matter, how it may come to stand apart from the penalizing matter

9. When the separation in point of material contiguity between parcels of matter which in idea are so inseparably interwoven is once effected and becomes permanent, the two parcels will naturally acquire different names. Thus accordingly has it happened in the case before us. Of the circumstantiative matter which concerns the description of the several sorts of acts which are made offences a great part has been frequently separated from the rest of the body of the law under some such appellation as that of *civil* law or the civil branch of jurisprudence: while the rest together with the greatest part of what concerns the description of the bare acts that have been made offences, or of the act of punishment, as also the greatest part of what concerns the circumstances affecting the description of the punishment, has been kept together under some such name as *penal* law, or the penal branch of jurisprudence. It

The circumstantiative matter forms the civil branch of the law: the penalizing the penal

199

will not be wondered at, if the boundaries of these two compartments should be in a considerable degree different in different countries: and indeed very unsettled in every country. It will not therefore be wondered at if the account here given of those boundaries should be found to be neither very particular nor very correct. Loose as it is, it may however, even at this stage of it, serve to give such an idea of the distinction as shall be rather more precise than any that has been given of it before. To render it however still more clear and satisfactory it may be worthwhile to give it a more particular application. For this purpose let us take a short review of the several divisions of the whole mass of law as marked out by the several classes and other subordinate divisions of offences: observing under each division what part of the matter necessarily comprehended under that division is most likely to be referred to the civil branch, and what part to the penal.

Circumstan-
tiative matter
belonging to
the several
penal titles.
1. In offences
against
person–it
excepts power
viz. over
persons

10. (1) To begin with offences against person. With regard to a man's person, it may be laid down as a general proposition that in most cases it is unpleasant to him to have another meddle with it. Every act therefore by which the person of another man is affected ought *prima facie* to be treated as an offence. If he thinks it gives him pain, it does give him harm: if he thinks it is productive to him of any such a mischief, it thereby does produce a mischief. Every body knows that in general it is unpleasant to a man to have his person meddled with in any way or another. If there be any exception to the above position it is where you consent that your person shall be dealt with in such or such a manner. Here your consent (provided it be neither unfreely nor unfairly obtained) shows that the act was not unpleasant to you: and therefore that there is no mischief in the case. The case of consent then forms one exception to the rule.

But though there should be a mischief in the case, this mischief may be outweighed: it will be outweighed whenever it is the necessary means of a more than equivalent good. This it is presumed to be in the several cases in which the power of exercising such and such acts upon your person, let them prove ever so disagreeable to you, is conferred upon such and such individuals by the law. When the law exempts a man from punishment in case of his dealing with your person in a manner that either stands a chance or is certain of being disagreeable to you, it thereby confers on him a *power*: it gives him a power over you; a power over your person. Now this is what it may find it necessary to do for various purposes: for the sake of providing for the discharge of the several functions of the husband, the parent, the guardian, the master, the judge, the military officer, and the sovereign: not to mention those extra-ordinary and accidental cases in which for the sake of averting some calamity or other mischief more serious than any which would probably be occasioned by the exercise of the power, it may be expedient to entrust a power of the like stamp to individuals at large. These powers then form so many exceptions to the general rule that no man has the right to meddle with the person of another. Accordingly until the rule which threatens punishment to him who shall meddle with the person of another has specified and made allowance for such exceptions, it can not be regarded as complete: the specification therefore of these exceptions belongs virtually and substantially to the penal branch of the law. But the collection of the sentences which are necessary to the expression of all these specifications must necessarily occupy a very considerable space. They will constitute the matter of several bulky titles, in none of which perhaps shall the general word punishment or the name of any particular sort of punishment make its appearance. If therefore there be [a civil] branch, these titles will of course constitute a part of it. And thus it is that the penal and civil branches share between them so much of the matter of the laws as regards offences against person.

11. (2) In offences against property the distinction between these two branches of law stands upon a somewhat different footing. The objects of property (I mean such as are *corporeal*, into which always may be resolved these other fictitious objects which are styled *incorporeal*) are either things or persons: things by the uses which they may be put to: persons in some few cases also by the uses they may be put to, but more commonly by the services which they may be obliged to render. Offences against property in things are acts whereby a man goes about to meddle or does that which has a tendency to exclude another who has a right from meddling with some object which belongs to the class of things. Now with regard to things no such general rule obtains as the above mentioned one concerning persons. On the contrary concerning every object of the class of things (concerning every such object at least with which a man's meddling or not can be material) the general rule is that there is always some one person at least who *has* a *right* to meddle with it. So far is it from being true that every act by which an object of the class of things is affected, ought *prima facie* to be an offence. You have done so and so with such or such a thing: are you the person who has, or of the number of those persons who have, or are in a way to have, a right to meddle with it? If you are, then you have a *title to* or an *interest in* the thing in question. This lets in all

2. In offences against pro-perty it excepts title, viz. power over things

201

the law relative to the various sorts of *titles*. This branch of the law is commonly an object of infinite variety and prodigious bulk: and may of itself furnish matter for a multitude of volumes. In none of these volumes, unless by accident will any mention be made of punishment. The very idea of punishment will therefore be out of sight: and the whole of this matter will of course be referred to the civil branch of law.

3. *In offences against repu-tation, there is little place for it*

12. (3) With regard to offences against reputation. Reputation is a fictitious entity: it cannot in strictness of speech be meddled with, as a man's person and his property may be meddled with. To meddle with a man's reputation is to propagate some notion to the advantage or to the prejudice of his reputation: to propagate some notion the tendency of which is either to augment or to diminish that portion of good-will which the circle around him may be disposed to bestow upon him. If the tendency of what is done be to augment that portion, no offence is committed: at least no offence against the reputation of that man. If to diminish it, the notion conveyed is either true or false. If true, the general rule is, or at least ought to be, that every man has a right to convey such notion. For the sort of behaviour to which the world in general is wont to annex its ill-will is for the most part that sort of behaviour which in some way or other is pernicious to society. To annex this ill-will to any sort of behaviour is in other words to punish that sort of behaviour with the punishment of the moral sanction. To contribute to the spreading abroad such notion is at the same time to prosecute the delinquent as it were before the tribunal of the public and to bear a hand in the infliction of that punishment. But the fear of the punishments and the hope of the rewards derivable from this source, or in one word the love of reputation, is one of those standing tutelary motives, of which the regular and ordinary tendency is to restrain men from every sort of behaviour which is pernicious to society: not to mention the tendency which it has to prompt men to actions which are of a beneficial tendency. It is the very best in point of general tendency, of all the tutelary motives after that of benevolence: and in point of force it is superior even to that.

There are some cases however in which it is not right that a notion to the prejudice of a man's reputation should be propagated, though it be true. These are in the first place where the fact charged upon a man although it be more or less disreputable, is not pernicious to society: the dictates of the moral sanction happening by reason of some prejudice to be at variance with the dictates of utility. In the next place where the fact is of such a nature that the pain given to individuals by the disclosure of it would outweigh the benefit resulting to the public from the punishment of it. If the notion, being prejudicial to a man's reputation, is at the same time a *false* one, the general rule is that no man has a right to propagate it: and to this there can scarcely be any exception.

Of this complexion are the rules which serve to mark out the acts that are to be deemed offences against reputation. These rules, will scarcely take up more words than may without inconvenience be included under a single title. The expository matter will take up so little room that there will be no need of sending it to a title apart, and severing it from the mandatory.

13. (4) With regard to offences against condition. In whatever way an offence is committed whereby a man's condition in life is liable to be affected, in such cases before the description of the offence can be completed a great many details must be entered into which are too multifarious, too minute and too voluminous to be all of them comprised within the penal branch of jurisprudence. Of what description are the persons between whom the relationship by which the condition is constituted can exist? By what means is the relationship formed? By what may it be dissolved? What are the powers which one of the parties has over the person or which each perhaps has over the property of the other? What are the rights which that one of them has who has no power? What are the duties of each of them towards the other? These and various other questions belong all or most of them to each of the relationships or conditions in question, and form altogether a quantity of matter too bulky to be included within the limits ordinarily allotted in the narrow title of the penal branch of law. Many of them also, we may have observed, must already have been brought upon the carpet under the head of offences against the person. Those, I mean, the answers to which exhibit the several *powers* which furnish so many exceptions concerning the general rule against one man's meddling in any way with the person of another. Many of them likewise require to have been settled under the head of offences against property; the privileges incident to these relationships being so many means of limiting or extending the power of the parties interested, in respect of their property. To instance in the case of the matrimonial condition. To ascertain what the ceremonies must be by which a marriage is constituted is necessary for three purposes: 1. in order to determine when it is that a man is to be understood to possess that power over a woman's person which constitutes one of the exceptions to the general rule concerning

4. In offences against condition

offences against person; 2. in order to determine when it is that a man is to be understood to possess those powers which the law in such a case gives a man over a woman's property; 3. in order to determine when it is that he has a right to cause another to be punished for having carnal knowledge of the woman without marrying her, as in the case of adultery, or by marrying her as in the case of polygamy, and so forth.

Many therefore, we may see, are the cases in which a number of different mandatory clauses in the body of the law may have one and the same assemblage of circumstantiative clauses belonging to them in common. Now so long as this circumstantiative matter is upon the carpet, the idea of punishment though all the while necessarily connected with it, lies concealed however and out of sight. It is not to be wondered at therefore that such a congeries of mere circumstantiative matter should ordinarily be kept apart from the penal branch of the law, and aggregated to the civil.

Thus much with regard to private offences.

5. In semi-public offences it is of the same tenor as in the corresponding private ones

14. (5) As to semi-public offences, these are determined in a great measure by the relation they bear to private ones: being but so many ways of producing the same mischiefs as are apt to result from private offences, only with less certainty and upon a larger scale. Concerning these it will not be necessary to be very particular. It may easily be conceived that the matter of the law relative to these offences like the matter of the law relative to the preceding offences will be in some proportion or other divided between the civil branch of the law and the penal.

The truth is that the same expositive matter that was involved in the mandatory matter relative to private offences, must be involved afresh in the mandatory matter relative to semi-public offences. A man *steals* lead or iron work from off a public bridge. The case must have been there that he was conscious of his having any *title* to the thing so taken. This lets in the whole of the law relative to titles. There are fifty different ways suppose of gaining title to a thing: and as many different ways of parting with it. In order then for the man to be convicted of theft it must appear either 1. that in no one of the first fifty ways could he have supposed himself to have acquired a title to the thing: or 2. that if in any one of those fifty ways he had supposed himself to have acquired such a title, yet in some one or other of the other fifty ways he must have supposed himself to have parted with it.

6. In self-regarding offences

15. (6) With respect to self-regarding offences. The law relating to acts of this description, such few of them, if any, as it may be requisite to constitute offences, will be apt to wear more of a penal complexion upon the face of it than the law relative to any of the preceding divisions of offences. What little there may be occasion to define, there will be little need probably to define for any purpose than that of furnishing matter for the prohibitions established by the laws relative to their title.

16. (7) We come now to public offences. And first with respect to offences against the external security of the state. Suppose the offence to consist in aiding a foreign power with whom the community in question is at war: and suppose war to have been declared. How does it appear that any such declaration has been made? In what persons is the authority of making such a declaration vested? Suppose the offence to consist in a personal or other injury offered to an alien. Who are aliens—who are citizens? Suppose it offered to a foreign ambassador. What are ambassadors? How do they come to be, how may they cease to be ambassadors? *7. In offences against the external security of the state*

17. (8) With regard to offences against the preventive branch of the police. Offences of this division will in the point in question stand upon a footing very little different from that of offences against justice; to which head as being the most important of the two the consideration of them may for the present purpose be referred. *8. In offences against the preventive branch of the police*

18. (9) With regard then to offences against justice. The power of administering justice (under which may be included the power of taking the several steps that are requisite to be taken in subservience to the administration of justice) is a species of trust: a species of public trust. An offence against justice is an offence against this species of trust. What the possible offences are that are capable of being committed against trust has been already shown. The mandatory part of the law relative to this division will consist then in the designation of these several offences and their punishments. But under this mandatory matter a great deal of expository matter will necessarily be involved. A man is guilty of resistance to the orders of a judge. But what sort of person is a judge? How does it appear that the person whose orders are in question, is that sort of person whose orders are at the time in question in the place in question, with reference to the persons and the things in question, to be treated as the orders of a judge? This lets in so much of the public or constitutional branch of the law as concerns officers of justice. How and by whom are judges to be appointed? What are to be their numbers? Where are they to sit? Over what extent of territory, over what sort of offences, over what person, and over *9. In offences against justice* what things are they respectively to have jurisdiction? Are the orders they give to be regarded as definitive or are they subject to reversal? If subject to reversal then again come the same string of questions concerning the superior judges in whom such power of reversal is to be lodged. All this we see is so much expositive matter which must be settled before the mandatory matter can have any application.

Let the person offended against be a person employed under a judge or set of judges whether to record the proceedings that are carried on before them, or to register their orders. Let the offence consist in disturbing them in the execution of their respective offices. One may easily conceive a similar string of questions to be repeated.

10. *In offences against the public force*

19. (10) With regard to offences against the public force. Suppose the offence to consist in the endeavour to withdraw one's self from military service. Military service is the sort of service which is rendered by a soldier. What is a soldier? How is it that he may cease to be so? A soldier is a man whose name is enrolled on a certain list as one who is bound to serve the public in a certain way. But who is it that has the power of enrolling soldiers? Such or such a military officer? How comes he by that power? By commission from the King for example: or from such or such a council etc., according to the nature of the government. This lets in so much of the public or constitutional branch of the law as concerns the appointment and discharge of military officers, and in general of persons engaged in the military service: all which is so much circumstantiative matter as before: and belongs therefore to the civil branch of the law in contradistinction to the penal.

11. *In offences against the positive increase of the national felicity*

20. (11) With regard to offences against the positive increase of the national felicity. These consist chiefly of offences of which the tendency is to impede or misdirect the operations of certain classes of officers who are invested with so many branches of public trust. What are the respective natures of those offices? By what means does a man become possessed of them? By what means may he cease to be so? The answers to these questions constitute so much circumstantiative expositive matter which may be referred to the constitutional branch of the law, and is of a civil nature.

12. *In offences against the public wealth*

21. (12) With regard to offences against the public wealth. A man omits, for example, to pay his quota to a tax. What is a tax? Who has a right to impose taxes? Who is to receive the produce? Such or such a person perhaps for some purposes: such or such another person for other purposes: the sovereign for all or any purposes. Or

206

let it be an offence touching the office of those persons who have the management of such or such an article of the public stock moveable or immoveable. What is the nature of those respective offices? By what means does a man acquire them, by what means may he cease to be in possession of them?—More circumstantiative matter belonging to another part of the constitutional branch of the law.

22. (13) With regard to offences against population. This is a title which is here inserted rather out of deference to current notions, than with a view to any offences which there will be occasion to place under it. Population (in due time, there will be occasion to shew) is a business that will go on extremely well of itself, so long as the legislator does nothing to disturb it. It is scarcely in the power of an individual to do any thing that can materially affect it, unless by offences which come under one or another of the preceding heads. If it were not a solecism to speak of the legislator's committing an offence, one might say perhaps with some degree of truth that there is no offence can be committed against population but what is committed by the legislator. Suppose however for example sake the legislator should think fit to have recourse to coercive methods, and under the notion of favouring population, should command or prohibit certain practices. In the description of those practices the words, *husband, wife, child* (meaning legitimate child) *nun, monk*, and so forth, might probably occur. It hath already been observed that the circumstantiative matter relative to these several sorts of persons is to be sought for in the civil branch of the law; that which belongs to the words *husband, wife*, and *child*, in that part of it which is of a private nature: that which concerns the words *monk* and *nun* to that which is of a constitutional or public nature.

13. In offences against population

23. (14) With regard to offences against the national wealth. Let the offence consist in exporting goods without a licence. The licence meant is one that must be given by certain officers: officers belonging to the Board of Trade. Who are these officers? By whom appointed? This introduces another string of questions, the solution of which belongs to another part of the public or constitutional branch of the law, and is still of a civil nature as before.

14. In offences against the national wealth

24. (15) With regard to offences against the sovereignty. Let the offence consist in taking up arms against the sovereignty. In whom does the sovereignty reside? in a single person, or in a number of persons? Whence does he, or whence do they derive this power? from succession or from election? More civil matter, belonging to the constitutional branch as before.

15. In offences against the sovereignty

16. *In*
offences
against
religion

25. (16) With regard to offences against religion. Let the offence consist in usurping the character of a clergyman. Further repetitions are needless. This we see lets in a great abundance of civil matter belonging to the constitutional branch as before.

17. *In*
offences
against the
national
interest in
general

26. (17) The last division of public offences, that of offences against the national interest in general may just be mentioned on this occasion, for the sake of shewing that it has not been forgotten. Let the offence be one that concerns the office of a Privy Counsellor. What is the office of a Privy Counsellor? By what events may a man be invested with it, and by what others may he be divested of it: and so with regard to the office of an ambassador, as hath already been observed. Or let it consist in taking a present from a foreign sovereign, without a licence from one's own. This we see, necessarily refers to so much of the expositive matter as concerns the description of the person or persons from whom the licence is to come.

CHAPTER XVII

DIVISION OF THE LAWS INTO CIVIL AND CRIMINAL[1]

§ i. *Distinction between Civil Law and Criminal*

1. Thus much concerning the meaning of the word *penal* when applied to a branch of law, and put in opposition to the word *civil*. But there is another word, the word *criminal*, which is also put in contra-distinction with the word civil and which at the same time is in many cases used interconvertibly with the word *penal*. In some cases, that is, but perhaps not in all. Therefore although no very explicit line of distinction is to be drawn between the civil branch and the penal, may not there however be a line somewhat more explicit drawn between the *civil* branch and the *criminal*? Let us see then what is to be understood by the word *criminal* as applied to a branch of law.

2. The criminal branch of law is that which concerns crimes. What then do we mean by crimes? Do we mean offences? But we have seen that there is no law whatsoever which does not terminate in the creation of an offence. If the word *criminal* then is to distinguish the branch of law it is applied to from any other, it is only some particular class of offences that can be meant by the word *crimes*. I know of but three circumstances that seem ever to have served as marks to distinguish them from other offences: 1. the magnitude of the mischief they occasion or are thought to occasion. 2. the quantum of displeasure or disapprobation which is annexed,or thought to be annexed to them by the community in general. 3. the punishment annexed to them by the law. An offence is spoken of as a crime, sometimes under the notion of its being *very* mischievous, sometimes because it is *very* odious, sometimes because the punishment for it is *very* heavy. The circumstances are apt not unfrequently to concur in one and the same offence: more especially on

Is criminal law more distinct from civil than penal is[2]

Three senses of the word crime–it imports 1. mischievousness, 2. odiousness, 3. penalty

---

[1] The Mss. for this chapter present certain problems. The division of the material into three sections has been adopted as an editorial device to distinguish three distinct groups of Ms. material. Only the first of these—corresponding to § i—was unequivocally destined by Bentham for final inclusion in the present work. See below for notes on the Ms. basis of §§ ii and iii.

[2] Bentham in fact reversed the order of *civil* and *penal* in this marginal heading. The Ms. for the whole paragraph shows frequent corrections of mistakes in the terminology.

account of the tendency which the one of them has to produce the other. The notion of an act's being mischievous is one cause at least, as it ought to be the only cause, which makes it odious: and its being odious is perhaps the most frequent though never otherwise than the improper cause of its being made punishable.

Magnitude of the punishment alone no source of distinction between offences considered with a view to punishment

3. As to the magnitude of the punishment, it is evident that from this circumstance no mark of distinction can be taken to separate one division of offences from another for the present purpose. For the business here is to consider in the first place what the offences are in themselves, and it is from thence that we are afterwards to determine what treatment ought to be given to them. As to the treatment actually given to them, this as every one knows is in great measure different in different countries; so that it never can come under any one single description whatsoever.

–nor the degree of odiousness

4. The degree of popular odium under which an offence is also in a high degree variable, to say nothing of the difficulty of measuring and collecting it.

–nor the degree of mischievousness

5. The degree of mischievousness of an offence though liable to some variation is however liable to less variation than either of those other circumstances.

Whether an act be a crime depends on all three circumstances together

6. It has been already observed that these circumstances are found frequently to attach in conjunction upon an offence: as it were to be wished they always did. It is not indeed without some force put upon language and some appearance at least of impropriety that an offence can be called a crime if any one of them be wanting. If it be mischievous without being odious, if it be not proportionably odious, you would scruple to call it a crime for fear of being understood to represent it in the light of an offence which was actually odious; a fact which by the supposition is not true. Are you persuaded of its being odious, without looking upon it as mischievous, you would not without reluctance be willing to call it a crime lest you should be understood to represent it as being mischievous, and thereby join in increasing an odium which you look upon as unjust. Were the case even such that you deemed it mischievous at the same time that you were sensible of its being odious, yet if it were not treated with severity by the laws, you would scarce perhaps think yourself warranted in point of verbal accuracy in speaking of it as a crime. To call it a crime would seem to be a trick of oratory.

Easier to point out some acts that are crimes, than to say what are not

7. If the word *criminal* is to be employed, it seems impossible therefore so far to mark out the boundaries of the criminal branch of the law as to determine with precision what offences it shall *not* extend to. To find some which it may not improperly be determined to extend to seems however not to be alike impossible. Such for instance are the offences of robbery, incendiarism, certain species of homicide, and calumniatory perjury: these being offences to which it is not likely that on any of the three grounds above-mentioned any person will be disposed to deny the appellation of crimes. Several articles more might perhaps be added to the catalogue: it would be impossible however to proceed any great length in it without getting into controversy: a controversy which, as there is no assignable standard to appeal to would be indeterminable.

8. What makes this the more indisputable is that in drawing the line between offences which are crimes and offences which are not, the consideration of *degree* enters everywhere into the question: it was for this reason that it seemed necessary a little higher up to make use of the word *very*. In point of mischievousness to entitle an offence to the appellation of a crime it is not enough that it be mischievous, it must be *very* mischievous: in like manner it must be *very* odious: so also must the punishment be *very* severe: at least it is not any *very* slight punishment that will suffice. This consideration alone is enough to make the application of the word crime altogether uncertain. *Particularly in as much as it depends upon degree*

9. It seems therefore that the word *criminal* will not serve to characterize any branch of law as subsisting in contradistinction to that which is called the civil. It seems therefore that we must come back to the word *penal* after all. But the word *penal* as applied to this purpose does not seem to have as yet acquired any determinate application, as we have already shewn. To settle the matter and save ourselves from the inconvenience of running into continual contradictions and obscurity there seems to be no remedy but to propose a new and in some measure arbitrary line. To the civil branch therefore may be understood to belong exclusively such offences as it is not judged necessary to punish with any extraordinary degree or species of punishment: to the criminal, such offences as it is judged necessary to punish with some extraordinary degree or species of punishment. *Offences if punished with an ordinary measure of punishment may be deemed civil offences; if with an extraordinary, criminal*

10. Let the immediate standard then be the supposed demand for the quantum of the punishment. The punishment considered in respect of its quantity may be distinguished into *ordinary* and *extraordinary*. Under the name of ordinary punishment may be comprised the least proportion of punishment that can in any case be made use of in point of quantity, and consequently of the mildest *Punishment ordinary, and extra-ordinary*

quality: that is pecuniary punishment: and that in such proportion as but just to outweigh the profit of the offence: for less than that, as has been shewn, would only do harm, and could not possibly be of any use: which must be substituted in case of the offender's not having wherewithal to undergo this sort of punishment, some other punishment, such as imprisonment, of the next mildest nature that can be devised. By extraordinary punishment may be understood any quantity or mode of punishment which it may be proper to substitute in certain cases to the ordinary mode and measure of punishment.[a]

Grounds for extra-ordinary punishment

11. As to the grounds upon which it may be proper to have recourse to extraordinary punishment: these herein before hinted at—viz.—1. any extraordinary mischievousness on the part of the offence, when it is so great as may make it necessary and worth-while to hazard an extraordinary expense in point of punishment for the sake of purchasing the better chance of combating it with effect: 2. the deficiency of the punishment in point of certainty as resulting from the difficulty of detection: which difficulty depends in great measure, as is evident, upon the nature of the offence. 3. the presumption which the offence may afford of the offender's having already been guilty of other offences of the like nature. 4. the accidental advantage in point of quality of a punishment not strictly meted in point of quantity. 5. the use of a punishment of a particular quality in the character of a moral lesson: 6. an extra-ordinary want of sensibility on the part of the offender to the force of such standing tutelary motives as are opposed to the offence whether on the part of the law itself, or on the part of the other auxiliary sanctions.[b]

Punishment must be extra-ordinary, where the profit is not pecuniary

12. It is to be observed that it is only where the profit of the offence is all of it pecuniary that there can be any very entire certainty of outweighing it by a given quantity and mode of punishment. When what a man gets by his offence is money and nothing else, take from him that money and so much more, and you

---

[a] See Ch. xiv (Proportion) 27.[1]

[b] See Ch. xi (Dispositions) 31, 32, 33.[2] It will be observed that with a view to the aggregating an offence to this or that branch of law this last circumstance can operate no otherwise than as far as the nature of the offender's disposition may be indicated by circumstances comprisable in the description of the *species* of offence: circumstances that happen by accident to accompany the offence in this or that accidental instance cannot for this purpose be taken into consideration.

[1] *An Introduction to the Principles*, Ch. xiv, para. 27 (in *CW*, 172–3).
[2] *An Introduction to the Principles*, Ch. xi, paras. 31–3 (in *CW*, 135–6).

may be certain enough of not leaving him a gainer. But when the profit is any part of it not pecuniary, there the case is different. Take for example the case where the motive or one of the motives is ill-will, and the profit of the offence is the gratification of the irascible appetite. A man falls upon you and beats you: what pecuniary loss is there that you could be sure would give him just so much pain as the satisfaction of giving vent to his ill-will promised to afford him pleasure? It is plain that between quantities so incommensurate there is no striking a sure balance. In such cases therefore it will not be safe to trust to pecuniary punishment altogether. Some other punishment therefore must be allowed of as applicable to such offence: which other punishment, according to the line of division here assigned to the two branches will exclude the offence from the civil branch by aggregating it to the penal. And this is one among other reasons why the slightest offence against a man's person though frequently of less mischief than even a very trivial offence against property can scarcely be referred to any other than the penal branch of law.

13. Thus far then we are arrived, that any offence may be deemed a civil offence, to which there seems to be no need of annexing any extraordinary species or degree of punishment. So much then as concerns an offence of this description belongs to the civil branch of the law, and not to the penal. On the other hand every offence to which it seems to be necessary to annex any extraordinary species or degree of punishment may be termed (it would be too much to say a crime, but however for want of any less inapplicable expression) a criminal offence or misdemeanour. Is it then true accordingly that whatever part of the law goes to make up the description of a criminal offence, belongs to the penal or criminal branch of law? Here, we see, the correspondency must fail. In many articles it is a part only of what belongs to the description of a criminal offence that can be included with any degree of propriety or convenience within this latter branch. For wherever the directory part of any law of which the comminatory part threatens an extraordinary degree of punishment runs out into details, those forming long and separate titles, those titles carrying nothing that belongs to punishment upon the face of them it must be aggregated to the civil branch of law. The necessity of this will appear the more manifest in the instances where we see an offence which by the change or addition of a single circumstance may be attended with such diversity of effects, as in the one case shall rank it under the head of civil, in the other under the head of criminal offences.

The directory (circumstantiative) part of every law belongs to the civil branch—the comminatory to the criminal

Intentionality makes the difference between civil and criminal offences

14. The circumstance I am speaking of is of one sort, a circumstance respecting the state of the offender's mind with reference to the obnoxious event, a circumstance relative to intentionality and consciousness: the circumstance that takes place where the offender is conscious of his being acting against the law, and intends accordingly to avoid if possible the being amenable to law for what he has done. It is this consciousness and the intention which is in a manner inseparable from it, that added together make up the idea which seems hitherto to have been but vaguely expressed under some such terms as *dolus, prava intentio, malus animus, malitia,* and the like.

Influence which this has on the mischief of the act

15. That this circumstance is intimately connected with the mischief of the act will be readily apprehended by anyone who recollects what is said on that subject in a preceding chapter.ᶜ There are two ways then in which this circumstance may enhance the demand for punishment. One is by enhancing the mischief of the act: the other is by diminishing the certainty of the punishment. When a man is conscious beyond a doubt that the act he is about to commit is within the prohibition of the law, that accordingly it is of the number of those acts which are marked out for punishment, his ingenuity will of course be set to work to escape detection. The punishment will therefore be attended with every degree of uncertainty which he can give it: for which uncertainty it is necessary, as has been already intimated, to make up in magnitude.

This uncertainty is an additional circumstance which contributes afresh to increase the mischief, to wit the secondary mischief, of the offence. For the better chance an offender learns to give himself of concealing the offence, the more apt he will be to commit it, and the more apt men are to commit offences, the more those offences will be dreaded: the more secret the offence may be from the nature of it, the more will people be afraid of it.

§ ii. *Limits between the Criminal Branch and the Civil*²

Some cases appear more manifestly to belong to the criminal branch than others

1. In some cases prohibition comes of course, and the only question is concerning the quantum and nature of the punishment. This

ᶜ Ch. xii (Consequences) § 2.¹

¹ *An Introduction to the Principles,* Ch. xii, § ii (in *CW*, 152–7).

² The Mss. for this section (U.C. lxxxviii.347–8) differ markedly from most of the Mss. for the present work in that they are (apart from some marginal insertions) in the hand of a copyist. They are headed 'Limits between the Criminal branch and the Civil' and some deleted passages suggest that they represent a partially superseded draft for §i above.

happens where the mischief of the act or (in cases where the legislator has suffered himself to be governed by principles other than that of utility) where the ground of antipathy or displeasure whatever it be is very apparent. Instances of this sort are most abundant among offences against individuals, semi-public offences against a class or neighbourhood, self-regarding offences against one's self, offences against the sovereignty, against justice, against the external security of the state, against the public force, and against religion. In other cases the question is not only in what manner the offence shall be punished but whether the act shall be so much as constituted an offence: whether punishment shall be applied to it at all. And yet even in these cases if it be once determined to place the act in the catalogue of offences it may be necessary to make the punishment which is employed to combat it a severe one: owing for example to the powerfulness of the seducing motive. Instances of this sort are most frequent among offences against the revenue, against the national wealth, and against the national interest in general. Thus much applies only to principal offences: offences that are obnoxious of themselves: offences that are constituted such in the way of *direct* legislation: but with regard to accessory offences, offences that consist in the breach of such regulations as are made in the view of withdrawing men by oblique methods from the above principal offences, in short from acts that are constituted such in the way of *indirect* legislation, the question 'shall the act be prohibited or no?' must be open to debate in every instance throughout the whole circle of such offences whatever the class or division they belong to.

2. This improbity of intention may in some instances be presumed from the nature of the act itself, when the mischievousness of it is so plain, that no man, it is supposed, can possibly be at a loss to know that it stands prohibited by the law. Thus it is for instance with all acts that affect a man in his person, in all cases in which they are not accompanied by some special ground of justification. For with regard to a man's *person* the general rule is that no one else has any right to meddle with it.

The case is not the same with regard to *things*. With regard to such things as are of value (that is all such things as with which a man's meddling can be *material*) the general rule is, that there is always some one person at least who *has a right* to meddle with them: and the only question is *who* is it that has that right: who is it that is in such manner favoured by the law, as to have that right conferred upon him. The party thus favoured may at one time be

Consciousness of criminality or criminal consciousness presumed from the nature of the offence: where it affects a person —not where it affects a thing

one person, at another time another. It is not therefore for meddling with the thing that a man is ever punished, but for meddling with a thing with which he has no right to meddle. The circumstance therefore of his having no right to meddle with it must be expressly stated in the definition of the crime. More than that, it is very possible that he may not *know* but that he *has* a right to meddle with it; if that were the case it would be wrong to punish him with any extraordinary degree of severity: for, if that were done, the best disposed man that ever lived could not be sure of conducting himself for any length of time without falling under the censure of the law: the circumstance, therefore, of his possessing this knowledge, must be included in the notion of the offence, when put upon the footing of a criminal one.

−unless the circumstance of his having no right to meddle with it be too clear to admit of doubt

If however it be any particular kind of act with relation to a thing that a man is forbidden or commanded to engage in, and that act can be so particularly described that there shall appear no doubt but that he must understand it to be prohibited or commanded; in any such case the circumstance of his knowing it to be prohibited or commanded will naturally be taken for granted, and there will appear no occasion for stating that circumstance in the definition of the offence.

The line is drawn by the magnitude of the punishment

3. If it be asked then what it is that constitutes the positive factitious distinction between the criminal branch and the civil, the answer is, in the first place the magnitude of the punishment: in the next place the quantity of space which it may be necessary to bestow upon the directory part of the law. If it be asked what is the natural distinction upon which the above positive one is grounded, the answer is that it is for the most part the criminal consciousness abovementioned: I say for the most part; for from the bulk of legislators neither on this point nor any other can anything very uniform or determinate be expected.

−which is made to depend in most cases upon criminal consciousness

−which is sometimes taken for granted as following of course

This criminal consciousness is sometimes looked upon as being in a manner inseparable from the intention of committing the offence, and then there is nothing said about it; at other times it is looked upon as accidental to that intention and then the circumstance of its being present is expressly taken notice of as one of the circumstances which must accompany the offence in order to put it upon the rank of criminal ones.

To mark out rights belongs not to penal law

4. The business therefore of establishing and limiting rights as well over persons as over things belongs not to the criminal branch of the law: all such business it supposes to be performed already by the civil branch.

5. This seems to be the most general rule that can be laid down with truth, but on both sides it admits however of exceptions. In certain cases where the mischief is such as appears to be very great, rashness and heedlessness, without criminal consciousness, are put upon the footing of criminality. The reason is that from rashness or heedlessness in cases of such danger society may have as much to fear as in cases of less danger from wilful criminality. In other cases where the mischief is very little or the means of redressing it certain, even the presence of criminal consciousness will not make it necessary to put the offence upon the footing of a crime. This happens principally with regard to offences which none but such as are responsible can commit. Where compensation is certain, punishment is needless.

Sometimes punishment where no criminal consciousness: sometimes no punishment where there is

6. After all, it cannot but be observed that the same offence at different times and places will stand, and to different persons will appear to stand, in a different light in point of criminality. So that nothing can be less stable than the distinction between the civil and the criminal branches of the law. Some however there will be, which will be sure always to keep their station in the criminal, while others will be vibrating as it were between that and the civil. These last, wherever they occur it will be proper to take some notice of— lest by passing them over our plan should appear imperfect.

Variableness of the distinction

What has been said is rather a display of the difficulty than a solution of it. But when a difficulty is insuperable the best thing that can be done is to acknowledge it.

§ iii. *Limits between the Criminal Branch and the Civil. Offences against Property*[1]

1. The taking or keeping, or using, or damaging a thing by one who though he has no title to take, or keep, or use, or damage it, is not conscious of his having none, is the common and ordinary offence against the law of property: it is punished by the ordinary allotment (or rate) of punishment, to wit the obligation of restoring the thing so dealt with and as far as that is impracticable or in-

Difference between criminal and civil offences against property

---

[1] The Ms. for this section (U.C. lxxxviii.349), like that for § ii with which Bentham has paginated it, differs from the other Mss. for the present work in that its opening passages are in the hand of a copyist. The continuation, however, is in Bentham's hand. The Ms. seems originally to have been headed (by the copyist) 'Offences against Property', to which Bentham later added 'Limits between the Criminal Branch and the Civil'. It seems likely that the Ms. is a fragment either of the *Plan of a Penal Code* or of the *Treatise on Offences* which preceded it; and that Bentham subsequently adapted it as an illustration of the points made in this chapter of the present work.

sufficient, of making amends to the party injured for what he has suffered by its being so dealt with: to which is commonly added the obligation of paying the expense necessarily incurred by the party injured in obtaining such restitution and compensation: that is his costs of suit. Such an offence is called a civil offence: and the consequence of such offence belongs to that branch of the law which in contradistinction to the *criminal* branch is called the *civil*.

The taking or keeping, or using, or damaging a thing by one who is conscious of his having no title so to do or which comes to much the same thing in consequence of an apparent title obtained by suggestions which he knows to be false constitute under different sets of circumstances so many extraordinary offences against the law of property. These are punished by so many extraordinary allotments of punishment. Such offences are styled *criminal* offences or *crimes*: and these are the offences against property which belong to that branch of the law which is called the *criminal* branch.

A line if drawn could not be permanent

2. That no settled line can be drawn between the civil branch and the penal is most manifest. Suppose a line to be drawn between them anywhere: an act of a general description having no punishment annexed to it or none above the ordinary, falls without the penal branch and belongs only to the civil. But now let the legislator make a law against such act, annexing to it a severe punishment. It is plain that the same act which before belonged to the civil branch, belongs now to the penal; and the boundary set up between them is broke down.

Limits with the penal branch marked out by the manner in which punishment is concerned

3. The law can do nothing without exercising power somehow or other; power of some sort or other then must be concerned in every act which it proposes. Now it cannot exercise power over one man but by means of power which it confers or has conferred upon another. Power is either over things or persons: and in either case it is either beneficial or fiduciary. When fiduciary it is coupled with trust. What concerns beneficial power, whether over things or over persons, and fiduciary where the benefitee is an individual, or an assemblage of individuals, belongs to the private law: what concerns a class of unassignable individuals, belongs to the public or constitutional branch.

But power can no other wise be constituted than by means of punishment. This punishment is either ordinary or extraordinary. Where either the means of enforcing the obligation or variety in the means of enforcing the obligation does not come in question, but the provision of the law turns upon the question concerning the acts which a man is to perform or abstain from, or the person by whom, or the circumstances in which they are to be abstained from or performed, it comes under the head of the civil branch: where the nature of the punishment is the principal object that strikes the eye, and the business is to mark out the different cases where different punishments are to take place, then that matter belongs to the penal branch.

4. To ethics it belongs to ascertain the cases in which on the one hand the punishment, and on the other the reward of the moral sanction ought to apply: and to instruct a man how to avoid the one and obtain the other. But wherever the punishment of the political sanction ought to apply, there also ought that of the moral: in this respect therefore this whole work belongs still to ethics. On the other hand there are divers cases in which although the punishment of the political ought not at any rate to apply, howsoever it may be with the moral, there are others in which neither the one ought to apply nor the other, nor in short any punishment at all. These cases have already been marked out. Where any punishment is groundless, there all punishment is groundless: there neither that of the political nor that of the moral ought to apply. So also if the punishment of the political sanction is inefficacious, the feebler punishment of the moral sanction must be so likewise: but it may very well happen that all punishment on the part of the political sanction may be unprofitable or needless, where that of the moral shall be both requisite and profitable.

Dictates of ethics include what ought to be dictates of jurisprudence and something more

CHAPTER XVIII

DISTINCTION BETWEEN PENAL AND CIVIL PROCEDURE

Division of judicial procedure into penal and civil

1. The nature of the power exercised by a judge depends upon the nature of the cause or case in which it is exercised. In every cause there must be at least two parties, a plaintiff and a defendant: and if there are more parties than two the cause may be considered as a complex one; and may be accordingly resolved into a proportionate number of simple causes in each of which there shall be but one plaintiff and one defendant. The nature then of every cause depends upon the manner in which the interest of the defendant is affected by the last act, the ultimate or definitive act which comes to be performed on the part of the magistrate in the course of the proceedings relative to that cause. This act may be termed the judgment.

[1]In other words every judgment has reference to some obnoxious act, which is a name that may be given in common to an act which having actually been committed is actually an offence, and an act which were it committed would be an offence. This obnoxious act then at the time of instituting the suit either had been committed or had not: if it had, the object of the suit and the business of the judgment belonging to it may be to punish it: and if it was the suit was a penal suit: if it had not, the object of the suit and the business of the judgment in that same suit as such, can not have been to punish it: it can only be to prohibit it.

To consider the matter in another point of view. On what occasion soever the law does any thing in favour of any person, it thereby confers on that person a right.[a] But there is no law whatsoever that does not operate in favour of some person or other: consequently there is no law whatsoever that does not confer on some person or other a right. Now the violation of a right is an offence: nor is there any thing else but the violation of a right that is an offence. In other words, by whatever act an offence is committed, a right is violated: and vice versa by whatever act a right (meaning

---

[a] It follows that a power is a species of right.

[1] Against this and the next paragraph Bentham has pencilled a marginal query, having apparently been in doubt as to their inclusion. They are preceded and followed by deleted passages.

always a legal right) is violated an offence is committed.[1] Whatever judgment then has relation to [an] offence has thereby also relation to a right. This right then which the judgment has reference to is either constituted by the judgment or it is not: if it be created by the judgment it could not have been violated before the judgment, consequently there could not have been any offence created or committed on the score of that right previously to the judgment; it did not subsist before, consequently the offence corresponding to it could not subsist before: if it be not created by the judgment, it must have subsisted before, it may have been violated, and the judgment may be styled a judgment of adjudication.

This judgment may be considered either with respect to its influence on the interests of the plaintiff or with respect to its influence on the interests of the defendant.

2. To consider it first in the latter point of view. Affecting the interests of the defendant it will affect them either in a favourable or an unfavourable way. Let it be in an unfavourable way: either then the intention is that it should affect him in the way of punishment or it is not: in either case if it affects him at all it must operate on him either with or without the intervention of his will[b]: if with such intervention it may be said to affect him in respect of his active as well as his passive faculties, if without, in respect of his passive faculties merely. If then the intention is that the judgment should affect him in the way of punishment in such case by what means soever it affects him the judgment may be styled a punitory or penal judgment, or judgment of conviction: if not by what means soever it may affect him it may be styled, in conformity to common usage, a *civil* judgment: taking the word civil in one of the many senses in which this very vague and ambiguous appellative is employed. We shall inquire a little further on whether some other epithet somewhat less uncharacteristic may not be found. *—with respect to the defendant* *Judgment of conviction*

3. Next let the judgment be in favour of the defendant: of this case little need be said: it is only in a negative way that a defendant can as such be favoured by it.[c] If the judgment had it been against *Judgment of acquittal*

[b] See supra (Division).[2]

[c] I am speaking here all along of one simple cause independent of every other that may by accident be combined with it. A sort of accessory suit which in most cases is combined with the principal one is that concerning costs: the costs incurred on each side in the carrying on of the principal one. Inasfar as

[1] At this point the Ms. has the following sentence, subsequently bracketed by Bentham for tentative deletion: 'So that the ideas of (a law, a definitive judicial act) an offence and a right are inseparable'.

[2] *An Introduction to the Principles*, Ch. xvi.

him would have been a penal one, a judgment of conviction, being in his favour it may be termed a judgment of acquittal or absolution. To find a name for a judgment given in favour of the defendant in a cause in which had it been against him it would have been not a penal but only a civil judgment, we must consider it in respect to the influence it may have on the interests of the plaintiff.

Judgment of adjudication

4. First then, let it have been given in his favour. Whatever is done by one man whether a magistrate or not in favour of another whether a plaintiff or not is done with or without the assistance of a third person: if without such assistance the magistrate or other person may be said to have done it with his own hand, *manu propria*, if with such assistance, he may in so far be said to have done it by the hand of another, *manu aliena*. Now what is done by a judgment can never be done *manu propria*: for a judgment in the sense in which it is an expression of will is a kind of occasional law, an order made upon such or such persons requiring them to do so and so: requiring them in the present case to comport themselves so and so for the benefit of the plaintiff. It is therefore from the conduct that is maintained by the persons in question in consequence of such judgment, and not from the judgment itself independent of such conduct that the advantage accruing to the plaintiff takes its rise: it is not ever *manu propria* that a judge acts as such, but always *manu aliena*. It is not therefore by any action of his own that the judge produces the effect resulting from his judgment any further than by means of some action which it produces on the part of some one else. The action then which is produced on the part of some one else must be produced either by physical or by moral influence: by physical influence it is not by the supposition: for then it might be said to be produced *manu propria* by the judge himself. It must therefore be by moral: that is by the force of certain *motives*. Now motives must be either of the coercive or the alluring kind[d]: those of the latter kind are, as hath been shewn already, inapplicable to the purpose in question; there remain those of the coercive kind. But to give birth to action of any kind on the part of any person by the force of coercive motives, is in other words to lay him under an obligation: which obligation is by the supposition in the case in question a legal one, and the judgment

the business of a judgment is to give costs to the defendant it may be considered *pro tanto* as a judgment given in a cross cause in which he is not the defendant but the plaintiff.

[d] See Ch. (Motives).[1]

[1] *An Introduction to the Principles*, Ch. x.

by which it is imposed may be considered as a kind of law. Now this obligation under which the party is laid, is by the supposition imposed on him for the sake of another person. But when in favour of one person an obligation is laid on another, such other person is said to have a right conferred on him or to be invested with a right. Since then the effect of the judgment is to *invest* the plaintiff with a right it may be termed a *judgment of investiture*: and since the investment in question is performed by a person acting in the capacity of a judge, it may be termed *a judgment of adjudication*.

5. Lastly, let the judgment have been given *against*, that is in disfavour of the plaintiff. Of this case little need be said. As all that it could do in favour of a plaintiff as such is to invest him with a right, so all that it can do against a plaintiff as such is not to invest him, or in other words to refuse to invest him with a right: it may therefore be termed a judgment of *non-investiture* or *non-adjudication*. *Judgment of non-adjudication*

6. It appears then that every legal judgment by which a period is put to a cause is either a penal or a civil judgment: if a penal judgment a judgment of conviction or a judgment of acquittal: if a civil judgment, a judgment of adjudication or a judgment of non-adjudication. *Recapitulation*

Let us try whether it might not be possible to find out some epithet which in its application to the subject of procedure might be opposed to *penal*, and which might be somewhat less uncharacteristic than the word *civil*. In a civil suit the two parties are both of them of course petitioners: the plaintiff or claimant requesting that a judgment of adjudication to such or such an effect may be given in his favour, the defendant or repugner that it may not be given: they may therefore both of them indifferently be styled *competitors*: and by analogy the branch of procedure which concerns the steps that may respectively be taken by them for the purpose of obtaining the object of their respective petitions may be styled *competitorial procedure*.

It cannot be denied but that in every case penal as well as civil there is a competition, so that neither that which is here in question nor probably any other epithet that could be found would be quite so characteristic as could be wished: all that can be said in favour of it is that when the suit is of a penal nature the circumstance of the punishment which is peculiar to it is of so striking a nature as to eclipse as it were and put out of sight the other circumstance which is in common.

It has been already stated, that to give a judgment of adjudication in favour of one man is to impose an obligation on some other. The person on whom this obligation is imposed is in most instances the defendant. Let it have been a right of property for instance that is adjudged to the plaintiff: to confer on him that right, the defendant is inhibited from performing any act the effect of which would be to disturb him in the enjoyment of that property. Let it have been a condition or station in life: the defendant is inhibited from performing any act the effect of which would be to disturb him in the enjoyment of the advantages belonging to that condition. But there may be cases in which the obligation is imposed not on the defendant but on other persons: usually on the special ministers of justice. Let it for instance have been a right of guardianship which is adjudged to the plaintiff as against the defendant, who is thereby treated as a lunatic: to give effect to this adjudication it may be necessary to lay an obligation on other persons to lay hands on the defendant and deliver him into the plaintiff's custody; in such case to trust to the effect of any obligation laid on the defendant himself, to trust altogether to the effects of mental coercion on the mind of one on whom such coercion may perhaps have no hold, would be evidently absurd. So where a delivery is to be made of the physical possession of a thing which perhaps the defendant has no longer in his possession, or where a nuisance is to be removed, which perhaps were he ever so well disposed, it exceeds his power to remove. In both cases indeed it is the defendant whose interests are principally affected: but in as far as the obligation is laid on himself alone, it is through the medium of his active faculties that he is affected: in as far as it is laid on third persons it is through the medium of his passive faculties merely.

All suits reducible to the above standards

7. In fixing the idea of a suit at law the business is to pitch upon such a model as shall be at once complete and simple. To this model if properly delineated every other less regular specimen may be reduced and made conformable: if imperfect by complexion, if complex by decomposition or resolution.

Suits defective by the want of a plaintiff

8. In some cases it may be proper or customary or both for the judge to take up the matter of himself: in this case he may be considered as acting himself in the double capacity of plaintiff as well as judge, until the former function be made over to a third person. This is the case for instance where the investitive event in a civil concern or the act of delinquency in a penal concern happens under his eye, so that there is nobody can tell him any more of the matter than he knows already: as where a lunatic is seen raving or a rioter doing mischief in the court in which the judge is sitting. So in case of a contempt of court.

224

9. But the cases are much more frequent in which a suit in order to be reduced to the ideal standard requires to be decomposed. Thus in matters penal many distinguishable offences may be included in one claim. This may be the case even from the very commencement of the suit; from the date of the first step that happens to be taken in it. Besides this there is scarce an instance of a principal suit but what gives birth to a number of incidental contestations which may be reckoned as so many collateral suits growing out of the principal one and which are successively determined by judgments which in this case are styled *interlocutory*.

Many accusations in one, many claims in one

Incidental suits arising out of the principal

Moreover there are few accusations of a penal nature which are not originally or incidentally intermixed with claims of a civil nature. This is the case in most of the instances where there is room for the operation of any of those subsidiary laws which we have had occasion to characterize under the names of catapaustic, metaphylactic and compensative laws.[e]

10. Lastly in many or perhaps most civil causes there are cross claims; the defendant insisting not only that the right in question ought not to be conferred upon the plaintiff, but that some other right ought to be conferred upon himself. In this case also there are two suits going on together in which the parties are the same: only he who appears in the one capacity in one cause appears in the opposite capacity in the other.

Cross claims

11. It should be understood that in many perhaps in most instances it is precisely the same judgment that is given in a penal suit and in a civil one: at least the interests of the defendant are affected by it in precisely the same manner: the only difference lies in the *cause* for which and the intention with which it is so given. Thus where money (that is a right to the absolute use and disposal of a sum of money) is given to the plaintiff at the expense of the defendant: if the event on account of which it was given, the event by means of which the plaintiff stands invested with the right of calling upon the judge to make over to him or to compel the defendant to make over to him this amount, if this event was one that

The judgment may be the same in a civil suit as in a penal one

---

[e] See Ch. | | (Limits).[1]

[1] The form of this reference shows that this material was not originally intended to form part of the chapter on 'Limits' out of which the present work grew. The Mss. for the present chapter are in fact headed 'Corpus', and were thus intended for what at various stages of Bentham's plan figured as Ch. xix, xxxviii, or xl of the expanded *Introduction to the Principles*. The chapter on the 'Idea of a complete *Corpus Juris*' was dropped from the plan for the separate work *Of Laws in General*. (See above, Introduction, xxxii–xxxiii: and below, Appendices E and F.) For Bentham's terminology at the end of this paragraph see above 149–50 and nn., b, c, d.

happened so much without the consciousness of the defendant as not to subject him to the imputation of delinquency, the suit can be called nothing but a civil one; for instance when the cattle of the defendant without any default of his do mischief to cattle belonging to the plaintiff: if on the other hand that event was of such a nature as to subject him to the imputation above-mentioned, as if he had driven the cattle purposely into the plaintiff's field, the suit may be termed a penal one: in short the delinquency of a defendant is but one out of the vast variety of *titles* on which, under any system of laws in being, a plaintiff may ground himself in praying a judgment of the nature in question against the defendant.[f]

What it is that civil suits have to do with offences

12. Recollecting that upon the plan here given of the law, everything that is or can be done by law supposes an offence, it may still be asked perhaps how is it that the judgment in a civil suit, in a suit in which nobody is held up to view in the character of a delinquent has anything to do with any offence? The answer is, by creating one: by turning into an offence the act of anyone who according to the nature of the judgment whatever it be should not comply with it.

A judgment must pass into an act of the will

13. A judgment although by its name it should be nothing but an act of the understanding, yet before it can have any effect must be understood as having been transformed into a mandate, which is an act of the will. A judgment then if it be a civil one, must if it does anything create an offence: it must pitch upon some act or other as one which in case of its coming to be performed in future is to be treated in that light. All the difference is that (according to the distinction here laid down) where the judgment is of a civil nature, what offence there is in the case comes after it; there is none to ground

[f] Writing on the law in the English language, I am not writing in the language of the English law. Under the English law in certain cases (for instance in case of the beating of a clergyman) by judgment of three different courts on three different accounts a man may be made to pay a sum of money to the same amount three different times for one and the same offence: by the Court of Common Pleas ten pound for example, to the plaintiff in satisfaction for the injury: by the Court of King's-Bench, a second ten pound to the Crown for the punishment of the offence: by a court called an ecclesiastical court and filled by laymen (the Court of the Dean of the Arches) a third ten pound to the officers of the Court, for the good of his own soul. The founders of the English law were unable to conceive how the being made to pay money should be any punishment to a man when his adversary is to receive it: how seeing a man punished should be any satisfaction to his adversary although it should be all he prays for: or how the being made to pay money to anybody but the officers of the pretended ecclesiastical court should be of any service to his soul. This same act forbidden as it is by the law, yet when a man is sued for it in the Common Pleas they will not allow to be an offence: or if they allow it to be an offence they will not allow the suit to be a penal one.

it upon: where it is of a penal, an offence is alleged to have been committed against a mandate already subsisting at the time: and it is this offence which is the ground of the judgment, in consequence by which judgment, if not complied with another distinct offence will have been committed just as there would in the case where a civil judgment is not complied with. In short, in a penal judgment there are two offences supposed: one precedent and therefore certain, the offence on which it is grounded: the other consequential and contingent as to any individual instance of it, the one which it creates: in a civil judgment there is but one offence concerned; viz: that consequential contingent one which it creates.

14. Rights then may for this purpose be distinguished into two kinds: the one which may be termed *inchoate, inconsummate, unliquidated* or *liquidable*: the other *consummate, liquid* or *liquidated*. The latter is the only one which is susceptible of being violated. A right of the former kind is nothing but a right which a man has to the being invested with a right of the latter kind by the hands of some other person: in some cases in the first instance by the judge: in other cases by a private individual in the first instance, but depending always ultimately for its effectivation upon the assistance of the judge: the former is a right to a right: the latter is the immediate right itself. The immediate right may in many or indeed most cases be violated by anybody whatever: the more remote right is of such a nature as not to be violated but by the judge or other person by whose hands the right-holder of the first right ought to be invested with the second. In a penal suit as such the plaintiff's complaint is that some right of his which is already liquid and needs not the intervention of anyone to liquidate it, has been violated; the which violation is of course an offence. In a civil suit as such he does not allege that any liquid right of his has been violated; but says that he has a right not yet liquid which he prays the judge to liquidate. Now the liquidation of this as yet unliquidated right would be a *service* rendered him by the judge: this service, he says the judge, upon his demanding it, already owes him: so that to this service he has already a liquid right; which if the judge in due time refuse to render him, will have been violated by the judge.

Rights unliquidated and liquid

15. It is not to be wondered at if it should be frequently a matter of doubt whether a right does or does not stand in need of liquidation; and consequently whether the suit proper to be brought by a man who wants to enjoy in future the benefit of the right should be of the penal or of the civil kind. The natural partiality of men in their own favour and their natural propensity to be angry with those

Sometimes the suit may be indifferently a civil or penal one

who oppose their wishes will naturally dispose them to prefer the penal course to the civil. They will therefore be apt to institute a penal suit in cases in which considering the doubtfulness of the title and the *bona fides* of the defendant, the civil might have been the more proper remedy. This propensity may be so strong that in certain cases suitors may desert altogether the path of civil procedure, and give every application they make relative to the right in question a penal form. Judges, who as such can follow no other course than what is marked out to them by the suitors, will be apt to give in to the same propensity, will swim naturally with the stream : so that in certain cases titles instead of being tried by a civil, will be tried by a penal action, the judge being supposed to have done that which if called upon by the plaintiff in a civil way, he would in so clear a case in spite of the reclamation of the defendant have deemed himself obliged to do: or to speak more unexceptionably, the plaintiff's unliquidated right being supposed so clear that the judge if called upon could not (as must have been manifest

A suit may be tried either way when there is no punishment

to the defendant) have refused to liquidate it. By this means there might in the cases in question be no other means of trying a civil claim than by a penal action, nor of obtaining the liquidation of a claim but by supposing it already liquidated: insomuch that if two men living in perfect amity but having rights which for the sake of persons connected with them perhaps rather than their own they wished to have liquidated by some impartial hand but which they could not of themselves contrive to liquidate wished to obtain the decision of the judge, they had no other way left for it than to agree that one of them should pretend the other had committed an offence. In this way a penal suit may come without difficulty to be employed indifferently instead of a civil action, provided the punishment be reduced so low as not to amount to any greater inconvenience than in a civil action the unsuccessful party would be obliged to bear on account of costs: in which case the defendant would have no motive for contesting the propriety of the one rather than the other.[g]

Example in claims to land

[g] To take an example or two from the English law. Originally titles to land were tried by what were called *writs of right*: these came under the notion here given of civil actions: these having been spoilt for use by impertinent niceties and delays, succeeding judges instead of clearing them of their defects abandoned them and suffered the plaintiffs to bring the same question to trial or one that answered the purpose nearly as well by an action of *novel disseisin*: this was what according to the principles here laid down we should call a penal action: this also becoming clogged with difficulties was dropped in its turn and the actions of trespass and ejectment (two other sorts of penal actions) substi-

16. Where no act has yet been performed which would be a violation of the right which the plaintiff claims, supposing it to belong to him, there it is plain there can be no true ground for a suit of the penal kind: and if his claim be tried in such an action it can only be done by means of a false representation given of the matter of fact, in which falsity the defendant must concur.

Cases where there is no ground for a penal suit-1. *where the right claimed has not been violated*

17. So likewise where it is clear the plaintiff can derive no title but through the intervention of the judge. Thus in the common case of a debt. A man is indebted to you ten pound: of what nature is the right you have in this case? it is not that any one specific thing that once was his belongs now to you: there is not a single thing in the world that in virtue of this debt you have as yet any right to meddle with: all the right you have is a right to call upon him to pay you money to that amount[h]: or in his default to call upon the Judge to take measures either for compelling him so to do, or for doing the same thing in your favour out of his effects by authority of the court. Now which ever of them it is that discharges the debt by making over to you the money, whether the debtor himself in the first instance, or the judge at his expense, by the payment of the money you acquire a new right which you had not before, a right to the exclusive disposal of the individual pieces of coin in which you are paid. Now then the pieces of coin being yours you may count them over and keep them or throw them away and in short do almost what you will with them without committing an offence; which he who has paid them over to you can no longer do without

2. Where it is as yet unliquidated as in the case of a debt

tuted in the room of it. These not answering the purpose after all of securing to either party a quiet and uncontrovertible title, the ingenuity of their advocates directed them to a new court of comparatively modern date, called a court of equity, where at length they obtained the security they sought for in a civil action under the name of a bill for a perpetual injunction. Other instances might also be mentioned in which titles to land may be tried in the court last mentioned still in a civil way by methods which it would here be to no purpose to insist upon.

Thus also partial rights to the use of land in certain cases in which originally they used to be tried in a writ of *quod permittat prosternere*, a civil action, are now tried in an action on the case for a nuisance, a penal action: and where the public is the party interested on one side, by an indictment, a mode of proceeding so decidedly penal as to be styled a criminal one: in which latter mode also it is common to try the right of the public to compel an individual or a parish or other corporate body to render those services which consist in the repairing of a road.

[h] See Ch. (Division).[1]

[1] *An Introduction to the Principles,* Ch. xvi: the reference is to para. 35 of that chapter (in *CW,* 227, n. e3).

your leave. But till the payment was made it was he that had the right of keeping the money and so forth: you had no such right.

−unless it be for the offence of not conferring the right
18. Had you offered to meddle with any of them it would have been an offence, an act of wrongful occupation. For him to meddle with them was *no* offence: at least no *such* offence. If indeed he was bound to make the payment in question to you without your demand, his keeping them, or rather his forbearing to make over to you the right of keeping them, was an offence: it was the offence of wrongful non-investment; but then it was an offence that had no more relation to the individual pieces of money in question than to any other.

It is plain then that when a debt is due to you, which debt if paid at all can no otherwise be paid than by making over to you the ownership of certain pieces of money, no title can be derived to any of those particular pieces of money but with the concurrence of the debtor or by the intervention of the judge. In this case there can be no pretence for charging the defendant with the commission of that sort of offence which a man would commit who should violate the right demanded by the suit: viz: the right of exclusive ownership with regard to certain pieces of money to be determined by the judge. This then is a claim which can not properly be prosecuted in any other manner than by a civil suit: unless it be in a penal suit where the offence alleged is the offence of wrongful non-investment; the offence of forbearing to render a man those services which are necessary to be rendered to him in order to his being invested with the right to which he has a right.

Even this foundation fails where the right which a man seeks to be invested with could not be conveyed to him otherwise than by the judge himself in consequence of the very suit by which it is claimed. The suit itself is instituted in order to obtain it: if the judge deems him to have a right to it, a right to this right, a preliminary right to this conclusive one, he gives a judgment investing him with this conclusive right. This right then takes its commencement from the end of the suit: it therefore had no existence at the beginning: it therefore never could have sustained a violation. Previous therefore to the judgment there neither is nor can have been any offence whatever in the case.

Recapitulation
19. The cases therefore where a claim may at the option of the plaintiff and consistently with the truth of things be made to bear either a penal or a civil form indifferently, are these: viz: where in point of law the right claimed is such an one as is capable of subsisting without the intervention of the judge: and where at the same time in point of fact an act has really been committed in viola-

tion of such right. You have as you think, a right: which right an adversary of yours has already violated: perhaps advisedly; perhaps through mis-supposal. For this violation you have a right to have him punished: but this right you are at liberty to desist from, just as you might from any other: you may forbear taking any notice of what is past and confine your endeavours to the securing yourself against violations of the like kind in future.

20. There are many instances therefore in which a penal action and a civil action are equally competent to the case: and what is more the steps proper to be taken in the one differ but little from those proper to be taken in the other. This however does not throw any obscurity over the distinction between the two branches of procedure themselves. A man may have recourse to the one of them only or to the other, as he pleases: but whichever he does recur to, it will always be known whether it is that he recurs to or the other. *A civil and a penal suit are distinguishable even where either may be brought indifferently, and where the steps taken in them may be the same*

21. To conclude then, whatever right is capable of being determined upon in a penal action is equally capable of being determined upon in a civil action: but there are cases proper for a civil action, which cannot without a departure from truth be determined in a penal action. *Conclusion*

Wherever a man has a right to a penal suit he has already a right not perhaps to a civil suit but to all the benefit that is attainable from a civil suit: unless 1. the right violated is expired, and unless 2. in the case the civil suit is of a definitive nature: viz: of the nature of a bill of injunction to quiet possession. The judgment in a suit strictly civil may be as burthensome to the defendant as the judgment in a penal suit, and even more so.

CHAPTER XIX

USES OF THE EIGHTEEN PRECEDING CHAPTERS[1a]

Uses

1. To conclude and at the same time apologize in some manner for the long-winded and abstruse discussions contained in this chapter[2] it may be not amiss to give some account of the uses that may be made of it. These may be as follows

(1) To draw some sort of line between the penal and the civil branches of the law-system.

(2) To lay the foundation for the plan of the complete body of laws supposing it to be constructed *ab origine*, according to a method of division grounded on natural and universal principles. The field of legislation is a trackless wild which how often so ever traversed has never hitherto been surveyed by rule.

(3) To exhibit a plan to work upon, a standard to be guided by in digesting or reducing a body of customary law or a mixed body of customary and statute law together into a pure body of statutory law.

(4) In point of matter—to exhibit a clue whereby the legislator may be guided in his endeavours to avoid the great imperfections which a body of laws is liable to fall into, weakness on the one hand, tyranny and oppressiveness on the other. Weakness from want of qualifications, tyranny from want of clearness, the one or the other as it may happen.

(5) To restrain the licentiousness of interpretation. Legislators may travel with their eyes open over a plain and level road: instead of groping their way blindfold through a wood. Expository jurisprudence, the art of finding clear ideas to annex to the expressions of a man whose ideas were not clear, instead of being the only branch cultivated would be thrown aside. The legislator might need a censor but would need no interpreter. He would be himself his

---

a After a discussion so abstruse and so fatiguing, something may be expected by way of apology from the writer, something by way of satisfaction to the reader. Labour is sweetened by utility.

1 This is the title of the chapter in both Bentham's 1782 lists of contents (cf. Appendices E and F below). In the text, however, written as a concluding section for Ch. XVII of *An Introduction to the Principles*, the rest of the work is referred to as 'this chapter'.

2 See n. 1 above for this and similar references below.

own and sole interpreter: the task of censure he would leave, and the exercise of it he would give encouragement to, in others.

(6) To exhibit a common standard, by which the several systems of law prevailing in every country may respectively be compared, and thereby their mutual agreements and disagreements represented, their comparative excellences and defects exhibited to view: to the end that what is excellent in one system may be transferred into every other, that improvements in the most important art of all, the art of legislation, may like other arts make the tour of the globe, and that each legislator may add to his own wisdom the wisdom of his neighbours and contemporaries.

(7) That the method of teaching the art of legislation may be improved, or rather that such a method may be invented, and thereby an acquaintance with the principles of this art may be diffused and rendered common among the body of the people. It is thus that in time the labours of the legislator may make room for the judgment and industry of the professor: and the fruit of Invention be made the subject of Science.

2. First then, it gives the plan of a complete and regular body of statute law: and thereby, as we shall have occasion to show in the next place, a complete body of law for every purpose. Laws are either obligative or de-obligative: commands or countermands. As to de-obligative, in a regular body of law there will be neither need nor room for them: their only business is to destroy others: and they perish when they have performed their office. There remain such as are obligative, and such alone we shall henceforward speak of under the denomination of a law. Every law turns an act into an offence: and one law creates but one offence: so many offences, so many laws: for every law there is an offence: for every offence there is a law. Now of the several sorts of acts which it may be proper to invest with the character of offences an account has been already given: thereby therefore an account was also given, though without announcing it, of the purport of the several laws which it might be proper to establish. Take this chapter then and the preceding one,[1] lay them together and we have, such as it is, a complete and pretty detailed plan of a complete body of the laws. The former chapter, taking the lead, gave an idea of the nature purport and *substance* or matter of the laws: the business of the present has been to give an idea of the *form* into which it might be proper that substance should be cast: of the expressions or shapes of discourse with which it

It gives the plan of a complete body of statute law

---

[1] I.e. the present work together with Ch. xvi of *An Introduction to the Principles*.

seems necessary that the several laws as determined by the principles contained in the preceding chapter, should as it were be
clothed, in order that the true nature and mutual connections of
those laws might be made apparent, and of the order in which it
seemed most convenient those masses should be arranged. It is to be
remembered that by this parcelling out what relates to the several
offences, the whole law is parcelled out. Not but that every law may
have, and it will probably be found convenient that every law
should have, a civil branch as well as a penal: a part which holds
an act up to view in the character of an offence: and a part which holds
not up to view any act in any such character. But the civil branch of
each law, as hath been shewn, is but the *complement* of the penal:
it is on the penal that every proposition which may be found in a
book of law depends for its obligative force. When the imperative
clause or clauses to which a clause that is not imperative relates is
traced out and understood, the true nature and efficacy of such
clause is clearly understood: till then, it remains in darkness. Not
that the order in which these two branches follow one another in
point of importance is necessarily determined by that in which it is
most convenient they should follow on in idea for the purpose of
intellection. In point of importance the civil branch (if it be possible
to draw a line between matters so intimately and inseparably
connected) might possibly be found to precede the penal: but it is
the penal at any rate that claims the head in the order of intellection
and enunciation.

Every law may then be distinguished from every other. Indeed as
the same division of civil or expositive matter belongs in common to
a multitude of divisions of penal or mandatory matter, many laws,
any two laws almost, will have a vast portion of their substance in
common: they will be like contiguous triangles, like the diagrams of
pyramids represented as standing upon the same basis: but the
matter of each will be separately describable: as in pyramids so
represented the parts of each are separately assignable.

The several laws that in a new code shall be established or that in
an old one may be conceived to be established upon this plan will be
the integrant or aliquot parts of that vast and complicated whole:
the several parts of a law as herein above described being the constituent parts of the above-named integrant ones. The number and
description then of the several laws of which the system is composed
being once given, the whole code will be given likewise: the parts
or contents of it will be an object of arithmetic: the lineaments
and limits of it an object of mensuration. They may be placed

contiguous: they may be connected together: and one book will hold them. On that one book any man may lay his hand and say, 'Within this cover is the sole basis of my rights, the sole standard of my duties. Duties and rights together, here I shall be sure to find them: elsewhere I have no need to look for them.'

3. In the second place, it will exhibit at the same time a plan for the digestion of the customary law. The customary law as hath been shewn is not any essentially distinct branch of the body of the law, it differs not from statute law in substance, but in as far as it is at all intelligible, in as far as it has any force or efficacy, it must be considered as a miscellaneous branch of statute law ill-expressed and ill-defined. To speak of it at all it must be spoken of though inaccurately and in the way of fiction as if it were a portion of statute law. It must be spoken of under the same language as the statute law of which it is the precarious and delusive substitute: as paper is brought to account under the heads of pounds, shillings and pence like sterling money. It must be represented if at all as containing such and such parts; as containing imperative, expositive, limitative, exceptive, and extensive clauses. And what then are these clauses? if apt in point of expression as well as of substance, they will be nothing more than so many portions of discourse which are proper to be adopted into the body of the statute law: that is into the body of the code: blanks of sterling bullion, which want nothing but the stamp of authority to give them currency. Whatever then antecedently to the enactment of a new code was customary law, the same being stamped with the seal of authority, becomes statute law with the rest. At present we may boldly affirm that among all the systems of law which prevail among the several nations of the world, there is not one which does not exist more or less of it in the form of customary law: so that as yet no instance of a complete code of statute law is any where to be found. It follows not however by any means that if a complete code of that kind were given to any nation it must thereby be deprived of so much as a single article of those ancient and respected institutions to which the people in many instances with great reason are so strenuously attached. If they lose their present form by such a change, it is only in order to be invested with a better: if the unessential parts of their nature are changed, it will be only in proportion as the essential parts are brightened and improved. Conceive a complete code to be established *uno flatu*. If in any point it be re-enactive of the old law, it will *pro tanto* be a digest of such old law: if the old law were in

—which includes a complete digest of the customary law

235

the statutory form, of the statute law: if in the customary form, of the customary law.

The customary will thus be destroyed indeed: but how? as the old king in the fable by the pious care of his children was destroyed: by changing a life of decrepitude and deformity into a life of strength and beauty.

It gives room for making amendments without inconvenience

4. In the third place, it gives room for making alterations without inconvenience. No system of laws will ever, it is probable, be altogether perfect: none so good but that a greater share either of information or judgment or of probity might make it better. Even if at any given instant it were really perfect, at the next instant, owing to some change in national affairs it might be otherwise. Every system of law then may from time to time be requiring alterations: and though it never were to require any, yet owing to the fluctuation of human councils, alterations would in fact be made in it. In a body of laws as in every other complex piece of mechanism a great part of its perfection depends upon the facility with which the several parts of it may be altered and repaired, taken to pieces, and put together. But such a system if constructed upon a regular and measured plan such as that appears to be which we have been attempting to sketch out, would not only have the advantage of every other which remained untouched, but alterations, whenever any were made, would give less disturbance to it: provided that such alterations, as often as any were made in point of form, were accommodated as they easily might be to that of the original groundwork.[b] The effects and influence of every such provision whether it were an entire law, a provision expositive, limitative, or exceptive, might then with certainty and precision be traced on and coloured by reference throughout the whole body of the laws. At present such is the entanglement, that when a new statute is applied it is next to impossible to follow it through and discern the limits of its influence. As the laws amidst which it falls are not to be distinguished from one another, there is no saying which of them it repeals or qualifies, nor which of them it leaves untouched: it is like water poured into the sea.

To distinguish different things we must give them different names: of that which has no name nothing can be said.

It will serve to ensure their propriety in point of matter

5. In the fourth place, the regularity which it would give to the laws in point of form would be a test and by that means a sort of pledge of their propriety in point of matter.

[b] See Append. tit. (Conservation).[1]

[1] This appendix is not extant in the manuscripts. Cf. above 170, n. 1.

It is plain that in a body of laws the main object, and the sole object of intrinsic importance, is the matter: what it is in point of form is no otherwise of importance than in virtue of the influence which the form has on the nature or efficacy of the matter. But it is the particular use and design of the plan here in question to exhibit and display the matter of the law in the clearest light and in its genuine colours. The fundamental principle which is the basis of the system of laws here sketched out is the principle of utility: and the method here proposed is particularly calculated to shew how far that principle has been deferred to, and where if anywhere it has been deviated from. It is the business of that principle to mark out all along the proper line for the steps of the legislator to pursue: it is the design of a plan like this to throw the strongest light upon those steps, and to shew on every occasion in the clearest manner how far they have been governed by that line.

The catalogue of the laws is made out from the list of the acts which are held up to view in the character of offences: the acts which are thus held up, being selected on account of the mischief they seem calculated to produce, are arranged according to the different modifications of which that mischief is susceptible. In the cases in which an act is deemed mischievous upon the whole it is made the object of the imperative part of a law: in the cases in which it is deemed not to be mischievous upon the whole it is made the object of a qualificative part of the same law. The amplitude of a law is as the amplitude of an act which it makes an offence: the original amplitude of the law as the original amplitude of the act, antecedently to the qualifications by which it is narrowed: the residuary amplitude of the law as the residuary amplitude of the act, deduction made of what is subtracted from it by those several qualifications. Now the amplitude which is given to a law manifests itself in the imperative provisions: the discrimination which is given to it, in the qualificative provisions. Take then on the one hand all the imperative provisions belonging to the several laws that compose the code, add together their respective amplitudes: take on the other hand all the qualificative provisions belonging to the same laws, add together in like manner their respective amplitudes, on the other side; from the sum of the one combined with the sum of the other results the general character of the whole system. If it be weak and insufficient in any part it is owing to the total absence or narrowness of some imperative provision: if it be tyrannical and oppressive it is owing to the absence or narrowness of some qualificative clause.

Considered in a general view, to the imperative clauses[c] it owes its vigour; to the qualificative its mildness: to a happy proportionality and correspondency between the two, its wisdom, and thence whatever share of utility remains to it upon the balance.[d]

Moreover in proportion as the law is deficient in any of those qualities which are necessary to it in order to its being present in its proper form to the conceptions of those whose concern it is to be appraised of it, it becomes chargeable with one or other of the foregoing imperfections as it may happen. If from a failure in all or any of those respects, a substantive law escapes altogether the apprehension of all parties whatsoever who are concerned in it, of those who are to *execute* it as well as those who are to *obey* it,[e] the whole code becomes *pro tanto* weak and simply insufficient: if it escapes the apprehension of those alone who should obey it without losing the obedience of those who are to *execute* it upon the others in case

[c] Under this head we must include those clauses which give to one set of men power over another: because whatever acts of authority a man to whom such a power is committed may exercise in virtue of such power, the law allows of: whatever mandates he may issue it adopts. When exorbitant powers are unnecessarily bestowed, and those powers are exercised in the performance of tyrannical acts, or the issuing of tyrannous mandates, it is the same thing as if so many tyrannous laws had been established *ab initio*.

[d] It must not be expected that an idea so general as this of the dependency of the character of the law upon the extent of the imperative and qualificative provisions in it should be altogether an exact one. It should be understood for example that a law which gives powers or authority of any kind exercisable over persons or over things that in the main are the property of other persons, adopts in effect all the acts of coercion that can be exercised by the person in authority over the persons subjected to it without abuse of trust: and has therefore *pro tanto* the effect of an obligative provision. It is in this way that the law may incur the charge of tyranny merely by conferring powers: which indeed is the most formidable and vexatious kind of tyranny: and yet powers will upon this plan have been constituted, as may have been observed, rather by the exceptive, that is by the qualificative matter of the code than by the imperative.

Moreover it is by obligations, partly compulsive and partly restrictive, and therefore by matter of the imperative kind, that the powers mentioned above are guarded against abuse. The quality of mildness then with reference to the subject at large depends partly upon the slackness of such part of the obligative branch of the code as relates to them, partly upon the strictness of such part of that branch as relates to their subordinate rulers: remembering always that the same person who is to some purposes a ruler is to other purposes a subject.

A tyranny of man it has often and justly been remarked, though less discernible, yet when once discerned is more formidable and at any rate more baneful than a tyranny of the laws. A tyranny of man is that which is established by permission to command, or what is equivalent, by vague mandates.

[e] To obey a punitive law is to execute the substantive.

of its being disobeyed (the frequent and deplorable lot of laws too complicated and obscure to be sufficiently promulgated), it becomes insufficient and oppressive both at once: insufficient in the first instance, tyrannical and oppressive in the second.

Now the qualities of precision, perspicuity and conciseness in the parts are all connected either in the character of causes or effects, or both, with the regularity of the method which happens to be adopted for the whole. As to promulgation, this indeed is in itself an operation distinct from that of composition. Though distinct they are however to such a degree connected that unless composed upon a regular plan the whole code take it all together never can possess a hundredth part of the publicity it ought to have. A plan, therefore, however excellent in other respects, would be very imperfect after all, unless it were composed with a particular view to promulgation: that essential and much neglected branch of administration by the abandonment of which the greater part of the legislative matter that subsists is continually rendering itself worse than useless. Now to disentangle one law from another, that which concerns one class of persons from that which concerns a different class of persons, a man must know how to describe them separately: the means of doing which it has been one part of the design of this chapter to afford.[f]

6. In the fifth place, it tends to check the licence of interpretation. *It tends to check the licence of interpretation* I mean of course what has been distinguished by the name of *liberal* interpretation: that delicate and important branch of judiciary power, the concession of which is dangerous, the denial ruinous.

Now this necessity, supposing it to exist, from whence does it arise? From the want of circumspection or advertency, from the want of amplitude or discrimination in the views of the legislator. In the beginning, one might almost say till now, legislators have felt their way rather than seen it, taking up the ground by bits and parcels and without so much as attempting any general survey of the whole. In consequence no order, no connexity: no steps taken for guarding against oversights and omissions. The best-imagined provision might perhaps have done more mischief than good unless moulded into form by the prudence of the judge. On the one hand, the obligative part was not wide enough to embrace the mischief: on the other hand, the qualificative parts were not wide enough to yield shelter to innocence or to afford the necessary range to power. But the incidents which foresight could not present to the legislator,

[f] See further Ch. xix (Corpus Juris).[1]

[1] For this reference cf. 124 n. 1 above.

experience would from time to time be presenting to the judge. What was to be done? Was the continual recurrency of partial evil to be suffered to reduce, to fritter away into nothing the hopes of general good? This was not to be endured. Here then in the very cradle of legislative empire grew up another power, in words the instrument of the former, in reality continually its censor and not infrequently its successful rival. How difficult to distinguish what the legislator would have adopted had he adverted to it, from what he did actually advert to and reject. How easy to establish the one under pretence of looking for the other? especially when if truth refused her aid, fiction was ready at their call. The legislator, perhaps an unlettered soldier, perhaps a narrow-minded priest, perhaps an interrupted, unwieldy, heterogeneous, unconnected multitude: the judicature, a permanent, compact, experienced body, composed of connected individuals, participating in the same affections and pursuing the same views. And thus sprung up by degrees another branch of customary law, which striking its roots into the substance of the statute law, infected it with its own characteristic obscurity, uncertainty and confusion.

For disorders proceeding from the want of plan, a regular plan may at length, it is hoped, provide a powerful palliative at least, and in time it is hoped, a complete and effectual remedy. To supersede as far as may be the necessity of discretionary interpretation, the business is to give amplitude enough in the first place to the imperative matter in the code: and it is for this purpose that a general survey of acts fit to be made offences taken upon an exhaustive plan, was presented in the last chapter[1]: in the next place to the qualificative matter: for which purpose an analysis of the possible grounds of justification conducted in the same manner, will be given farther on.[g] By these processes when laid together, such a degree of comprehension and steadiness might one day perhaps be given to the views of the legislator as to render the allowance of liberal or discretionary interpretation on the part of the judge no longer necessary.

[g] See Ch. xx (Plan). B. I. Tit. (Justifications).[2]

[1] *An Introduction to the Principles*, Ch. xvi.

[2] The first reference is to a chapter entitled 'Plan of Book I' (i.e. the first book of the *Penal Code*) intended originally to be Ch. xx of *An Introduction to the Principles*. It appears as Ch. 41 in the March 1782 table of contents referred to in the introduction (xxxii above: cf. Appendix F below), but had disappeared from the list incorporated in the draft letter to Ashburton (Appendix E below), having naturally been dropped when the idea of separating *An Introduction* and the present work from the *Code* developed. The second reference is to one of the 'titles' of Book I of the *Penal Code* itself.

But in an analysis of so extensive and intricate a nature, errors would unavoidably insinuate themselves: nor supposing it perfect would there be any assurance that the lights afforded by it should always be steadily pursued: and even though a plan were eventually to prove perfect, yet antecedently to experience, it would be rashness to proceed upon the presumption of its proving so. Human reason does not seem to be yet far enough advanced to warrant our laying the discretionary mode of interpretation under an absolute prohibition in all cases whatsoever. It remains therefore to contrive some expedient for guarding that power from abuses during the exercise of it, from the inconveniences it is attended with, and confining it within its proper limits. For these purposes a plan is contrived, which will be developed at length in a subsequent part of the work.[h] Let the judge be required wheresoever he determines in the way of liberal interpretation, to declare openly his having done so: at the same time drawing up *in terminis* a general provision expressive of the attention he thinks the case requires, which let him certify to the legislator: and let the alteration so made if not negatived by the legislator within such a time have the force of law. By this means the legislator would see what the Judge was doing: the Judge would be a counsel to him, not a control, the sceptre would remain unshaken in his hands. The experiments of the one would be corrected by the experience of the other: the simplicity of the legislative plan would be preserved from violation: the corrective applied would be applied, not in the obscure, voluminous and unsteady form of customary jurisprudence, but in the concise and perspicuous form of statute law.

As to the individual case by which the propriety of the general alteration comes to be suggested, the authority of the judge in this line should be confined to operations of the remedial kind: it should not extend to positive punishment [but] should be confined to the case in which whatever burthen was thrown upon one party would be so much taken off the shoulders of the other: and that no man be left in possession of a clear profit reaped in fraud of the old law: for by punishment past mischiefs cannot be recalled and whatever is yet to come may as effectually be prevented by a new law which may be made on purpose.[i]

[h] See Appendix Tit. (Interpretation) and (Conservation).[1]

[i] It is a common rule that penal statutes ought to be construed strictly. This as we have seen seems consonant to utility as applied to the substantive laws

[1] 'Interpretation' was one of the subjects destined for the Appendix according to the Prospectus of Bentham's *Plan of a Penal Code* drawn up in the summer of 1780 (cf. *Correspondence*, ii, 488–9 n. 18). For 'Conservation' cf. above 170 n. 1.

*– and to
facilitate a
comparison
between the
laws of dif-
ferent nations*

7. In the sixth place, it would facilitate a comparison between the laws of different nations. At present not only the jurisprudence of any given nation is a labyrinth in itself, but each one of those systems is a different sort of a labyrinth of a different form from every other. Few nations who can boast of having any considerable part of the body of their laws reduced by authority in any such order as to bear the name of a code: none who can shew the whole of that body reduced to any such form. But of such codes as there are take any two and compare them together; and run over the list of the divisions that are respectively contained in them: in no instance will you find the titles of those divisions the same throughout or in the same order: nor where the titles themselves happen to be the same, will the contents of the divisions so entitled be found to be ranged upon the same plan. And yet if upon any occasion any part of the legal systems of two different nations come to be confronted by any person, some common plan he must necessarily form to himself to which he will reduce them in his own mind. But if that which is taken for a standard is confused, his idea of the other will in like manner be confused: if the parts of the former were indistinguishable, equally so will those of the latter. This then is a difficulty the remedying of which will be another advantage derivable from a natural and regular plan of legislation. To every one of those labyrinths it would afford an uniform and consistent clue. By this means a set of tables might be formed exhibiting the provisions made by the several governments of the world (such of them whose policy was thought to be worth attending to) under the several heads included in the natural syllabus in question: a comparative view of the several systems of legislation confronted together in their correspondent parts and digested into one work: a work which to borrow an expression from divines might be styled a sort of universal *harmony of the laws.*[j]

themselves: otherwise when applied to the adjective laws which concern the steps to be taken for carrying them into execution. There is reason why a man who upon the footing of the old law was not guilty should not be punished: there is none why a man who to the satisfaction of the judge can be proved guilty should be suffered on account of a flaw in the process or in the law relative to it, to triumph in impunity.

[j] In the year 1727, 1162 years after the death of Justinian in 565, Heineccius Heince, a Dutch civilian lawyer, published a digest of the compilations of that Emperor reduced to the order of the Pandects. In the year 1767, 40 years after, Beyer, a German lawyer of Ulm in Franconia, published a digest of the same compilation reduced to the order of the Institutes. Sad proof of the slow growth of human reason! that after an interval of so many hundred years no better

As to the uses that might be made of such a comparison, those have been already touched upon in the preceding chapter.[k]

8. In the seventh and last place, it may be made to facilitate the communication and thereby the gradual improvement of the science to beginners. When once an improvement has been made in any science and the utility of it ascertained, [when] it stands confirmed by the suffrages of the experienced in that line, the next care is to facilitate the communication of it to the rising generation. In its turn every intellectual production undergoes this course of husbandry. If while in the nursery of invention it is found to bear the blasts of criticism, it is taken up by somebody, pruned into form, and transplanted into the garden of science. *—and to facilitate the communication of the science to beginners*

In that department of logical science which goes by the name of grammar (for between what is commonly called logic and what is commonly called grammer there seems to be no clear line of separation) many helps are made use of for the purpose of teaching the rules of speech in general, which might be transferred and adapted upon occasion if it were worth while to any particular branch of discourse in particular. Such is that exercise which consists in ranging particular words and combinations of words under general classes and uses, and which when applied to words in the light of which they are considered by grammar goes commonly under the name of *parsing*.

The several general propositions or grammatical rules as they are called, however abstracted and abstruse as they are in themselves, being repeatedly exemplified over and over again upon different models, the purport of them may, as experience testifies, be enabled by degrees to make a lasting impression upon the least susceptible conceptions. A word being proposed to the scholar, he is required to point out the classes to which it is conformable. Each word and combination of words is thus referred to a particular class invented and named for the purposes of discourse in general. This process is equally applicable to every other branch of logic as to the elementary branch which is called grammar.

As words of any sort may be *parsed* by referring them to the

idea should have been devised than that of copying, following the ideas of a sovereign who for the purpose of pointing out to the subject the base of his duty has laid before him two different arrangements of the same matter altogether unconnected and incommensurate.[1]

[k] Ch. xvi (Division) 60.[2]

[1] The first of these editions was the work of Johann Gottlieb Heineccius (1681–1741). The Beyer edition of 1767 has not been traced.

[2] *An Introduction to the Principles*, Ch. xvi, para. 60 (in *CW*, 274).

classes entitled by the words a *verb*, a *noun*, *a verb in the infinitive mood*, *a noun in the accusative case* and so forth, so words of a particular stamp considered in a particular point of view may be parsed by referring them to the classes entitled by the words *genus*, *species, subject, predicate*, and the like: as may also entire propositions of the argumentative stamp by referring them to the classes entitled by the words *Barbara, celarent, darii*, and so on. In the same manner may propositions of the legislative stamp be parsed by referring them to the classes entitled *Law against simple personal injuries, law against semi-public offences, law against public offences*: *imperative provision, qualificative, limitative, exceptive, justificative*; *substantive law, adjective law, remedial law, punitive law*; and so on through all the variety of appellatives above exhibited, as well as of such others as upon a maturer and more particular examination it might be found advisable to add or substitute to the foregoing.

School

When these rules and exercises were prepared and brought into order, a sort of school might be established: a school, of which the business should be to teach, not the art of forensic disputation for the emolument of individuals, but the art of legislation for the benefit of empires.

Model

If a model of a complete code, applied for exemplification's sake to the circumstances of some one nation in particular, were once formed, and students of various nations were to meet together under one roof (as hath so often been the case in the schools of medicine, of botany, of chemistry, and other branches of the

Harmony

physical department of science) a harmony of the laws actually in force upon the plan above mentioned might form one part of the business of such a school, each student taking in hand the jurisprudence of his own state. By this work the old laws of each country would be arranged upon a new plan. This being accomplished the next and finishing achievement would be to frame for each nation a

New code

complete code new in point of substance as well as form, copied from the general model above mentioned with such alterations as shall be deemed requisite to adapt it to the particular manners, sentiments, and exterior circumstances of each respective state. If the time when an institution of such a sort could be proposed with any probability of its adoption is yet at a great distance, the idea of it however can not be thrown out too soon: the sooner it is exposed to public view, the sooner it takes rank among those embryo projects which chance will sometimes bring into life and a happy concurrence of talents and resolution sooner or later brings onward to maturity.

As grammar is taught by sentences thrown on purpose out of regimen, and geography by dissected maps, in like manner might the art of legislation, particularly what may be styled the mechanical branch of it, be taught by means of shapeless laws, to be taken to pieces and put together again after the manner of the model. As to making examples on purpose it is what there could be no need of here: since enough and enough might be found ready made among the laws that are anywhere in being.

A school boy (of the higher forms) is thought to have made but a small proficiency in grammar, if when a grammatical sentence is set before him, there be a word which he is unable to refer to the place that belongs to it in that sentence. If the science of legislation were as far advanced as that of grammar, and it were the custom for legislators to be as well acquainted with that science as it is for school boys to be with grammar, a statesman would be thought to have made but a small proficiency in legislation, if in any book of law that were set before him there were a word which he knew not how to refer to the place that [it] occupies in some mandate. But to love power is one thing: and to love the labour which alone can qualify a man to exercise it as he should do, is another.

9. But to pursue these visions any farther, would be to wander too far from the proper track of this design. It is time we should resume the regular thread of the discourse which leads in the next place into the examination of the different plans which the legislator may form to himself for the attack of the mischiefs which he has to combat, and the steps which it may be in his way to take for bringing the whole of the force he has at his disposal to cooperate together and act in subservience to the principal design. *Connection of this and preceding chapters with the next ensuing*[1]

Legislation is a state of warfare: political mischief is the enemy: the legislator is the commander: the moral and religious sanctions his allies: punishments and rewards (raised some of them out of his own resources, others borrowed from those allies) the forces he has under his command: punishments his regular standing force, rewards an occasional subsidiary force too weak to act alone: the mechanical branch of legislation, the branch we have been treating of in the present chapter, the art of tactics: direct legislation a formal attack made with the main body of his forces in the open field: indirect legislation a secret plan of connected and long-concerted operations to be executed in the way of stratagem or

---

[1] This heading and the associated paragraph relate to Ch. xvi of *An Introduction to the Principles* and Ch. xvii, out of which the present work developed, and their connection with what was originally conceived as Ch. xviii on 'Indirect Legislation'.

petite guerre. All these heads except this last have been discussed already. It remains that we should say something of this irregular system of warfare: a system which on account of the economy with which it may be used and the ingenuity which it is thought to require and which it often gives occasion to display stands in much higher favour with men in general than that which is carried on by open force.

Plan   10. In a system thus constructed upon this plan, a man need but open the book in order to inform himself what the aspect borne by the law bears to every imaginable act that can come within the possible sphere of human agency: what acts it is his duty to perform for the sake of himself, his neighbour or the public: what acts he has a right to do, what other acts he has a right to have others perform for his advantage: whatever he has either to fear or to hope from the law. In this one repository the whole system of the obligations which either he or any one else is subject to are recorded and displayed to view: delineated either actually by the commands it pronounces contained in it, or potentially by the powers it confers: powers of manual governance, or powers of issuing commands either permanent in the shape of laws or transient in the shape of executive mandates.

Nothing need be omitted, nothing un- prepared for   11. The acts to the performance of which a man is actually obliged are embraced by the commands that are delineated upon the face of the law itself: the acts to the performance of which a man may *come* to be obliged are embraced by the powers of imperation which are conferred by the law. The commands issued in virtue of these powers will be either of the permanent or of the transient kind: those which are of the former kind go to augment the body of the laws: the latter quit the stage one after another and vanish altogether in proportion as the purposes they are designed to answer come to an end.

In a map of the law executed upon such a plan there are no *terrae incognitae*, no blank spaces: nothing is at least omitted, nothing unprovided for: the vast and hitherto shapeless expanse of jurisprudence is collected and condensed into a compact sphere which the eye at a moment's warning can traverse in all imaginable directions.

Such are the fruits of a method planned under the auspices of the principle of utility, in which the laws are ranged according to the ends they have in view.

APPENDIX A[1]

DISTINCTION BETWEEN PENAL LAW AND CIVIL

1. So much for private ethics on the one hand and jurisprudence on the other. We come now to speak of what is called civil law or jurisprudence on the one hand and penal law or jurisprudence on the other: or more properly to the art of legislation in civil matters on the one hand, and the art of legislation in penal matters on the other. Between these two branches which are so often set in opposition to one another where then lies the distinction? Nowhere. They are inextricably interwoven. What individual law is civil and not penal? There is no such thing. What law is penal and not civil? There is no such thing. In every law must be comprised two things: 1. a specification of the cases in which the punishment is to attach; 2. a specification of the punishment itself: without punishment, no such thing as law: without a motive no such thing as action. *Limits between penal law and civil indiscernible*

2. The individuation of a law, I mean the description of that which is to be looked upon as neither more nor less than one entire law, is as yet a matter altogether unsettled and obscure: nor is this a place for entering into those details which would be necessary to clear it up. But be it settled anyhow, still it will be equally impossible to draw any precise line between the penal branch [and the civil branch] as shall discriminate effectually what is delivered concerning the art of treating one of those branches from that of treating the other. Let every assemblage of words that forms a sentence and composes a part of the body of a law be looked upon as constituting an entire law: the proposition would not be the less true. On this supposition every such sentence in which no mention was made of punishment should belong to the civil branch of the law: every sentence in which punishment was mentioned, to the penal branch. Would this be admissible? Certainly not. For never was there a code called a penal one which did not contain abundance of sentences in which there was not the least mention of such a thing as punishment. *It is not every sentence of the penal law that mentions punishment*

3. Is law to be deemed a species of command? and is that to be deemed one law which constitutes one command? Neither in this way could we find any distinction between what is called the civil *Nor is there any command that belongs exclusively to the civil branch supposing there were two distinct*

[1] See Introduction, xxxvi above, for a discussion of the textual problems connected with this appendix.

branches of juris-prudence

branch and the penal. In this case if every law must have a punishment to back it, part of every law would belong to the civil branch, while the other part belonged to the penal.

A law may be penal without men-tioning punishment

4. Suppose even a law to which no punishment was annexed by the legislator; still however a punishment it must have. It might derive it from the moral sanction: it might derive it from the religious sanction: but some punishment at any rate it must have; else it would not be a law; else it would not obtain obedience: else it could not have any of the effect of what is really a law.[a]

The distinc-tion between penal and civil applies not to the laws them-selves, but to the books that treat of them

5. In the law itself then there is no such distinction to be met with. What distinction there is respects the books that happen to be written on the subject of the law. That book belongs to the subject of penal jurisprudence which has most in it about punishment: that book belongs to the civil branch which has least in it about punishment itself, and most about the cases in which punishment is or is not to be applied.

The book indeed may be a large book; it may indeed be of any size, and yet be a book of law, and yet not say a syllable in any part of it about punishment: still however it has a tacit reference to punishment: else the law which it delivers or professes to deliver would be nugatory, and the book useless.

Example in the law rela-tive to wills

6. A great book for example is written about wills: a subject in fact which has given birth to many a great book. It says a great deal about the nature of a will: about the sort of persons who are em-powered to make them: about the cases in which these persons may

Ambiguous import of the epithet civil *as applied to law*

[a] This is so true that there is no such thing as any tolerably significant name for that branch of law which is so often spoken of as contra-distinguished from the penal. The only word to use for this purpose is the word *civil*; than which nothing can be more inexpressive. The word *civil* it must be confessed is put to very hard duty. It is to be met with everywhere: and wherever it comes it brings confusion. The word *civil* (*civilis*) comes from *civis* the member of a commonwealth or state or community of people such as when the word was first framed were frequently collected all together within the walls of one city. *Civilis* then means belonging to a commonwealth. In what respect then does it characterize that branch of the law which is not penal as contra-distinguished from that which is? That which is not penal concerns the community, true: but does not that which is penal concern the community full as much? Some-times it is used as synonymous to political which in its original signification has precisely the same meaning in Greek as civil has in Latin. Sometimes it is put in opposition to political, meaning every branch of the law besides what is meant by the political. Sometimes it is put in opposition to ecclesiastical: meaning every branch of law besides what is meant by the ecclesiastical. Some-times it is put to express this law, the whole jurisprudence of ancient Rome: Sometimes as much of that jurisprudence as is adopted into the law of this or that modern state. Other senses might undoubtedly be found besides these.

and those in which they may not exercise that power: about the different sorts of wills when made: about the number of witnesses which must attest them: about the places where they must be registered: about the construction that is to be given them, and so on for evermore: all this while without intimating a syllable about punishment. Has punishment however no concern in this? If that were the case the whole affair would amount to nothing. In fact all this is of no further use than as it serves to fix the application of punishment: distinguishing the one person who would *not* be punished in case of his meddling with and using that thing in question, from the multitude of other persons (amounting in fact to no fewer than all the rest of mankind) who would. You claim to be the sole proprietor of yonder house: that is, the only person of all mankind who according to the disposition of the law, in case of his occupying it would not be liable to punishment. You maintain that you are the person named in their behalf by the will of your deceased friend: who possessed the house: who was of the number of those persons who are allowed to make a will: who was so circumstanced as to have a right to dispose of this house by his will: who made such and such a will accordingly in your favour; took care to have it attested by so many witnesses, etc. etc. All this is only to give other persons to understand that were they to offer to meddle with the house they would be punished, and that you alone are left free to deal with it as you please.

7. All this holds equally good with regard to what may be called the constitutional branch of the law, or that which concerns the designation of persons invested with public trusts, and of the powers they are invested with. Are you a king? a judge? or general? Then upon your commanding me to do so and so, in case of my not obeying I am liable to be punished for it. Are you not a king? a judge, a general? Then in case of your commanding me to do so and so as if you were, I am not liable to be punished for disobedience: but you perhaps are liable to be punished for your presumption. *So in the law concerning the appointment of persons to public trusts*

8. Whatever business the law may be conversant about, may be reduced to one sort of operation, viz: that of creating duties. To make duties, in the first place it must define them: in the next place it must mark out the punishments to be inflicted for the breach of them.[b] Here then are two operations distinguishable in *The whole business of law reducible to that of creating duties – This*

[b] It is by creating duties and by nothing else that the law can create rights. When the law gives you a right, what does it do? it makes me liable to punishment in case of my doing any of those acts which would have the effect of disturbing you in the exercise of that right. *Rights created by prescribing duties*

takes two operations

themselves, though for use they must always be conjoined. In point of expression it may take more words to perform them or it may take fewer.

Which however may be expressed in one sentence

9. After a manner, they may be performed, both of them together in a single sentence: in which case they will shew as if in substance they were but one.

Instance in a law against theft

10. 'Whosoever stealeth, shall be hanged.' That might do, after a certain sort, for a law against theft. In saying thus much an inexperienced or negligent legislator might think he had done enough. In this style accordingly were conceived the first crude attempts at legislation.[c] But what is meant by stealing? for the ideas meant to be represented by this word are certainly not so obvious to present themselves to every man alike without difficulty or danger of mistake. To explain this sufficiently will at any rate take up another sentence: it may take up a paragraph, a page, a volume.

Or a part of it may take up volumes in many of which nothing should be said about punishment

11. Were a man to put together all that has ever been written in this view, it might perhaps take up a multitude of volumes. Suppose a single one: it is plain that in this whole volume there need not be a syllable about punishment. Yet to punishment it must have reference: and before it amounts to as much as any one single law it must be conjoined with some clause by which punishment is appointed. It is a part however of the mass of jurisprudence: that which has been written with or without authority upon the subject of the laws in general. Is it then a part of the penal branch of jurisprudence? But it contains not a syllable about punishment. Is it a part of the civil branch? But it has a necessary reference to punishment, without which it would be nugatory and unavailing. Will this necessary reference then which it has to punishment serve to confine it to the penal branch? Not so either: for the same necessary reference has everything that comes under the head of law. A regulation belonging to the constitutional branch of law has it as much as any other.

Conclusion— that book relates to penal law, which dwells most upon punishment

12. What then after all is the difference, such as it is, between the penal branch of the law and the civil? or rather between a book written on the subject of penal law and a book written on the subject of civil law? That book belongs to the penal branch which dwells upon the subject of punishment: that to the civil which without making any mention or at least without making much mention of the article of punishment, dwells most upon the cases in which punishment is or is not to be applied.

[c] The style of the laws of the 12 tables, and of such of the Greek laws as were handed down to us, was as concise and inexplicit, as this example.

APPENDIX B[1]

PART I

1. Power, right, prohibition, duty, obligation, burthen, immunity, exemption, privilege, property, security, liberty—all these with a multitude of others that might be named are so many fictitious entities which the law upon one occasion or another is considered in common speech as creating or disposing of. Not an operation does it ever perform, but it is considered as creating or in some manner or other disposing of these its imaginary productions. All this it is plain is the mere work of the fancy: a kind of allegory: a riddle of which the solution is not otherwise to be given than by giving the history of the operations which the law performs in that case with regard to certain real entities. Would a man know what it is that the law really does in every case, and in what condition it leaves the parties that are concerned? He must know in each case the acts which it takes into contemplation, and the aspect which it bears to them. He must know who the persons, and what the things, if any, which are in question: what the acts are of those persons, whether for their termination they look to other persons or to things: and in what circumstances if in any the act is prohibited or permitted, commanded or left uncommanded. Knowing thus much, we shall have ideas to our words: not knowing it, we shall have none. The ingenuity of the first authors of language which if not compelled by necessity was at least invited by convenience, has thrown a kind of veil of mystery over the face of every science, and over none a thicker than over that of jurisprudence. This barrier it will not be practicable perhaps not even expedient altogether to remove. We must however have learned upon every occasion how to pierce through it at pleasure before we can obtain a clear perception of the real state of things. These phantastic denominations are a sort of paper currency: if we know how at any time to change them and get sterling in their room, it is well: if not, we are deceived, and instead of being masters of so much real knowledge as by the help of them we mean to supply ourselves with, we possess nothing but sophistry and nonsense.

Rights, powers, and other fictitious legal entities to be explained by their relation to real entities

The ideas annexed to the words *person* and *thing* are ideas

---

[1] See Introduction, xxxvii–xxxviii, for the textual problems presented by the Mss. for this appendix.

251

copied immediately from the impressions made by real entities. The ideas annexed to the words and phrases, *act of the will, sign of an act of the will, physical act* or *act of the body, event, circumstance,* etc. are either like the former, ideas copied immediately from the impressions made by real entities or copies of the sensible affections of determinable real entities. The ideas annexed to the words *command* and *prohibition* are resolvable immediately into ideas of the number of those just mentioned. Now there can be no such thing as an act which is not the act of some person or of some sentient thing: nor can there be any act of law which is not either a command or a prohibition, or the reverse of the one or the other of those operations: nor lastly, can there be any command or prohibition which has not for its object some sort of act. It follows that whatever other words besides these may be made use of in expressing the matter of a law or body of laws and that are not names of real entities or of the sensible affections of determinable real entities, the import of the words just mentioned will serve as a key to the import of such other words: and while it lays open the import of each will lay open the connection between every one of them and that of every other. By these means alone can the import of such words as *duty, obligation, power, right* and other names of fictitious moral entities be laid open: by these means alone can a regular analysis of the contents of a body of laws be exhibited. I may be excused for announcing in so peremptory a manner the necessity for the ensuing disquisitions, since nothing less than necessity could have excused the exhibition of so uninviting a detail. It is to this abstract way of speaking, these fictitious entities alone that the law owes all its obscurity. Avoid them or explain them by the relation they bear to real ones and the law is clear.

Legal fictitious entities are created by creating offences

2. We have already had occasion to shew that the division of offences is in fact the division of the whole law: and that a complete analysis of all the offences that can be treated includes a complete account of everything that can be done in the way of law. It follows that whatever number and variety of these fictitious entities may be created or brought into play, it must all be done in the course of some or other of those operations by which the several sorts of offences are created. They are a sort of vapours which during the course of the legislative process are as it were generated and sublimed. By every operation which the law performs some one of them at least is exhibited or produced: by most operations two or even three: according to the number of persons or rather of the parties whose interest is concerned, and to whom the law during the

process bears a different relation. On the one hand whatever the law does in any case, somebody or other there must be (if it has any views at all) somebody or other there must be whom it is meant to favour: on the one hand, whatever it does, if in a positive way it does any thing, to somebody or other it must issue prohibition or command: somebody or other in a word it must be intended to coerce. If the party whom it is meant to favour be the same whom it coerces, there may be but one interest concerned: if different, there must at least be two: and if at the same time that it favours one party it coerces a second party in one way and a third party in the opposite way (which we shall see is frequently the case) there may and indeed must be three.

In giving an explanation then of the several fictitious legal entities, our plan will be to go over the several heads of delinquency, state the operation which the law performs in creating the offence and so exhibit the fictitious entity which is the result.

3. As yet there is no law in the land. The legislator hath not yet entered upon his office. As yet he hath neither commanded nor prohibited any act. As yet all acts therefore are free: all persons as against the law are at liberty. Restraint, constraint, compulsion, coercion, duty, obligation (those species I mean of each which issue from the law) are things unknown. As against the law all persons possess as great a measure of this great blessing of liberty as it is possible for persons to possess: and in a greater measure than it is possible for men to possess it in any other state of things. This is the first day of the political creation: the state is without form and void. As yet then you and I and everyone are at liberty. Understand always, as against the law: for as against one another this may be far from being the case. Legal restraint, legal constraint and so forth are indeed unknown: but legal protection is unknown also. You and your neighbour, suppose, are at variance: he has bound you hand and foot, or has fastened you to a tree: in this case you are certainly not at liberty as against him: on the contrary he has deprived you of your liberty: and it is on account of what you have been made suffer by the operation which deprives you of it that the legislator steps in and takes an active part in your behalf. Since the legislator then takes an active part, how is it that he must demean himself? He must either command or prohibit: for there is nothing else that he can do: he therefore cuts off on the one side or the other a portion of the subject's liberty. Liberty then is of two or even more sorts, according to the number of quarters from whence coercion, which it is the absence of, may come: liberty as against the

Before the law acts liberty is universal

253

law, and liberty as against those who first in consideration of the effect of their conduct upon the happiness of society, and afterwards in consideration of the course taken against them by the law, may be styled *wrong-doers*. These two sorts of liberty are directly opposed to one another: and in as far as it is in favour of an individual, that the law exercises its authority over another, the generation of the one sort is, as far as it extends, the destruction of the other. In the same proportion and by the same cause by which the one is increased, the other is diminished.

Restraint produced on the one part: personal security and protection afforded on the other

4. The law, after certain exceptions made, prohibits in me and in others all such acts as it thinks advisable to prevent in consideration of their being liable to produce on your part either bodily imperfection (the source of future pain or loss of future pleasure) or actual pain of body or actual pain of mind proceeding from any of the specific sources which are here mentioned: in other words all such acts as come under the denomination of simple corporal injuries, irreparable corporal injuries, homicide, menacement, or simple mental injuries. What then is the result? To me and the rest of the community, restraint: to you, personal security and protection. To speak more at length, it takes measures for affording you personal security, it makes provision for the security of your person: it affords you its protection for your person against those injuries: and (to introduce the word *right*) it gives you, when corroborated by the requisite apparatus of subsidiary laws, a right of being protected by the hands of its ministers against the endeavours of any who would inflict on you such injuries.

Restraint produced on the one part— liberty on the other

5. After certain exceptions as before, it prohibits in me and in others all such acts as it thinks advisable to prevent in consideration of their being liable to restrain you from doing such acts, from the doing of which it is a prejudice to you to be by such means restrained, or to constrain you to do acts which it is a prejudice to you to be constrained to do: in other words, it prohibits all such acts as come under the denomination of simple injurious restrainment, simple injurious compulsion, wrongful confinement, and wrongful banishment. What is the result now? To you, liberty: to me restraint as before. Personal liberty is accordingly either liberty of behaviour in general or liberty of locomotion. Liberty of behaviour again is either the absence of restraint or the absence of constraint: and liberty of locomotion either the absence of confinement or the absence of banishment.

Restraint on the one part— protection for reputation on the other

6. After the like exceptions as before it prohibits in me and in others all such acts as it thinks advisable to prevent in consideration of the tendency they appear to have to diminish your reputation. What is the result? To me and the rest of the community another species of restraint: to you another species of protection.

7. Thus far we have been treading on plain ground. As to the fictitious entities which are the result of the processes whereby offences against property and offences against reputation are created, these and the processes by which they are produced are of a more various and more complicated nature. To begin with property. Now property before it can be offended against must be created: and the creation of it is the work of law. To shew how the several modifications of it are created by law we may thus proceed. Conceive any material thing at pleasure: a piece of land for instance. The law issues no mandate at all to me or anyone with respect to that piece of land: on the one hand it does not command us, or any of us, to exercise any act upon the land: on the other hand neither does it command us to forbear exercising such an act. It does nothing at all in short in relation to the land: and of course, nothing in your favour. What is the result? On all sides liberty as before. Moreover, considering that it might have commanded us all, you and me and others, not to exercise any act upon that land, and that such are the commands which to you, to me, and to everybody but one or a few it actually does give with respect to by far the greatest part of the land under its dominion, it is on that account frequently spoken of as if it had done something in favour of those whom it has left thus at liberty: it is spoken of as having given them or rather left them a *power over* the land: it may also be said to have left them a *property in* the land. As this same sort of property is given not to you only, but to me and everybody else, no restraint with respect to the use of the land being laid on anybody, that which is given to you may on that account be styled *inexclusive*: an inexclusive power over the land: an inexclusive property in the land. The land in this case is said to be the common property of us all: and each of us is said to have a property in it in common with the rest: and each man may even be said to have *the* property of it, so as this phrase be added '*in common with the rest*'.

To all an inexclusive power over or property in a thing

8. Again. The law prohibits me and certain others from exercising any act upon the land: leaving you and certain others at liberty as before. In this case it gives you a power or property which, according to the persons with reference to whom it is spoken of, is at once inexclusive and exclusive. It is inexclusive with reference to your own associates: it is exclusive with reference to me and mine. You and they have each of you a power over, a property, an estate,

A power over a thing inexclusive as against some, exclusive as against others

an interest, in the land: we have not any of us any such property or power, nor (for anything that appears) any interest or estate in it.

A property exclusive with respect to all

9. The law forbids everybody but you from exercising any act upon the land. In this case it gives you alone a power over the land: it makes the land your property, your estate: it makes you sole owner, the proprietor of the land: it gives you not only *an* estate, *an* interest, *in* the land in severalty, but *the* property *of* the land, *the* estate *of* the land, both also in severalty.

This case is never strictly verified

10. As to this case it may be proper to observe that in reality it is never completely verified. Under any system of law some occasions there are in which for the carrying on of government it is necessary that any man's ownership over any object of property would be liable to be suspended: as if for instance there were need to make use of the land in question for the encampment of an army. But when these periods are not long, and the commencement of them is casual only and contingent, as in the case just stated, such slight exceptions are not in common speech considered as derogating from the general rule.

Power over things, corroborated by prohibition of disturbance

11. The law having left you a power over the land, no matter whether in severalty or in common, prohibits me and others from doing such and such acts in consideration of the tendency which they appear to have to annihilate or at least to diminish the benefit which you might otherwise reap from the exercise of your power over the land. It forbids me for instance not only from walking on it, or carrying away turf or stone from it, but also from making a wet ditch all round it though on the outside, or building a wall close to the windows of a house which you have built on it. In this case the law not only permits you to exercise such power over the land as without its interference you were enabled to enjoy, but interferes itself in your favour, and takes an active part in your favour in securing to you the exercise of that power by taking measures for averting such obstacles as might be opposed to the exercise of it by the enterprizes of other men. The power or liberty you had before as against the law may now be said to be corroborated or assisted by the law: corroborated by the mandate it issues to other persons, prohibiting them from such acts as it thinks fit to prevent in the consideration above mentioned. The acts thus prohibited it will be proper to specify. In general they will be any acts whatever which appear to possess the tendency above mentioned. But the catalogue of them will require various exceptions, as well in favour of the general interests of the community as in favour of the liberty and property of other persons whose interests may interfere with those which you have in the occupation of that land.

12. It has been seen that there are acts which interfere with your *One though not the only way of cor-*
enjoyment of a piece of land without being acts exercised upon that
very piece of land. But among the acts which may interfere with *roborating a*
that enjoyment there are few which are so likely to interfere with it, *power over things is by*
as any acts of another person when exercised upon the same land. *rendering it*
At Athens there were certain spots which were the common pro- *exclusive*
perty of the whole Athenian people: such were their amphitheatres
or places which among them answered the purpose of an amphitheatre. It is evident that the right which was enjoyed by particular persons of choosing the best station in such an amphitheatre, the
prohedria as it was called, was a right which in general would contribute more materially to narrow and impede the right which another
Athenian citizen possessed of placing himself in the same station than
the right of opposing any of those indirect impediments that have
been exemplified above. It appears therefore that rendering the power
which a man has over a thing exclusive is one way though not the
only way in which the law may corroborate that power. Exclusive
power and inexclusive power are both capable of being corroborated: and that without altering their nature: but a power
when exclusive is already corroborated in some degree by being
exclusive: and a power which is as yet but inexclusive can scarcely
by any means be so materially corroborated as by being rendered
exclusive. Powers (property and so forth) when thus corroborated
whether exclusive or inexclusive, may be said to be corroborated
by *prohibition of disturbance*, or simply, by *prohibition*.

13. All this is not enough: in order to give you the complete *Powers sub-*
enjoyment of the land which is made your property, something more *servient to powers over*
effectual should be provided than the precarious expedient of a *things*
legal mandate. In order to give a further degree of corroboration to
a power over things, there are two other powers that have been provided. It is intended you should have the complete enjoyment of
your land, it is necessary therefore if any impediments to that
enjoyment should arise such impediments be removed. Now the
causes, or instruments rather, from which such impediments may
arise must be either *things* or *persons*. Hence the occasion for two
other sorts of powers, the one over other things, the other, over
persons. These additional powers may be styled by the common
appellation of *subservient powers*: in contradistinction to the power
you have over the land itself: which again, in contradistinction
to these may be styled the *principal power*.

Subservient powers over things impeding

14. First with regard to things. The things that may be the object of this power are any things which happen to be in any situation which prevent or impede your exercising the power you have over the principal thing the piece of land in question. You have a power of travelling over a road: a man sets up a fence across the road: in corroboration of the power which he is thus impeding, the law permits you to beat down and remove the fence. In this way it is that the law creates a subservient power over impeding things in corroboration of a principal power already given.

It is the essence of such power to be but occasional

15. It is obvious that this subservient power may in the same manner as that to which it is subservient be corroborated by prohibition of disturbance. The only point in which it is essentially distinguished from the principal one is that of constancy. The power you have over the land, the power of travelling over it may either be immediate and uninterrupted, or may be constituted so as to be brought to appear or disappear by any variety of events of any sort: on the contrary with regard to the power you have over the things which may happen to stand in the way of your exercising the power you have over the land: such former power if subservient to the latter can be only occasional. Upon all other occasions perhaps the only power possessed by anybody over the wood of which the fence is composed would have been possessed by your antagonist: no power at least would be possessed over it by you: it is only upon the occasion of its being so situated as to prove an impediment to the exercise of the power you have over the land, that the law gives you this power over the wood which is upon it.

Power over persons is either over their passive or their active faculties

16. Next with regard to the subservient power over such persons as may chance to be circumstanced in a manner to impede the exercise of the principal one. This application of power over persons must be explained in its turn as well as any other: but as this is but one among a great variety of applications and modifications of which that branch of power is susceptible, it will first be proper to give a general explanation of the whole together.

To understand the nature and possible modifications of that sort of fictitious entity which is called a power over persons it will be necessary to make a distinction between the corporeal or purely passive faculties of man and his mental or active faculties. By the first I mean those which are common to man's body with the rest of matter: by the second I mean those which are common to him with other sentient beings only, and which either belong to or constitute the mind. By the first he is assimilated to the legal class of *things*: it is by the second only that he stands distinguished from that class.

Of the power which may be exercised over his passive faculties we have therefore in effect been already speaking. That which may be exercised over his active faculties requires a further consideration.

17. In the former case in order for the power to be exercised, needs but one person to act, to wit the person by whom the power is to be exercised, and one act to be performed, to wit the act of that person: For the latter case there must be two persons who act, and two acts to be performed. In the first place on the part of the person by whom the power is exercised there must be one act: in the next place, on the part of the person over whom the power is exercised, there must be another: the first of these when spoken of with reference to the power may be styled its *subservient* or *instrumental* object: the latter its *ultimate* or *final* object. The first may be spoken of as the means by which the power operates: the latter is the end in which it terminates. The latter may be termed an act of power, the former an act of compliance. From each of these acts a source of distinction may be derived. From the nature of the act of compliance, the power may be either *productive* or *preventive*: it may be styled productive if that act be of the positive kind: preventive, if of the negative kind. (As to the act of power it may be of a nature to produce a change in the condition of the body of the party from whom the compliance is sought, without affecting his will, or by means of its influence on his will.) As to the means whereby the power may operate, these may be either of a *physical* or a *mental*, in which latter case it may otherwise be said to be of a *moral* nature: those may be said to be of a physical nature which tend to produce the effect by the influence they exert over his body or the adjacent bodies, independent of any which they may exercise on his will: those may be said to be of a mental or a moral nature which tend to produce the effect no otherwise than by the influence they exert upon his will. Now for acting upon the will of a sentient being there are but two sorts of means, the prospect of pain and that of pleasure: those which act by holding out the prospect of pain may be termed *coercive* motives, those which act by holding out the prospect of pleasure may be termed *alluring* motives. When the means by which a power of the sort in question operates are such motives of the coercive kind as persons in general are prohibited from applying in so much that were it not for the creation of such power the application of them would be an offence, the power (whether it be of production or prevention) may be said to act by the *power of punishment*: when they are such motives of the coercive kind as persons in general are not prohibited from applying,

Distinctions observable in regard to power over the active faculty

it may be said to enforce itself by *coercive influence*: when they are of the alluring kind, by *alluring influence*. And in particular when the motives which are applied are of the nature of those which result from a change made in the condition of the body, the power may be said to enforce itself by the *power of corporal punishment*.

Power over the active faculty precarious

18. It may be observed that of the two sorts of acts which must be performed in order for a power of this sort to have been exercised the performance of the former stands upon the whole on a much higher footing in respect of certainty than that of the latter. This footing will again be different according as the act which is the final object of the power is of the positive kind or of the negative. For causing a man to forbear exercising acts which it is intended he should abstain from there are very effectual expedients: physical means have their application here: and the efficacy of those operations which apply themselves directly to the body is much more certain than of those which before they can produce any change in the condition of the body are forced to make their way to it through the mind. The law can be much more certain of giving birth to an act which has its termination in the person of any man than of giving birth to an act which takes its commencement from that person. Indeed properly speaking it is the power of giving birth to the act which is the instrumental object which is all the power that the law can be said to confer upon a man: the power of giving birth to the act which is the final object of the productive or preventive order, it can no otherwise give him than by giving him the power before mentioned. The truth of this observation will be perceived when we come to give an account of the several operations by which the several modifications of power are created and confirmed.

Power over the passive faculties of persons, un-corroborated

19. In the general mandate above mentioned, the law has prohibited you from doing any such act to the body of any person as that person does not like. It now takes a certain person in particular under consideration, and in derogation of that general mandate permits you to exercise certain acts on his body whether it be his pleasure they should be exercised or no. In this case it gives you a power over the body or in other words over the passive faculty of that person. This power being constituted by bare permission is as yet uncorroborated. As all other persons but you are excluded from exercising the acts in question upon the person in question, the power is exclusive and so entirely exclusive as to belong to you in severalty. It is plain enough that if the general mandate of which this particular permission is an exception had never been estab-

lished, every other person in the community would have had the same power over the person in question: as on the other hand so would that person over every other.

20. The law having given you the power above mentioned, prohibits me and others from doing such and such acts in consideration of the tendency which they appear to have to annihilate or at least diminish the benefit which you might otherwise reap from the exercise of your power over the person in question. By this means the uncorroborated power you had before is now corroborated: corroborated exactly in the manner of a power over things, by prohibition of disturbance. What is the result? To you a species of liberty as well as of power: the liberty of exercising such acts upon such persons, in other words a property in the use of his body: to others restraint. As to the person himself on whom the power is to be exercised on his part nothing ensues: his personal security, insofar as your power over him extends, is diminished, but his liberty as against the law remains on the same footing as before: you are left at liberty to exercise the acts in question upon his person; but he is left at liberty to resist you.

−corroborated by prohibition of disturbance

21. But now then the law addresses itself to the person himself over whom the power is to be exercised and includes him under a prohibition similar in its design to that just mentioned to have been addressed to other persons. By this means your power secures a further degree of corroboration: it may be said to be corroborated by prohibition of noncompliance, or which comes to the same thing, by command of submission.

−by prohibition of disobedience

22. It may have been observed that in giving you a power over the passive faculty of a man the same operation gave you virtually a power over the active faculties of the same person. Of this latter power the amplitude, as far as depends upon that act of yours which is the instrumentary object of it, is in proportion to the uneasiness which can be produced on your part by the acts in which the exercise of the power you have over the passive faculties of the person consists: as far as concerns that act of his which is the final object of the former power the amplitude of it depends upon the nature of the acts which he can be brought to perform by the apprehension of such uneasiness. On the other hand the converse of this proposition does not hold good. It is not true that a power over the active faculties of a person involves in it of necessity a power over his passive faculties. This may have been inferred already from the analytical sketch that has been given above: and it will unavoidably be made appear in a more particular manner by the

Power over the passive faculty includes power over the active. Power over the active faculty constituted by power of punishment

statement of the several operations by which a power over the active faculties of a person may be given in other ways.

Power over the active faculty constituted by power of coercive influence

23. Of the number of the sorts of acts which tend to produce uneasiness in a person by the influence they have on his person, reputation, property or condition in life, the law leaves you still at liberty to perform such articles as in affording him its protection in those several points it left unprohibited. In so doing it gives you such and so much power over his active faculties as is constituted by what may be called coercive influence: or more at length, the liberty of applying coercive influence: the liberty of endeavoring to determine him to perform or not to perform such and such actions by the application of coercive influence to his will.[a]

–by power of alluring influence

24. The law, (after such exceptions as it thinks proper) leaves you at liberty to perform what acts you please of the number of those which are attended with such effects as are of a nature to prove agreeable to him. In so doing, it gives you that sort of power over his active faculties which is constituted by what may be termed alluring influence. Of this and that last mentioned permission, what is the result? To you, liberty of behaviour as before; to the person over whom the power is given and to others, nothing.

No property constituted by either kind of influence

25. Upon considering these two last species of power it will be observed that they are neither more nor less than what every man in proportion to his physical faculties possesses of course over every other. Accordingly they do not either of them constitute any species of what is commonly called property: any more than would any power over things while it remained inexclusive and uncorroborated, except in virtue of the contrast which the condition a thing is in which a man has this sort of power over makes with the condition of the thing over which no power is left him by the law.

Yet both come under the notion of power
Power of coercive influence–what sorts of acts (instrumental) it may extend to

26. It would have been an omission however not to have mentioned them under the head of power: they are commonly comprised

[a] It may be wondered what acts of the nature above specified can upon the principle of utility remain unprohibited? The answer is certainly not many, in comparison at least with those which ought to be prohibited. Of the number of those which affect a man in his person, perhaps none: of those which affect him in his reputation almost all, provided there be no mixture of falsehood in the proceeding. The like may be observed with respect to such as affect him in respect of his property or in respect of his condition in life, but no otherwise than in virtue of the tendency they may have to intercept some benefit which might otherwise devolve on him. Let the law have done everything for you which it ought to do, every man will still be left at liberty to endeavour to persuade your customers not to deal with you, your mistress not to give you her hand, or your electors not to give you the place you wish for, so long as neither force nor falsehood, nor in the last-mentioned case bribery, be employed.

under that name: they make as much figure in the world nearly as any other sort of power[b]: and although it requires no express and positive operation on the part of the law to constitute or confer them, yet by the law they may be, and in many instances are, taken away.[c]

27. Let us return to power over things: we are now prepared for obtaining a primary idea of the manner in which it may be corroborated by an occasional power over persons. As to mere influence whether coercive or alluring this as hath been already observed is no more than any man, unless it be expressly taken from him, possesses of course upon all occasions: it is therefore what every man has of course to corroborate any share that may have been given him of power over things: to give it him therefore on the present occasion requires no express operation or aspect of the law. There remain power over the passive faculty, and power of punishment.

28. First, with regard to power over the passive faculty. The persons who may be the objects of this power are any persons who happen to be in such a situation as to prevent or impede your exercising the power you have over the thing in question: the occasion of its accruing to you is the time at which they are thus employed.[d] You have the power of travelling over a piece of land. A man cometh designing to prevent you, watches the moment when you are making your way through a narrow pass and plants himself in your way: the law permits you hereupon to push him aside. In this way it is that the law gives a power over the passive faculty impeding persons in corroboration of a power over things. *–by power over the passive faculty*

29. Next, with regard to a power of punishment over persons. A man is obstructing you as in the case just mentioned: the law permits you to threaten to beat him for example, or do him some *–by power of punishment*

[b] In Great Britain for example the greatest and most effective part of the King's power is of these two kinds: nor is the efficacy of it thought in general to be too little. The King of Great Britain has abundance of places to put a man into, such as men love to be put into; but he has no Bastiles. Possessing this power he is the object of a constant and not unsalutary jealousy: without it, he would be a cipher.

It may be said that he has this power from the law: since he possesses it in virtue of his possessing the power of appointment to these offices (a particular species of property of which hereafter) which is given him by the law. True, but it is not by any separate operation on the part of the law: the same operation which gives him those powers gives him this unavoidably and of course.

[c] For example when the influence, assuming the shape of *bribery* or other species of *corruption*, tends to produce a breach or abuse of trust: or when in the shape of *subornation*, it tends to give birth to any offence at large. *Power of alluring influence–what acts of power it does and does not extend to*

[d] See supra, 258.

*By what
powers over
persons
powers over
things may
be cor-
roborated*
other harm which, were it not for this particular occasion, it would be an offence in you to bring upon him: and in case the threat proves ineffectual the law permits you to carry it into execution. In this way it is that the law may give you a power of punishment in corroboration of a power over things.

*Subservient
power cor-
roborated—1.
by permission
of assistance,
2. by com-
mand of
assistance*

30. Thus far the corroboration that has been given to powers by powers whether over persons or over things has been given by operations of which the parties only have been the immediate objects[e]: by permission given to the party favoured: by prohibition denounced to the party restrained. But the resources of the law are not yet exhausted. Against the attack of a number of invaders or even of a single invader the force of a single person taken at random will often be unsufficient, and as to the force of the law, the force of which the application is implied in the act of prohibition it can seldom be applied till after the mischief has been incurred. In most cases if not in all it will be requisite to make provision for affording further assistance to him whom it is meant to favour: to wit such assistance as is to be met with on the spot, and in the way to be applied at the very time at which alone assistance can be of use. This assistance may be afforded of whichever nature the impediment is which it is requisite to overcome: whether in the first instance it arises from a person or a thing. In either case the force of the corroboration is susceptible as it were of two degrees: it may apply itself in the way either of simple permission, or of positive command. The occasional powers, which persons are permitted to exert in corroboration of a principal power, may themselves receive a further degree of corroboration: in the first place by a power given to third persons to render their assistance: in the next place by a command given to the same purpose: in the first case the power in question may be said to be corroborated by permission of assistance: in the other case by command of assistance.

*Restraint or
constraint on
one part—a
right to
services on
the other*

31. We come now to speak of right to services. In order to have given you by means of the power of punishment a power over my active faculties, the legislator should have permitted you of your accord to perform in a certain contingency certain acts of the number of those which on account of the prejudice which it is in the nature of them to impart to me (in respect either of my person, my property, my reputation, or my condition in life) he is disposed in general to prohibit. Instead of this he reserves this power in his own

---

[e] On these as on other occasions in the giving powers over persons various precautions will be requisite: but to enter into such details suits not the present purpose.

hands. He causes me to perform certain acts for your benefit, that is, for the sake of the benefit which such acts seem calculated to produce to you: but he leaves not the motives by which I am to be induced to perform these acts, nor the time of applying those motives, to your choice. He intends for example that I should plough your field for you; and that I should be caused to do it whether I like to do it or not. As a means of causing me to do it he intends accordingly that upon the contingency of my not doing it I should be turned out of a field of my own or kept in confinement. But he intends not to leave me exposed to as much suffering as I should be exposed to were you permitted to judge in every case in the first instance whether I had failed or not in doing what I ought to do in the way of ploughing it, or to determine the time during which I should be kept out of the possession of my field, or the time during which or place at which I should be kept under confinement. He therefore reserves these points to the determination of the magistrates who in cases like this are specially commissioned to execute his will. Accordingly, he either of himself commands me at once to perform the acts in question, or shows himself to be in readiness to adopt any command issued on your part to the same effect in case of your thinking fit to issue such command: reserving in his own hands in either case the enforcement of such command. In so doing he gives you a right to my services in the behalf in question: a right to certain *services* on my part. Wherein consists the exercise of such a right? In the demanding of the services only or in the demanding and receiving them accordingly?

31a. The varieties of proprietary interest are not yet exhausted. *Rights to the use of things* In what manner and by what operations powers are created, whether over things or over persons, has been already shewn. But powers are not the only things of which property may consist. It may consist also of rights, a sort of fictitious objects which in some cases indeed coincide with powers, but in other cases are essentially distinct from them. In order to give you a power over a thing the law permitted you to exercise certain acts having their determination in that thing: and that, at any time, without waiting for the consent of any one. To give you a right to a thing, or to the use of a thing, the law takes a different course. It does not permit you to exercise any act on it in the first instance: it however shews itself resolved that upon the performance of a certain act on the part of some other person, it will thereupon immediately give you such permission: and in the meantime it commands that person to per-form that act. As soon then as he performs that act you have a power over the thing: till he performs it, you have none. Or (which is but to express the same meaning in other words) if before he has performed the act you should take upon you to meddle with the thing, you would be liable to be punished: as soon as he has performed it, you are exempt from being punished on that score.[f] This is in effect to command him to execute, in your favour, an act of investitive power over that thing: which power we shall have occasion to explain more particularly a little further on. It is also giving you a right to a service on his part: to wit, the service which consists in his performing in your favour the act just mentioned: another sort of right which will be considered immediately after the present. But as the service to be performed is referable solely to no other object than this particular thing, and is no otherwise of importance than in virtue of its having the effect of giving you a power over this thing, it will be convenient to consider the right in question in the class of a right to things, then in that of a right to a service: for it will be convenient to have a class of rights to things in order to contrast with the class of rights to services.

To constraint correspond active services, to restraint services of forbearance

32. Now an act, we may remember, may either be of the positive or of the negative stamp: services may accordingly be either active services or services of forbearance. When the legislator in order to procure you a benefit commands me to do certain acts, the services to which he thereby gives you a right are of the active stamp: when in the same view he commands me not to do such or such an act the services to which he thereby gives you a right are services of forbearance. He commands me to plough your field for you as before: it is thereby that he gives you a right to active services: he commands me not to cut certain trees which though growing on my own land are of use to you affording shelter for your field: he thereby gives you a right to services of forbearance.

Services corporal and mental

33. Services may be considered again, in two other points of view: according to the faculties by which they are performed; and according to the object on which they are performed. With regard to the first of these points it is plain enough that being the result of

[f] I owed you yesterday ten guineas. I have just been paying you with ten pieces of that name. I took them out of my pocket and counted them into your hand: or I laid them down on the table and bid you take them up. You now have a power over those pieces; you have the property of the pieces. But before I performed those acts in virtue of which I am deemed to have paid you, (that is to have invested you with that power) you had no such power: you had only a right to any such pieces of money amounting to that value, as I might think fit to give you. Had you taken the pieces in question off the table before I bid you, and gone off with them, you would have committed an offence.

the active faculty, there is no sort of service in the rendering of which the mind must not be concerned as well as the body. Although the acts in which they consist should have originated in the mind, yet these acts, before they can have been productive of any effect beneficial or otherwise in society must have been communicated to the body. On the other hand, let the concern which the body has in the business be ever so considerable, the production and regulation of its motions must still have originated with the mind. For distinction's sake, however, where the share which the body has in the production of the effect appears the most considerable, they may be referred to the body; where that which the mind has, to the mind. The service, for instance, which a husbandman renders to his landlord by ploughing his field for him may be referred to the head of corporal service, notwithstanding the attention which it is necessary the mind should give to the guidance of the plough: the instruction which is given by the professor to his pupil may be referred to the head of mental service, notwithstanding the part which it is necessary the lips or the hand should take in communication of it.

34. Secondly, as to the object on which the service is to be performed. As the commencement of the act whereby the service is rendered is determined by the person whose faculties are in question, so the termination is determined by the object on which the service is performed. This object must belong of course to the class either of persons or of things. In the first case the service may be styled as service *in personam*, in the other case a service *in rem*.[g] The service rendered by a surgeon is a service *in personam*, that rendered by the husbandman as above, a service *in rem*. Each of these classes again may be divided indefinitely according to the nature of the persons or things on which the acts in question are to be performed, according to the nature and tendencies of those acts which are to be performed, and according to the occasion or circumstances in which they are to be performed.

Services in personam *and* in rem

[g] The division of services into *personal* and *praedial* as distinguished by the Roman law is ambiguous and inexhaustive. It does not quadrate with either of those given in the text.[1]

[1] The distinction to which Bentham refers is that between personal and praedial *servitudes*, servitude in general being a right *in rem* over the property of another. Praedial servitudes rustic and (later) urban, were rights over one piece of land or building (the servient tenement) in favour of another (the dominant tenement): a typical instance was a right of way. These rights were perpetual, whereas personal servitudes were temporary. The most important form of personal servitude was *usufruct*—the right to use something and take its fruits, a right usually enjoyed for the life of the holder only.

35. Power and right considered with respect to the identical person by whom it is exercised may be distinguished again into direct and indirect. It may be styled direct, when the acts in which the exercise of it consists are the acts of the very person by whom the power is said to be possessed: in this case it may be styled the power or right of occupation: it may be termed indirect, when those acts though still taking their origin in some measure from his will, are not his acts but those of some other person.

Power (and right) direct and indirect

36. Indirect power or right may again be divided into investitive and divestitive. It may be styled investitive power when the will of the one person is that such or such another should perform the act in question: divestitive, when the will of that person is that the latter having exercised them should exercise them no longer: in the former case we see the acts which result from the will of that person considered as being in possession of that power are of the positive kind: in the other, of the negative kind. Let us see how these powers are created.

Power indirect–investitive and divestitive

37. The law shows itself resolved that, upon the event of my declaring that such is my will in this behalf, it will issue those mandates, that set of permissions, prohibitions, dispensations, and commands by the issuing of which it will have given you a power of occupation over the land in question. It is by so doing that it gives me investitive power over the land in question. By these means it in a manner adopts the expression of my will, and turns it into a law.

Power investitive how created

38. You are already in possession of the direct power over the land; or what comes to the same thing you are about to possess it. The law shows itself resolved that upon the event of my declaring that such is my will in this behalf it will revoke or forbear to issue those mandates by the issuing of which it gave or would have given you such power of occupation. It is by so doing that it gives me a divestitive power over the land in question.

Power divestitive

39. It will be proper to observe that the exercise of either branch of the indirect power is a very different thing from the exercise of the direct power. The act by which a direct power is exercised is by an act which terminates in the person or thing which is the object of the power. The act by which the indirect power is exercised is any act which serves as a sign of my entertaining the desire in question.

Exercise of an indirect power, what

The exercise of an investitive power is one sort of investitive event. The exercise of the divestitive power is one sort of divestitive event. Of these two events considered in a general point of view more will be said a little further on.

40. This division into direct and indirect is applicable to unconsummated rights as well as to powers.

Rights direct and indirect

41. The law shows itself resolved that upon the event of my declaring it to be my will that upon the event of your declaring it to be your will that a third person should have a direct power over the land it shall happen accordingly. In this way it gives me sort of a indirect power which may be styled an investitive power of the 2d order: and so with respect to the divestitive power. In the same manner it may constitute investitive powers of the third, fourth or fifth orders, and so on.

Investitive and divestitive powers of the 1st, 2nd, 3rd, etc. orders

42. When the law showed itself resolved to give me the direct power over a thing in the event of my declaring such to be my will, such declaration of will on my part may be considered as a kind of signal which the law waits for, in order to invest me with such power. But in the same manner it might have taken the expression of any number of wills or of any proportion of any such number of wills for the signal. In this case, the investitive power may be considered as residing in the whole number of such persons in conjunction together, each of them having a joint share in it: or what comes to the same thing a conditional investitive power may be considered as residing in any one of them, each one of the rest having a power of control by non-assent.[h]

Conditional investitive power— power to control by non-assent

43. The law shows itself resolved that in the event of my declaring it to be my will that you should have a direct power over the thing in question, it will at the end of a certain time after such declaration confer on you such power, provided a third person does not within that time declare it to be his will that you should not possess such power. In this case I may be said to have a conditional investitive power over the land in question: and such third person may be said to possess another sort of power of control over the investitive power: a power of control by dissent.

Defeasible investitive power— power of control by dissent

44. It appears then that the investitive and divestitive powers may each of them be possessed either exclusively or inexclusively: when inexclusively each of the sharers may exercise it indiscriminately or in association only, that is not but in conjunction with the rest: if in association, the share he has may either be a power of control by non-assent, or a power of control by dissent.

Principal modifications of which the indirect powers are susceptible

45. Moreover the persons who share in the power in question may on the occasion of their exercising it be divided into groups, which groups may be indefinitely diversified: but the consideration

Other modifications of indirect powers dismissed

[h] This is the sort of power which the members of a corporation possess over the lands and other articles that are the property of the corporation.

of these and the other variations that may attend the constitution and operations of corporate bodies is not necessary to the present purpose.

Buying and selling, a mutual exercise of the investitive power

46. A mutual exercise of the investitive power by two persons in favour of each other is called *buying and selling*. Or more fully thus. You have the investitive power over a measure of corn: I have the like power over a measure of wine. You exercise in my favour the investitive power that you have over the corn, in consideration that I exercise in your favour the investitive power I have over the wine: Doing thus we may each of us be said to buy and to sell: you buy my wine with your corn: you sell your corn for my wine. I buy your corn with my wine: I sell my wine for your corn.

Buying and selling, where money is concerned

47. If either of the articles consists in what is called money or in what serves as money, the application of the words buy and sell is not thus reciprocal: he who buys the money is not said to buy, but only to sell: he who sells the money is not said to sell but only to buy: the one of them only is accordingly styled the buyer, the other only the seller: just as if buying and selling were two different operations. The reason for this peculiarity in language is not to the present purpose: it is sufficient to observe the fact.

Giving, what

48. If the power in question be exercised on one side only, he who exercises it is said to *give*: and sometimes where it is necessary to distinguish the present case from a case in which the word give has been made use of in speaking of buying and selling, he is said to give the thing *gratis*, or *for nothing*.

Conveying, what

49. The word *convey* is used indifferently in either case: in that of buying and selling, or in that of giving.

Different modes of buying and selling

50. The terms *buying* and *selling*, *giving*, and *conveying* are applicable to any other direct power or right as well as to the general or residuary power over a thing: buying services with things is called *hiring* services: rendering services in return for things or selling a right to services for things is called doing work *for hire*: buying the use of a thing for a time is called *hiring* it: selling the use of a thing for a time is called *letting* it, or *letting* it out to hire.

A compact or contract is to be distinguished from a conveyance

51. A *conveyance* ought to be distinguished from a *pact* or *covenant*: whether it be a covenant to render services one's self, or to convey a right to services or any other property: a pact or covenant is the expression of an intention to do some act or other, for the benefit of some person or other, and in the case of the not doing to incur certain penalties to be inflicted by the law. Let the act in question be an act of conveyance: such a sort of act whereby any thing, suppose a dwelling-house is conveyed. If I convey to you a house of mine and then enter into it without your consent, I am punishable as for a trespass upon your house, just as I should have been, had the house never been mine: if I only covenant to convey it before such a time and have not conveyed it by that time and the law gives its sanction to the promise contained in my covenant, in such case although I enter into the house without your consent I am punishable not as for a trespass upon your house, but in another manner as for the breach of this my covenant.[1]

52. So much with respect to the nature of the powers and rights themselves in which property consists. We now come to speak of the party or parties for whose benefit they are to be exercised. For the benefit of somebody they must have been designed, so long as the legislator has acted with a view to utility, or in short with any view whatever. This party or parties must have been either the person himself to whom the power is given or some other: in the first case the power may be styled a beneficial power or simply a power; in the other case a fiduciary power or trust. *Persons for whose benefit a power is designed. Power beneficial or fiduciary*

53. In this latter case again the beneficiary as hath been already observed may be either 1. an assignable individual or individuals: 2. a subordinate class of persons individually unassignable, or 3. the public at large: trusts may accordingly be distinguished into private, semi-public and public trusts. *Fiduciary private, semi-public or public*

54. The law permits me to enter upon and walk over a field, of which the general property is in you: thus much it might do for my sake, in which case the power it gives me would be of the beneficial kind. But it does not stop there: it does not content itself with permission: it commands me to enter into your field in order to plough it for you: it thereby renders the power a fiduciary one. The legal operation by which the power is constituted is in the first case a permission alone: in the other case it is a permission with a command super-added to it. *Power fiduciary how created*

55. Let us observe the several results of this operation of the law. To me it affords liberty as against restraint: but at the same time it takes away a portion of the liberty I have as against constraint: to *Power fiduciary imports right to services*

[1] What renders it the more necessary to advert to this distinction is that the word contract which in English is used only in synonymity with covenant is in Latin and some of the other European languages put in synonymity not only with covenant but with conveyance: at least certain particular conveyances or instruments of conveyance are called contracts.[1]

[1] Bentham may have had in mind the French use of the term *contrat de cession* for conveyance.

you it affords a right to my services. If the beneficiary be a person different from him against whom the trustee is left at liberty, that is in the present case from the present proprietor of the land, there are three persons concerned in point of interest in the operation: and with reference to these three it produces so many different results. I have a power, for example, of taking turf out of your field in trust, that is for the use of another person. In this case if the power I have is backed as it will commonly be by a prohibition of disturbance addressed to you, the metaphorical results produced by the law will stand as follows: to me in the first place liberty as against restraint as before: in the next place constraint, as before: to you, restraint: to the third person, a right to my services, as before.[1]

The operations of the executive magistrate are liable not to quadrate with those of the legislative

56. Hitherto it has been all along taken for granted that in the establishment and maintenance of property the legislator and the executive magistrate go hand in hand: that the prohibitions and commands whereby those several sorts of property are created are constantly enforced; and that accordingly the adjective commands by which the substantive commands given to the above purport are enforced, are constantly and punctually observed. But from various accidents it will every now and then happen otherwise: the course taken by the executive magistrate will be unconformable to that marked out to him by the legislator. It is this distinction that seems to be the source of certain distinctions which the whole phraseology of the law of property is continually bringing upon the carpet. These distinctions being to be explained now, this is the time for exhibiting the import of the word *possession* as well as certain other words which could not till now have been conveniently display'd.

Occupation, what

57. To understand what it is to possess, we must understand the nature of what it is to *occupy*.

A man may be said to *occupy* a thing when he performs any acts having their termination in that thing: the case is nearly the same with the word *to use*. The words *use* and *occupation* are in most cases nearly synonymous.[j] If a man occupies a thing it will be for the sake of some benefit to be thereby derived from that thing to either himself or some other person: the nature of the thing and the nature of the benefit to be derived from it will determine the nature of the act which is termed occupation. A piece of land is made use of

[j] Use extends to transfer.

[1] At this point in the Ms. the following pencilled note occurs: 'Weakness of the investitive power alone, strength of it when coupled with the divestitive.' The fact that there is a gap in Bentham's numbering of paragraphs here—what appears below as para. 56 is numbered '59' in the Ms.—suggests that Bentham intended but failed to develop these points more fully.

in one way, a house in another, a garment in another, a piece of household furniture in another, an article of food or fuel in another.

58. *Possession* must be distinguished into *physical* and *legal*: physical again into physical possession as against physical obstacles and physical possession as against human obstacles: and legal into legal possession *de jure* and legal possession *de facto*. Possession in general in a loose way of speaking may be said to be the absence of obstacles opposed to occupation: or in other words it is the liberty of occupation. As far as this liberty results from the situation which the thing is in, setting aside the interference of law, the possession may be termed physical: as far as it results from the aspect of the law, it may be termed legal. So much for a general idea of the nature of possession: but a subject so intricate demands more particular explanations.

Various senses of the word posses-sion analysed

59. You may be said to have the physical possession of a thing as against physical obstacles, when it appears that in the event of your exerting your endeavours to use it, you will occupy it accordingly: in this sense you are in possession of the water at the bottom of your well, if you have health and strength and time enough, and so forth to draw it up: of a horse which is on a common, provided the common is near enough for you to go upon it presently, and provided that if you have got upon it you can catch him: of the stone which is in a quarry upon the common, provided the stone does not lie too deep for you to dig it out. Now as the strength of the endeavours that are necessary to produce the effect in question, or in other words the difficulty of producing it will be apt to vary by insensible degrees, it will be difficult in most instances to draw the line between the cases in which a man has and that in which he has not this species of possession: so that if two persons were disposed to dispute upon the question whether a given person were or were not in this sense in possession of a given thing, they might go on disputing without end.

Physical pos-session as against physical obstacles

60. You may be said to have the physical possession of a thing as against human obstacles at large when there is not on the part of the will of any other person any impediment sufficient to prevent you from occupying or making use of it. Thus you are physically speaking in possession of the coat which is on your back at any rate: of a coat which is in the next room to you provided nobody hinders you from getting at it: of a coat which is at the tailor's, provided the tailor and everybody else is disposed to let you have it.

Physical pos-session as against human obstacles

61. You may be said to be in the legal possession of a thing *de jure* if you are in such a case that the law has issued such mandates

Legal posses-sion de jure

as have the effect of prohibiting other persons from disturbing you in the physical possession, or what comes to the same thing in the occupation of it: or at least of preventing its own officers from giving you such disturbance.

Legal possession de facto **62.** You may be said to be in the legal possession of a thing *de facto*, when it appears that the executive magistrate to whom the secondary mandates of the legislator are addressed will in case an occasion should take place do that which he ought to do upon the supposition that the mandates above mentioned are established in your favour: or in other words will in case of disturbance do what is requisite to maintain you in the physical possession of it as against human obstacles.

Title may be good, lawful, valid: or actual, effectual **63.** To have the legal possession of a thing, is in other words to be entitled to it, or to have a title to it: this title may, if the legal possession in question is the legal possession *de jure*, be termed a good, lawful or valid title: if the legal possession in question is the legal possession de facto, an actual or effectual title.

Investitive and divestitive event **64.** Now the time during which any given person is in possession of any given thing must it is evident have certain boundaries: if no others, those at least which limit the man's life. It must have accordingly on the one hand a commencement, and on the other a termination. The moment of its commencement must be marked out by one of them: that of its termination by another: the former of these may be termed the investitive event with respect to the period of time: the latter the divestitive.

The two species of legal possession and title commonly go together **65.** It appears then that in every case the fictitious entity called a title is constituted by some investitive event; and so many sorts as there are of investitive events, so many sorts are there of titles. From the happening at which any article in the catalogue of these investitive events takes place to the time at which every article in the catalogue of divestitive events takes place, the title subsists: upon the happening of any article in the latter catalogue, it is at an end. During this same period also you are said to possess the thing in question, or to be in possession of it, meaning legal possession: in the legal possession *de jure* if the aspects of the legislator are in favour of your occupying it: in the legal possession *de facto* if the conduct or procedure of the executive magistrate be or appear likely to be in favour of your occupying it: in both together if both the aspects of the legislator are and the administration appears likely to be in favour of it. Now it is but by accident that the administration of the executive magistrate fails of being conformable to the mandates of the legislator: the design and expectation is that it should always be conformable to them: and so it actually is in common even in the worst ordered governments that are. In common then these two species of possession go together: and so they may of course be deemed to do when nothing is said to the contrary. Whenever then the phrase legal possession is introduced it may be taken for granted if nothing is said to the contrary that what is said of legal possession in general is meant to be applied to both these kinds of it.

66. The investitive event may either be voluntary or natural: it may be termed voluntary when it consists of the commencement of the title as effected by the will of some person purposely manifested in the intention of causing it to commence: as if you were expressly to declare it to be your will that I should have such or such a portion of your land: it may be termed natural where the commencement of the title is effected by an event in the production of which the will of man has ordinarily no concern: as if you were to die; whereupon according to a rule of law established in that behalf, I were to succeed to the legal possession of your land. Now it is in the case where the investitive event is voluntary that the person whose will is in question is said to have the investitive power over the thing in question. And the case is the same with divestitive events and divestitive power. *Investitive event purely natural or voluntary*

67. Hitherto in order to avoid perplexity we have been speaking of the investitive event as if it never consisted of any more than one single event at a time. But the truth is that it may be either simple or complex: and that to any degree of complexity. It may consist either of one single event, such as the death of a man or of the sum of any number of events of any sort natural or voluntary: such as the death of a man produced by the sentence of a court of justice: the performance of the ceremonies necessary to confiscation: or of the ceremonies instituted for the purpose of establishing the authenticity of his testament; and so on. But as the unity of an act or other event depends solely upon the custom of language any number of such events may to certain purposes be spoken of as one. *Investitive event may be simple or complex*

68. It will be proper to observe the difference between possession and occupation: between possessing a power of occupying a thing, and exercising that power. To occupy a thing you must perform some act: an act having its termination in the thing in question. To possess a thing it is not necessary that you should yourself perform any act: possession is not any real but only a fictitious mode of action. It is not necessary so much as that any body else should perform any act: all that is necessary is that things should be so *Possession is permanent—occupation instantaneous* circumstanced as to make it appear that in case such or such another person were to take such and such steps of which the tendency would be to prevent your occupying it were you so disposed the executive magistrate would do or at least according to law ought to do what depended upon him for preventing or punishing such transgression. Occupation therefore is the exercise of a power characterizable and diversified by the acts of which it may consist: possession of a power or right is characterizable by nothing but the time during which it lasts. Possession is something permanent and continual: occupation and exercise are instantaneous.

Right of possession is the same as right to a thing

69. Along with the word *possession*, we hear also of the *right of possession*: the nature of this right will easily be apprehended from what has been said of a right to things. Right to a thing and right to the possession of a thing are expressions of the same meaning: and perhaps the case is, that the latter alone is the original and proper phrase of which the former is but an elliptical abridgement.[1] To have possession of a thing is to have the power over a thing: to have a right to the possession of a thing, is to have a right to the thing.

When a man has actually the legal possession of a thing in this case too it is common to speak of him as having the right of possession also, but in this case the phrase right of possession has a different meaning from what it has in the former. To give him what is meant by the right of possession as explained above would in this case be narrowing his interest in the land instead of enlarging it. In this case then to say that he has the right of possession, or in other words a right to the possession along with the possession itself means only as much as to say that the possession he has of a thing is *not* defeasible by eviction: to say that he has the possession without having the right of possession is as much as to say that the possession he has *is* defeasible by eviction. The right of possession is not to be confounded with what was spoken of just now under the appellation of the legal possession *de jure*. A man may have the former without having the latter; as in the case above exemplified. A man may have the latter without having the former: in truth if he has the latter he can not be said to have the former as above explained: if he has already the permission to do what he pleases with the thing in question he can not be said to be in the same condition with one who as yet has not that permission, but waits to have it conferred on him by the act of another person.

Protection for property

70. We may now perhaps be in a condition to ascertain what the operations are by which the law gives protection for property. For

[1] Ms. reverses the order of 'latter' and 'former'.

such species of property as consist in a power over things, the protection it gives in the first instance is afforded by prohibition: by the prohibition of any acts by which the possession or the exercise of such power would be disturbed. For such as consist in a right to certain services on the part of certain persons, if those services be of the negative stamp, also by prohibition: by prohibition of the acts in the abstaining from which those services consist. For such as consist in a right to certain services of the positive kind, by command: to wit by command to render such services to the person in question.

71. So much for the several modifications of which property is susceptible. Take a certain number of them and lay them together, and there are I imagine few species of incorporeal property established under any system of law which may not be made out. To make sure of getting them all, the way I have taken has been to take for an example that system concerning the state of which I had the best opportunities of being informed with certainty, I mean the English law. I have accordingly examined all the several species of incorporeal property of which mention has been made by the most approved writers on that law: and these I have found to have been all of them explainable by means of the above mentioned list of distinctions. The truth is I went to work upon the several complex species of incorporeal property themselves as characterized by the several names in use; and it was by analyzing each of them into the simple modifications of which it appeared to be made up that I came to form the entire catalogue here delivered.

Impossibility of ascertaining the whole number of possible modifications by an exhaustive process

The plan of investigation here pursued it may be observed is not of the exhaustive kind: it is nothing more than that of simple enumeration. But the case seems to be that such a plan is inapplicable to the present subject. To find the limits of any subject nothing more can be done than to ascertain the real or semi-real entities, the substances or motions or situations it relates to. These may be analyzed in an exhaustive method without danger of the omission of any article. The several possible subjects of corporeal property were accordingly distinguished in the first place into the two great classes of things and persons. Under one or other of these two heads one might be perfectly sure that every whole article in the catalogue of these material subjects would be comprised. But it is impossible to set any limits to the number of parcels into which this immense mass may by possibility be divided. A surveyor may measure the whole circuit of a field: but to count the paths that may be made across it is impracticable: even a simple line may be divided into an infinity of parts. As impracticable is it to determine the sum total of the sources of distinction with regard to property by any exhaustive process.

As far however as I can perceive, the plan of enumeration I have here pursued will perform pretty well what is required for practice: and if in any other of the established systems of law in Europe there are any incorporeal objects of property in the composition of which any modifications are to be found other than those which have been here enumerated, I believe the list of such omissions will be found at any rate to be a short one.

Conclusion.
Intricacy of
this subject

72. So much for the several fictitious entities which may be brought to view in speaking of the various modifications of property. I can not pretend to have exhibited the whole catalogue of them, much less to have exhibited all the various groups and phases in which they may be combined. The sum total of all these combinations taken together forms a wilderness in which the most piercing eye will be incessantly exposed to lose itself in: the parts of it are altogether disparate and incommensurable: take them each by itself and their bearings to each other are altogether unascertainable. To give some sort of clue to this labyrinth is all that I can hope to have accomplished here. To exhibit an entire plan of it would require an entire work, a work perhaps the most laborious but by no means the least useful of any within the pale of jurisprudence. To explain every article in this catalogue is impracticable: at the same time it was not without regret that I saw myself forced to leave a number of articles unexplained which perhaps stood not in less need of explanation than those to which it has been given.

Thus much may be affirmed with certainty of them all, that to render them intelligible there is no other expedient than the showing of the relation which the import of them bears to the import of the group of real entities, simple modes, and qualities that have been already mentioned: with these real entities modes and qualities we must therefore begin. So far the road is plain: but when we proceed further and endeavour to ascertain what is the most convenient order for arranging them one with another there seems to be nothing to afford us light: there is no seeing where to begin such a work, nor where it would be ended. There is no end to the variety of phrases that may be made out of them to express the same signification. They may be used separately: they may be used in long strings of four or five or six strung one upon another.

We may even go so far as to say of a man that a man is entitled to possess a condition or station in life which gives him a title to possess the right of exercising such or such a power over such or such a thing. Obscure as they are, they are at the same time so familiar as to be meeting us as it were at every turn we take. As if this were not enough, from these fictitious entities have arisen a secondary race of entities still more fictitious and characterized by the same names. Even the most common words we have, words that enter and that indispensably into the composition of almost every sentence; auxiliary verbs and possessive pronouns, are words of this stamp, sophisticated as it were and turned aside from their original signification: to *have* is to possess: the pronouns *your, my, her, his, their,* and so forth imply possession: even a fragment of a word, the two or three concluding letters in it envelop the same meaning: for so it is that in many languages that *case* is formed which is called possessive. All this while, so essentially do these words enter into the composition of all language that in explaining any one of the original ones here spoken of, we are obliged to make use of other words of which the import is not to be clearly delivered but through the medium of those very words which we are endeavouring to explain: such is that illogical and vicious circle in which it seems probable that we shall forever be condemned to run.

Thus it is that the tyranny of language makes its sport of scientific industry. In some places it has regularity enough to tempt the ingenious mind to endeavour at subjecting the science to the rules of exhaustive method; while in other quarters it is deformed by such a degree of irregularity as sets up an insuperable bar to his most strenuous efforts.

Part II

It may be observed by the bye that although it should be clearly known for example that such or such a magistrate being the magistrate to whom it belongs in the first instance to maintain you in the possession of it is not disposed so to do, you might nevertheless be said to be apparently in the possession of it *de facto* and to have apparently an *effectual title* to it, provided it appears that such or such another magistrate would: to wit any magistrate who is superior, or paramount in the scale of jurisdiction to the former. *Actual title depends upon the disposition of the judge paramount*

By the help of the above distinctions it may now be ascertained how far and in what sense a man may be put out of possession, meaning legal possession, of a thing by an act which notwithstanding shall be treated upon the footing of an offence. It is possible that a man may by such an act be made to lose the legal possession even *How by an offence a man may lose the legal possession de jure*: by the English law, for instance, if a man steals a thing yet if the thing be afterward sold even by the thief in open market, he who at the time of its being stolen had the legal possession of it *de jure*, loses that possession. But more commonly when it is by an offence that a man loses the *de facto* legal possession of a thing, that is the effectual title to it, *de jure* legal possession of it, that is the valid title to it, remains, for a considerable length of time at least, unchanged.

The duty of the executive magistrate is to make the legal possession de facto coincide with that de jure

Now the effectual title we see depends upon the disposition of the magistrate: the disposition to observe, or not to observe that conduct which consists in the maintaining the person in question in the physical possession of the thing in question. But the duty of the executive magistrate on this as on all other occasions is to act in conformity to the law: that is, on an occasion like the present, to give the effectual title, the legal possession *de facto*, to him who has the just title, the legal possession *de jure*.

Ways in which it may happen that he fails of doing so

Now in order thus to conduct himself on the present occasion as on any other, there are three qualifications or endowments which as we shall often have need to observe it is necessary he should possess: I mean knowledge, power and inclination, a certain species and measure of knowledge, a certain species and measure of power, and a certain bent of inclination. If then he possesses them all, he cannot *but* act in conformity to the law: if he fails in respect of any one of them, he can *not*. Now when he does not, the failure may either be his fault or not his fault: and when it is not his fault it either be the fault of some other person, or the fault of nobody. The knowledge in question is again of two sorts: 1. knowledge of the *law*. 2. knowledge of the *fact*. Knowledge of the fact is in the present case the knowing that such or such a particular event has happened: and that such and such other particular events have not, any of them, taken place. Knowledge of the law is the knowing that the law has provided that an event of such or such a description shall be regarded as having in favour of such or such a sort of person and with respect to such or such a sort of thing, the effect of an investitive event: and that the event above mentioned to have happened is of that description, and that the individual person and thing in question are each of the sort in question: as also that such or such sorts of events and no other are according to law to have the effect of so many divestitive events as against that person and with reference to that thing: and that none of any events that have happened are of any of those sorts.

Means by which such failure may be brought about

Now there are various means by which the magistrate may be

deprived of the above requisite endowments: some of them by his own fault, others of them without it. *Knowledge* of the fact may be withheld from him by suppressing or destroying written or other permanent evidences of it: by forging or fraudulently procuring counter-evidence: by suppressing oral testimony: by giving or procuring false testimony: *power*, by a failure on the part of those whose duty it is to assist him, by the surreptitious evasion of those on whom it should be exercised, or by the opposition of a superior controlling force: *inclination*, in a remote way as before by with-holding true information from him, by supplying him with false, or in a direct way by applying the force of any sort of motives alluring or coercive, in such manner as to act upon him in any direction other than that of the line of his official duty.

Of these various natures then are the means by which the possession of a trust or any other article of property may be offended against: and the offences thus committed are of a very different nature from those which regard the exercise of the right of property in question. The exercise of this right is the same thing with the occupation of the thing which is the object of the right. Now the idea of occupation is always a positive idea: it includes the idea of some act as performed by the person who is said to occupy. On the contrary the idea of possession is in the case of the first mentioned sort of possession, to wit physical possession, a purely negative one. It imports nothing more than the absence or the negation of such acts on the part of other persons as would have the effect of preventing the possessor from occupying the thing in question. For a man to occupy a thing he must act: for him to possess it physically, there is no need that either he or any one else should act at all. No more is there in order for him to possess it legally *de jure*: at least from the time that this investitive event by which his title was created has taken place. No more is there in order for him to have the legal possession of it *de facto*: unless where he has lost the physical possession of it, in which case a certain course of conduct is requisite on the part of the magistrate and his assistants in order to bestow it on him anew.

The exercise of the right consists in an act: viz in the occupation of the thing

As to the word *occupation* it may be applied as well to an object of incorporeal as to an object of corporeal property: but between the ideas that are annexed to it in the two cases there will be a little difference. Where the object is corporeal the nature of the act signified by the word occupation will easily enough be apprehended: where it is incorporeal, not without some difficulty. In the former case the material body in which the act of occupation terminates is

Occupation of an in-corporeal different from a corporeal article

suggested immediately by the very word expressive of the thing which is said to be occupied and which is spoken of as the object of the property: in the latter case, no such material body is immediately suggested. Suggested however by some means or other it must be before any distinct image can be painted in the mind, in short before any clear idea of the termination of the acts in question can be obtained, and consequently before any intelligible idea annexable to the word *occupation* can be found. In the case of that species of incorporeal property which is here in question viz: a trust, the corporeal object will in different cases be different according to the nature of the power or the right in the exercise of which the

Occupation of a person

performance of the trust consists. If it be no more than a power over things, things only will be the objects in which the act of occupation can terminate: if it be a power over persons, the objects in which the acts of occupation terminate will belong to the class of persons. Now when this is the case with an act the idea of its progress is a little different from that of the progress of an act which terminates in a portion of unsentient matter: it admits of more varieties, and is more difficult to conceive. Where the act is to terminate in a mass of unsentient matter, a considerable quantity of motion must be produced for the purpose in the body in which the act originates, and continued during the whole progress of the act until it arrives at the body in which it is designed to terminate: a motion sufficient to produce that effect without the help of any other motion originating from volition. In the case where the act is to terminate in a human person, or other sentient being, no such motion is requisite to be produced. Not but that even here, some sort and degree of motion is necessary; but this motion may be of so slight and subtle a nature as could not produce the effect it is attended with on any other body than that of a creature endowed with volition, nor in virtue of any other power than that of acting on his will. Mentor, when in order to withdraw Telemachus from the enticement of Calypso's Island, he had determined to convey him on board the Phoeacian ship, had nothing left for it but to treat him on the footing of an irrational being and to take advantage of the instant when they were standing together on the brink of a promontory, and to push him headlong into the sea.[1] Had he possessed the same influence on the inclinations of the young prince as on so many other occasions he had exercised, a nod or a wink might have been sufficient. Now even this

[1] A reference to Fénelon's *Aventures de Télémaque*, which Bentham had first read at the age of seven and to which (he suggested in old age) might be traced the first dawning in his mind of the principle of utility (cf. Bowring, x, 10).

nod or this wink would have been a motion: but such a motion as could not have been attended with any material effect but by means of the association which custom has established between such signs of volition on the part of *one* sentient being, and the volitions and thence the physical actions of *another*.[k]

[1] We come now to offences against trust. A trust is a species of

Trust a species of property

[k] Judging according to the fashion of language it might be thought that there are sorts of offences against trust besides those above specified: for example where a man exercises a power which lawfully belongs to him, but in a *manner* in which it is not lawful to exercise it. But this distinction between the power itself and the manner of exercising it would hardly I believe stand the test of examination. It would be found impracticable, I take it, to give any clear and intelligible account of the matter whereby it should appear that there are two distinguishable cases, in one of which the power itself is illegal, and in the other the power itself legal, but the manner of exercising it illegal: for at bottom where is the difference between exercising such and such a power and exercising a power in such or such a manner? In one case the *possession* of the power (i.e. of the condition to which it stands annexed) is considered: in the other the *exercise* of the power, viz: the performance of a certain act. To have an idea of a power exercised, we must have an idea of some action which is performed: of some action by the performance of which a man exercises a power. A man exercises a certain power by performing a certain action. Now every action (taking the circumstances into the account of its description) must either be lawful or unlawful. If then the action be unlawful, it will be as proper to say that the power of performing it does not belong to him as that the exercise of it is unlawful. If the action be lawful it will be no more proper to say that the exercise of the power is unlawful than that the power itself is. I may here perhaps be accused of subtlety: but is it not rather the popular usage that is chargeable with subtlety in setting up a verbal distinction which has no foundation in point of fact? If ever it should be necessary to speak of a power as one thing and the manner of exercising it as another, or in other words to speak of the same power as a thing that may be exercised in divers manners, it ought at least to be remembered that the only way to analyse the expression and clear up the ideas that belong to it is to point out the act which is performed when the power is said to be exercised in such or such a manner, and to consider each different manner of exercising what is called the same power as constituting a separate power of itself.

It is with language in general as with mathematical language in particular. Algebraical notation may on many occasions be made use of with advantage for the sake of expedition: but it never is clearly understood until it be translated into the language of geometry or plain arithmetic. In like manner abstract phraseology must on many occasions be tolerated for the same reason: but on no occasion can it be clearly understood unless it can be translated into such expressions as have a direct reference to the sensible objects that are in question.

[1] The Mss. from here to the end of the Appendix bear at several points the numeral 'ccxix'. This evidently refers to the pagination of *An Introduction to the Principles* as printed in 1780 and thus confirms the suggestion made in the Introduction to the present work (p. xxxviii) that Part II of Appendix B is an early draft of part of

property. To discover the offences to which a trust may stand exposed we discover the offences to which property in general may stand exposed.

Articles to be considered in relation to property

In speaking of property there are four things to be considered: 1. the nature of the thing which is spoken of as the object of the property; 2. the person who is said to possess the property, or to whom the property is said to belong, who is styled the proprietor and whose property the thing is said to be; 3. the nature of the relation or proprietorship which subsists between that person and that thing[1]: and in virtue whereof the person is said to be the proprietor, owner or possessor of the thing; and the thing to be the object of the property or of the possession, or more briefly, the property or the possession of that person; 4. the acts in which the exercise of the property consists.

The object of property – Property corporeal and incorporeal

First then with regard to the object of property. This, according to the distinction which is commonly made, may either be a corporeal object or an incorporeal one. But the only objects which have any real existence are those which are corporeal. It follows that those which are styled incorporeal objects of property can be nothing but so many fictitious entities. Now to possess a fictitious entity, were the matter to rest there, would be to possess nothing. Property therefore must either amount to nothing at all or it must relate somehow or other to some corporeal object; that sort of property which in common speech is said to have only an incorporeal thing for its object as well as that which is said to have a corporeal one. To have a clear idea of what is meant by any of the names applied to an incorporeal object of property we must look further: we must push on till we come to the corporeal object or objects which are its sources. That which is styled a corporeal object is one single and entire corporeal thing: that which is styled an incorporeal object is either one or several corporeal objects considered in some particular point of view. Where the object of the property is said to be corporeal that object, the real corporeal object, presents itself necessarily and immediately upon the mention of the property. Where it is said to be incorporeal, the real corporeal object does not thus immediately and necessarily present itself. It is not necessary

---

[1] There are a great variety of other phrases which are made use of on this occasion: but it would be foreign to the nature of the present design to attempt giving a full and perfect catalogue of them.

Ch. xvi of *An Introduction to the Principles*. It is not, however, the earliest version, and would seem to have been written when a substantial portion of Ch. xvi, already in print, had had to be discarded (cf. *Correspondence*, in *CW*, ii, 488). •

upon the present occasion to enter into the examination of the necessity there may be for setting up this fiction: it is sufficient that it be actually and universally set up, and that it is so firmly engrafted into every language that it is now impossible to carry on discourse without it. The fact is then that wherever the thing which a man is said to have for his property is either less or more than one entire single and determinate corporeal object a fictitious entity is created as it were for the purpose and spoken of as being the object of a man's property: as being the object of which he is said to have the property, and what he is said to possess. This fictitious entity, to distinguish it from the real entities that may strictly speaking be the objects of property, is styled an incorporeal object of property. In these cases then the immediate object of the property is a fictitious entity: ultimately however the property must always relate to some really existent objects capable of being the objects of corporeal property; otherwise the property as has been above observed would amount to nothing.

The modifications of which the several incorporeal objects of property are susceptible must therefore have reference to and be determined by those of which the several sorts of corporeal objects of property are susceptible: and to give an idea of the former we must begin with obtaining an idea of the latter.

In the first place then, the object of property when corporeal is either rational or irrational: in other words it is either a *person*, that is a human creature, or a *thing*. Things again are either animate or inanimate. Inanimate things again are either immovable or movable. By immovable things are meant those objects whether natural or artificial which in order to be made use of do not in their totality require to be moved: such as a piece of dry land, a piece of land covered with water, a house and so forth.[m]

1. Object of a corporeal property—a person or a thing

Secondly, with regard to the nature of the relation which subsists between the proprietor and the object which is his property. This relation is what may be called a *legal* one. A man may be said to bear a legal relation to any object when either he on his own account or on account of some other person, or some other person in his favour are either commanded or forbidden to exercise any act having its termination in that object. If this definition be just, it

2. Relation— A legal relation what

Number of the relations is equal to that of the persons

[m] Upon examination it would be found that in the nature of the things themselves there is no clear line drawn between these two classes of objects, since there is no one particle of matter that can be used but what can be moved. To ascertain in all cases to which of them a given article is to be referred it will therefore be necessary that the line should be drawn by positive law.

Line between movable and immovable objects not clear

concerned multiplied by that of the aspects

follows that the legal relation which the same person may have to the same object of property may be as many as there can be changes run upon the following articles: 1. two persons concerned and each of them commanded to do the act or not commanded: forbidden to do it or not forbidden.[1]

3. Acts of occupation – property direct or occupied per se, indirect or occupied per alium

[Thirdly,] with regard to the acts in which the occupation of the property consists. These acts may be exercised either directly by the very person himself who is here considered as the proprietor, without the intervention of any other person, or indirectly through the intervention of some other person: in other words either by the immediate acts of the proprietor in question, or the act of another who stands appointed by such proprietor: in the former case the property may be said to be occupied direct, in the latter case indirect.

Legal relation constitutes a condition

Now according to the custom of language whatever legal relation a man bears with respect to any object, whether it be a person or a thing, he may in virtue thereof be said to possess a kind of fictitious entity called a *condition* in life, or more briefly a *condition*. In this case such condition so long as he continues to possess it is oftentimes considered as a kind of clothing or covering with which he is said to stand *invested*: for such are the shifts to which the authors of language have been forced to recur in their endeavours to extend the application of that subtle instrument to the various purposes of life.[n] Now the time during which a man continues to stand thus invested can not be unlimited, since even the time during which a man continues to act is never unlimited. It must therefore be limited, and that by two events, the one marking its commencement and the other its termination: the former of these may be styled with reference to the condition in question the *investitive* event: the other, the *divestitive*. Now when a man in the pursuance of the will of any proprietor exercises any act on a thing which is the object of his property, such agent also may on that account be said to bear at least a temporary kind of legal relation to it, and in virtue of such relation to stand invested with at least a temporary condition.

Condition – its commencement and termination – an investitive event x[2] a divestitive event

Act of investment communicates a legal relation, and a condition however transient

Investitive event purely natural or voluntary

It appears then that incident to every condition there must be an investitive and a divestitive event. These may each of them be either

[n] *Invested*, from the Latin *investio*, to clothe. Under the feudal law, where a person had an estate given to him to be paid for by certain services which were styled feudal, he was said to be *invested* with the fief or feud.

[1] A gap in the Ms. at the end of this paragraph indicates that Bentham intended, but failed, to continue the numbered series of 'articles'. The unfinished state of these Mss. is further shown by the fact that the next paragraph in fact opens with the word 'Fourthly', though the marginal heading is numbered '3'.

[2] Bentham uses this symbol for *versus* or 'as distinct from'.

voluntary or purely natural. They may be styled voluntary when they depend in any sort upon the will of any person; purely natural when they have no such dependence. When either of them is voluntary, the person on whose will it depends is in virtue of such dependence spoken of as possessing a certain sort of power, viz: an investitive or a divestitive power with reference to the condition in question.

It is evident that although a man should possess the investitive, yet if he possess not the divestitive power with reference to any condition, the acts done in virtue of such condition by the person who stands invested therewith have but a slight dependence on his will; and it is only by a sort of extension given to the import of the terms that they can be referred to him as their author. *Weakness of power investitive without the divestitive—in this case the interest remaining to the investor is next to nothing*

On the other hand when a man possesses the divestitive power with regard to any condition conferring property and no limitation in point of time is set to the exercise of that power, so that he may exercise it at any time, the dependence which the acts of occupancy in question have upon the will of the original proprietor is very strong, and the interest if such it can be called which is possessed by the derivative occupant is almost too precarious to come under the denomination of property, or to cause him to be spoken of in ordinary discourse as one who on that account stands invested with a condition. One who in the character of a guardian or other trustee takes care of a man's house shall be considered as having a certain sort of interest or even property in the house; while a servant taking precisely the same care of the house shall not commonly be spoken of as possessing any sort of interest in it: yet all the difference there is between the condition of the trustee in the one case and that of the servant in the other may be that the right which the former has of occupying the house has a certain duration, while that of the latter may be put an end to at any time at the pleasure of the beneficial owner. *Strength of, when accompanied by the divestitive—in this case the interest of the derivative occupant is what is nothing* *Example—servant and guardian*

In the latter case the influence which the will of the original proprietor has on the nature of the acts exercised on the subject in question by the derivative occupant is so strong and so obvious that the thing is considered as being the property of the former in virtue not merely of such acts as may have been exercised on it by himself, but even in virtue of the acts exercised on it by the latter: in so much that the very acts of the latter are in common discourse spoken of as being the acts of the former, and the former is considered as continuing the sole proprietor of it all the time. *It is in the latter case only that the acts of the derivative occupant are spoken of as being the acts of the original investor*

On the other hand where the divestitive event is in no respect *In the former case the occupa-*

tion is considered as totally severed from the exercise of the investitive power

dependent on the will of the original proprietor, the influence which he has on the acts of the derivative occupant is in comparison feeble and precarious: the acts of the latter are no longer considered as being the acts of the former: the property of the thing is conceived as being divided between the two parties, all the property the original proprietor has is considered as being confined to the investitive power, which power being once exercised is from thenceforward at an end, from which period the whole property of it that remains centers exclusively in the derivative occupant.

Not that the investitive power has no influence on the acts of occupation

Not that this influence is in every case absolutely nothing. On the contrary where the property is of that sort in which the description of the acts in which the occupation of the object consists is limited by the obligation of rendering them subservient to the benefit of some other person, the original wish and intention of the original proprietor is a circumstance that may have a considerable influence on the conduct of the derivative occupant. This we may see exemplified in a particular manner in public trusts: in which the right or power of investment or as it is commonly called of election or appointment is found not to be altogether insignificant even though no divestitive power be lodged in the same hands.

Recapitulation – Power either direct or indirect

Upon the whole then it appears that the power which belongs to a man in virtue of his possessing property is either direct or indirect. By the direct power is to be understood the power of occupation. The indirect is either investitive or divestitive. These are distinctions which apply alike to every sort of property, of whatsoever nature be the object of it: as also to every sort of right and every sort of power; words of which the import is included indeed in that of the word property when taken in its most extensive signification.

APPENDIX C[1]

1. Thus inextricably is the penal branch of the law interwoven with the civil: that with which we are here immediately concerned, with that with which here we have no such immediate concern: in order to settle and arrange the former, it became therefore unavoidably necessary to look through all the latter: so toilsome and so arduous when pursued with care and industry is the business of arrangement. Before we conclude it may be not amiss to gather up in the way of recapitulation the broken hints that have been given in the course of this chapter and thereby to give a sort of analytical sketch of the whole business of the art of legislation. *Connection*

2. The art of legislation has two general objects or purposes in view: the one direct and positive, to add to the happiness of the community: the other indirect and negative, to avoid doing anything by which that happiness may be diminished. *Objects of legislation – producing good, avoiding to produce evil*

3. To enable it to compass the former of these purposes it has two great instruments or engines: 1. coercion and 2. remuneration. Coercion is either 1. physical or 2. moral, viz: by punishment. Physical coercion, by which a human being is treated upon the footing of an inanimate machine, it is evident enough can be made but little use of, by reason of the vast and incessant expense it would cost in labour and attention on the part of those whose business it must be made to apply it. Remuneration is also in comparison employed but little, for various reasons, one of which is the boundless expense it would require, and the absolute want of a fund from which that expense could be supplied. *Two instruments – coercion and reward; coercion is either physical or by punishment*

4. Having these instruments to work with, the way in which the law promotes the happiness of men, is by influencing *actions*. Take any individual for example. The actions which it influences must be either his *own* or those of *other* individuals. His own actions it cannot influence in any material degree by reward, on account of the expense. In what instances it can be consistent with the above mentioned *collateral* purpose of legislation, in other words, whether it can be worthwhile to attempt to influence them by coercive methods, is a matter that in most cases lies very open to dispute. *Method of operation – imposing obligations*

As to the actions of other men, the way in which it may promote his happiness by influencing those actions is either by causing such *Obligations positive and negative*

---

[1] See Introduction, xxxix above, for a discussion of the textual problems connected with this appendix.

as would be productive of *inconvenience* to him to be *abstained from*, or by causing such as are productive of *advantage* to him to be *performed*. In as far as by coercive methods it causes or endeavours to cause an action to be abstained from or performed it thereby creates a *duty*. Duties accordingly are either duties of *abstinence*, i.e. negative duties, or duties of *performance*, i.e. positive duties.

Objects of the conduct regulated things or persons

5. Now the objects in which the actions are capable of *terminating* are either *things* or *persons*. It is by causing certain actions to be abstained from on the part of other men which would lessen the advantage you are capable of reaping either for yourself or others from certain things, at the same time that you, or such and such persons of your appointment, are not caused to abstain from certain actions by which that happiness may be promoted, that you have *power* given you over those things. This power according to the amplitude of it is termed either the *property* of, or a property or *interest* in, the thing in question. Power over things is constituted then by the imposing of duties of abstinence on other persons. This power then either you are left free to exercise or not according as may contribute most to your own advantage, in which case it may be styled a beneficial power, or it is coupled with a duty, in other words you are bound to exercise it for the sake of some other party, in which case it is called a *trust*.

Power over things
Power over persons, three degrees of it

When the acts you are left free to perform are such whereby the interests of other individuals is liable to be affected, you are thereby said to have a power over those individuals. In this case in as far as you possess the power in question you possess an exemption from the duty of *abstinence* as far as concerns the acts to the performance of which your power extends. This exemption then on your part may either stand single or it may be coupled with an assistant duty (subservient to the same design) on the part of other men. In the first case it may be styled a *naked* or *uncorroborated* power: in the other case it may be styled a *corroborated* power. This assistant duty will either be a duty of forbearance, viz: the duty of abstaining from all such acts as may tend to prevent you from exercising the power in question, or 2. a duty of performance, viz: the duty of performing such acts as may enable you to overcome any obstacle that may oppose itself to the exercise of that power. Power over persons may accordingly be considered as susceptible of three degrees of perfection. Power in the first, lowest, or least perfect degree, is where it is not made any body's duty to oppose you, in case of your going about to exercise it. Power in the second or middle degree is where not only it is not made any body's duty to oppose you in case of your going about to exercise it, but it is made every body's duty not to oppose you in case of your going about to exercise it. Power in the third, highest, or most perfect degree is where not only it is made every body's duty not to oppose you in case of your going about to exercise it, but in case of your meeting with any obstacle to the exercise of it whether from the party over whom it is to be exercised or any other person or in short from any other cause, it is made the duty of such or such persons to enable you to overcome such obstacles.[a]

6. If the legislator goes further and in the view of preventing you from suffering any such prejudice as you might be exposed to suffer in any of those respects from any other cause, such as the agency of irrational or unsentient beings, commands me[1] in certain cases to exert my[2] endeavours for that purpose, he thereby for every act so commanded gives you a distinct sort of right and one which has a different name, viz: a right to a certain service on my part.

The law where it creates negative offences corresponding to the above positive ones gives right to so many sorts of services

7. I have been speaking of the manner in which the legislator acts in order to give you protection for your property and your condition in life. But in thus speaking I have been obliged to consider your property and your condition as objects already established and subsisting. But to establish you in possession of those privileges requires a distinct and various series of operations.

To give protection to different kinds of property may require different operations

8. Suppose that it is only certain particular acts that the legislator permits you to exercise upon the land: for instance to walk over it; to drive a carriage over it; to build on it; to dig stone out of it— prohibiting you accordingly from exercising upon it all other acts not comprised in such permission. In such case the power he gives you over the land may be said to be partial in point of use: and to distinguish it from the case next mentioned it may be said to be created *per exceptionem*: that is, by an exception annexed to the general rule whereby you are prohibited from meddling with the land.

Power particular or partial in point of use, and given specially or per exceptionem—property in a thing

9. Suppose that in a general view he permits you to exercise upon the land any acts that you have a mind to exercise: specifying only

Power general or partial in point of use, but given generally or sub exceptione—property of a thing

[a] In point of fact it is not always that where power over persons is given it is given in the highest degree. In that degree however it ought always to be given where it is given at all, since upon no other terms can a man be assured of the enjoyment of it. Power and the benefits for the sake of which it is conferred are left in a very precarious state where the enjoyment of it is made to depend upon the physical strength of the person on whom it is conferred or on the caprice of those who may happen to be about him.

[1] Ms., 'you'.
[2] Ms., 'your'.

certain acts in particular which he prohibits you from exercising. In such case also the power he gives you over it must still be said to be partial in point of use: but to distinguish it from the former it may be said to be created *sub exceptione*: that is by an exception annexed to the general rule whereby you are prohibited from meddling with the land.

Power given generally usually more ample than power given specially

10. It may be observed that a power given in this latter way will commonly be more ample than a power given in the former way: since it is not likely that the sum of the uses which can be specified by a few particular words will be so ample, that is that the sum of the acts will be so various as that of the acts and corresponding uses which remain unspecified.

Power is not necessarily ample in point of value, in proportion to what it is in point of use

11. But though the power that is given should in point of use be more ample than that which is withholden, it does not necessarily follow that it should be so in point of value. It contains for instance a considerable quantity of rich ore: but it is unfit for building on; it leads to no place that a man would wish to go to, and in short it is of scarce any value but what arises from the stone. In this case it is plain that he who should have the power of taking ore from it, without having any other power would have a power which although not very ample in point of use would be very considerable in point of value: at the same time that he who should have the power of doing every thing else with it but taking ore would have a power which though ample in point of use, might in point of value be next to nothing.

Power partial in point of substance

12. Suppose that the permission given to you had reference only to a part of the land. In this case the land may be conceived to be divided into two portions; over one of which you have such a power, and over the other, not. It may seem therefore not to be a distinct case of itself. But as the limits of things must in legal as well as other discourse be determined by their names, and since where the whole quantity of land contained within such and such limits is known only by one name, and since therefore the power which you have must be referred either to the whole of what is known by that name or to nothing, it will oftentimes be necessary in discourse to refer your power to a greater portion of matter than in point of reality it extends to: when this is the case the power you have may with respect to the whole of that which is so comprised under one and the same be said to be partial in point of substance. It is thus that the power you have over a house may extend only to one room in it: or the power you have over a wall, only to one side of it. With regard to power which is partial in this way, it is evident that like

that which is partial in point of use it may be created either *per exceptionem* or *sub exceptione*.

13. With regard to fiduciary power, whether it be power over things or power over persons, the party to be benefited may consist either of a single individual, or of divers individuals. When it consists of divers individuals, these individuals may be either assignable or unassignable. When unassignable, the number of them may either be limitable to a multitude less than the whole multitude of individuals in the state, or it may not. First then, where the party to be benefited consists of a single assignable individual or a number of assignable individuals, in either case the trust may be termed a private one. 2. Where it consists of an unassignable number of persons limitable to a multitude less than the multitude which compose the state, it may be termed a semi-public trust. 3. Where the number of persons to be benefited is not limitable to a multitude less than that which composes the state,[b] it may be termed a *public* trust. *The beneficiary may be an individual, a class, the public*

14.[1] Acts of which the tendency is mischievous in the first instance are either mischievous upon the whole, or not. Those which are not mischievous upon the whole are either simply innocent, that is indifferent, or else beneficial upon the whole. Those which are indifferent, if any such there be, are not worth taking any account of. Those which are mischievous upon the whole are so either to one assignable individual or individuals, or to individuals unassignable. Those which are so to an assignable individual are so, either to the agent himself or to some other person. Those which are so to individuals unassignable are so either to the whole state, or to a subordinate class or division of its members. Those which are so to an assignable individual, whether it be the agent himself or another, affect him either in point of person, in point of property, in point of reputation, or in point of condition in life. As to acts which, though they may be mischievous (as well as beneficial or innocent) in the first instance, are permitted, whether under the notion of their being beneficial upon the whole, or because the interests of those to whom they may be prejudicial are neglected, the performance of these acts is termed the exercise of a *power*. Power is either over persons or over things. And in both cases it is either beneficial or fiduciary.

15. An act is a real entity: a law is another. A duty or obligation *Right—how resulting out of duty*

[b] Included within the class of persons or a number of persons determined by a natural (political) local division.

[1] No marginal heading in Ms. for para. 14.

is a fictitious entity conceived as resulting from the union of the two former. A law commanding or forbidding an act thereby creates a duty or obligation. A right is another fictitious entity, a kind of secondary fictitious entity, resulting out of a duty. Let any given duty be proposed, either somebody is the better for it or nobody. If nobody, no such duty ought to be created: neither is there any right that corresponds to it. If somebody, this somebody is either the party bound, or some other. If it be he himself, then the duty, if such it may be called, is a duty he owes to himself: neither in this case is there any *right* that corresponds to it. If it be any other party then is it a duty owing to some other party: and then that other party has at any rate a right: a right to have this duty performed: perhaps also a *power*: a power to compel the performance of such duty.

Notion of duty a common measure

16. What is it that every article of law has in common with the rest? It issues commands and by so doing it creates *duties*, or, what is another word for the same thing, *obligations*. The notion of duty is a common measure for every article of law. It is from hence that the differences and resemblances of the various branches of law are to be traced as from this common source.

The notion of command leads to that of duty: that of duty to that of right: and that of right to that of power. Right is either naked or armed with power. That of exemption to that of privilege: power and duty together to that of trust.

Of duties some are productive of a power; others not: those which are not may be styled barren. Barren duties might subsist were there but one person in the world: suppose Adam. Duties constituting power require at least two persons: if the power be coupled with a trust, and the beneficiary of the trust be not the same person with the person on whom the duty is imposed, they require three.

Necessity of the above definition

17. Of all the words that occur in language there are few that are more familiar, that is, occur more frequently, than those of which I have been giving an explanation: at the same time I think it may be observed with confidence that there are few that are so far from being clearly understood. If it be true that our ideas are derived all of them from our senses and that the only way of rendering any of our ideas clear and determinate is to trace it up to the sensible objects in which it originates, the only method that can be taken for explaining them to the purpose is the method I have just been taking here. This method is that of defining these and other names of fictitious entities not *per genus et differentiam*, nor by any other of the methods which are applicable to real entities, but by a method which I have ventured to style that of paraphrasis: a method new in itself and which therefore if mentioned at all must be mentioned by a new name. Now this method is one that most assuredly has never been taken hitherto: if therefore they are now properly explained this is the first time they have ever been so. These explanations then, dry and tedious as they are, seemed indispensable: since without them no part of what follows could have been clearly and perfectly understood. No wonder that legislators should not any where have done precisely what they ought to do when they have never hitherto had a clear understanding of what it is they themselves have actually been doing. No wonder they have so often handled their instruments improperly when as yet they have not so much as learnt to distinguish one of them from another.

18. With regard to the powers hitherto spoken of we have seen by what operations on the part of the law they are constituted: it is in every case by *permission* only in as far as the agency of him to whom the power is given is concerned. Where the power is in its highest degree of force, a command indeed as we have seen must be superadded. But who is the person to whom such command is issued? not to you, the person to whom the power is given, but to me, the person who am commanded to assist you. You have a power given you to draw water out of a neighbouring pond. For you to possess this power the law has no need to do anything more with respect to you than to permit you: that is in effect to do nothing. This is all it can do with respect to you in order to give you such a power with respect to the thing in question as shall be beneficial: beneficial that is to you. And when it does no more with respect to you, the effect of what it does upon the whole, if it does anything, this effect, I say, can not fail to be beneficial to you: for if upon any occasion you find that a benefit is to be obtained by doing of the act which you are empowered to do, you do it, and reap the benefit accordingly: if not, you forbear to do the act, and at the worst you are but as you were.

Power over persons howsoever corroborated imports not of itself any command addressed to the persons to whom it is given

19. But now, besides permitting you to do the act, let the law command you to do it, and the case is very different. It is very likely that now the power given you may not be beneficial to you. To judge from so much of the case as has been stated, it should rather seem that it really were not: for had it been your own benefit that the law had in view it would generally speaking have been sufficient to have left you at liberty to exercise the act if you had thought proper. A man is sure to have the inclination to do what is beneficial to himself, so as he has but the knowledge of what is best calculated

Difference between power beneficial and power fiduciary

for that purpose. If then there be any case in which the law in the view of causing a man to procure himself a benefit by any act takes upon itself to compel him to do that act, it must be upon the supposition that although he has (as he cannot but have) the general inclination to do what seems beneficial to him, yet he has not the inclination to do the particular act in question, for want of knowing that it will be beneficial to him. But these cases in which the interference of the legislator is to supply the want of knowledge are comparatively but rare: where in the direction of a man's actions it takes an active part it is much more commonly for the sake of supplying not so much the want of knowledge, as of inclination. Now this is the case where the act which the law wishes to see done is the act of one person, and the person for whose sake it wishes to see the act done, the person I mean whose benefit it has in view is another: in this case therefore it is necessary that it should command. Where this is the case then the power which is given to a man may be styled a fiduciary power, or in one word, a trust: if the design being that it should be done for the benefit of the party himself who is left at liberty to exercise it or not as he thinks proper, it is styled a beneficial power: if it be for the sake of both parties that the command is issued, the power may be styled a beneficial power as well as a fiduciary one. On your neighbour's land there is too much water: on your land there is not enough: the law permits you to draw water from his land upon your own: it thereby gives you or confers on you a power: but besides that it commands you to draw off the water: it thereby renders the power fiduciary, or in other words confers or imposes on you a trust: but in as much as the doing of the act is by the supposition for your advantage, the power may be styled a beneficial one with respect to you at the same time. Suppose the water not to be wanted on your field: and the power is purely fiduciary merely and not a beneficial one: meaning always with respect to the person who is empowered.[c]

---

[c] It may appear a different case in words, but in fact it will come to the same thing, if the case be that the person empowered to do an act is not absolutely commanded to do it, but only commanded that if he does it he shall do it in such or such a manner: this is only making the command not absolute but conditional: so long as the condition, that is the event the happening of which or the circumstances the existence of which is the condition, does not take place, the command does not take place: but if the condition takes place the command thereupon takes place as before. You are not obliged to bring water upon your field at all; but if you do you are obliged to fetch it from your neighbour's: or to take it another way, your neighbour is not obliged to remove the water from his field at all; but if he does he is obliged to transfer it upon

yours: or to put another case, you are not obliged to remove water from your neighbour's land at all; but if you do remove it, you are obliged to remove it at a particular time when the absence of it will be most advantageous to him: or on his part he is not obliged to convey any water upon your land at all: but if he does he is obliged to convey it at a particular time when the presence of it will be most advantageous to you. Language is hardly precise enough to furnish a rule for determining in every case whether a man shall be said to perform two different acts, or to perform the same act in two different manners. It should seem then that in every case in which it would be proper to say that a man performs an act in two different manners it might be at least equally if not more proper to say that he performed two different acts. Upon this latter supposition, the circumstance which is common to the two may be considered as the condition which must take place in order for the command in question to attach: so that all the difference between the being obliged to do such an act absolutely, and the being obliged if he does it at all to do it in such or such a particular manner, is that in the former case the obligation is absolute, in the latter case conditional. In both cases there is a command; and it is by this command that the trust or fiduciary power, what there is of it, is constituted. Of the circumstances that may be considered as entering into the constitution of an act known by a certain name, take any one in particular and suppose it absent, the act is left free and the power that is given is beneficial only: suppose it present and the act is commanded and the power of performing it becomes fiduciary.

In point of language any two acts may be considered as being the same when any one phrase can be found that will serve to indicate them both: but in point of fact no two acts are perfectly the same. To be perfectly the same, they must be the same with regard to the particles of matter in which they commence, the particles of matter in which they terminate, the particles of matter through which the action which they consist in is propagated during its progress, as also in respect of time and of place: but that they should be the same in respect of all these constituent circumstances is impossible: which impossibility is recognized by the common axioms that no body can be at the same time in different places, nor any two bodies at the same time in the same place.

But this is not peculiar to a fiduciary power nor to that sort of act in which the exercise of a fiduciary power consists, nor to that sort of command whereby a fiduciary power is constituted: to be conditional is no more than what may happen to any sort of command, one as well as another.

APPENDIX D[1]

. . . prohibition or *forbiddal*: and the act is said to be prohibited or forbidden. In both cases the expression of the will[a] is styled some-

Imperfection of the nomenclature relative to expressions of the will

[a] To make use of the words *command* and *prohibition* to denote the mere aspects of the will without regard to the motives which it may happen to rely on for its accomplishment, is, it must be confessed an impropriety. But there are no other words that could have been made use of for the purpose without giving in to a still greater degree of impropriety: constituted then as language is at present the impropriety was unavoidable: and being immediately confessed and held up to view, it will not, it is hoped, be productive of any mistake.

To obtain a clear view of the ideas that are included or liable to be included under the notion of a law, it will be necessary to take them one at a time: the aspect for example now, and the motive by and by. As to the act which is the object of the will in question, it is evident enough that if it be a voluntary act, some motive or other to give it birth it must have had. As to the will however which may have taken that act for its object it is possible for it to have been conceived without averting to that motive, or even to any motive at all: the will, the *wish* as it is called may even be expressed, without particularizing any thing of the motive. As the two objects, viz: an expression of will, and the expression of the motive relied on for the accomplishment of that will, may actually exist the one without the other, of course they may be conceived to do so.

The business then is to find words that will convey the one idea without the other: the former without the latter. This is what the word *command* will not properly do: for it limits the nature of the motive relied on, intimating it to be of the coercive kind, and thereby excluding every expression of will which does not place its reliance on that motive: and the word *prohibition* is in the same case.

Now true it is that where the will in question is, as here, the will of a sovereign, the motive or at least one of the motives which it relies on, is commonly of the coercive kind: the reasons of this will be stated in their proper place. True it is therefore that whatever be the motive actually relied on, any will the expression of which appears to come from such a source will in general be apt to appear as if it were accompanied with an intention of employing such motives for the purpose of providing for its accomplishment. This however is not necessarily the case: the two circumstances of sovereignty, and an intention to coerce, though closely connected, are not by any means inseparable. Hold up to view a motive of the alluring kind, and no other, the connection will be much weakened: disclaim in expressed terms all intentions of a coercive kind, it will be entirely dissolved: and it can not so much as have

[1] See Introduction, xxxix above, for a discussion of the textual problems connected with this appendix. The Ms. for what precedes the phrase with which the text here opens is not extant, but Bentham's numbering shows that it must have comprised three paragraphs, the fourth beginning with the words 'Next let the aspect be inactive'.

times a *command*: and for distinction's sake it may be termed, in the former case an *affirmative*, in the latter a *negative*, command. To prevent ambiguity, where both cases are meant to be included, instead of the word *command* we may make use of the word *mandate*. Moreover in either case the provision made by the law may be said to be *imperative* or *obligative*: or the mandate itself may be styled an imperative or obligative provision.[b] 'Every man shall export corn'

been formed, where the act is such that it is plain from the nature of it no intentions of that kind could ever have been entertained: as is the case for instance where if the act be not performed there is no harm done, and at the same time the probability is against its being in a man's power to perform it.

Conceive a law to this effect—'Give information against all such as you shall suspect to be deserters'. This, as coming from the sovereign, might carry the appearance of an intention to punish in case of noncompliance, although nothing were mentioned about punishment. Let it go on say—'and you shall have 40s. for each', such intentions may possibly indeed be apprehended, but it is not probable. Let it go on still further and say 'but whether you do or no you shall not be punished'; it is certain no such intentions can be apprehended: I mean so long as any confidence is put in the declaration of the law. But take another act, and let the law be 'Exert yourselves, ye men of science, and let the longitude be discovered'. It is plain enough that not the smallest apprehension of punishment could ever be excited by an address like this; even although no reward were proffered nor indemnity proclaimed.

It appears then that strictly speaking it does not follow that where the aspect of the will is active and affirmative, the expression of it must because it is the will of the sovereign be of that limited species which is commonly brought to view by the word *command*: and so vice versa with regard to a *prohibition*.

These however are the only words we can make use of: unless we were to invent an entire set of new expressions and lay aside the current language altogether.

The word *invitation* for instance if that were used would be as bad on the other side: it would intimate that the motive relied upon were not of the coercive kind, but of the alluring.

The word *requisition* indeed stands pretty clear of the idea of a motive: but then there are no words for expressing any of the correlative aspects: nor has it any *conjugates* (as the logicians call them) for expressing the states of the act which correspond to them. No words which are to *requisition* what *prohibition* and *permission* are to *command*. We could hardly say 'an act required': and even if we could, still there are no phrases which are to the phrase 'an act required,' what the phrases 'an act prohibited', and 'an act left free' are to the phrase 'an act commanded'.

The like or stronger objections would I am pretty well satisfied appear against any other terms that could be assigned.

[b] The difference between what I mean by a legislative provision and what I mean by a law is as follows: A legislative provision may be a whole law or only a part of a law. Every law contains one or more legislative provisions: but it is not every legislative provision that amounts to a law. See 126.

—may serve as an example of a command. 'No man shall export corn':—this may serve as an example of a prohibition.[c]

Aspect in-active—a non-command—an inactive permission

4. Next let the aspect be inactive. Here then there is nothing to express: there is neither command in the case, nor prohibition: and the act, being on the one hand not commanded, and on the other hand not prohibited, may be said to be *left free.*

This however seems to be one of the cases in which the word *permission* has been employed: what others there are we shall come to presently. A man is about to perform an act, no matter what: you, being an authority, do not prohibit him: he may thereby be said in a certain sense to have your permission for doing it. In this case to distinguish it from another which we shall come to presently, the permission may be styled an *original* or *primordial* permission: and it may be said to be *inactive.* To match with this it is plain there should be some word opposed in like manner to *command.* But there does not seem to be any such word in use: to answer the purpose of it there seems to be as yet no other expedient than that of having recourse to circumlocution and saying *a permission not to perform* or *a permission to forbear performing* such or such an act. But how then to distinguish this sort of permission from the former? It might be styled perhaps though not very characteristically a negative permission. But if on any occasion an univocal appellative (I mean an appellative comprised in a single word) should be necessary, we must make one for the purpose: such for example as the word *non-command.*[d] This would tally pretty well with the word *countermand*: a word already in use, for which we shall have occasion presently.[e] Moreover as a command or a prohibition may either of them be termed indifferently a mandate or provision obligative, so a non-command or an inactive permission

[c] The provisions here exemplified, while they remain thus unqualified, appear equally absurd when considered in the character of laws actually enacted: but the absurdity of the law is a matter that need not be regarded. It seemed conducive to perspicuity to take the same act throughout for all the modifications of which the aspect of the will is susceptible: and it would be singular indeed if there should be any act towards which the law could without absurdity bear indifferently all sorts of aspects. The argumentative logicians in their explanations of the forms of syllogizing exhibit every form that is conceivable, absurd as well as rational. The act here specified was preferred as being simple in its conception.

[d] A little further on[1] we shall see there is as much occasion for finding a name for the expression of these inactive aspects, as for any of the others. See 111.

[e] See 110.

[1] I.e. in Ch. x, for which the Mss. printed in this appendix were an early draft.

may be termed indifferently a *non-mandate* or a provision *un-obligative*. 'No man is obliged to export corn':—this may serve as an example of a non-command. 'Every man may export corn':—this may serve as an example of a permission, which in the present case is supposed to be a primordial one.

5. So much for the case where the aspect of the will is *primordial*: let it now be superventitious: this superventitious aspect is either conformable to the primordial one or unconformable: in the former case the expression of the superventitious aspect may be said to be *consentaneous* to that of the primordial: in the latter case, *alterative* of it.

Superventitious provision—consentaneous—alterative

6. Let us begin with the former: and first let the primordial aspect have been active: the expression of it may then be either a command or a prohibition: the expression of the superventitious aspect will therefore be either a command or a prohibition likewise: and the act is commanded or prohibited as before.

Primordial aspect—active, superventitious provision if consentaneous a command or a prohibition

In all these cases the reiteration may most commodiously be performed, and indeed most commonly is performed, by reference: but from various causes it may chance to be performed *in terminis*. When it is performed by reference, the repetition, if such it may be called, is not, if properly managed, productive of any inconvenience: the great inconvenience is when the statute book is loaded with superventitious laws made in terms the same with those of the old, or what is worse, in terms which, without taking any notice of the old, differ from them so little as to leave it doubtful whether they were or were not meant to convey the same meaning: but of this hereafter.

As many terms then as there are in the primordial law which have other terms or combinations of terms that stand in logical subalternation with respect to them, so many sources, as it were, are there from whence provisions which are *re-iterative in specie* may take their rise. An expository provision then which is reiterative *in specie* if couched in the same form with the primordial one will be a mandate differing from the primordial one only in respect of some one term: or, if it differs in respect of more terms than one, it may be resolved into a set of provisions which shall each of them exhibit no other than that difference. Let us take for an example as being the simplest the law respecting corn: 'Let no person export corn.' Taking the word *person* as the source of specification it may be resolved into the following reiterative mandates: 'let no man export corn': 'let no woman export corn.' Taking the word *corn*, into the following: 'let no person export wheat': 'let no person export rye':

'let no person export barley': and so on. By adding more terms (expressive of the constituent circumstances of the act) other sources of specification may be added still. Corn cannot be exported but it must be exported in or upon some vehicle. Let the primordial law then be 'Let no person export corn in or upon any vehicle': taking the word *vehicle* then for the source of specification we have the reiterative mandates following: 'let no person export corn in any waggon': 'let no person export corn in any navigable vessel': and so on without end. Other sources of specification may be taken from the constituent circumstances of place and time: in point of place from the *locus a quo*, and the *locus ad quem*: and so on again without end.

How by abbreviation a cluster of provisions reiterative in specie may drop the imperative form for the assertive

7. All this is exposition: exposition performed by reiteration of the whole mandate except as to the term expounded. But this course though exemplified in order to make out the chain of demonstration is evidently more verbose than is necessary: accordingly it never is pursued in practice. For expressing one and the same will the forms of expression which there are are innumerable. Accordingly where in a primordial provision that part of the sentence or discourse which is particularly appropriated to exhibit the volition is once expressed, in the superventitious provision, so as the connection which the terms of them are meant to have with that volition be by any means made out, it is sufficient. The volitional part then, if one may so call it, of the discourse may be set down once for all; and thenceforward the reiterative provisions may be couched in sentences which taken by themselves and independently of such connection might pass for ordinary assertive sentences. The reiterative provisions above mentioned by being thrown out of the imperative into the assertive form might for example be expressed as follows. 'It matters not who the person be, whether male or female: nor what the corn, whether wheat, or rye or barley, or any other: nor what the vehicle in or upon which the exportation is performed; whether a navigable vessel or a waggon, or any other.' And thus we may perceive for the first time, how imperative matter may be masked under the assertive form: an observation that suggests the fundamental idea of the distinction we shall hereafter have occasion to explain between the matter of a penal and that of a civil code. In these examples we may perceive two things affected by this change of form; the abbreviation, and the conversion of the imperative form into the assertive. The abbreviation is of a piece with those which are remarked in the ordinary treatises of general grammar and without which no discourse on

302

any subject could well be carried on: it is the conversion of the imperative into the assertive form that bears a more particular relation to the subject of jurisprudence.

Convenience requiring that provisions which are reiterative for the sake of explanation, that is expositive, should be in the abbreviated and assertive form, in considering them we may drop the idea of the imperative form altogether; considering them as if the natural as well as original form of them were the assertive: still bearing in mind that in some way or other to some sentence or other of the imperative form they are convertible, and that it is to that convertibility that they are indebted for the capacity of entering into the composition of a legislative code.^f In order for the proposition or, as in this case it is called, the provision to have the effect of a mandate, by every term in it must be expressed either a person, act or thing, which in some part of the code or other is spoken of as being the subject or object agible or passible, direct or indirect, of the legislator's will: and when this is the case that is an effect which it can not fail of having.

f From the not sufficiently attending to this consideration arises a capital blemish that runs through the whole of the compilation to which Justinian lent his authority. Imperfect as it is, it would have been infinitely less so could the compilers have taught themselves to observe the simple rule of knowing their own minds. Lawyers themselves, and mere lawyers, they seem to have forgot they were speaking in the person of a legislator. Accordingly instead of deciding, they conjecture, they debate where they should decide: they quote, where they should command: they reason upon the import of words instead of fixing it. Instead of a will of their own they give you the opinions of other men: without having so much as the sense to decide between such as are in contradiction to each other. When laws of different aeons are at war, the strife is quieted by an obvious and acknowledged rule:—the recent supersede the old: but how shall it be when they are both of the same date? When this is legislation, what is jurisprudence? It is the art of knowing the mind of a man who knew it not himself. Yonder lies a field which I have pretensions to: a neighbour contests it with me: which of us shall have leave to occupy it will depend upon the decision of the judge. To know what the judge will decide I wish to see what the legislator has ordained. I open the code, and there I find that in a case parallel to that in dispute Paulus (who is no legislator) was for deciding it one way, and Caius another: and that as to the legislator himself, further than the recording of those irreconcilable opinions, he has never troubled his head about the matter.

APPENDIX E

JEREMY BENTHAM TO LORD ASHBURTON

3 June 1782[1]

My Lord

The Book (printed sheets) herewith inclosed waits upon your Lordship at the desire of Ld Shelburne who had the patience to read them over with me last summer at Bowood: Since then he has frequently intimated to me his wishes that it might come under your Lordship's eye: and last Tuesday he desired I would myself take upon me to furnish your Lordship with a copy without delay. Thus much, my Lord, I thought necessary to account for the liberty I take in putting into your hands a book which is not only without beginning or end but which must undergo several alterations before it faces the public eye: circumstances which I reminded him of but which he was pleased to overrule. The approbation of so enlightened a judge as Ld Ashburton would naturally have been one of the first objects of my ambition: but if left to myself I should certainly not have thought it advisable [to have] produced my titles to that honour in so imperfect a condition. I inclose in another paper a short account of the views with which it was written as well as of the undertaking of which it makes a part. To contrast in some measure with that dry cargo of speculative metaphysics I take the liberty also of including a pamphlet written three or four years ago upon the spur of the occasion on the subject of a measure or detail which happened to come then upon the carpet.[2] This and an anonymous book entitled a Fragment on Government of which I have no copies left is all I have yet ventured to make public.

[1] U.C. clxix.124–8. The Mss. embody in fact drafts for two letters, though these were evidently to be sent together. The first was to accompany a copy of the printed text of *An Introduction to the Principles* as it stood at the end of 1780; while the second, sent with a copy of the Prospectus for Bentham's *Plan of a Penal Code*, was designed to explain the proposed extension of the *Introduction* on which the present work is based.

An incomplete text of these Mss. is printed by Everett (pp. 7–10). The text given here is complete in substance; but it has not been thought necessary to present all the deleted passages, variant readings and insertions which will be found in the version to be published in *Correspondence*, iii in this edition. Where alternative readings or interlineations are printed here they are enclosed between oblique strokes. In accordance with the practice adopted in the present edition when dealing with Bentham's letters, the original spelling and punctuation are preserved.

[2] *View of the Hard-Labour Bill*, 1778.

P.S.

Of the loose proof sheets herewith inclosed there exists no other copy either in print or manuscript than this, which your Lordship will therefore have the goodness to preserve.[1]

My Lord[2]

The sheet in a different hand contains a prospectus of my plan as it stood about a year ago: since which a number of alterations have unavoidably taken place in it.

As the distinction between the penal branch of the law and the civil is so familiar, I had all along taken for granted that the line of separation between those objects might be traced within the compass of a page or two. When I came to make the experiment, I found that such separation could scarcely be said as yet to exist: and that to set up one of my own in such a manner as to answer as nearly as possible the purposes for which the verbal distinction is made would involve a multitude of problems of the most intricate kind which nobody seem'd hitherto to have thought of solving. I found in short that the substance of the penal law was almost inextricably interwoven with the civil on one hand and the constitutional on another: and it became necessary to carry my eye through the whole mass of the law ere I could disentangle from the rest the part to which I had originally intended to confine myself. By this means what I had originally designed for sections to the chapter which your Lordship will find unfinished, grew to such a bulk as to be some of them almost too big for chapters. I had however the satisfaction of finding that the additional matter I had thus been forced to introduce would as far as it went serve for an introduction to the principles of legislation in general as well as to the penal

[1] A deleted sentence in this postscript identifies the 'loose proof sheets' as pp. 313–320 of *An Introduction*. It is not clear why Bentham possessed only one copy of these pages, which represent the penultimate sheet of what had been printed in 1780.

[2] The draft of the second letter mentioned above begins here. The 'sheet in another hand' mentioned in its opening paragraph is not extant, but it must have been a prospectus for the *Plan of a Penal Code* similar to that sent by Bentham to his brother in Russia in the summer of 1780 (cf. *Correspondence*, in *CW* ii, 488–9 n. 18). What alterations had taken place in the plan between 1780 and 1782 we do not know. So far as the *Introduction* is concerned, however, we do know that the difficulties Bentham goes on to indicate to Ashburton were already perplexing him in the summer of 1781. A passage drafted for (though not included in the final text of) his letter to Shelburne of 18 June 1781 refers to 'a provoking chapter which still sticks with me: and of which the object is to exhibit the possible branches in the texture of a complete body of laws quelconque, to settle the individuation of a law, what it is that makes one entire yet single law, and what parts of the total mass of the laws belong to the three great branches into which that body is commonly divided . . .' (U.C. clxix.116).

branch in particular: and that the branch which I had happen'd to take up first was the very branch which in a natural arrangement would take the lead of the other two and serve best to exhibit the lineaments of the whole[;] for this being the branch in which those characters of imperation which are essential how much soever they may be obscured to everything that bears the name of law were most distinct; it would form a natural center of aggregation for the disjointed (heterogeneous) parts of the civil branch on the one hand, and either a centre of aggregation or a standard of comparison for the equally heterogeneous parts of the constitutional branch on the other.

The chapters then which contain the remaining part of the matter designed for the introduction stand at present as follows

Ch. 18 (dismembered from Chap. 17) Jurisprudence its branches.

Ch. 19. A law defined and distinguished. See Ch. | | Here the difficulties are stated which occur in common speech from the want of distinction between acts of legislation, acts of administration and acts of judicial authority, and acts of any settled.[1]

Ch. 20. Source of a law or of the persons of whose will it may be the expression. (Here it is shewn) in what manner covenants, conveyances, judicial orders, orders of executive magistrates, by-laws, treaties entered into by the executive magistrate with foreign states etc. connect with those permanent laws which emane directly from the sovereign legislature: and how in the current language covenants and conveyances are confounded together under the name of *contracts*.

Ch. 21. *Ends* or purposes to which a law may be directed.

Ch. 22. Of the *things* and *persons* which a law may take for its *subjects*.

Ch. 23. Of the *acts* which a law may take for its *objects*.

Ch. 24. Of the parties on whom a law may operate. (Here it is shown) by what means the chief/executives/magistrate and even the entire sovereignty may stand in the capacity of parties bound.

Ch. 25. Of the modifications a law is susceptible of in point of local extent.

Ch. 26. Of the modifications a law is susceptible of in point of *time*.

Ch. 27. Of the modifications a law may admitt of in point of generality. Here the nature of the several sorts of privilegia is placed in a new light, and the indeterminateness and instability of the distinction between public and private acts is brought to view.

---

[1] The last two words are a marginal insertion, but the sentence remains incomplete.

In the course of this and the 24th chapter I found it necessary to give an analytical view of the several simple modifications of which the powers of government public as well as private are susceptible: for the modifications expressed by the common division into legislative executive and judicial I found to be very complex in themselves, and very ill distinguished from one another.

Ch. 28. Of the *aspects* of a law. Here are exhibited the several *aspects* which laws and parts of laws may bear to one another as well as to the acts to which they bear a common relation, as also of the several changes and combinations of which they are susceptible: such as command, prohibition, permission, repeal, alteration, confirmation, continuation etc.: likewise when it is that there is a repugnancy between the acts of a superior and the subordinate legislature.

Ch. 29. Of the force of a law: of the ways in which a law exerts its force. Herein is given an idea of the connection of the laws of procedure with the rest.

Ch. 30. Of certain remedial *appendages* with which laws of a certain class may be provided. These are of less extensive application than the penal. Herein of procedure *in praeveniendum, in compescendum,* and *in compensandum.*

Ch. 31. Of the words or other *signs* by which a law may stand *expressed.*

Ch. 32. What it is that constitutes a *compleat* law.

Ch. 33. Of the common and customary law: that no such thing as *a* compleat law is to be found in it.

Ch. 34. Of the *separation* of the civil branch of the law from the penal—That the former is only a development of certain parts which belong in common to the other.[1]

Ch. 35. The division of the laws into civil and criminal—That this division as it stands at present is arbitrary and unsteady and productive of confusion.

Ch. 36. Of the distinction between civil and criminal *procedure.*

Ch. 37. Uses of the eighteen preceding chapters.[2]

[1] The following somewhat obscure marginal note occurs about here, beginning opposite Ch. 34.:

'From where it enables the legislator to know how far any given body of laws he has before him is compleat[;] if compleat to see at once[?] the whole effect and influence of any amendments as well in point of amplitude as discrimination.

'Hence any impropriety in point of substance may be the easier discover'd. Tendency which such a method has to check the licence of interpretation—to facilitate the confrontation of the laws of different nations—and the communication of the science of legislation to beginners.'

[2] I.e. Chs. 19–36, which form Chs. i–xviii of the present edition.

Ch. 38. Idea of a compleat *Corpus Juris,* and of the different ways in which it may be divided for different purposes into the internal and the international; and the former into the penal, civil, & constitutional branches—into the general code and the system of particular codes as determined by the particular classes of persons interested: into the law of procedure or adjective law as it may be called, and the substantive, or that to which the adjective is subsidiary: into the main body of the law, and the appendix or book of *formularies,* including precedents of conveyances, pacts, covenants, judicial orders etc. all which as far as circumstances admitt should be settled by the legislator.[1]

Ch. 39. Of Indirect or preventive Legislation: or of the several ways of preventing misdeeds otherwise than by punishment immediately applied to the very act which is obnoxious. Indirect Legislation may be levelled 1. against *delinquency*: or 2. against *misrule.*

Ch. 40. Influence of *time* and *place* on the expediency of a law. Some parts of a perfect body of law would be equally adapted to all times and places: others not.

The plan being thus enlarged, so as to take in the whole body of the law as well as the penal branch, it occurred [to me] that the subject of reward would now require the same development as that of punishment had received before: the one being as much a spring of action and instrument of government as the other. But several considerations concurred in determining me to allott to this subject a separate work. The most proper place for it which would have been immediately after the chapters relative to punishment (Ch. 13, 14, and 15) was pre-occupied. 2. As the influence of this spring of action in government lies comparatively within a narrow compass, the whole of what I should find to say about it would I thought form a work/volume/of itself which from the nature of the subject might be rather more readable than the rest. In this volume might even be comprised what relates to the application that may be made of the instrument in question towards the production of particular services: whereas the whole of the penal and civil

[1] The following marginal note occurs at this point:
'These 19 chapters taken together [i.e., presumably, Chs. 19–36 together with Ch. 38, excluding the 'Uses' chapter] form a sort of universal anatomy of the entire body of the law whatsoever considered nakedly as a collection of expressions of will, abstraction being made of the propriety of the volitions so expressed. In this part of my course as well as in that which your Lordship has before you I found there was no trusting for a single step to the beaten tracks. I was travelling a new road and had every step of the road to make. This would of course render the business the more toilsome: both to myself in writing and to the few if any who may have patience to read.'

branches of law is included in what concerns the application of punishment.

Of all the matter above spoken of no more is printed off than what accompanies this address. However Book the first containing the whole of the penal code except what relates to procedure was at one time thought to be finished in readiness for the press: but the analytical view I took afterwards of the system of offences in the introduction suggested the necessity of a multitude of additions and corrections which have not all of them as yet been made. There are however titles enough in a legible state to serve as specimens of the manner in which the general principles contained in the introduction are applied, and of a method by which I have attempted to reconcile plenitude with discrimination and brevity, with perspicuity and precision. Indeed any one in which the law is produced in *terminis* may be considered as an integrant part of the whole. Book 2 relating to procedure is not in equal forwardness: however the leading principles are settled, the outlines marked out, most of the matter determined in idea, and some of the titles set down *in terminis*. The case is nearly the same with the several titles destined for the appendix.[1]

My present design is to publish what is printed of the Introduction by itself: making only a few inconsiderable alterations in the last chapter in consequence of the enlargement which the whole plan has undergone since this part was printed off. I propose to wait however for the completion of the book on Indirect Legislation. These I propose to publish together, in order to take at the same time the sense of two different sets of readers: the Introduction is destined for the few who have strength of mind to embrace a set of fundamental principles in all their extent, and patience to follow up a long thread of metaphysical discussions. The Essay on Indirect Legislation being like that on Reward full of propositions of detail and illustrations drawn from the actual laws of different nations, will I hope like that be somewhat less unpopular and less ill suited to the relish and the powers of the bulk of readers. What I shall finish next whether the Essay on Reward, or that on the influence of place and time which I think likewise of throwing into a small but separate work, or Book the 1st of the penal code, or whether before I publish the latter I shall wait till I have settled the terms as well as the plan of the civil code, in order that the boundary between that

[1] According to the prospectus mentioned above (305 n. 2), these titles were to deal with the text of laws—its 'Composition—Promulgation—Interpretation—and Improvement'.

and the penal code may be distinctly and specifically marked out in every part, I have not yet determined.

Your Lordship will easily perceive that a work of law upon this plan is virtually a project of reformation addressed to any nation to the circumstances of which it is meant to be applied, and that every title of it may be considered as a proposal for the alteration of the laws at present in force in so far as they differ from the model of supposed perfection which it is the design of such title to exhibit. In the construction of this model the law of England was of course the principal but by no means the only established body of law of which I studied to avail myself of the excellencies as well as to provide a remedy for the defects: abstraction being made of all local prejudices which whatever tenderness they may claim from the hand of the legislator ought never to stop the eye of the individual inquirer. But the most signal and perhaps impracticable reformation of all is that which would be effected were the present indeterminable prospect and immeasurable bulk of the whole reduced to the moderate dimensions within which upon this new plan it would be confined, an improvement the proposal of which cannot be considered as [... ?] in any of the titles taken separately but which must be looked upon as the general result [of the] method and expression which will have been given to the whole. It is evident that the plan as far as it went could in a certain sense be the destruction of the *customary* or as it is so uncharacteristically termed by us, the *common* law: since whatever goes at present under that name would either be abrogated or *homologated* as the Flemish writers call it, that is expressed in assignable authoritative terms and thereby converted into the form of statute law.

[1]If the form be what I have endeavoured to make it, the *substance* of the law would by being thrown into any other form lose a great part of any utility it otherwise possess[ed]. But the *form* might be given to any body of laws whatsoever were its imperfections in point of substance those excepted that depend upon the want of amplitude and discrimination, the indeterminateness, contradiction, tautology, ambiguity, and obscurity which it is the special purpose of the form in question to remove. As a model of a digest it might have its use although as a system of legislation (new code of law) it should be deemed useless or impracticable.

I shall trouble your Lordship no further at present: but in the

---

[1] This paragraph is written at the end of the draft without any clear indication of where it should be placed.

course of a day or two I shall take the liberty of sending one sheet more containing the titles of the chapters of the three essays on indirect legislation, on reward, and on the influence of time and place, in the state they are in at present, exhibited at one view.

I have the honour to be etc.

APPENDIX F

OF LAWS IN GENERAL: TABLE OF THE CHAPTERS[1]

17.   I[2]. Limits between Ethics and Jurisprudence
18.   II. Jurisprudence its branches
19.   III. A law defined and distinguished
20.   IV. *Source* of a law or—Of the *Sources* from whence a law must issue
21.   V. *Ends* to which a law may be directed
22.   VI. Subjects of a law—or. Of the things and persons which a law may take for its subjects
23.   VII. Objects of a law—or—Of the *acts* which a law may take for its objects
24.   VIII. Of the *parties* which may be affected by a law
25.   IX. Of the local *extent* which a law may have
26.   X. Of the *duration* of a law—or—which a law may have
27.   XI. *Generality* of a law or—Of the modifications which a law may admit of in point of *generality*
28.   XII. Aspects of a law—or—Of the aspects which a law may bear towards an act
29.   XIII. *Force* of a law—or—Of the ways in which the law exerts its force
30.   XIV. *Appendages* of a law—or—Of the *appendages* with which a law may be provided
31.   XV. *Signs* of a law—or—Of the signs by which a law may be expressed
32.   XVI. *Completeness* of a law—or—What it is that goes to the making of a complete law
33.   XVII. No *customary* law complete—or—of a customary law —that it can never be complete
34.   XVIII. *Separation* of the civil branch of a law from the penal

[1] U.C. xxix.1. The heading of the sheet is as above. The sheet is ruled into columns of which cols. 2–5 contain the headings reproduced here. The first column contains the following deleted 'false start':

> '17. Limits between ethics and jurisprudence
> 18. A law distinguished and defined
> 19. Sources of a law
> 20. Ends etc.[?] to which a law may be directed
> 21. Subjects of a law
> 22. | |'.

[2] The Roman numerals appear to have been later insertions.

35. XIX. What laws may be termed *criminal* or—The division of laws into civil and criminal incomplete
36. XX. Distinction between penal and civil *procedure*
37. XXI. Uses of the eighteen preceding chapters[1]
38. Idea of a complete *Corpus Juris*[2]
39. Plan of Book I[3]
38. Of Indirect Legislation
39. Influence of *Place* and *Time* on the *expediency* of a law
40. Idea of a complete *corpus Juris*
41. Plan of Book I[4]
Ordo March 1782[5]

1. Objects
2. Local extent[6]
3. Duration[7]
2. Generality
3. Extent in place
4. ——— in time
5. Aspects
6. Parties

---

[1] Here, as in the Ashburton letter, the 'Uses' chapter is linked to the material constituting Chaps. i–xviii of the present edition.

[2] Deleted; but cf. 40 below.

[3] Deleted; but cf. 41 below.

[4] I.e. of the *Penal Code*.

[5] This heading and date, together with what follows, occupy the fifth column. It is not quite clear to which stage in the evolution of the document the date (which may be later than the heading 'Ordo') refers. Nor is the purpose of the 'Ordo' below clear. It differs not only from the two main tables of contents in the sequence of topics, but also from various other shorter lists of topics to be treated in this context: cf. U.C. xcii.107 and B.M. Add. Ms. 33, 549 f. 287.

[6] Deleted; but cf. the second item 3 below.

[7] Deleted; but cf. item 4 below.

INDEX OF SUBJECTS

Note. The symbol 'vs.' is used below to indicate 'as distinct from' or 'as opposed to'. Other abbreviations for frequently occurring phrases are:

pl(s). and pn(s).: pleasure(s) and pain(s)

pun.: punishment

References to Bentham's notes are given by means of the page and identifying letter (or letter and number). Where a note extends over more than one page and the reference is to a part of it only, the general reference is followed by a specific page number or numbers in brackets, thus: 123h2 (124). References to matter excluded from the main text but included in editorial footnotes are given by means of the page, the letter 'n.' (indicating an editorial footnote) and the number of that footnote, thus: 14n.1.

ACTIONS AND ACTS:

I. *In general.* an act as a real entity 2a (3), 252, 293; positive vs. negative 36, 38, 58, 95–6, 121, 137, 266, 268; negative have no commencement or termination 36, 38; termination of an act: pathological vs. physical effects 35–7; acts with one or both of these, distinguished 36–7; pathological termination is in abeyance and contingent in certain cases 37; termination, how assigned to an act 37k; names of, by reference to effect 40m; grammarians' examples of active verbs misleading as to termination of acts 40m; and progress of 34, 50, 282; termination when act operates upon will 282; acts of discourse vs. physical 37k; all acts of body (external acts) comprise (*i*) agible subject in which action begins (*ii*) passible subject in which it terminates (*iii*) abstract act or motion 47–8, 50, 282; and examples 48–51, 282; acts of belief 47; acts declarative of belief 47g; no act at all times pleasurable for a man to perform 54; acts of an intransitive nature 57e; generality and particularity of 76; subalternation of, when species of one another 100; no rule for determining when two acts performed or one act in different manner 296c (297); no two acts the same in fact though may be in point of language 296c (297)

II. *As objects of a law.* 18b, 34, 34a, 39, 41–52 (Ch. v), 58; subjects of a law are subjects of acts 39; direct vs. indirect

ACTIONS AND ACTS (*cont.*)

objects of a law 41; acts opposite to objects are offences 58, 120–1; the local extent of a law depends upon territory where acts terminate 72; are essentially objects of a law 93, 94; vs. laws themselves as only incidentally objects of a law 94; unity of classes of, determines the unity of the law 170–1; as objects of imperative part of the law (where deemed mischievous on the whole) or of qualificative part (where deemed not) 237; amplitude of law is amplitude of act 237; law promotes happiness by influencing 289. *See also* ASPECTS OF A LAW

III. *Their genera, species and circumstances.* circumstances by means of which they are diversified 39; acts and circumstances specificant and unspecificant 41, 42, 43, 44, 45, 47–50; genus and species of: species distinguished from genus by circumstances 43, 44, 46–7, 47f, 52, 112, 115; species of, included under or excluded from genus characterised by name of offence, by inculpative or exculpative circumstances 175; every act attended by circumstances 44; whether it appears so or not depends on wording 51–2; name of one species of, may suggest wider species 51–2; and case 44–6, 47f; vs. circumstance 46

As offences: *See* OFFENCES; consequences and effects of: *See* CONSEQUENCES AND EFFECTS; mischief of: *See* MISCHIEF AND HARM. *See also* CIRCUMSTANCES

315

ADMINISTRATION: *See* EXECUTIVE AND ADMINISTRATIVE FUNCTION

ADOPTION AND PRE-ADOPTION: of will or mandate: vs. original conception of 21; forms of, distinguished: (*i*) in respect of time: susception vs. pre-adoption 21; (*ii*) in respect of persons 21–7; (*iii*) in respect of degree: bare permission vs. ulterior corroborative laws 27; (*iv*) in respect of form: primordial vs. superventitious 27–8; sovereign only suscepts mandates of predecessor 21–2; but may suscept or pre-adopt mandates of subordinate power-holders 22; end of sovereign must be good of the community 31; adoption by sovereign of constitutional laws *in principem* made by predecessor's covenants 65–7; such adoption generally expected 65–6. *See also* POWER, II (*i*); POWER-HOLDERS

ADVICE AND COUNSEL: vs. exhortation 14n.1; vs. law 14n.1

AFFECTIONS: *See* SENTIMENTS AND AFFECTIONS

AGENTS (AGIBLE SUBJECTS OF A LAW) AND PATIENTS (PASSIBLE SUBJECTS OF A LAW): 34–40 (Ch. IV); the terms explained 34; as beings in which acts have commencement (agible subjects) 34; or progress 34; or termination (passible subjects) 34–7, 50; acts of body always comprise both 47–8; community as the passible subjects of acts 37; sovereign as the passible subject of constitutional laws *in principem* 64. *See also* ACTIONS AND ACTS, I; PERSONS; THINGS

AGREEMENT: *See* CONVEYANCES AND COVENANTS

ANIMALS: properties of, are similar to those of both persons and things 35d; legislation protecting 48h; persons as rational animals 49–50; their pathological and intellectual faculties too often disregarded 137h (138); hence thought like things subject only to power of contrectation 137h (138)

APPREHENSION: *See* EXPECTATION AND APPREHENSION

ARCHETYPATION: of case 45c; of circumstances 123g2

ASPECTS OF A LAW:
I. *In general.* is the aspect or phase of the legislator's will expressed by the law in relation to the acts which are its ob-

ASPECTS OF A LAW (*cont.*)
jects 93; aspect and act are the only essential ingredients of a law 93, 94; four aspects of, distinguished 95; nomenclature for aspects imperfect 298a

II. *Aspects (and hence laws or mandates) classified.*
(*i*) as primordial (where law has only acts for its objects) 95, 126, 301; and superventitious (where law applies to mandates) 95, 126, 301

(*ii*) as decided or undecided 95; decisive mandates comprise commands and prohibitions 95, 298–9; indecisive comprise non-commands 95, 119, 300 and non-prohibitions (or permissions or inactive original permissions) 95, 110, 119; decisive mandates are imperative, obligative or coercive 96, 299, 300 or efficient *per se* 119b2; indecisive mandates are unimperative, unobligative or uncoercive 96, 119, 300–1 inactive 300 or inefficient *per se* 119b2; certain distinctions in legislator's will for which no corresponding mandates 97; may be expressed partly by silence 98–9; their use 99–100, 119; inactive vs. active permission or repermission 110; non-command vs. countermand 110; unobligative distinguished from de-obligative 119

(*iii*) affirmative vs. negative 95–6, 298–9

III. *Logical relations between aspects.*
(*i*) equivalencies (equipollencies) between commands and prohibitions 95–6; not less and not more than two presented to same act at same time 97, 98

(*ii*) relations of inclusion and exclusion (opposition and concomitance) 97

(*iii*) relations of contradiction and contrariety 110–11, 129; mandates simply contradictive (or revocative) 110, 121; or contrariant (or reversive) 110–11, 121; de-obligative provisions (or countermandates) 110; comprise countermands 110, 300 and repermissions (or superventitious active permissions) 110; repugnancy 129–32

IV. *Aspects considered in relation to exceptive and limitative provisions* (q.v.). logical equivalencies (equipollencies) between them 116; and other logical relations 120–3. *See also* ACTIONS AND

ASPECTS OF A LAW (*cont.*)
  ACTS; COMMAND AND COUNTER-
  MAND; PROHIBITION AND PER-
  MISSION; WILL AND VOLITION
ASSOCIATION: of ideas, and wording of
  acts 51–2
AUTHENTICATION: of a provision 126;
  this may involve ceremonies of
  authentication 126l2
AUTHORITY: of the sovereign, founded
  on or influenced by custom vs. con-
  tract 109. *See also* DISPOSITION AND
  PROPENSITY

BELIEF: acts of, vs. acts declarative of,
  are not objects of a law 47g
BENEFIT AND FAVOUR: end of a law may
  be benefit of author 31; proper end of a
  sovereign who adopts, is general good
  32; beneficial effects of an act 35; all
  laws must favour one or more persons
  55–6; and thereby confer rights on
  those persons 220; may favour legislator himself 56; whether party enjoys
  intended benefit depends on the event
  56; person merely not coerced by a law
  negatively favoured in point of agency
  56–7; primordial law benefits only if it
  imposes duty or obligation on someone
  57; if duty extra-regarding, law confers right to services 57–8; party
  favoured by a law may be an individual,
  a subordinate class of persons, or
  the community 58; but coercion
  attaches only to individuals 58–9;
  favour in point of agency vs. in point
  of interest 59; party favoured for own
  sake or for another's, hence resulting
  power or right beneficial or fiduciary
  59; benefit derived from a law may be
  remote or indirect (example: tax law)
  62; and is in proportion to acquaintance with it 63–4; every law productive of no benefit pernicious 71; beneficial power, *see* POWER, III (*iii*). *See
  also* RIGHTS
BENEVOLENCE: social motive of (as
  internal vs. external motive) 31b;
  tutelary motive of 202
BODY: liability to be made to suffer in
  and subjection to sovereign 20d; acts
  of, *see* ACTIONS AND ACTS, I

CASE: vs. circumstance 44–6; distinction
  compared to that that between species
  and property 45; as a fictitious entity

CASE (*cont.*)
  45; archetypation of 45c; constituted
  by circumstances 47f; idea of, connected with idea of genus and species
  of an act 47f
CAUSE: disposition to obedience as
  efficient cause of all power of imperation 18b; cause of law is design to
  favour 63. *See also* CONSEQUENCES
  AND EFFECTS
CERTAINTY: *See* PROBABILITY AND
  CERTAINTY
CIRCUMSTANCES:
  I. *In general.* by means of which description of acts as direct objects of law
  is diversified 39; as modes of being of
  indirect subjects of law 46; are fictitious entities 42, 45; the word 'circumstance' is to act as 'property' is to substance 42–3; contrasting usage of
  people at large vs. of logicians and
  naturalists 43; the word is applied to
  fictitious entities only 45d; by which
  species of act distinguished from genus
  43, 44, 46–7, 52, 112, 115; whether or
  not an act appears attended by circumstances depends on wording 43–4,
  51–2; but in fact every act so attended
  51; constituent circumstances, of which
  acts are made up 44, 302; vs. case 44–
  6; distinction between conditional and
  unconditional mandates by reference
  to 45; distinction between circumstance and act depends on manner in
  which objects are regarded by law, not
  on their nature 46; circumstances to
  which will of the legislator may apply
  46–52; archetypation of 123g2.
  II. *Classifications and subdivisions.*
  specificant and unspecificant 41, 44;
  examples 41–2, 48–50; specificant,
  render commands etc. conditional vs.
  unconditional 112–13; limitative and
  exceptive 113–14, 123–4; both these
  narrow an act identified by generic
  name and are qualificative 115; de-
  obligative 121; exculpative or justica-
  tive 121; inculpative (or criminalising
  or criminative) 122; whether inculpative or exculpative comes first depends
  on whether law conditional or unconditional 122; they may be of different
  orders 123, 124; compared to nest of
  boxes of different colours 123g2; they
  include or exclude species of actions in
  or from genus characterized by name

CIRCUMSTANCES (*cont.*)

of an offence 175; forms of pleading explained by reference to inculpative and exculpative 123h2; and in civil cases, by reference to investitive and divestitive 123h2; re-inculpative (or convictive) 124, 175, 189; exemptive 145–6, 167, 168; latter distinguished from disexemptive 147, 167; or condemnative 189; aggravative or extenuative 173–4; invalidity of covenant or conveyance has effect of exculpative or exemptive 189; invalidity of formulary has effect of exemptive or disexemptive 189; laws incomplete because of failure in various ways to specify kinds of, and this left to discretion of judge 183. *See also* CLAUSE OF A LAW; LIMITATIONS AND EXCEPTIONS; PROVISION OF A LAW

CIRCUMSTANTIATIVE MATTER: is the most voluminous part of expository matter 198–9; that which is common to different sorts of offences is separated from the rest and made the civil branch of the law 199. *See also* EXPOSITORY MANDATE OR MATTER

CIVIL AND PENAL: *See* PENAL AND CIVIL

CLAUSE OF A LAW: defined and distinguished from words and provisions and propositions 114; limitative and exceptive 113–15; these as qualificative 115; examples 116v; their effect on a provision 121–2; annexed to punitory laws, are limitative 147; upon which residuary amplitude of a law depends 161; every law in which there is an exceptive clause is resoluble into two provisions 177; to which the system of laws owes its mildness 238; exculpative or justificative 121, 123; de-obligative 121, 123; inculpative (or criminalizing) 122–3; circumstantiative 198; imperative 198; to which the system of laws owes its vigour 238; comminative 298. *See also* CIRCUMSTANCES; LIMITATIONS AND EXCEPTIONS; PROVISION OF A LAW

CODE: laws in a complete, cannot be otherwise than complete 158–9; whole code given if number and description of laws given 172, 234; no instance of a complete code of statute law any where to be found 235; is weak and

CODE (*cont.*)

insufficient and/or oppressive if it escapes apprehension 238–9; model of a complete, use in teaching art of legislation 244; framing of new 244; idea of a complete *corpus Juris* 308

COERCION AND COMPULSION: act of issuing an illegal mandate backed by coercive motives an offence 19; kinds of offence which it constitutes 19c; all laws must coerce one or more persons 54; coercion of a law may not be felt because of benefit of concomitant laws 54–5; but can attach only to individuals, not the community 58–9; except where offence is against laws that are universal *ex parte subiecti agibilis* 59g; idea of, why inseparably connected in minds of mankind with that of law 136; but these may be separated 136, 298a; coercive and alluring motives, the only means for acting on will 259–60; these constitute power over active faculties 262; coercion, by means of which legislation compasses its direct purpose 289; may be physical or moral (pun.) but the former is little used 289; motives and influences of a coercive nature, *see* MOTIVES AND INFLUENCES; offences against the public force, *see* OFFENCES, V (*iv*). *See also* DUTY AND OBLIGATION; PUNISHMENT

COMMAND AND COUNTERMAND: *privilegium*: Latin for command 6; the word, why an inadequate substitute for the word 'law' 10; vs. order 10d; positive (or affirmative) vs. negative 19c, 299; laws belonging to the legislator by way of conception readily perceived as commands 26; laws by which he adopts are imperfect mandates 26 left to subordinate to fill up 26 and appear solely to give descriptions 26; every efficient primordial law is a command 58; every legal command imposes a duty 58, 294; command of the sovereign, conveyed through language 82; as a decisive mandate 95; vs. prohibition and permission 95–6, 97, 110–11; property and essence of law 105; imperative mood only one of ways of expressing 105; varieties of expressions of 154; sovereign's habit of commanding 109; no complete correspondence between the words 'countermand' and 'permission' 110o; the

COMMAND AND COUNTERMAND (*cont.*)
word 'dispensation', where used instead of 'countermand' 111o (112); conditional and unconditional (or absolute) 112–13, 115–16, 296c; points at pun. 134; completeness of 164–5; bare act commanded or prohibited by laws vs. expository matter takes up small space 179t and is a very small object 198; exposition of law concerning conveyances may be transformed into 180–1; connection between assertive matter of law and command 181; permanent vs. transient 246; no command belongs exclusively to penal or civil branch of the law 247; affords protection for property and creates right to positive services 277; law commanding or forbidding creates obligation or duty 294; renders power fiduciary 295, 296c (297); the word, its imperfections for expressing aspects of will without regard to motive 298a; may be termed indifferently a mandate or provision obligative 300; a non-command may be termed indifferently a non-mandate or a provision unobligative 300–1. *See also* ASPECTS OF A LAW; IMPERATIVE AND IMPERATION; LAW OR MANDATE; LOGIC; PROHIBITION AND PERMISSION

COMMANDMENT: the word, why an inadequate substitute for the word 'law' 10

COMMON LAW AND CUSTOMARY LAW: mandates declaratory of 107–8; vs. of statutory law 108; in way of which notice of reward or pun. may be given by the judge 134; nature of, hitherto not understood 152; as unwritten law 152–3; vs. written and vs. traditionary law 153; incompleteness and other imperfections of 184–95 (Ch. xv); under which no certain right and wrong 184; sources of, are *records* 185–6 and *reports* 186–7, 190, 192; from which treatises are worked up 188; their deficiencies made up by manuscript reports 188–9; greatest part of the business done in the way of *ex post facto* law 187d, 190; utility and *stare decisis* 190–1; other authorities for, listed 192e; uncertainty of 192–4; as a fiction 193, 194; rules of, are quasi-laws 194; plan for the digestion of 235–6; as an ill-expressed and ill-defined

COMMON LAW AND CUSTOMARY LAW (*cont.*)
branch of statute law 235; which it infects with uncertainty 240; liberal or discretionary interpretation of the law as a branch of 240. *See also* JUDGE

COMMUNITY: considered as constituting the passible subjects of an act 37; whole community may be only partly favoured by a law 58; but is favoured by every law and injured by every offence 58; good of, *see* GOOD AND EVIL; happiness of, *see* HAPPINESS

COMPACT: *See* CONVEYANCES AND COVENANTS

COMPENSATION: vindictive 55; a course a law may take in obviating mischief of an offence 149–50; only mischief of private offences admits of or requires 150f; where certain, pun. is needless 217; compensatory laws, *see* LAW OR MANDATE, V (*vi*)

COMPLETENESS (OR INTEGRALITY) AND UNITY OF A LAW: 156–83 (Ch. xiv); individuality refers to both completeness (or integrality) and unity 156; difference between these illustrated 171; complete body of laws includes the whole body of conveyances 179–80; what is needed to make a law appear complete 182–3; why laws fail to be complete 183; no instance of a complete law without perfect plan of legislation 183; customary law not complete 184–95 (Ch. xv); unity of a law not determined by unity of sentence or proposition expressing it 143–4

Completeness and unity considered in relation to obligative laws of four different patterns: (*i*) consisting only of a directive part 156–67; (*ii*) including also a comminative part 167–8; (*iii*) including temperative provisions 168; (*iv*) including satisfactive provisions 168

Completeness may be in point of expression 157–9; connection (by juxtaposition vs. by reference) 159; or design 160; incompleteness in point of design may be deficiency in amplitude (original vs. residuary) or discrimination 160–1; example of this 161–2; completeness of a law and of a command 164–5; completeness of a de-obligative law 168–9; but the number of laws depends upon obligative laws only 169–70

COMPLETENESS (OR INTEGRALITY) (*cont.*)

Unity determined by reference to unity or *species infimae* of offences 166, 170–3; these are monadic or narrowest assignable laws 172; need to distinguish *infima genera* as well as *infimae species* 174–5; dependence of these distinctions upon language 166, 174

Infinitude of laws of property 177–8; reducible by translating laws out of imperative into assertive form 178–9; clusters of provisions reiterative *in specie* similarly reduced 302–3

COMPLIANCE: *See* OBEDIENCE AND COMPLIANCE

COMPULSION: *See* COERCION AND COMPULSION

CONCEPTION: original, of a will or a law or mandate, vs. adoption 21; in which way, laws belong to the legislator alone 26. *See also* ADOPTION AND PRE-ADOPTION

CONCESSIONS: of sovereign, not laws but treaties with the people 16. *See also* SOVEREIGN AND SOVEREIGNTY; TREATIES

CONDITION IN LIFE: in which a man may be made to suffer by the sovereign 20; of indirect subjects of the law, form circumstances diversifying description of acts 39; made up of duties, powers, rights and their negations 61; a fictitious entity 286; legal relation constitutes a 286; an investititive and a divestitive event incident to every condition 286–7; in point of which an assignable individual may be affected by a mischievous act 293; offences against, *see* OFFENCES, II (*iv*). *See also* INVESTMENT AND DIVESTMENT

CONSCIOUSNESS: of offender, circumstance influencing mischief of act and enhancing demand for pun. 214; line between criminal and civil depends mainly on 216; its connection with intention 216; its presence does not necessarily make the offence a crime 217; and its absence makes offences against property civil vs. criminal 218

CONSENT: to an act, shows it to be not unpleasant 200; forms exception to law concerning offences against person 200

CONSEQUENCES AND EFFECTS: pathological effects of an act: vs. physical 35–7; pathological and physical effects

CONSEQUENCES AND EFFECTS (*cont.*)

on persons vs. physical effect on things 35; pathological effects consist in sensations 35; may be pleasurable or beneficial or painful 35; certain or contingent 35; and are manifested in passible subjects of an act 50; beginning and end of chain of causes and, not ascertainable 37k; sensible signs reporting an act as a continuation of its effects 37k. *See also* ACTIONS AND ACTS

CONSTITUTION AND CONSTITUTIONAL LAW: or *jus publicum* 12; a fictitious entity 12; the word 'constitution', why an inadequate substitute for the word 'law' 12; constitutional law, including laws *in principem* (transcendent laws) 64–71; these, divided into royal covenants and recommendatory mandates 64–5; how adopted by successors of the sovereign 65–7; how binding on sovereign himself 67–70; structure of, explained by distinction between general and particular laws 81; liberties founded on undecisive mandates of sovereign 99; a law *in principem* may have custom as foundation 109; how related to the distinction between civil and penal branches of the law 137h (139), 249; concerns designation of persons invested with public trusts 249. *See also* LEGISLATORS AND GOVERNMENT; SOVEREIGN AND SOVEREIGNTY

CONSTRUCTION: *See* INTERPRETATION AND CONSTRUCTION

CONTRACT: *See* CONVEYANCES AND COVENANTS

CONVEYANCES AND COVENANTS: the distinction between the two 23g, 270–1; covenant distinguished from promise, agreement, engagement, stipulation, pact, compact, and contract 23g; covenant and contract in English and Roman law 23g (24), 271i; covenant an expression of will 24, 65; or of intention to do an act or to incur penalties for not doing 270; imposes obligation on covenantor 24; a species of conveyance of a right to covenantor's services 23g (25); converted into mandates by sovereign's adoption 25, 26, 78; fundamental laws by which each is adopted 27i; multitude of species of, is reason for not including

CONVEYANCES AND COVENANTS (*cont.*) them in the general discussion 30; royal covenants as constitutional laws 64–5; and how a man can impose obligation on himself 67–8, 78–80; international covenants 70; parties bound by covenants always determinate individuals 78c but not so in the case of conveyances 79; conveyance meaningless without pun. 136f; sense in which conveyances are laws 179–80; whole body of, included in complete body of laws 179–80; good and valid vs. void 180; law relating to, may be comprised in exposition of words such as proprietary subject, proprietary rights, title, etc. 180; such exposition, how translated into commands 180–1; invalidity of covenant or conveyance has effect of exculpative or exemptive circumstance 189. *See also* CIRCUMSTANCES; TREATIES

COUNSEL: *See* ADVICE AND COUNSEL

COUNTERMAND: *See* COMMAND AND COUNTERMAND

CRIMINAL OR PENAL LAW: whole system of, indirectly contained in system of constitutional law through procedure 144n.2. *See also* OFFENCES; PENAL AND CIVIL BRANCHES OF THE LAW

CUSTOM: force and efficacy of law may depend on 109. *See also* DISPOSITION AND PROPENSITY; HABIT

CUSTOMARY LAW: *See* COMMON LAW AND CUSTOMARY LAW

DANGER: positive mischief may consist of 150f; private offences produce both pn. and danger, but danger only produced by semi-public and public offences 150f

DECREE: the word, why an inadequate substitute for the word 'law' 11

DEFINITION: only of classes of object 52; as narrowing of a genus by reference to circumstances constituting specific properties 52; import of names for fictitious entities, how explained 251–2, 294; paraphrasis as new method of 294. *See also* ENTITIES, fictitious; METHOD OF ANALYSIS

DESCRIPTION: when legislator preadopts mandates, laws may appear to be solely giving 26; of acts, how diversified 39; varieties of, of acts and cir-

DESCRIPTION (*cont.*) cumstances 41–2; of act, narrowed by circumstances 46–7. *See also* EXPOSITORY MANDATE OR MATTER; IMPERATIVE AND IMPERATION

DISCOURSE: *See* LANGUAGE AND DISCOURSE

DISPOSITION AND PROPENSITY: to submission and obedience, by which power and authority of sovereign are constituted 16, 18b, 109, 137h (138 and 139); is weakened if sovereign violates concessions 16; is ultimate efficient cause of all power of imperation 18b; modifications of, and divisions of sovereignty 18b, 68n (69); disposition to expect obedience as part of foundation of authority 109. *See also* CUSTOM; SOVEREIGN AND SOVEREIGNTY

DIVESTMENT: *See* INVESTMENT AND DIVESTMENT

DUTY AND OBLIGATION: as fictitious entities 2a (3), 251, 293–4; are imposed by laws commanding or forbidding 54–5, 121, 294; extra-regarding vs. self-regarding 57, 294; every legal command imposes 58, 294; law creates rights by prescribing 58, 249b, 294; affirmative vs. negative 58, 61; an element in condition in life 61; how imposed by sovereign upon himself 67–8; meaningless without pun. 136f; business of law reducible to creation of 249–50; duty of magistrate is to act in conformity with the law 280; duties of abstinence (negative duties) vs. duties of performance (positive duties) 290; a common measure for every article of law 294; obligation means same as duty 294; are productive of power or barren 294. *See also* COMMAND AND COUNTERMAND; POWER; RIGHTS

EDICT: the word, why an inadequate substitute for the word 'law' 12

EFFECTS: *See* CONSEQUENCES AND EFFECTS

ENDS AND PURPOSES: of a law 31–3 (Ch. III); of the art of legislation, *see* LEGISLATION

ENGAGEMENT: *See* CONVEYANCES AND COVENANTS

ENTITIES: fictitious vs. real 2a (3), 251–2; fictitious entities: rights and wrongs 2a (3); duties and obligations 2a (3),

ENTITIES (*cont.*)
293–4; laws of nature 2a (3); constitution 12; law 16; circumstance 42, 45; property 42, 45; case 45; reputation 202; power over persons 258; title 274; incorporeal objects of property 284; condition in life 286; right 294; secondary fictitious entities 279, 294; legal fictitious entities: power, right, prohibition, duty, obligation, burthen, immunity, exemption, privilege, security, liberty 251; explained by reference to real entities 251–2, 278, 294; as a result of operations creating offences 252; law owes its obscurity to fictitious 252; real entities: pain 2a (3); person 2a (3), 251; act 2a (3), 252, 293; thing 251; act of will 252; sign of an act of will 252; law 293. *See also* DEFINITION

ESSENCE OF A LAW: *See* LAW OR MANDATE, I

ESTABLISHMENT: the word, why an inadequate substitute for the word 'law' 13

ETHICS: ascertains whether pun. or reward of the moral sanction should apply 219; instructs how to avoid pun. and obtain reward 219; dictates of, include those of jurisprudence and more 219. *See also* SANCTIONS, II

EVENTS: prospect of certain events as a motive 1; every event contingent while future 37; upon which depends whether a party enjoys benefit intended by legislator 56; give titles 180; investitive vs. divestitive 274; the former. voluntary vs. natural 275, 287; and simple or complex 275; limit condition in life 286–7. *See also* INVESTMENT AND DIVESTMENT

EVIDENCE: extrinsic to a code of laws as to meaning of words cannot outweigh intrinsic 158

EVIL: *See* GOOD AND EVIL

EXCEPTIONS: *See* LIMITATIONS AND EXCEPTIONS

EXECUTIVE AND ADMINISTRATIVE FUNCTION: orders issued by the executive power 4, 7–8; executive mandates or orders vs. legislative mandates or laws 78; promulgation of the law a neglected branch of 239; executive magistrate sometimes takes a course unconformable to that marked out by legislator 272; but commonly conformable to it 274–5; which is his duty 280

EXHORTATION: vs. advice 14n.1; vs. law or mandate 14n.1

EXPECTATION AND APPREHENSION: of adoption by sovereign of predecessor's covenants 65–6; of pl. and pn., motives as 133

EXPOSITORY MANDATE OR MATTER: style of imperation dropped in 104–6; used in translating laws out of imperative into assertive form 106, 179t; included in civil part of the law 198; and contains circumstantiative matter (q.v.) 198–9. *See also* COMMAND AND COUNTERMAND; IMPERATIVE AND IMPERATION

FACULTIES AND ABILITIES: of persons: active (or self-moving), power over, is power of imperation 18b, 137h (138); volition is active 35; vs. passive, of body or mind, power over is power of contrectation physical or hyperphysical 137h (138); of sensation (experience of pn. and pl.) and perception are passive 35; of animals: their pathological and intellectual faculties are too often disregarded 137h (138); hence thought subject only to power of contrectation 137h (138). *See also* POWER, III (*xvi*)

FAVOUR: *See* BENEFIT AND FAVOUR

FELICITY: offences against the positive increase of the national: *See* OFFENCES V (*v*)

FICTIONS: common or customary law as a 193, 194. *See also* ENTITIES, fictitious

FORCE: *See* COERCION AND COMPULSION

FORCE OF A LAW: *See* LAW OR MANDATE, II; MOTIVES

FREEDOM: *See* LIBERTY AND FREEDOM

GENERALITY AND PARTICULARITY OF A LAW: 76–92 (Ch. IX); law particular in any respect is necessarily temporary 74–5; ordinary language imperfectly marks distinction between 76a; meaning of distinction 76–7; a law may be particular in one point and general in another 76–7; which mandates general, which particular 77–8; the distinction important for understanding constitutional law 80; corresponds to distinction between powers of imperation *de classibus* and *de singulis* 80; legislation commonly thought of as power of enacting general laws 81; generality

GENERALITY AND PARTICULARITY OF A LAW (*cont.*)
and particularity of customary or unwritten laws 153–4. *See also* POWER, II (*ii*)

GENUS AND SPECIES: subalternation of acts 100; mandate reiterative *in genere* or *in specie* 100–1, 106, 301–2; *species infimae* and *genera infima* of offences 171–5 (*see also* COMPLETENESS etc. OF A LAW); of acts, *see* ACTIONS AND ACTS, III; CIRCUMSTANCES, I

GOOD AND EVIL: good of the community as end of law adopted by sovereign 31–2; and of subordinate issuing a mandate 32; promotion of negative good as equivalent to averting positive mischief and *vice versa* 32–3; law as a necessary evil 54. *See also* BENEFIT AND FAVOUR; MISCHIEF AND HARM

GOOD NAME: *See* REPUTATION AND GOOD NAME

GOVERNMENT: *See* LEGISLATORS AND GOVERNMENT

HABIT: of obedience, *see* DISPOSITION AND PROPENSITY; SOVEREIGN AND SOVEREIGNTY

HAPPINESS: of the community, the positive end of the art of legislation 289; negative end is the avoidance of diminution of 289; law promotes by influencing actions 289

HARM: *See* MISCHIEF AND HARM

IDEA: of a law, vs. of a statute 12; of a law, may be of purely intellectual object 12; this must be formed for analysis of statutes 12; association of, and wording of acts 51–2; idea of pun. separable from law only with difficulty 136; of coercion, is inseparably connected with that of law in minds of mankind 136; all ideas originate from the senses 160c; of mischief: general vs. particular 160; ideas of law, offence and right are inseparable 221n.1; of occupation vs. of possession: as positive vs. negative ideas 281

IMAGINATION: must have sense as a ground to work on 160c

IMPERATIVE AND IMPERATION: logic of, vs. logic of judgement 15h; imperative mood only one way of commanding

IMPERATIVE AND IMPERATION (*cont.*)
105; translation of laws out of imperative into assertive form 106, 178–9; forms of, may be directly imperative or indirectly imperative or comminative or declarative 154; vigour of law due to its imperative clauses 238; imperative matter may be masked under assertive form 302, 303f; power of, *see* POWER, III (*xii*); imperative provisions, *see* PROVISION OF A LAW. *See also* COMMAND AND COUNTERMAND

INDIVIDUALITY OF A LAW: *See* COMPLETENESS etc. OF A LAW

INFLUENCES: *See* MOTIVES AND INFLUENCES

INJUNCTION: the word, why an inadequate substitute for the word 'law' 11

INSTITUTION: the word, why an inadequate substitute for the word 'law' 13

INTEGRALITY OF A LAW: *See* COMPLETENESS etc. OF A LAW

INTENTIONS AND INTENTIONALITY: of the legislator: oblique vs. direct vs. ultimate 55; he must intend to confer a benefit on someone 55–6; and difference between civil and criminal offences 214; of the offender: two ways in which it enhances demand for pun. 214–16; improbity of, may be presumed from act 215; covenant as expression of intention to do an act or to incur penalties for not doing 270

INTEREST: in point of which a party may be favoured by a law 59; latent 64; man governed by his own, in what sense true 70p; extensive vs. confined sense of the word 70p; offences against the national, *see* OFFENCES, V (*xi*)

INTERPRETATION AND CONSTRUCTION: of a law 158–9; nature, necessity and mischief of 162; strict vs. liberal (or discretionary) 162; strict refers to actual will of legislator, liberal to hypothetical will 162, 163; attribution of will of legislator except on ground of inadvertency is not to interpret but to overrule 162; a virtual act of autocratic power 162i (163); liberal, is extensive or restrictive 163; how its licence checked 239–41; important and delicate branch of judiciary power 239; dangerous but necessary 239; as a branch of customary law 240; cannot yet be absolutely prohibited

INTERPRETATION AND CONSTRUC-
TION (*cont.*)
241; plan for guarding against abuse
of 241

INVESTMENT AND DIVESTMENT: power
of aggregating to a class is power of
investment 83–4; investitive power
includes but not identical with accensitive 83i (84); investitive vs. divestitive 85, 268; investment may subject a
man to obligations 87; wrongful non-
investment or divestment an element
in offences against trusts, or condition
151g, or property 230; investment
provided for by therapeutic law 151g;
judgment may invest persons with
rights (judgment of investiture) 222,
223, 227, 230; or may refuse investment
(judgment of non-investment) 223; a
right to a thing may include right to
performance of an act of investitive
power 265; title is constituted by investitive events 274; these may be
natural or voluntary 275, 286–7;
simple or complex 275; commencement and termination of a condition
marked by investitive and divestitive
event 286. *See also* POWER, III (*xi*)
INVOLUNTARY: *See* VOLUNTARY AND
INVOLUNTARY

JUDGE: rules and orders made by 7;
investitive and divestitive powers over
judicial offices 87; incompleteness of
law leads judge to assume place of
legislator 183; judges do not publish
and may prevent publication of laws
193; nature of power of, depends on
nature of cause 220; his experience
supplements legislator's foresight in
reducing mischief of a provision 239–
40; but his relations with the legislator
should be open and should be confined
to operations of the remedial kind 241;
legal possession and title, how far dependent on inclination of 274, 279–81.
See also COMMON LAW AND CUSTO-
MARY LAW; PROCEDURE
JURISPRUDENCE: scope of, vs. of logic of
imperation of the will 15h; general 23g;
Roman vs. English 23g (24); contrasted with general metaphysics 45–6;
distinction between general law and
particular law helps us find our way
through the labyrinth of constitutional
80; authoritative vs. unauthoritative

JURISPRUDENCE (*cont.*)
153; expository, the art of finding clear
ideas to annex to expressions 232;
ingenuity of first authors of language
has thrown a veil of mystery over 251
JUSTICE: ministers of, bound by punitory laws 61; offences against, *see*
OFFENCES, V (*iii*)

KNOWLEDGE AND PROMULGATION OF A
LAW: parties needing to be acquainted
with a law 63; their need proportionate
to their benefit or detriment from it
63–4; notoriety of a law ought to be
even more extensive than its binding
force 71; need for publication universally disregarded 71; notice of pun. or
reward may be given in text of law by
legislator or in way of customary law
by judge 134; deficiencies in reports of
law cases 186–8; English judges fail
to publish their laws and may prevent
publication 193; laws too complicated
or obscure to be promulgated are often
disobeyed 238–9; but unless properly
composed cannot have adequate
publicity 239; a neglected branch of
administration 239. *See also* COMMON
LAW AND CUSTOMARY LAW

LANGUAGE AND DISCOURSE: influence
of local establishments and local action
on the idiom of 8–9; advice as the language of the understanding 14n.1:
exhortation as the language of the will
14n.1; irregularities of language 39–40,
143–4, 279; language of logicians vs. of
natural science vs. of familiar speech 43;
importance of wording of description
of acts and circumstances 43–4, 51–2;
political discussion is endless and
profitless while men are unaware of the
ambiguity of words 68n; imperfection
of language in expressing the distinctions relative to generality of a law and
particularity of a law 76a; and Bentham's suggested alternatives 76a;
objections to coining new words 76a,
122d2; language as the assemblage of
conventional signs 82, 152; imperative
mood in all languages 105; language of
the will vs. of the understanding 105;
want of symmetry in all languages between the words 'countermand' and
'permission' 111o; unity of a law not
determined by unity of sentence or

LANGUAGE AND DISCOURSE (*cont.*)

proposition expressing it 143–4; but depends in part on words used in classification of offences 166; no trusting to mere words 144; discourse an assemblage of signs which may be transient sounds or written or graphical symbols 152; parsing, or the ranging of particular words under general classes 243–4; use of this in science of law 244, 245; tyranny of language 279; need to translate abstract phraseology of 283k; comparison with algebraic notions 283k; imperfections of language relative to expressions of aspects of the will 298a. *See also* COMMAND AND COUNTERMAND; COMPLETENESS etc. OF A LAW; DEFINITION; ENTITIES, fictitious; IMPERATIVE AND IMPERATION; LOGIC

LAW OR MANDATE:

I. *Definition.* defined 1; so as to include more than what is usually called law 3; reasons for this extensive definition 9–10; and for rejecting various other appellations 10–16; law so defined compared with meaning of *legislation* and *legislative power* 3–4; is wider than these terms since it includes: (*i*) domestic orders 4; (*ii*) temporary orders of administration 4; (*iii*) judicial orders 4–5; (*iv*) particular orders of the sovereign 5–6; (*v*) regulations, rules and orders made by judges 6–7; (*vi*) regulations made by King or executive 7–8; (*vii*) regulations made by subordinate executive magistrates 8; idea of a single complete vs. idea of statute 12; idea of, is purely intellectual object 12; the word 'mandate', why an adequate substitute for the word 'law' 13–16; vs. advice or counsel and exhortation 14n.1; vs. concession 16; law as abstracted from genus of laws is a fictitious entity 16; but *a* law is a real entity 293; essence of, variously described as: there being a party bound or coerced 54, 63; an aspect of legislator's will and an act as its object 93, 156; a command 105. *See also* COMMAND AND COUNTERMAND; IMPERATIVE AND IMPERATION

II. *Considered in various respects.* eight respects distinguished 1–2; source of a law 18–30 (Ch. II) (*see also* ADOPTION;

LAW OR MANDATE (*cont.*)

CONCEPTION; SOVEREIGN AND SOVEREIGNTY); ends of a law 31–3 (Ch. III); subjects of a law 34–40 (Ch. IV) (*see also* AGENTS etc.; PERSONS; THINGS); objects of a law 41–52 (Ch. V); not only acts but laws themselves may be 94 (*see also* ACTIONS AND ACTS; CIRCUMSTANCES); parties affected by a law 53–71 (Ch. VI) (*see also* BENEFIT AND FAVOUR; COERCION AND COMPULSION; DUTY AND OBLIGATION; SUFFERING); extent of a law: (*i*) local 72–3 (Ch. VII) (*see also* PERSONS; THINGS); (*ii*) extent in point of time 74–5 (Ch. VIII); generality of a law 76–92 (Ch. IX) (*see also* GENERALITY etc. OF A LAW); aspects of a law 93–132 (Ch. X) (*see also* ASPECTS OF A LAW); force of a law 20, 133–48 (Ch. XI) (*see also* COERCION AND COMPULSION; DUTY AND OBLIGATION; SANCTIONS); appendages of a law 149–51 (Ch. XII); expressions of a law (signs of a law) 152–5 (Ch. XIII) (*see also* LANGUAGE AND DISCOURSE); completeness and unity of a law 156–83 (Ch. XIV) and of customary law 184–95 (Ch. XV) (*see also* COMPLETENESS etc. OF A LAW)

III. *In general.* parts of a law: Blackstone's analysis of, into declaratory, directory, remedial and vindicatory criticised 2a; parts are directive 134, 137, 144, 156, 214; incitative or sanctional 134, 144, 156; which may be comminative, where motive furnished for compliance is pun. 134, 167, 213, or invitative where motive is reward 134, or satisfactive 151, 168; incitative is only a prediction 137; comminative must be supplemented by subsidiary punitory laws addressed to judge 137–40; all laws must affect persons in way of coercion, suffering and favour 53–6; no law without a motive 56; essence of vs. cause of vs. efficacy of 63; whatever the law permits a man to perform or abstain from, it inhibits all others from compelling him to abstain from or perform 131–2; uses pun. rather than reward 134–5; has no means of administering pl. by its own immediate operation, or of producing pl. without pn. at the same time 135e; idea of pun. separable from

LAW OR MANDATE (*cont.*)

law only with difficulty 136; but this is possible 136, 298a; may sometimes be backed by both penal and praemiary sanctions (law with an alternative sanction) 136–7; its three courses in obviating mischief (compensative vs. therapeutic or catapaustic vs. meta-phylactic law) 149–50; what offences admit of these 150f, 151g; one law creates one offence 233; amplitude of 237; laws of different nations can be compared by means of a natural and regular plan of legislation 242–3; this comparative view as a harmony of laws 242, 244; law must have a pun. 248; business of law reducible to the creation of duties 249–50; produces on the one hand restraint 254 and on the other personal security or protection 254 or liberty 254 or protection for reputation 254–5; conception of, *see* CONCEPTION; adoption of, *see* ADOP-TION AND PRE-ADOPTION; mischief of, *see* MISCHIEF AND HARM; against offences, *see* OFFENCES; of a sovereign, *see* SOVEREIGN AND SOVEREIGNTY; mandates of subordinate power-holders, *see* POWER, II (*i*); POWER-HOLDERS; tendency of, *see* TEN-DENCY. *See also* ASPECTS OF A LAW; COMMAND AND COUNTERMAND; DUTY AND OBLIGATION; IMPERATIVE AND IMPERATION; LOGIC; POWER; SANCTIONS

IV. *Classification of laws or mandates.*

(*i*) *by reference to sources:* sovereign vs. subordinate 29; private or domes-tic 29, 77–8; public or civil 29. *See also* ADOPTION AND PRE-ADOPTION; CONCEPTION; POWER; SOVEREIGN AND SOVEREIGNTY

(*ii*) *by reference to logical relationships with other mandates*

(*a*) primordial 27–8, 57, 95–100, 301–302; and superventitious 27–8, 57, 301–2; the latter may be reiterative 25, 100–110, 301–2 (*in genere* vs. *in specie* 100–1, 106; *in toto* vs. *pro tanto* 100–1; *in tenor* vs. *in terminis* 102; four purposes of 101–2); alterative 110–24, 301; or extensive 125–9

(*b*) principal and subsidiary 137–45; subsidiary as proximate vs. remote 140; subsidiary includes punitory laws 2, 61, 140, remunerative laws 140,

LAW OR MANDATE (*cont.*)

144–5, and occasional appendages or remedial laws 149–51; as adjective or enclitic vs. substantive or self-subsis-ting laws 142

(*iii*) *by reference to aspects of the will:* decisive (imperative, obligative and coercive) 95–6; or undecisive (unim-perative, unobligative and uncoercive) 95–6; decisive, either command or prohibition 95–6; undecisive, either non-command or non-prohibition (per-mission) 95; affirmative or negative 95–7; uncoercive or undecisive man-dates, various forms and uses of 99–100, 119–20

(*iv*) *by reference to degree of fullness:* first or simplest pattern comprises only a directive part when force derives only from auxiliary sanctions 156; com-pleteness and unity of 156–67; three other patterns distinguished 156; their unity and completeness 167–8

v. *Further classifications and sub-divisions.*

(*i*) adjective: punitory vs. compensa-tive 55, 61–2; may be named enclitic 142; *See also* IV (*ii*) (*b*)

(*ii*) agathopoieutic 160b

(*iii*) anaetiosostic 148

(*iv*) catapaustic 149–50, 225

(*v*) common or customary: *See* COMMON LAW AND CUSTOMARY LAW

(*vi*) compensative 149–50, 225. *See also* (*i*) adjective; (*xxviii*) substantive; COMPENSATION

(*vii*) conditional and unconditional 45, 112–13, 115–16, 122–4; examples 182; no unconditional affirmative 122p, 144u, 116

(*viii*) contradictive or revocative 110. *See also* ASPECTS OF A LAW, III

(*ix*) contrariant or reversive 110, 121; these, where repugnant 132. *See also* ASPECTS OF A LAW, III

(*x*) corroborative 27

(*xi*) declaratory 107–10; the term usually employed with unwritten or customary laws 107–8. *See also* (*xxxi*) written and unwritten

(*xii*) de-obligative 100; these, either countermand 110, 119 or repermission 168; and are not needed in a regular body of law 233. *See also* IV (*iii*)

(*xiii*) expository 102; in which lan-guage changes from imperative to

LAW OR MANDATE (*cont.*)

assertive form 104–6. *See also* EXPOSI-TORY MANDATE OR MATTER

(*xiv*) *ex post facto* law 187d; mischief of 190–1

(*xv*) general and particular: *See* GENERALITY etc. OF A LAW

(*xvi*) immediate vs. potestative 26–7

(*xvii*) invitative or praemiary 136, 140, 145

(*xviii*) legal vs. illegal mandates 15–16; act of issuing an illegal mandate 19c

(*xix*) legislative vs. executive 78

(*xx*) metaphylactic 149–50, 225; vs. preventive or prophylactic 150d

(*xxi*) monadic or narrowest assignable: *See* COMPLETENESS etc. OF A LAW

(*xxii*) obligative 157, 233; must contain an imperative provision 157; upon which number of laws depends 168; commonly annexed to de-obligative laws 170n. *See also* IV (*iii*)

(*xxiii*) occasional judgment as 222

(*xxiv*) permanent vs. temporary: *See* GENERALITY etc. OF A LAW

(*xxv*) preventive or prophylactic 150d

(*xxv*) punitory: *See* (*i*) adjective *and* IV (*ii*) (*b*)

(*xxvii*) statutory 108. *See also* STATUTES AND STATUTORY LAW

(*xxviii*) substantive 61–2. *See also* IV (*ii*) (*b*)

(*xxix*) therapeutic 149–50, 151g

(*xxix*) traditionary 152–3

(*xxxi*) written and unwritten: the former as graphical discourse 152; modifications in words expressing it 154; the latter as declaratory law 108–9; and the frequent name of customary law 153. *See also* COMMON LAW AND CUSTOMARY LAW

LAWS OF NATURE: *See* NATURAL LAW AND LAWS OF NATURE

LEGISLATION: meaning of term 3–4; business of judicature constantly opposed to that of legislation 4–5; power of 81–2, 137h; no instance of complete law without perfect plan of 183; deficiencies in current systems of 183; field of, a trackless wild 232; teaching of art of, how to be improved 233; and use of model of complete code in 244; advantages of natural and regular plan of 242; as a state of warfare against mischief 245–6; the mechanical branch of 245; direct vs. indirect 245–6, 308;

LEGISLATION (*cont.*)

art of, aims to add to happiness of community and prevent its diminution 289; the former (direct) purpose compassed by coercion and remuneration 289. *See also* LAW OR MANDATE; LEGISLATORS AND GOVERNMENT

LEGISLATORS AND GOVERNMENT: laws belong to the legislator in the way of conception, and to legislators and power-holders conjunctively in the way of pre-adoption 26; circumstances to which will of legislator may apply 46–52; legislator's business is to discover latent interests 64; his two courses in giving efficacy to his laws: force of auxiliary sanctions or his own 133; may give notice of pun. or reward in text of law itself 134; business of government cannot be carried on otherwise than by pun. 135; six reasons for this 135e; incompleteness of law leads judge to assume place of legislator 183; use of this work for guidance of 232; lack of amplitude and discrimination in legislator's views creates necessity for interpretation 239–40; plan for control of latter 241; legislator contrasted with judicature 240; judge should be his counsel, not a control 241; executive magistrate sometimes takes course unconformable to that marked out by the legislator 272; but commonly conformable to it 274–5; intentions of the legislator, *see* INTENTIONS AND INTENTIONALITY; will of the legislator, *see* WILL AND VOLITION; ASPECTS OF A LAW. *See also* JUDGE; LEGISLATION

LIBERTY AND FREEDOM: all laws must curtail liberties of one or more persons 54; this is a mischief 62; liberties founded on uncoercive mandates of sovereign 99; pre-established universal law of liberty 119–20; a fictitious entity 251; is universal before legislator commands or prohibits an act 253; the two sorts of liberty: against law and against wrong-doers 253–4; liberty of occupation, *see* OCCUPATION

LIMITATIONS AND EXCEPTIONS: circumstances, words, clauses and provisions (or propositions) may be limitative or exceptive 113–14; these generally termed qualificative 115, 129; a limitation is an indirect ex-

LIMITATIONS AND EXCEPTIONS (*cont.*) ception, and an exception is an indirect limitation 114, 128; interconvertibility of conditional commands and unconditional commands with limitations and exceptions 115–16; qualifications may appear on either side of a law, according to phraseology used 116; words of limitation and exception 116v; every efficient law may be considered an exception or a limitation to universal law of liberty 119–20; limitations and exceptions to preceding limitations and exceptions 120; chains of such provisions alternately narrowing and extending predecessors 120, 123, 126; and exculpative or justificative circumstances 121, 122–4; to punitory laws 147. *See also* CIRCUMSTANCES; CLAUSE OF A LAW; PROVISION OF A LAW

LOGIC: logic of the will vs. of the judgment 15h; common logic, in which the word 'substance' is more frequently used than the word 'act' 43; and 'property' (vs. 'circumstance') more frequently used of substances than of acts 43; logician of ordinary stamp versed in dialectics but not in terminology 68n (69); the term 'logical extent' rejected as an alternative for 'generality' 76a; grammar as a branch of 243

MAGISTRATE: *See* COMMON LAW AND CUSTOMARY LAW; EXECUTIVE AND ADMINISTRATIVE FUNCTION; JUDGE
MAGNITUDE: *See* QUANTITY AND MAGNITUDE
MANDATE: *See* LAW OR MANDATE
METHOD OF ANALYSIS: need to form idea of a law as purely intellectual object to serve as pattern 12; analytical sketch of mandates 15, 29–30; analytic sketch of provisions according to exhaustive method 128–9; why such analysis not applicable in case of species of incorporeal property 277–9; but only simple enumeration of species 277–8; method of paraphrasis 295. *See also* DEFINITION; ENTITIES, fictitious; LANGUAGE AND DISCOURSE
MIND: in which a man may be made to suffer by sovereign 20d; simple mental injuries 20d; religious biases of the mind 20d; mental vs. physical quali-

MIND (*cont.*) ties 35; as locus of pathological termination of an act 36 (*see also* ACTIONS AND ACTS, I). *See also* INTENTIONS AND INTENTIONALITY; WILL AND VOLITION

MISCHIEF AND HARM: averting positive mischief is promoting negative good 32–3; of an offence, according to which offences are classified 33; and laws are thus classified by ends of preventing 33; of private offences alone admits of or requires compensation 150f; of semi-public or public offences, may be stopped or guarded against 150f; circumstances affecting 183; secondary mischief of an offence increased by uncertainty of pun. 214; of an act: semi-public and public 37; these generally attend private and semi-public offences 58; enhanced by consciousness and intentionality of offender 214; of a law: produced by a law in first instance 54 but compensated by the good produced 54; restrainment of liberty as 62; of voluminousness of the laws 71; of *privilegia* 187d; of *ex post facto* law 187d, 190–1; actual and contingent, connected with individual offence by way of causality 149; measures against this may be taken in addition to measures against indeterminate and uncertain 149; the three courses the law may take in obviating 149–50; positive, consists of actual pn. or danger 150f; every law is made upon the consideration of 160; idea of, *see* IDEAS; quantity and magnitude of, *see* QUANTITY AND MAGNITUDE

MOTION: effect of act on things is either motion or quiescent state 35; abstract, an element in acts of the body 47–8; considerable motion required if act is to terminate in a thing 282; but only slight if in a person and operates on his will 282. *See also* ACTIONS AND ACTS, I

MOTIVES AND INFLUENCES: advice and exhortation, unlike a law, administer no new motives 14n.1; external 31; internal, enumerated: social motive of benevolence, semi-social motive of love of reputation, self-regarding motives of love of power and wealth 31b; no law without a motive 56;

MOTIVES AND INFLUENCES (*cont.*)
motives producing adoption by sovereign of predecessor's covenants added to by expectation of this event 65; as forces by which human will is influenced 68; solemn engagement of sovereign as 70p; no man acts without a motive or against a preponderant mass of 70p; as the expectation of pn. and pl. 133; of the legislator's own creation, vs. auxiliary force of the two foreign sanctions 133; sanctional or incitative part of law makes known motive furnished for compliance 134; in the nature of pun. vs. in the way of reward 134; tutelary motives of benevolence 202 and of love of reputation 202; coercive 18–19; act of issuing an illegal mandate backed by coercive motives an offence 19; kinds of offence which it constitutes 19c; alluring vs. coercive 133, 222; law trusts to coercive motives, invitation does not 136; coercive motives influence the will by holding out prospect of pn., alluring motives by holding out prospect of pl. 259; application of some of coercive kind of offence 259; these used in pun. 259; coercive and alluring influence vs. exercise of power of pun. 259–60, 263–4; the former constitute power over active faculties 262; motive relied on distinguished from aspect of the legislator's will 298a; will of sovereign commonly relies upon the coercive motive, but may rely upon the alluring 298a. *See also* BENEVOLENCE; COERCION AND COMPULSION; POWER; PUNISHMENT; REWARD; SANCTION

NATURAL LAW AND LAWS OF NATURE: as fictitious entities 2a (3)
NATURE: state of, subjects acting as in, exert the moral sanction and coerce sovereign 70
NOTICE: *See* KNOWLEDGE AND PROMULGATION OF A LAW

OBEDIENCE AND COMPLIANCE: laws often disobeyed if too complicated and obscure to be promulgated 238–9; act of compliance as an object of power over active faculties 259, 260; power over passive faculties corroborated by prohibition of non-compliance 261;

OBEDIENCE AND COMPLIANCE (*cont.*)
disposition to and habit of, *see* DISPOSITION AND PROPENSITY. *See also* IMPERATIVE AND IMPERATION; SOVEREIGN AND SOVEREIGNTY
OBLIGATION: *See* DUTY AND OBLIGATION
OCCUPATION: defined 272–3; absence of obstacles to, is possession 273, 276, 281; is instantaneous (vs. possession, which is permanent and continual) 275–6; idea of, is positive, and includes idea of an act performed (vs. idea of possession, which is negative) 281; the word, applicable to both incorporeal and corporeal property 281; but only with difficulty in the case of the former 281–2; of corporeal and incorporeal objects 281–2; of a trust, intelligible by reference to powers or rights exercised in its performance 282–3; acts of, are direct or indirect 286; of derivative occupant 287; this, if subject to divestitive power of the original proprietor, scarcely amounts to property 287; offence of wrongful occupation of property, *see* OFFENCES, II (*ii*). *See also* POSSESSION; PROPERTY
OFFENCES:
I. *In general.* offence of issuing an illegal mandate 19c, 20d; offences classified according to mischief they produce 33; to create an, is to make a law 33; and to impose an obligation 57; division of, and analysis of possible modifications of pathological termination of an illegal act 36; extra-regarding vs. self-regarding 57, 58; negative vs. positive 58; private, semi-public or public according as party favoured by law is an individual, a subordinate class or the whole community 58, 61; public injured by every offence 58; a new offence made by addition of specific circumstances to a command 113t; are acts opposite to those which are the objects of the declared will of the legislator 120–1; cases in which the offence is a continued act 151g; classes of, may be distinguished from one another *ad infinitum* 170–1; unity of, by which unity of a law is determined 170–1; *species infimae* and *genera infima* of 171–5; these, distinguished 172; the former constituted by application of

OFFENCES (*cont.*)

circumstances of aggravation and extenuation to the latter 173–4; principal vs. accessory 215; by whatever act an offence is committed, a right is violated and *vice versa* 220–1; judgment in civil suits only create offences 226; penal judgments are also grounded on offences already committed 226–7; one law creates one offence, and for every offence there is a law 233; mischief of, *see* MISCHIEF AND HARM; procedure against, *see* PROCEDURE; vs. crimes, *see* PENAL AND CIVIL BRANCHES OF THE LAW, II. *See also* BENEFIT AND FAVOUR; COERCION AND COMPULSION; DUTY AND OBLIGATION

II. *Private offences.* generally attended by semi-public or public mischief 58; produce pn. and danger 150f

(*i*) *against persons:* laws concerning 59–60, 150f; murder, adultery, simple corporal injuries, wrongful confinement are *genera infima* 172; division of matter comprised in them between the penal and civil branches of the law 200–1; consent forms one exception to general rule 200; powers over persons form further exceptions 200–1

(*ii*) *against property:* of wrongful occupation of property: law prohibiting is fundamental law by which conveyances are adopted 27i; includes theft 174; which is an example of a *genus infimum* 172, 174; by reference to which the nature of other offences against property may be most commodiously explained 176; definition of, requires the word 'title' 181, 201–2; law concerning, are infinite but reducible to one 181; this may be couched in conditional form or as unconditional provision with exceptive clause 181–2; example, a creditor inter-meddling with debtor's money 230, 266f; of wrongful withholding of services: law prohibiting is fundamental law by which contracts are adopted 27i; division of matter comprised in offences against property between penal and civil branches of the law 201–2; title referred to civil branch 201–2; laws concerning 60–1, 176–83; title forms exception to prohibition against intermeddling 201–2; differences be-

OFFENCES (*cont.*)

tween criminal and civil 217–18; of wrongful non-investment 230; an act which is an offence may cause loss of legal possession 279–81. *See also* CONVEYANCES AND COVENANTS; OCCUPATION; POSSESSION; PROPERTY; TITLE

(*iii*) *against reputation:* laws concerning 60; the rules marking them out 202–3; to which there are scarcely any exceptions 203; hence expository matter comprised in, not separated from, mandatory 203. *See also* REPUTATION AND GOOD NAME

(*iv*) *against condition in life:* 203–4; laws concerning 61; their circumstantiative matter must be aggregated to the civil branch of the law 204; example: matrimonial condition 203–4. *See also* CONDITION IN LIFE

(*v*) *against person and reputation:* laws concerning 150f

III. *Semi-public offences.* generally attended by public mischief 58; laws concerning 61, 150f; produce danger 150f; matter of law relating to, how divided between penal and civil branches of the law 204; same expository matter as in private offences 204

IV. *Self-regarding offences,* in laws creating them, same person is coerced, made to suffer and favoured 56; and they impose self-regarding duty 57; laws concerning 150f; little to define in them, hence are of mainly penal character 204–5

V. *Public offences.* laws concerning 61, 150f; produce danger 150f; division of matter comprised in the different public offences between civil and penal branches of the law 205–8

(*i*) against the external security of the state 205

(*ii*) against the preventive branch of the police 205

(*iii*) against justice 205–6; are offences against a species of trust 205; law relating to, consists in designation of the offences and their puns. 205; its expository matter part of public or constitutional branch of law 205

(*iv*) against the public force: its circumstantiative matter belongs to the civil branch of the law 206

OFFENCES (*cont.*)

(*v*) against the positive increase of the national felicity: its circumstantiative or expository matter referred to the constitutional branch of the law and is of civil nature 206

(*vi*) against the public wealth 206–7; its circumstantiative matter belongs to the constitutional branch of the law 207

(*vii*) against population: its circumstantiative matter belongs to the civil (private and constitutional or public) branch of the law 207

(*viii*) against the national wealth: comprises matter belonging to the public or constitutional branch 207

(*ix*) against sovereignty: comprises matter belonging to the civil (constitutional) branch 207

(*x*) against religion: comprises matter belonging to the civil (constitutional) branch of the law 208

(*xi*) against the national interest in general: comprises expositive matter concerning description of person(s) 208

VI. *Offences against trust.* against possession of distinct from against exercise of 281; identified by references to offences against property 284; language misleadingly suggests existence of other offences against, concerned with unlawful exercise of power 283k. *See also* TRUST

ORDER: domestic 4; issued by the executive power 4, 7–8; judicial 4–5, 7; of the sovereign 5–6; or rules and orders, as names of the regulations given by judicial power 7; the word, why an inadequate substitute for the word 'law' 10–11; vs. command 10d

ORDINANCE: the word, why an inadequate substitute for the word 'law' 12

PAIN: *See* PLEASURE AND PAIN

PARTICULARITY OF A LAW: *See* GENERALITY AND PARTICULARITY OF A LAW

PATIENTS: *See* AGENTS etc.

PENAL AND CIVIL BRANCHES OF THE LAW:

I. *In general.* 196–208 (Ch. XVI), 247–50 (Appendix A); every important law has a penal and a civil part 196; these inextricably interwoven 247; the distinction applies not to laws but to books about laws 248, 250; penal and civil parts separated for purposes

PENAL AND CIVIL BRANCHES OF THE LAW (*cont.*)

of convenience 197; but the distinction varies in different countries 200, is imprecise 247, vague and ambiguous 221, 248a

penal part: includes the imperative and comminative clauses 198 and the bare description of acts made offences and of acts of pun. and circumstances affecting pun. 199

civil part: includes qualificative and and expository matter 198; circumstantiative matter common to different sorts of acts made offences is separated from rest and forms civil branch 199

division into penal and civil branches of matter comprised in laws illustrated in case of various offences 200–8 (*see* OFFENCES, II, III, IV, V).

II. *Penal or criminal and civil offences.* senses of the word 'crime' distinguished 209–11, 214–16; provide no clear distinction 211, 217, 218, so new arbitrary line proposed 211–12; offences punished with ordinary degree of severity may be called civil 211, if with extraordinary severity may be called criminal 211 and assigned to penal or criminal branch of the law 213; but, if directory part is detailed, titles describing it belong to the civil branch 213, 216; offences against property if punished only with compulsory restitution or compensation are civil offences 217–18; if by extraordinary puns. are criminal offences 218

III. *Penal and civil procedure.* distinction depends on nature of judgment given in a suit 220; a suit is penal if its object is to punish an offence committed 220, and judgment is then punitory or penal 221 and either a conviction or an acquittal 223; suit is civil if no offence committed and object is to prohibit 220; judgment is then civil and either an adjudication or a non-adjudication 223; cases in which either a civil or a penal suit may be brought 227–8, 230–1. *See also* PROCEDURE; SUIT

PERCEPTION: as a passive faculty of persons 35

PERMISSION: *See* PROHIBITION AND PERMISSION

PERSONS: are real entities 2a (3), 251; as agible or possible subjects of a law 34, 54 (*see also* AGENTS etc.); have mental and physical properties (vs. things, which have only physical) 35; assignable vs. unassignable 37, 271, 293; as rational animals 49–50; affected by law by being (*i*) coerced; (*ii*) made to suffer; (*iii*) favoured by it 53–6, 84; and examples 59–62; this with regard to punitory and compensative laws 61–2; same person coerced, made to suffer, and favoured by laws creating self-regarding offences 56; if not coerced by law, is negatively favoured in point of agency 56 (*see also* BENEFIT AND FAVOUR); determines classification of offences as private, semipublic or public 58, 61; need to be acquainted with law 63–4; generality and particularity of 76; ideas annexed to word 'person' are ideas of impressions of real entities 251–2; benefited by beneficiary or by fiduciary power 271–2; in latter case, may be as assignable individuals or subordinate class of persons or public at large 271, 293; as corporeal (sentient) objects of occupation 282–3; and as objects of corporeal property 285; an assignable individual may be affected by a mischievous act in point of person, property, reputation and condition in life 293; faculties of, *see* FACULTIES AND ABILITIES; offences against, *see* OFFENCES, II (*i*) and (*v*); power over, *see* POWER, III (*xvi*)

PLACE AND EXTENSION: *See* TIME AND PLACE

PLEASURE AND PAIN: pn. a real entity 2a (3); pns. of the religious sanction 20d; experiencing of, as a passive faculty of persons 35; pleasurable vs. painful pathological effects of an act 35; catalogue of, use for analysis of possible modifications of pathological termination of an illegal act 36; pn. of privation 37; motives as the expectation of 133; drawn from the political sanction, upon which legislator relies for the effectuation of his will 133; any man at any time much surer of administering pn. than pl. 135e; power of administering pl. depends upon circumstances of the individual to whom it is applied 135e; scale of pl. very

PLEASURE AND PAIN (*cont.*) short and limited, scale of pn. unlimited 135e; sources of pl. few and soon exhausted, sources of pn. innumerable and inexhaustible 135e; law has no means of administering pl. by its own operation 135e; or of producing pl. without pn. at the same time 135e; more painful to lose a given sum than pleasurable to gain it 135e; positive mischief may consist of pn. 150f; pn. produced by private offences 150f; coercive motives influence will by holding out prospect of pn., alluring motives by holding out prospect of pl. 259

POLICE: offences against the preventive branch of, *see* OFFENCES, V (*ii*)

POSSESSION: meaningless without pun. 136f; physical (against physical vs. human obstacles) vs. legal 273; legal is either *de jure* or *de facto* 273–4; possession in general or roughly is absence of obstacles to occupation 273; the two species of legal possession commonly go together 274–5; is permanent (vs. occupation, which is instantaneous) 275–6; right to, distinguished from possession *de jure* 276; how legal possession lost by an offence 279–81; duty of magistrate is to give legal possession *de facto* to him who has it *de jure* 280; ways in which he may fail to do so 280–1; idea of, is negative (vs. of occupation, which is positive) 281. *See also* OCCUPATION

POWER:

I. *In general.* an element in condition in life 61; any branch of (even sovereign) may be shared 68n (69); but same branch cannot be possessed exclusively by two persons 68n (69); distribution of 68n (69); possible powers in a state reduced to two, viz.: power of contrectation (or impressive or autocheiristic) and power of imperation 81, 137h, 258 (*see also* III (*ii*) *and* (*xii*)); but power of imperation rests ultimately on power of contrectation 137h (139); a right in certain cases is a 84, 220a; meaningless without pun. 136f; a fictitious entity 136f, 251–2, 258; every power is a right, not every right a power 137h (139); powers and rights are leading terms in arrangement of civil and constitutional law 137h (139);

POWER (*cont.*)

distinction between lawful power itself and unlawful manner of exercise unreal 283k; power of the sovereign, *see* SOVEREIGN AND SOVEREIGNTY

II. *Powers analysed and classified in connection with three main topics.* (*i*) subordinate power-holders; (*ii*) distinction between general and particular laws or mandates; (*iii*) property and trusts.

(*i*) *subordinate power-holders:* their mandates are adopted by the sovereign 21–2, 137h (139); ultimate efficient cause of, is command or allowance of sovereign 137h (139); their powers are imperative or de-imperative 22, beneficial or fiduciary 22; conveyances and contracts are mandates adopted by the sovereign 23–6, 78–80; domestic mandates are often particular either wholly (domestic) or *ex parte* 77–8

(*ii*) *distinction between general and particular laws or mandates:* whole power of imperation includes both power of imperation *de classibus* (power of general legislation) and power of imperation *de singulis* (power of aggregation or accensive power) 26h, 80–2, 91–2, 137h; aggregative or accensive and disaggregative or disaccensive power, its branches, subdivisions and examples 83–91. *See also* III (*i*) *and* (*xii*)

(*iii*) *property and trusts:* involve direct power over things which may be exclusive or inexclusive 255; such powers may be corroborated or uncorroborated (or naked), 290; varieties of corroboration 256–61, 263–5, 290–1, 295; also involve indirect or investitive powers created and exercised in various ways 268–9, 275; varieties and examples of investitive powers 269–71; divestitive powers 268, 287–8; beneficial or fiduciary powers 271–2, 290, 293, 295–7; powers partial and general in point of use 291–2

III. *Classifications and sub-divisions.*

(*i*) accensive (or aggregative) and disaccensive (or disaggregative): *in personam:* 83–8; to aggregate a man to a class is to invest him with a condition 83; but power of investment, though it includes, is distinguished from accensive power *in personam* 84; includes

POWER (*cont.*)

jurisdative or dicaiodotic power (or power of conveyance) 84–5; and jurisademptive power 85–6; and potisdative power or dosidynamic or endynamistic power 65l (66), 84, 86; and disendynamistic power 85; *in rem:* examples 88–9; *in actum* 89; *in locum* 90; *in tempus* 90–1

(*ii*) autocheiristic 57e, 80, 86; which may be called contrectative or impressive 81, 87, 88; is over passive faculties 137h (138); vs. power of imperation 137h; of which it is the complement 137h; physical vs. hyperphysical (superphysical) contrectation 137h (138); pun. is an exercise of this power 137h (139)

(*iii*) beneficial and fiduciary 19c; the distinction regarding parties favoured in point of agency 59; the distinction between the two 271, 295–6; the latter as trusts (private, semi-public and public) 271, 293; affords right to services 271–2. *See also* II (*i*) *and* (*iii*)

(*iv*) contrectative: *See* (*ii*) autocheiristic

(*v*) constitutional and public 22, 86–7, 218

(*vi*) corroborated and uncorroborated (or naked) 268, 269. *See also* II (*iii*)

(*vii*) direct and indirect 268, 269. *See also* II (*iii*)

(*viii*) endynamistic: *See* (*i*) accensitive

(*ix*) exclusive and inexclusive 255–6

(*x*) executive: *See* EXECUTIVE AND ADMINISTRATIVE FUNCTION

(*xi*) investitive and divestitive 268; included in but not identical with accensive power 84; when to invest with a right is same as power of conveyance and of jurisdiction 85–7; of the 1st., 2nd., 3rd. etc. orders 269; may be possessed exclusively or inexclusively 269; may be subject to powers of control by non-assent or dissent 269; buying, selling, giving and conveying as exercise of 269; weakness and strength of 272n.1, 287; possessed by persons upon whose will depend voluntary investitive and divestitive events 287. *See also* II (*iii*); INVESTMENT AND DIVESTMENT

24*

POWER (*cont.*)

(*xii*) imperative and de-imperative (or of imperation and de-imperation) 18–22, 79–80; is over active faculties of persons 18b, 137h (138); complete power of, broken into shares 26h, 81–92; the two distinguished 81; vs. power of contrectation 137h (138). *See also* II (*i*) *and* (*ii*); IMPERATIVE AND IMPERATION

(*xiii*) impressive: *See* (*ii*) auto-cheiristic

(*xiv*) judicial 5–7. *See also* JUDGE

(*xv*) permanent vs. occasional 59–60

(*xvi*) over persons, divided into power over active and over passive faculties 18b, 137h (138), 258; conferred by the law as exception to offences against person 200–1; over their active faculties 18b, 137h (138), 258; requires exercise of two acts: of compliance and of power 259, 261; means whereby it operates: physical vs. mental or moral 259; physical more certain than mental 260; operates via power of pun. or via coercive and alluring influence 259–60; power is of pun. when application of coercive motives would, but for creation of power, be an offence 259; power of corporal pun. 260; this, given by law in corroboration of power over things 263–4; does not necessarily include power over passive faculties 261; since is also constituted by the mere liberty of applying coercive and alluring influence 262; these two last species of power possessed by every man over every other 262; do not constitute property 262 but they may be taken away by law 263; power over their passive faculties 18b, 137h (138), 258; exercise requires only the act of person having the power 259; this as an uncorroborated power 260 may be corroborated by prohibition of disturbance or of non-compliance (command of submission) 261; virtually includes power over active faculties 261; given by law in corroboration of power over things 263

(*xvii*) principal and subservient 257; the latter corroborates the former 257; and may itself be over things or persons 257; subservient corroborated by permission of assistance or command of assistance 264

POWER (*cont.*)

(*xviii*) private or domestic 19c, 218

(*xix*) productive or preventive 259

(*xx*) public and constitutional 22, 86–7, 218

(*xxi*) power of pun. 259, 260, 263–4. *See also* (*xvi*) over persons; PUNISHMENT

(*xxii*) over things 255; conferred by exception to offences against property 201; exclusive vs. inexclusive 255–6; corroborated in various ways 256, 257, 258, 263. *See also* PROPERTY

POWER-HOLDERS: subordinate power-holders, the term explained 22f; laws belong to power-holders conjunctively with legislator in way of pre-adoption 26. *See also* POWER, II (*i*)

PRE-ADOPTION: *See* ADOPTION AND PRE-ADOPTION

PRECEDENT: invalidity of formularies of, has effect of exemptive or disexemptive circumstances 189; collection of, may form branch of customary law 189. *See also* COMMON LAW AND CUSTOMARY LAW

PRECEPT: the word, why an inadequate substitute for the word 'law' 11

PREDICTION: vs. the directive part of the law 137; meaning of 137g; contained in the satisfactive clause 151; as the comminative part of the law 167

PRINCIPLE OF SYMPATHY AND ANTI-PATHY: suffering to which party exposed by law ultimately intentional only where legislator proceeds upon the principle of sympathy and antipathy 55n.2

PRINCIPLE OF UTILITY: upon which, the end of a sovereign in adopting a law must be the greatest good of the community 31, 32; as the fundamental principle of the system of laws sketched out 237

PRIVILEGIUM: Latin for 'command' 6; and for particular law: unfavourable (*odiosa*) vs. favourable (*favorabilia*) 77; mischief of 187d

PROBABILITY AND CERTAINTY: certain vs. contingent pathological effects of an act 35, 37; every event contingent while future 37; certainty of pun. diminished by consciousness and intentionality of the offender 214; uncertainty of pun. a circumstance

PROBABILITY AND CERTAINTY (*cont.*)
increasing secondary mischief
of an offence 214

PROCEDURE: laws relating to 2a;
meaning of 140; divisible into procedure *delicti causa* and procedure
petitionis causa (penal and civil) 140;
the word, its common substitutes 142k;
and exemptive circumstances 146–7;
ad puniendum vs. *ad satisfaciendum* vs.
ad compescendum 151; penal and civil,
see PENAL AND CIVIL BRANCHES OF
THE LAW, III

PROHIBITION AND PERMISSION: will of
sovereign validates mandates of subordinate power-holders by permission
27; this is the first degree of adoption
27; command and prohibition are
decisive, non-command and permission are indecisive mandates 95–6;
permission is non-prohibition 95, 97;
command includes permission, but
excludes prohibition and non-
command 97; use of indecisive mandates 97–8; original inactive permission
vs. superventitious active repermission
110, 300; no complete correspondence
between the words 'countermand' and
'permission' 111o; the word 'dispensation', where used instead of the word
'repermission' 111o; conditional vs.
unconditional 112–13, 115–16; point at
pun. 134; power constituted by bare
permission is uncorroborated 260;
power over passive faculties may be
corroborated by prohibitions 261; prohibition affords protection for property
(power over things and right to negative services) 276–7; the word
'prohibition', its imperfections for
expressing aspects of will without
regard to motives 298a. *See also* AS-
PECTS OF A LAW; COMMAND AND
COUNTERMAND

PROMISES: concessions of sovereign are
only 16. *See also* CONVEYANCES AND
COVENANTS; SOVEREIGN AND
SOVEREIGNTY

PROMULGATION: *See* KNOWLEDGE etc.
OF A LAW

PROPENSITY: *See* DISPOSITION AND
PROPENSITY

PROPERTIES: *See* QUALITIES AND
PROPERTIES

PROPERTY: a man may be made by the
sovereign to suffer in 20d; in things or

PROPERTY (*cont.*)
in services of persons 60; laws of property 60–1; parties affected by them
60–1; when fiduciary 60, 295–6; laws
of, how related to rest of system and
reducible to nature of a mandate 176–
82; law creating, simplest form of,
corresponds to offence of wrongful
occupation of 176–7; infinitude of laws
concerning 177–8; reducible by translation into assertive form 177–80; all
conveyances in force included in law
creating 180; how these comprised in
exposition of a few words like e.g. title
180–1; created by law 255; its several
modifications, how created 255–79; includes various kinds of power, their
corroboration 255–64, 290–1; consists
of rights as well as powers 265; these
are rights to use of things 266 and to
services 266–7; protected by prohibitions and commands 276–7; intricacies
of analysis of modifications of 277–9;
an enumeration but no exhaustive plan
of them 277–9; some articles left unexplained 278; its objects: corporeal and
incorporeal 281–2; trust is a species of
283; incorporeal objects are fictitious
entities and are corporeal objects considered under a particular point of view
284–5; this fiction grafted into every
language 285; objects of corporeal
property: persons or things 285; the
four articles to be considered in
speaking of 284–6; and powers over
things particular or partial in point of
use 291–3; offences against, *see*
OFFENCES II, (*ii*). *See also* OCCUPA-
TION; POSSESSION; POWER; RIGHTS

PROPORTION: between imperative and
qualificative clauses, to which system
of laws owes its wisdom 238

PROVISION OF A LAW: how distinguished
from words and clauses 114; either
contains a law in itself or goes towards
making up a law 124, 126, 299b; may
be issued *uno flatu* or *diverso flatu*
126–7; differences in this respect between a law and an edict, ordinance or
statute 126; summary view of various,
according to exhaustive method of
analysis 129. *See also* ASPECTS OF A
LAW, IV; CIRCUMSTANCES; CLAUSE
OF A LAW; COMPLETENESS etc. OF
A LAW; LAW OR MANDATE; LIMITA-
TIONS AND EXCEPTIONS

PUNISHMENT: inflicted upon a man: different senses of word 'upon' 38; is one case where persons purposely exposed to suffer by a law 55; vs. reward 133; must be announced 134 (*see also* KNOWLEDGE etc. OF A LAW); command, prohibition and permission all point at 134; comminative part of law gives notice of and predicts 134, 137; this supplemented by a subsidiary punitory law usually addressed to Judge 137–9; principal and punitory laws may be expressed in one sentence but are separate laws 142–4; as a motive furnished for compliance with a law 134, 167; of which great use is made in business of government 134–5; six reasons for this 135e; wherefore idea of pun. is separable from law only with difficulty 136; idea of, upon which depend the words obligation, duty, right, title, possession, conveyance 136f; an exercise of the power of contrectation 137h (139); its application limited by exemptive circumstances 145; and *species infimae* of offences distinguished by differences in quantity and quality of 171, 172–4; article of quantity of, includes that of intensity and duration 173o; certitude and propinquity of, ought in every instance to be kept to a maximum 173o; if varied, must be varied either in quantity or quality 173; often not fixed by legislator, wherefore laws are incomplete 183; circumstances affecting, left to discretion of judges 183; act of, all there is in customary law 184; ordinary vs. extraordinary, and distinction between civil and criminal offences 211–12, 217, 218; grounds for applying extraordinary, listed 212; must be applied if profit of offence is not pecuniary 212–13; demand for, how enhanced by consciousness and intentionality of the offender 214; is needless where compensation is certain 217; alone constitutes power 218; ethics instructs how to avoid 219; of the political sanction: where applied, there ought also that of the moral sanction 219; the latter is feebler than the former 219, but may still be requisite and profitable where the pun. of the political sanction is unprofitable or needless 219; and it may be the sole pun. of a

PUNISHMENT (*cont.*)
law 248; but without some pun. could not be a law or have effect of a law 248; hence no clear meaning for civil vs. penal law 248a; power of 259; and of corporal pun. 260, 263–4; as a power over active faculties of persons 261, 263–4; as moral (vs. physical) coercion 289; punitory law, *see* LAW OR MANDATE IV, (*ii*) (*b*), *and* V; quantity and magnitude of, *see* QUANTITY AND MAGNITUDE; uncertainty of, *see* PROBABILITY AND CERTAINTY. *See also* COERCION AND COMPULSION; DUTY AND OBLIGATION; SANCTIONS

PURPOSES: *See* ENDS AND PURPOSES

QUALIFICATIONS AND QUALIFICATIVE MATTER: includes both limitations and exceptions 115, 129; may be placed on either side of a law 116; used in translating laws out of imperative into assertive form 179t; is included in civil part of the law 198. *See also* CIRCUMSTANCES; LIMITATIONS AND EXCEPTIONS

QUALITIES AND PROPERTIES: physical qualities of things vs. mental and physical qualities of persons 35; properties of substances compared to circumstances of an act 42–4; are fictitious entities 42, 45

QUANTITY AND MAGNITUDE: relative, of pl. and pn. 135e; of mischief: of an offence 149; of mischief, odiousness and pun., as circumstances by which crimes are distinguished from other offences 209–11, 216; exceptions to this 217

REGULATION: issued by magistrates 6–8; the word, why an inadequate substitute for the word 'law' 12–13

RELATION: legal 285–6; in virtue of which a man possesses a condition in life 286

RELIGION: religious biases of the mind 20d; religious sanction, *see* SANCTIONS, V; offences against, *see* OFFENCES, V (*x*)

REMUNERATION: *See* REWARD AND REMUNERATION

REPUGNANCY: between laws 127, 129–32; when equivalent to alterative may be revocative or reversive: in each case either *in toto* or *pro tanto* 130; this not

REPUGNANCY (*cont.*)
the usual sense of repugnant 130; which carries with it the idea of incompatibility 130; none between laws made by independent sovereigns 131; spoken of where powers of legislation have been delegated from a superior to a subordinate authority 131; two cases of, and difference from alterative explained 132. *See also* ASPECTS OF A LAW, III

REPUTATION AND GOOD NAME: in which a man may be made to suffer by the sovereign 20d; love of, as a semi-social motive 31b; as an internal motive 31b; as a tutelary motive 202; as a fictitious entity 202; notions concerning, may tend to augment or diminish it 202; these can be true or false 202; should generally be a right to propagate them if true 202; exception to this if dictates of moral sanction are at variance with dictates of utility 202; or if pn. would outweigh benefit 202–3; in point of which an assignable individual may be affected by a mischievous act 293; offences against, *see* OFFENCES, II (*iii*) and (*v*)

REWARD AND REMUNERATION: is offered when motives of alluring kind held up as connected with an act (vs. pun., when motives of coercive kind) 133; as a motive furnished for compliance with the law 134; must be announced 134 (*see also* KNOWLEDGE etc. OF A LAW); invitative part of law gives notice of 134; little use made of, in business of government 134–5; six reasons for this 135e; pecuniary 135e; laws relying on, for efficiency, are invitative or praemiary 136; laws with alternative penal and praemiary sanctions 136–7; ethics teaches how to obtain 219; reward, by means of which the art of legislation compasses its direct purpose 289; but is little used 289; sovereign may rely on motives of alluring kind 298a; projected work on 309. *See also* LAW OR MANDATE, IV (*ii*) (*b*)

RIGHT AND WRONG: as fictitious entities 2a (3); question of right often confused with that of fact 67m; right is conformity to a rule, wrong is deviation from it 184; under customary law, distinction scarcely exists 184

RIGHTS: right to services conferred on

RIGHTS (*cont.*)
some party if law imposes extra-regarding duty on another 57–8, 291; such rights may be beneficial or fiduciary 59; person favoured by a law is invested with a 57, 63, 84; in virtue of which services are owed to him 84; an element in condition in life 61; in certain circumstances is a power 84, 220a; meaningless without pun. 136f; are either rights of dominion or mere liberties, which are rights of exemption from dominion 137h (139); the former as powers or shares of power 137h (139); in some cases they are essentially distinct 265; no law that does not confer a right on some person 220; every violation of a right an offence and every offence violates a right 220–1; distinction between penal and civil procedure and that between rights as inchoate, inconsummate, unliquidated or liquidable vs. consummate, liquid or liquidated 227–31; only latter susceptible of violation, former are rights to rights 227; law gives a right by creating a duty and makes disturbance of right punishable 249b; are fictitious objects 265; property in part consists of rights to things or to use of them 265; such rights analysed 265–71; right to a thing or to its use includes right to performance of an act of investitive power by some person 265–6; direct and indirect 268, 269; investitive and divestitive rights or powers 268; right to services imported by fiduciary power 271–2; of possession 276. *See also* PENAL AND CIVIL BRANCHES OF THE LAW; POSSESSION; POWER; PROCEDURE; PROPERTY; SERVICES

ROMAN LAW: limitation of dictator's powers in 18a (19); on conveyances and covenants 23g; Roman vs. English jurisprudence 23g (24); *furtum* in Justinian 118a2; discovery of Justinian at Amalfi 187; publication of Pandects and Institutes 242j; the word 'civil' used to refer to 248a; division of services into personal and praedial in 267g; defects in Justinian's compilation 303f

SANCTIONS:
I. *In general.* are the sources of motives

SANCTIONS (*cont.*)
68, 133; the relative efficacy of the different types of 70; penal vs. praemiary 136–7

II. *Moral.* upon which the force of treaties depends 16; by force of which sovereign binds himself 70; force of, distinguished into two great branches: that exerted by subjects of a state acting in a state of nature, and that exercised by foreign states 70; under the influence of intelligent and voluntary agents 133; pun. of, annexes ill-will to behaviour 202 and should be applied where that of the political sanction is applied 219; but if pun. of the political sanction is inefficacious, so must be that of the moral 219; yet the latter may still be requisite and profitable where that of the political is unprofitable and needless 219; and may be the sole pun. of a law 248; is the ally of the legislator 245

III. *Physical.* not directed by design, hence does not explain efficacy of laws *in principem* 68; not included among those under influence of intelligent and voluntary agents 133

IV. *Political.* inapplicable for purposes of enforcing laws *in principem* 68; unless a narrow sense given to expression 'sovereign' 68n; in which case he may be judged and coerced by another 68n; usually draws with it the force of the moral and religious sanctions 70; their efficacy usually less than that of political 70; under the influence of intelligent and voluntary agents 133; legislator relies for the effectuation of his will upon pl. or pn. drawn from 133; pun. of, where applied, so ought that of the moral sanction 219; but if former is inefficacious, so must be the latter 219

V. *Religious.* upon which the force of treaties depends 16; pns. of 20d; by force of which sovereign binds himself 68–70; under the influence of intelligent and voluntary agents 133; is the ally of the legislator 245; may be sole pun. of a law 248

See also COERCION AND COMPULSION; DUTY AND OBLIGATION; SOVEREIGN AND SOVEREIGNTY

SELF-REGARDING CONDUCT: love of power and of wealth as self-regarding

SELF-REGARDING CONDUCT (*cont.*)
and internal motives 31b; self-regarding offences, *see* OFFENCES, IV

SENSES AND SENSATION: as a passive faculty of persons 35; means the faculty of experiencing pn. and pl. 35; all ideas originate from the senses 160c. *See also* CONSEQUENCES AND EFFECTS

SENTIMENTS AND AFFECTIONS: because of which the will of the legislator may fail to be what it ought to be 162

SERVICES: doctrine of, extends over whole body of law 57–8; rights to services are created and protected by command and prohibition 58, 276–7; affirmative vs. negative 58; service of making a conveyance 23g (25); of liquidating unliquidated rights 227; of performing an act of investitive power 266; active services vs. services of forbearance 266; corporal vs. mental 266–7; personal vs. praedial 267g; *in personam* vs. *in rem* 267; right to, *see* RIGHTS

SIGNS: of a law 152–5 (Ch. XIII); sensible, as continuation of a physical act 37k; composing discourse: transient vs. permanent 152; sign of an act of will a real entity 252. *See also* LANGUAGE AND DISCOURSE

SOURCE OF A LAW: 18–30 (Ch. II). *See also* ADOPTION AND PRE-ADOPTION; POWER, II; SOVEREIGN AND SOVEREIGNTY

SOVEREIGN AND SOVEREIGNTY: law defined in terms of volition of 1; law as to person not subject to power of, has no force, yet is a law 20; such power constituted by the disposition of the people to obedience and submission 16, 18b, 68n, 109, 137h (139); may be divided so that different persons sovereign in different cases 18b; this explained by modifications in disposition to obey 18b; example 18b (19); orders of the sovereign 5–6; his mandates cannot be illegal 16; concessions of, as treaties with the people, depend for their efficacy on moral and religious sanctions 16; meaning of 18; a man is subject to any sovereign who can make him suffer 20d; sovereign may issue constitutional laws *in principem* 64; these are transcendent laws prescribing what sovereign should

SOVEREIGN AND SOVEREIGNTY (*cont.*)
do 64, 306; sovereign is the passible subject of such laws 64; these may be addressed to him alone or to him and his successors 64–7; his covenants vs. recommendatory mandates 64–5; how adopted by successors 65; he imposes obligations upon himself by assistance of moral and religious sanctions 67–8; but not by political unless sovereign used in narrow vs. popular sense of the term 68n; his engagements as real motives 70p; examples of binding laws *in principem* 71; use of declaratory laws in relation to laws *in principem* 108–9; examples 109–10; sovereignty not inseparable from the intention to coerce 298a; mandate of the sovereign, *see* ADOPTION AND PRE-ADOPTION; CONCEPTION; POWER, II; offences against sovereignty, *see* OFFENCES, V (*ix*). *See also* SANCTIONS

SPECIES: *See* CIRCUMSTANCES; GENUS AND SPECIES

SPEECH:*See* LANGUAGE AND DISCOURSE

STATUTES AND STATUTORY LAW: the word 'statute' an inadequate substitute for the word 'law' 11–12; idea of, vs. idea of law 12; provisions of, vs. of a law 126; statutory law: plan of a complete and regular body of 233–5; no instance of is anywhere to be found 235; penal statutes ought to be construed strictly 241i. *See also* COMMON LAW AND CUSTOMARY LAW

SUBALTERNATION: *See* GENUS AND SPECIES

SUFFERING: every law must expose one or more persons to suffer by it 54–5; if only party bound and coerced by it 54; persons may be otherwise exposed through necessity or purposely 55; purposely, if for purpose of pun. or of vindictive compensation 55; as oblique vs. direct vs. ultimate intention of legislator 55

SUIT: penal vs. civil 220–4; the latter may include interlocutory 225; judgment may be the same in a penal as in a civil 225–6; penal, involves complaint of violation of liquid rights, civil involves request for liquidation of unliquidated rights 227; may be tried in either way 227–8, 231; but in certain cases only by departure from truth 229–30, 231. *See also* PENAL AND

SUIT (*cont.*)
CIVIL BRANCHES OF THE LAW, III; PROCEDURE; RIGHTS

SUSCEPTION: vs. pre-adoption 21. *See also* ADOPTION AND PRE-ADOPTION

TENDENCY: of a law: prejudicial vs. beneficial 56; mischievous vs. beneficial, how traced out 63

TERMINATION: of actions: *See* ACTIONS AND ACTS, I

THINGS: as agible or passible subjects of a law 34 (*see also* AGENTS etc.); have only physical properties (vs. persons, who have both physical and mental properties) 35; animate vs. inanimate 35d, 285; ideas annexed to word 'thing' are ideas of impressions of real entities 251–2; immovable or movable 285; occupation of corporeal objects 281–2; only real objects are corporeal 284; corporeal object is one single and entire corporeal thing 284; as corporeal objects of property 285; power and rights over things, *see* POWER, III (*xxii*); POSSESSION; PROPERTY; RIGHTS

TIME AND PLACE: acts which sovereign may and may not take for his laws may be distinguished by place and time 18b (19); distinction between susception and pre-adoption by reference to time 21; time and space are accompaniments of everything that is 74; extent of a law: local 72–3 (Ch. VII); extent in point of time 74–5 (Ch. VIII); place and time as sources of specification of a law 302

TITLE: meaningless without pun. 136f; to proprietary subjects 180; variety of events constituting 180; exposition of words like 'title' contain all the law relating to conveyances 180; and also law relating to other modes of acquiring property 181; required in the definition of the offence of wrongful occupation of property 181 and of other offences against property 201–2; laws concerning, constitute exceptions to offences against property 201; are of prodigious bulk and referred to the civil branch of law 202; good, lawful or valid vs. actual or effectual 274; a fictitious entity constituted by an investitive event 274; actual, depends on disposition of the paramount magis-

TITLE (*cont.*)

strate 279; actual and effectual, how lost by an offence 279–80; effectual vs. valid equivalent to *de facto* vs. *de jure* legal possession 280; duty of magistrate to give effectual title to him who has just title 280

TREATIES: concessions by the sovereign as promises and treaties with the people 16; their force depends upon the moral and religious sanctions 16; and they are binding only upon the sovereign 16; made by one sovereign with another 16. *See also* SOVEREIGN AND SOVEREIGNTY

TREATISES: as set of general rules abstracted from sources of customary law 188

TRUST: a species of property 282–4; private vs. semi-public vs. public 293; offences against, *see* OFFENCES, V (*iii*) and VI; fiduciary powers or, *see* POWER, II (*iii*) *and* III (*iii*)

UNITY OF A LAW: *See* COMPLETENESS etc. OF A LAW

UNDERSTANDING: advice as the language of 14n.1; prediction as the expression of an act of 137g; because of state of, will of legislator may not be what it ought to be 162

USAGE: *See* LANGUAGE AND DISCOURSE

VOLITION: *See* WILL AND VOLITION

VOLUNTARY AND INVOLUNTARY: investitive and divestitive events, voluntary vs. natural 275, 287. *See also* INVESTMENT AND DIVESTMENT

WILL AND VOLITION: laws defined in terms of volition of the sovereign 1; exhortation as the language of 14n.1; logic of the will vs. of the judgment 15h; volition as an active faculty of persons 35; human will influenced by motives 68; of the legislator: its effectuation usually depends upon pl. or pn. drawn from the political sanction 133; modifications in its expression 154–5; actual vs. hypothetical 156–7, 163; failure to be what it ought to be must arise from the state of his understanding (inadvertency vs. wrong judgment) or from the state of his affections 162; two means for acting on will of sentient beings, viz.: holding out prospect of pn. (coercive motives) or of pl. (alluring motives) 259; imperfections of existing nomenclature for expressions of 298a; conception or adoption of, *see* CONCEPTION; ADOPTION. *See also* ASPECTS OF A LAW; COMMAND AND COUNTERMAND; IMPERATIVE AND IMPERATION; INTERPRETATION AND CONSTRUCTION

WORDS: *See* LANGUAGE AND DISCOURSE

WRONG: *See* RIGHT AND WRONG

INDEX OF NAMES

Note. This is an index of names of persons and places occurring in the text and notes, the latter (whether Bentham's or the editor's) indicated by 'n'. Where a note extends to more than one page and the reference is to part of it only, the general reference to the initial page of the note is followed in brackets by a specific page reference. Under Bentham's name only references to his other works are indexed.

AMALFI: 187 & n
AMERICA: 8, 109
AMSTERDAM: 5
ANJOU: 13n
ANTIOCHUS: 18n (19)
ANTISTIUS LABEO: 191n
APPIUS, the Decemvir, and VIRGINIA: 163n
ARISTOTLE: 77n, 152n
ASHBURTON, Lord: *See* DUNNING, John
ATEIUS CAPITO: 191n
ATHENS: 113n
ATTICA: 119
AUGUSTINE, St., of Hippo: 186n
AUGUSTUS, Roman Emperor: 191n

BARRINGTON, Daines: 66n
BEDE: 186
BENTHAM, Jeremy
  Correspondence: 96n, 144n, 151n, 241n, 284n, 304n, 305n
  Essay on Indirect Legislation: 62n (63)
  Fragment on Government: 18n, 67n, 194n, 304
  Introduction to the Principles of Morals and Legislation: passim
  Plan of a Penal Code: 102n, 240n, 241n, 304n, 305n, 313n
  Traités de Législation Civile et Pénale: 62–3n
  View of the Hard Labour Bill: 304n
BENTHAM, Samuel: 151n
BERNE: 5, 70n
BEYER, —, of Ulm: 242n, 243n
BIELFELD, Jacob Friedrich von: 165n
BLACKSTONE, Sir William: 2n, 18n
BOLOGNA: 161n
BUCKINGHAM, Duke of: *See* VILLIERS, George
BURN, Richard: 118n
BYZANTIUM (Byzantine Empire): 17

CALIGULA, Roman Emperor: 56 & n, 71

CATHERINE II, Empress of Russia: 144n, 151n
CHARLES V, Holy Roman Emperor: 10 & n
CHARLES II, King of England: 5n, 103n
CICERO, Marcus Tullius: 6 & n, 187n, 193 & n
CLARENDON, Earl of: *See* HYDE, Edward
COKE, Sir Edward: 187n

DEMOSTHENES: 193n
DUMONT, Etienne: 62–3n
DUNNING, John, 1st Baron Ashburton: 304
EUROPE: 48n
EVERARD, Nicolaus: 161n

FELTON, John: 46n
FENELON, François de Salignac de la Mothe: 282n
FORSTER, Rev. John: 144n
FRANCE: 17, 18n (19), 29, 70n
FREEMAN, Richard: 187n

GENEVA: 70n
GENOA: 5
GEORGE III, King of Great Britain: 109
GERMANY: German Empire 17, 29; Germanic body 18n (19)
GREAT BRITAIN: 17, 18n (19)

HALE, Matthew: 118n
HALIFAX: 8
HAWKINS, William: 118n
HEINECCIUS, Johann Gottlieb: 242n, 243n
HENRY III, King of England: 90n
HERODOTUS: 152n
HINDOSTAN: 48n
HOMER: 119n
HYDE, Edward, 1st Earl of Clarendon: 5n

IRELAND: 8

341

JAMES II, King of England 28 & n, 109
JOHN, King of England: 90n
JOUSSE, Daniel: 174n
JUSTINIAN, Roman Emperor; 10, 118n, 187 & n, 242n, 303n
LIVY: 163n
LOUIS IX, King of France: 13n
LOUIS (LEWIS) XIV, King of France: 18n (99)
LOW COUNTRIES: 17
LYCURGUS: 22 & n

MAINE: 13n
MAN, Isle of: 8
MASURIUS SABINUS: 191n
MAYNARD, Sir John, Serjeant: 187n
MONTESQUIEU, Charles Louis de Secondat, Baron de la Brède et de: 2n, 163n

ORLÈANS: 13n
OROSIUS, PAULUS: 186

PERIANDER, tyrant of Corinth: 152n
PETTY, William, 2nd Earl of Shelburne, (later 1st Marquess of Lansdowne): 304, 305n
PHILIP III, King of Spain: 165 & n
POBAR, Marquis de: 165n
POLAND: 5
PORPHYRY: 77n
POTTER, John: 113n
PUFFENDORF, Samuel: 161n
PYTHAGORAS: 49n

RICHARD II, King of England: 90n
ROME: 6, 18n (19)
RUFFHEAD, Owen: 104n

SANDERSON, Robert: 96n
SEMPRONIUS PROCULUS: 191n
SHELBURNE, Lord: See PETTY, William
SPARTA: 113n
SPELMAN, Sir Henry: 165n
STRAFFORD, Earl of: See WENTWORTH, Thomas
SUETONIUS Tranquillus, Gaius: 56n, 71n
SWEDEN: 5
SWIFT, Jonathan: 160n

THEOCRATES: 193n
THESEUS: 119 & n
THRASYBULUS, tyrant of Miletus: 152n
TIBERIUS, Roman Emperor: 191n

UNITED PROVINCES: 29

VENICE: 5
VILLIERS, George, 1st Duke of Buckingham: 46n
VIRGIL: 119n
VIRGINIA: See APPIUS
VIRGINIA, colony of: 131

WENTWORTH, Thomas, 1st Earl of Strafford: 5 & n
WESTMINSTER BRIDGE: 75 & n
WILLIAM I, King of England: 165
WILLIAM II, King of England: 90n
WILLIAM III, King of England: 109
WILLIAMS, William Peere: 187n

YORKSHIRE: 8

ZELEUCUS: 193n